Praise for Like What You Do

"Dr. Walt is truly 'a man for all seasons.' This memoir is an intimate look into the life and work of a Menninger man who, together with his family, forever altered the way we approach mental health all over the world."

—*Laura Kelly*
48th Governor of Kansas

"A warm and compelling story of a man, a family, and an institution that shaped American psychiatry in the twentieth century. Dr. Menninger's long and clear-eyed perspective on the world is balanced by his eternal optimism and deep compassion. In these times of psychobabble, the simplicity and humanity in his explicated solutions to both our individual and societal struggle are inspirational. He has returned much more than he has been given."

—*Jennifer F. Havens, MD*
Arnold Simon Professor and Chair, Department of Child
and Adolescent Psychiatry, NYU Grossman School of Medicine

"Explore the extraordinary life of Dr. Walter Menninger in this captivating book. From his formative years in a renowned family of psychiatrists to his groundbreaking contributions in mental health, Dr. Menninger shares his journey navigating the complexities of the human mind. With honesty and insight, he reflects on pivotal moments, professional triumphs, and the evolution of psychiatric care. A compelling narrative of resilience, innovation, and compassion, this memoir offers a profound look into the life of a pioneer in psychiatry."

—*Yvonne Maldonado, MD*
Taube Endowed Professor of Global Health and Infectious Diseases,
Stanford University School of Medicine

"Like What You Do is a compelling review of an amazing life and life's work. From Dr. Walt's marriage to his college sweetheart and parenting six children to his leadership of both the Topeka State Hospital and the Menninger Foundation at a time when mental health was often overlooked as an essential component of a healthy life, Dr. Walt had a profound impact on peers and patients. His new book is a great read."

—*Kathleen Sebelius*
44th Governor of Kansas,
21st US Secretary of Health and Human Services

"Dr. Walt's memoir, *Like What You Do*, reads like a history of psychiatry and the mental health professions in the USA during his 90-plus years; it is written from the unique view of a remarkable man standing on the shoulders of brilliant others in this preeminent family of the period who birthed a vision of alleviating human suffering. Yet his style is candid, humble, filled with wisdom, relatable, and infused with that amazing ability to distill complex concepts, both psychological and environmental, into common sense discourse that was Menninger. An uplifting volume conveying the deeply-held Menninger spirit of community and collaboration that provides hope in these difficult times and this troubled world."

—*Bonnie J. Buchele, PhD*
President-Elect, American Psychoanalytic Association

"Seldom does one book inform, inspire, educate, engage, enthrall, charm, and provoke. This one does! In addition to sharing his personal and family history, 'Dr. Walt' provides advice, guidance, and direction that offers a handbook for our own lives."

—*Ted D. Ayres*
Vice President and General Counsel Emeritus, Wichita State University,
producer and host of *Inside The Cover*, PBS KANSAS

"I guarantee you will like what you read, if you read *Like What You Do, The Memoirs of Dr. Walt Menninger*. What a privilege to be invited to take a journey at Walt's side, as he paints a vivid picture of his amazing life and career. Most interested readers will already know a lot about the remarkable Menninger dynasty and the truly international impact of the Menninger Clinic. But there's a lot you won't know, unless you read the book—from his very personal family tales, to his heady and influential leadership roles, serving as a rudder in the mental health and political winds of the world. Read it! You'll like it and you'll learn a lot!"

—*John M. Oldham, MD*

Distinguished Emeritus Professor, Menninger Department of Psychiatry and Behavioral Sciences, Baylor College of Medicine

---

"Dr. Walt's book is truly a tour de force. He combines a fascinating personal story with a compelling picture of how modern American psychiatry has evolved, and the challenges it has faced, from the early 1920s when his grandfather started the 'family business' with his two physician sons, Will and Karl, to the passing of the baton to Dr. Walt and before him his brother Roy, two sons of Dr. Will. And what a saga it is. Anybody interested not just in the evolution of modern psychiatry, but also in the meaning of a life well lived, should read this book."

—*Harvey Kurzweil*

Trustee, Menninger Clinic, 1998 to date; Fellow, International Academy of Trial Lawyers; partner, Winston & Strawn LLP law firm

---

"Anyone interested in the history of psychiatry, including an insider's perspective on the world-renowned Menninger Clinic, will not want to miss reading Dr. Walt Menninger's memoir."

—*Harriet Lerner, PhD*

Author of *The Dance of Anger* and *Women in Therapy*

"Dr. Walt Menninger shares with us the uniqueness and the commonness of the Menninger family as he recounts adventures and occurrences from his life and that of his family. His wisdom and life lessons are easily grasped as you read the stories. This is a historical work presented by a living legend of the psychiatric family dynasty. It is interesting and insightful, a book to be read and treasured, and the perfect gift to share with anyone interested in psychiatry, history, leadership, and humanity."

—*Linda P. Jeffrey*
President, Kansas State Historical Society

"In addition to being a full personal memoir, *Like What You Do* is an historical account of the Menninger Mental Health Clinic in Topeka, from its inception through the transition to Houston. Dr. Walter Menninger lived that history, both professionally and as a member of the family. The book is a multi-dimensional, fun, and remarkable read."

—*David Holloway*
Emeritus Director Apprentice Singers' Program, Santa Fe Opera

LIKE WHAT YOU DO

The Memoirs of Dr. Walt Menninger

BY WALT MENNINGER WITH TODD FERTIG

Flint Hills Publishing

Cover Design by Amy Albright

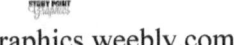

stonypointgraphics.weebly.com

Author headshot by Miranda Chavez-Hazim

Flint Hills Publishing

Topeka, Kansas
Tucson, Arizona
www.flinthillspublishing.com

Printed in the U.S.A.

Paperback Book ISBN: 978-1-953583-88-8
Hardback Book ISBN: 978-1-953583-90-1
Electronic Book: 978-1-953583-89-5

Library of Congress Control Number: 2024907124

Contents

Like What You Do

The Memoirs

of

Dr. Walt Menninger

Introduction

To whom much is given, much will be required, and from the one to whom much has been entrusted, even more will be demanded." Those words from Luke 12:48 have carried special weight throughout my life. When you've been born with a silver spoon in your mouth, your responsibility is not to tarnish it. I was blessed to be born into a family that had already accomplished much, earned a great deal of respect, and made a profound impact on many lives.

My responsibility, I felt, was to not tarnish that legacy, and to add to it where I could. My blessing came with an expectation. Life isn't a free ride. You really should leave the world a better place than you found it.

Many children are born into families that operate their own enterprises, be they farms, stores, or even large companies. It just so happens that my family's business was a psychiatric hospital and training program.

When I was born, the Menninger Clinic was a well-respected, yet relatively small, family business. It remained as such for most of my childhood. But suddenly, about the time I entered high school, the clinic expanded, seemingly overnight. So much so that, when I was ready to assume a role, it was world-renowned and influential.

Like my father, Will Menninger, and my uncle, Karl Menninger, I became a psychiatrist. But what I didn't anticipate was that I would follow in their footsteps outside of the family clinic. Like my father and my uncle, I wound up spending much of my time writing, speaking, participating in work groups in the civic arena, and consulting.

I had a multifaceted career that allowed me to travel to interesting places, meet interesting people, and engage in interesting work. I like to say that I frequently found myself in the right place at the right time. But being born into the Menninger family had a lot to do with that. In most circles, my family name was recognized and respected. My grandfather, Charles Menninger, my father, and my uncle were prominent leaders, earning world-wide recognition. The Menninger name gave me *entrée* into many circles and opened many doors for me.

To whom much is given, much is required.

I knew from my childhood that I wanted to become a psychiatrist like my father. I don't recall that it was ever discussed openly, nor am I sure when it became my definitive goal. But by the time I was in high school, I was certain it was what I would do. I knew from an early age that I wanted to help people. Having watched my father closely, it seemed psychiatry was a way to do that. The opportunity was there for me to join the family business, and I did my best to stick to that path. But I discovered many amazing and satisfying things along the way that I never planned for. It is from these adventures that many of the greatest lessons of my life were learned.

Perhaps the most valuable lesson I learned, applied repeatedly throughout my career, derived from the application of advice from Dr. Felix Wroblewski, at Cornell Medical College, who served as a mentor early in my career:

"It's more important in life to like what you do than to do what you like."

Adopting this attitude has been the key to much of the success I've experienced in life, and served as a fitting title for my memoir, written in my early 90s.

"Why write a memoir?" you might ask. I asked myself that question repeatedly as I put down these words.

Is it the self-gratification of saying you authored a book? No. I've published books before. I didn't need to write another one.

Is it nothing more than narcissism that produced this work? I hope not.

I was motivated to put these words on paper because, although many of my experiences seem like ancient history now, there are some nuggets of wisdom, some scraps of hope, and some embers of insight in those stories that are still meaningful. The Morale Curve, the TGIF Syndrome, the Myth of Happiness, reflections on tragedy and loss, violence and civil disobedience.... I don't want to take these lessons to the grave with me. I want to make one last effort to plant them like seeds, in hopes they will grow for generations to come.

Few people in life have had the opportunities I had. My task was to not tarnish the silver spoon. But beyond that, I realized that there is a responsibility to care for what you have been given and to pass it on.

I hesitated to write this book particularly because of my awareness of the much-researched "fallibility of memory." As old athletes are prone to say, "The older I get, the better I was." In my own case, I don't want to succumb to the fallibility of memory, remembering only my accomplishments and the good times in my life. I don't want to paint an unrealistic picture of the success of the Menninger Clinic over the decades, nor of myself as a doctor, husband, father, and contributor to my community.

But as I turned 90 in 2021, I determined that, to the best of my memory, I would tell my story in its entirety in hopes that I could honor the family business by recalling it from its humble beginning to the day it passed from Menninger leadership in 2003. Having watched the organization up close as a youth, having studied under extraordinary teachers, and having traveled the world to work with remarkable leaders on a variety of important projects as an adult, I hope to pass on a few lessons I learned along the way.

I owe a debt of gratitude to Todd Fertig, who helped me to record my memories and to artfully intersperse amongst the chapters a dozen talks and writings produced throughout my career which I deemed the most worthy of inclusion in the book.

It has been my pleasure to work with Flint Hills Publishing to bring this project to reality. Thea Rademacher and the staff have encouraged me along the final leg of the journey. Additionally, I thank my daughter Marian and my daughter-in-law Claire for their thorough and careful editing of the manuscript.

While I am grateful for many who have supported me throughout my life and career, I wish to say a special *thank you* to my eldest son, Fritz, who has been instrumental in allowing me to remain in my home and assisted me in living a vibrant life into my 90s. Without his help, my life these past couple of decades would have been much different. My "independence" has been largely dependent upon his assistance.

Writing a memoir brings recollections flooding back of so many people who impacted your life along the way. It would be impossible to acknowledge all of them in this book. Friends, relatives, and co-workers who don't find your names in the following pages, please know that your presence in my life is cherished.

The Menningers

It could be said that everyone is a product of his or her ancestry. In my case, while I sought to stand on my own two feet and make my own way in life, there is no question that I am a product of those who went before me. My story is inextricably intertwined with my parents' and grandparents' stories.

When your family history has been documented by outsiders like mine has, you find that other people know more about your ancestry than you do. Growing up, I was generally oblivious to the significance of our family story. It wasn't until much later that I understood that the lives and accomplishments of my elders left a permanent impact on mental health care in the United States.

How did it happen? That story has been told in countless articles, as well as in a few books. I'll provide only a brief account of the story here.

The German "Meiningers" crossed the Atlantic when Andreas (Andrew) Meininger, a widower, immigrated to Baltimore in 1844, bringing five children. He died in Ohio in 1852.

One of Andreas' children was Augustus Johan, who was born in Germany on November 21, 1826. He came with his father to the U.S. as an 18-year-old. Augustus became a blacksmith in a German-speaking section of Cincinnati. He married German immigrant Katarina Schmidtberger in 1850, and they had nine children. They never learned to speak much English, sticking to German communities everywhere they lived. It was with them that the spelling of Meininger became "Menninger."

The family eventually settled in a German-speaking community in Tell City, Indiana, where Augustus would become owner of a sawmill. Though he was in his mid-30s at the start of the Civil War, Augustus took up arms on the side of the North. He lived until 1904, two years after the death of his wife.

One of the nine children of Augustus and Katherine was my grandfather, Charles Frederick Menninger.

My grandfather was born on July 11, 1862. He was a dutiful son of a sawmill owner, but he was born to study. His passion for learning knew no bounds. Though he came from a family with meager means and limited education, he blossomed as a student.

Since he was the sixth of eight children, Charles had older siblings who could take over the family business. So, his parents encouraged his wide-ranging interests. He left home as a teen to clerk in a law office, and he seemed destined to become a lawyer. But he so enjoyed his undergraduate experience at Central Normal College in Danville, Indiana, Charles decided to become a teacher.

Perhaps because his family wasn't too thrilled with his career decision, Charles moved away from Indiana, taking a teaching position at Campbell Normal University in Holton, Kansas. Named after a wealthy local benefactor, Allen G. Campbell, the school had just opened in 1880. Today there is little left to remember of the college. It went through a couple of mergers, then moved to become Kansas City University in 1913. The school folded altogether in 1933.

At the age of 20, Charles began teaching at the small single-building college in Holton in 1882, and soon met a young student named Flora Vesta Knisely, who went by Flo.

Born in Pennsylvania on April 23, 1863, Flo was held in her mother's arms while Abraham Lincoln delivered his Gettysburg Address that November.

When she was ten, Flo's father died of cancer. With her mother, Flo moved to tiny Industry, Kansas, in a desperate attempt to survive by farming. The site they chose to resettle was fitting, because there were few people more industrious than my grandmother. Mother and daughter set to working the farm just outside of Abilene, which was pretty audacious for a couple of women in those days. Flo had several siblings she looked after from a young age. To make money to help support her mother, Flo started teaching school while still a teen.

As a 19-year-old, while still trying to contribute to the family's finances, Flo moved to Holton to further her education at Campbell College. Soon, her work ethic and fierce determination won over Charles, who was less than a year her elder. The teacher married the student on

January 15, 1885.

A few issues had to be resolved by the Campbell College couple. Grandfather was raised Lutheran by his German parents. They drank wine, smoked, played cards, and even danced. Flo was raised in the fundamentalist River Brethren sect, and she was a prohibitionist. In order to meet in the middle, they eventually compromised on the Presbyterian church once they made their home in Topeka. First Presbyterian Church at 817 SW Harrison has been the spiritual home of Menningers for more than 130 years, dating back to when parishioners used to rent pews!

———————————+———————————

My grandfather was a gifted learner. He could master just about any subject quickly, which was essential at tiny Campbell College. Whatever students needed to have taught, the professors had to quickly learn themselves. Charles taught German, geology, botany, mineralogy, physics, engineering, and studied everything from bird migration to telegraphy. When several young students required some basic pre-medical courses, it fell upon my grandfather to figure out how to teach them. He consulted with some local doctors and did some reading, and he quickly assembled a course that would pass the requirements of medical schools.

My grandfather enjoyed learning anything, but the medical courses piqued his interest in a unique way: he realized he could make more money as a doctor than as a professor. He and his new wife began talking over their long-term prospects, and they decided the sacrifices medical school would require would pay off in the long run.

In 1887, Charles headed to Chicago to attend a homeopathic program at Hahnemann Medical College. It was a big commitment for a young couple. Besides the separation, they had little money. Initially, Charles wanted to go to Cornell, but that was out of the question. Flo supported Charles' studies at the much-cheaper Hahnemann by teaching school in Holton. After one year of medical school, the couple calculated that Topeka would be a more profitable site for Charles to practice medicine. So, Flo took a job teaching at Branner Primary School in north Topeka in 1888 and moved into an apartment there. Charles finished medical college and returned to Topeka in 1889.

There he would become known to most as Dr. C.F. Menninger.

C.F. opened an office at 727 South Kansas Avenue and quickly developed a good business, partly due to the large German-speaking population in Topeka at the time. To save money, he and Flo lived in rooms adjoining the office. They even utilized the waiting room to host guests in the evenings.

C.F. quickly found his homeopathic degree from Hahnemann was looked down upon by the other doctors of Topeka, who had all studied allopathy. The difference between the two, which was somewhat contentious at the time, is that allopaths treat with medicines to counteract disease, while homeopaths expose patients to small doses of the same or similar disease to increase the immune system's ability to fight the illness. Dr. Hahnemann had developed the homeopathic concepts, and they were not widely accepted.

C.F.'s training made him unique in Topeka, but his medical school training in homeopathy might have been a blessing in disguise. While other doctors rested on their laurels, believing they had superior training, C.F. never ceased in his quest for further learning, perhaps driven by his own belief in the inferiority of his training. He realized he had only a rudimentary education, but he was smart enough to know what he didn't know. C.F. was so devoted to professional development that he occasionally referred patients to competitors so that he could guard his time for study.

With no major medical school in the state at the time, the doctors of Topeka established their own medical school in affiliation with Washburn College in a ramshackle building adjoining a livery stable. They contributed their own time and money to get it going. C.F. eagerly enrolled in classes at the brand-new Kansas Medical College when it opened in 1890. Additionally, he subscribed to journals and attended all kinds of continuing education programs to grow his knowledge.

As always seemed to be the case with C.F., his diligence and quickness in mastering subjects set him apart. After a while, he was asked to do more than attend classes at Kansas Medical College. They said, "You know more than we do. Why don't we give you an honorary degree, and you start teaching on the staff?"

That sounded like a good idea at the time, but things would soon get more complicated. In the early part of the 20th Century, there were many "proprietary" medical schools—small schools that were teaching medicine without accreditation or oversight. The medical college at Washburn operated in this manner until the Flexner Report came out. Published in 1910 by the Carnegie Foundation, the Flexner Report basically challenged medical schools to shape up. They wanted to clean up the myriad of diplomas floating around and ensure some oversight of the degree process. So, the University of Kansas Medical School invited doctors: "Send your medical diplomas in with $5, and we'll give you a KU diploma."

C.F. had his honorary degree from Kansas Medical College. A physician from Topeka wrote a letter to Chancellor Frank Strong, describing my grandfather as a good physician, wondering if he would be eligible for a KU degree. Chancellor Strong's response was "We don't do honorary degrees."

A little later, Chancellor Strong wrote again, saying, "I've looked into this Dr. Menninger. Have him send in his $5." Strong had obviously checked it out and realized what type of reputation my grandfather had. The diploma my grandfather received from KU doesn't say "honorary" on it.

With the medical practice established, and a little money finally saved, my grandparents were ready to start a family. Karl was born in July 1893. Edwin was born in 1896. A third boy—my father—was born in 1899.

Desirous of a girl child, my grandmother had the name picked out for her third baby before the birth—Clara Louise. But when the child was a boy, my grandparents had to choose a new name. I'm not sure why they didn't have a boy's name ready to go. When they had to choose on the fly, they named my father William Claire. Grandmother called him Claire for years.

As a general physician, C.F. fit the image of a 19th century doctor, driving a horse and buggy to make house calls. When they were young, Karl, Edwin, and Dad occasionally accompanied him on his rounds. They would tend to the horse while he visited patients. I'm sure they learned a lot talking with him about his work while making rounds. It's hard to know what Karl and my father witnessed from his practice, but certainly they seemed to model in their psychiatric practice the type of bedside manner and personal attention that you would associate with old-time medical care.

Legend has it that C.F. came back from a professional visit to the Mayo Clinic in Rochester, Minnesota in the summer of 1908 inspired to start a family clinic that would incorporate his three sons. The story goes that he returned from Minnesota, told the family over breakfast of his vision, and prayed with the family for God to bless the plan.

I'm not sure if he got the idea only after meeting the Mayos. But it seems pretty certain that C.F. wanted to work within a group practice. The life of an old-time doctor was grueling and pretty solitary. Adding in the fact that he felt isolated by his homeopathic training, it's easy to imagine why my grandfather would have longed for partners. He loved learning from others, but also realized that specialization was the future of medicine. In the Mayos, he saw how doctors could divide and conquer the vast field of medical learning, then share their knowledge. Once his sons Karl and Will began their medical training, the dream didn't seem far-fetched.

As the Menninger family grew in the 1890s, so did C.F.'s practice, and his prominence in Topeka.

Because Flo was a schoolteacher, many parents began bringing their children to C.F. for treatment. He had to quickly learn pediatrics, as well as how to deliver babies. The mortality rate for children was alarming at the time, and he often found parents resigned to accept the death of their sick children. But C.F. inspired hope in both the young patients and their parents, and that alone produced better results than what was common around the turn of the century.

My grandfather's relations with other doctors in Topeka were hot and cold. They would cooperate to form the Kansas Medical College and gather to read research papers to each other, but they were resistant to sharing their best practices, much less referring patients to each other. C.F had no patience for this competition between doctors. Not only did they look down on him for his training, they held him at arm's length when he sought out their advice. It's possible that it was this culture of competition that made my grandfather long for his sons to become doctors and join him in his practice. He probably believed that, like the Mayos, the Menningers could share responsibilities, specialize in different areas of medicine, and freely share their knowledge without fear of competition.

Regardless, his one-man practice flourished to the point that, despite my grandmother's frugality, they bought a large house at 1251 Topeka Avenue in the summer of 1898. This house had 13 rooms, finally allowing them the space to host gatherings.

Flo and C.F. always had a soft spot in their hearts for people who were without a home or family or were down on their luck. They took in numerous temporary boarders over the years, some of them staying for long periods and becoming like extended members of the family. Once, when the Kansas River flooded in 1903, C.F. brought more than 30 people to stay temporarily at his family home. When measles soon broke out among the children staying with them, the Menninger house became a makeshift hospital. The 23 children and four mothers wound up staying almost a month in the house.

Seeing such openness and generosity demonstrated during their childhood probably encouraged Karl and Will to be service minded. But beyond that, it may have opened their eyes to the needs—particularly the mental health needs—of members of their community. The poor and downtrodden who passed through their home over the years would have made the boys acutely aware of the hardships people suffer.

What might have seemed of little consequence at the time but would be monumental in our lives was the start of a Boy Scout troop in Topeka in 1910. Grandfather would certainly have appreciated the skills and discipline the Boy Scouts promoted, but I don't think he was involved with the start of the program in Topeka. He was too busy. Nonetheless, the three Menninger boys got involved, and my father became one of Topeka's first Eagle Scouts.

The open house policy extended to the Boy Scouts and other groups Flo's sons brought home. Anxious to be an influence in their peer groups, Grandmother made sure her sons could provide visitors with food and refreshments and a comfortable place to hang out. At the same time, Grandfather hosted professional gatherings and Grandmother hosted Bible study meetings, for which she gained considerable acclaim. Once she became a mother, she gave up education as a profession. But she never stopped teaching, and Bible study became the primary outlet for her talent.

The house wasn't just full of people. My father and his brothers were permitted to raise a variety of different animals. Of course, they were required to help take care of the horses that were essential to grandfather's practice. Even after the family bought a car—a Cadillac—in 1910, they had to keep horses because automobiles were unreliable.

It was as a boy that my father developed another passion he would cultivate for the rest of his life: stamp collecting. He was particularly fond of stamps from around the world that commemorated physicians and developments in health care.

There were a couple of interesting things that happened to my father as a child that nearly prevented my being here. First, Dad contracted scarlet fever when he was around three years of age and nearly died. My grandfather rarely left his side, and my father eventually recovered. But the family had to quarantine for six weeks during the scare. Second, Dad had another close call much more of his own doing. When he was a child, he discovered a bunch of Grandfather's sugar cubes drenched with various medicines. He ate a stomachful of these cubes and could have died. Somehow, he survived and kept the secret from his parents for many years. The family dog, to whom my dad fed some of the cubes, wasn't so fortunate.

One by one, Karl, Edwin, and Will graduated high school and faced the big decision: would they join my grandfather's medical practice, or would they take a different tack?

A fateful event put a damper on my grandfather's Mayos-inspired plan, reducing the potential workforce by a third. Edwin was badly injured in an accident as a student at Washburn College (which wouldn't be known as a "university" until 1941). An explosion of a test tube he was carrying outside of class badly damaged his left hand and his face. He lost some ability in the hand, and the sight in his right eye.

If I look at it with my psychoanalyst's lens, I might presume Edwin was ambivalent about becoming a doctor. This careless act made the decision for him and steered him in a different direction. What in heaven's name was he doing walking around toting phosphorus and potassium chlorate in a test tube? But he was an entertainer—he enjoyed trying to master magic tricks and sleight of hand, in addition to small chemical explosions.

With a medical career out of the question, Edwin pursued another of his talents—journalism. He had been successful as a youth at delivering newspapers, and he was active in the campus publication. After graduating from Washburn, he got a graduate degree from the Columbia University Pulitzer School. Subsequently, he worked for the *New York World Telegram* while Dad was in medical school at Cornell. Edwin wound up owning his own newspaper in Stuart, Florida—*The Stuart News*—and he rarely came back to Kansas. So, I didn't really get to know my uncle Edwin while I was growing up. As an adult, I had the opportunity to visit him a few times when we vacationed in Florida.

Edwin was much like my grandfather in that he loved studying nature. Edwin was passionate about horticulture. He was fascinated by flowering trees, and particularly in the fact that there were no flowering trees native to Florida. He made it his mission to perpetuate flowering trees in the state, teaching and writing books on the subject, running his own nursery, and distributing more than 10,000 seedlings and countless seeds to Floridians. For his efforts, he was given an honorary degree of Doctor of Science from Florida State University.

So, every son of C.F. and Flo Menninger did, in fact, become a doctor!

Dr. Edwin Menninger passed away in 1995 at the age of 98.

The first to graduate and move out of the house, my uncle Karl attended the University of Wisconsin. As an undergrad, he actually considered ministry as a career. But eventually, Karl decided to go to medical school at Harvard.

Third and last in line, my father graduated from Washburn in 1919, then attended graduate school at Columbia University before entering Cornell University Medical School. He considered pursuing employment with the Boy Scouts.

During his time at Columbia, my dad met my mother, Catharine Wright, while volunteering at a Presbyterian camp in New York, somewhere up in the Catskills. Mom was raised as a Presbyterian in East

Orange, New Jersey. I think her parents attempted to stave off the relationship as best they could. For nine months, they sent her to the Sorbonne in Paris. But the relationship survived.

After graduation from Teachers College at Columbia, my mom got a master's degree in nutrition at Johns Hopkins. While they were dating, my parents talked about going into missionary work, particularly to China. But the plan was frustrated by a lack of suitable placements in China, coupled with the fact that mission policy precluded their raising children in the field. When they asked both their sets of parents if they would help raise their future grandchildren, my parents were rebuffed. With roadblocks in the way of going to China, my father listened to Karl's appeal for help with the Topeka clinic. My father graduated from Cornell Medical School in 1924, then had an 18-month medicine/surgery residency at Bellevue Hospital in New York City. At the end of the residency, my father married my mother on December 11, 1925, then drove immediately to Topeka to become a partner in the Menninger practice.

With two sons becoming medical doctors, my grandfather's dream of sharing a medical practice with them was becoming a reality. But the direction that practice would take was not what he had envisioned.

A New Direction

It would be hyperbole to say that a decision by one member of the Menninger family changed the world. But a decision made by Karl Menninger in 1918 did more than just alter the course of the family. It improved the lives of thousands in need of mental health care. It changed the face of Topeka, Kansas. And it shaped the next generation of psychiatric care in America.

It helped to determine my career path, more than a decade before I was born.

Uncle Karl's decision to attend Harvard Medical School meant he was following my grandfather's wish that his sons become doctors. But his interests gradually turned to the nascent field of psychiatry. The force of his personality, combined with my grandfather's desire to partner with his sons, would turn the focus of the Menninger Clinic in a new direction.

———————————•———————————

Historically speaking, psychiatry wasn't exactly new in the 20th century. There had long been institutions to care for the mentally ill. In the late 1700s and early 1800s, the asylums of Europe gradually discovered that there was some hope for improvement for those institutionalized for psychosis. The term "psychiatry" was first used in the early 1800s, but the people who practiced it were called "alienists," because they treated "mental alienation."

Of course, my grandfather had some knowledge of mental health care prior to Karl's decision. Although he hadn't specialized in psychiatry, C.F. could observe it in his general practice. He had noticed over the years that some patients he treated for physical maladies responded better to his attention, kindness, and encouragement than they did to any physical remedy. Specifically speaking, he noted two things: patients often exhibited emotional suffering even when they had no physical symptoms, and that talking about their problems often elicited some relief.

Interestingly, my grandfather was fascinated by the Shakespeare character Hamlet. He saw the famous play while in medical school in Chicago and seemed to be struck by the prince's madness. After returning to Topeka, C.F. helped organize a group who shared papers on a regular basis. Thoughts about Hamlet stuck with my grandfather, and he decided to write an in-depth paper on the character. To learn more about mental illness, my grandfather sought out Dr. B. D. Eastman, superintendent of Topeka State Hospital, for input. Eastman happened to be in the process of planting trees at the property, and my grandfather, an expert in such things, volunteered to help. That led to hours working side-by-side. The friendship allowed my grandfather to pick the expert's brain on issues of mental health.

Technically, what my grandfather studied was primarily "neurology," which is the study of diseases and disorders of the nervous system. As a general practitioner, he observed how physical and mental health were linked. Particularly, prior to the advent of insulin, he worked with diabetics by managing their diet. C.F. noticed how important hope was in treatment. He knew that each day had to have meaning. Unlike other doctors who often made their patients believe there was no hope, my grandfather inspired belief in his patients that they could get better.

My grandfather believed in the words of Plato from a couple of thousand years earlier:

> So neither ought you attempt to cure the body without the soul; and this is the reason that the cure of many diseases is unknown to the physicians of Hellas, because they are ignorant of the whole, which ought to be studied also; for the part can never be well unless the whole is well...that is the great error of our day in treatment of the human body, that physicians separate the soul from the body. (Charmides)

————————————————

While my grandfather's Topeka practice thrived, Karl attended Harvard Medical School. He had been a weekend preacher in small churches while an undergrad at Wisconsin and seriously contemplated entering the ministry. But at medical school, those interests were surpassed by a new passion: psychiatry. This passion grew during his residency at Boston Psychopathic Hospital, where he was greatly influenced by Dr. Ernest Southard. Southard was one of the "new psychiatrists" who were finding success helping patients improve their mental health. It was under the influence of Southard that Karl decided to eschew surgery, preaching, and the mission field to devote himself to psychiatry.

As Karl treated people with syphilis at Kansas City General Hospital during his internship, he made special note of the psychological impact of diagnosis and treatment. It was similar to the physical improvements my grandfather noted when his patients exhibited either hope or despondence. Karl expressed his interest in psychiatry to my grandfather, who always encouraged his sons to follow their passions.

My father was at Washburn College during this time, and while he kept up on Karl's activities, he had no say in the direction of the Menninger family practice. My father graduated college in 1919 and went to graduate school at Columbia before starting medical school at Cornell. I don't think he had any intention of becoming a psychiatrist when he entered medical school.

At that time, most psychiatrists worked in state-run institutions, where the care provided was custodial. Most patients who entered with serious mental health issues weren't expected to recover. But a "new psychiatry" was taking off. Sigmund Freud had sparked a lot of interest in psychiatry among Europeans, and new research was inspiring belief that the mentally ill could be treated, not just managed.

Acknowledging that Karl would specialize in neurology and psychiatry, Grandfather welcomed Karl to join his practice at 727 S. Kansas Avenue in 1919. They branded themselves the Menninger Diagnostic Clinic.

While Karl's psychiatric practice developed, Grandfather continued his general practice, which helped financially support Karl's specialization in the early years. My grandfather created a safe place for Karl to develop his neurology and psychiatry practice, calming suspicions of this new-fangled specialization, and smoothing over the feathers Karl might ruffle.

The plan proved to be a wise one for a couple of reasons.

First, my grandfather was always eager to learn from others, and he understood that a recent graduate of medical school would bring fresh, innovative ideas to the clinic. Despite all his efforts to keep up with new developments, my grandfather knew that incredible advancements in medicine had occurred since he had graduated. My grandfather knew his medical school training at Hahnemann Medical College was subpar. He believed the training to be had at a place like Harvard or Cornell was far superior.

Second, it followed a plan to integrate his sons into the practice. While Karl got established, my grandfather created a place for my father to practice as well. It was always his desire to bring both his sons into the fold. To accommodate the growth, in 1920 he and Karl moved their office to the Mulvane Building—a six-story edifice built in 1909 at the corner of 6th Avenue and Kansas Avenue. (It would be torn down in 1931.) Unlike most men, whose pride wouldn't have allowed them to take a back seat, my grandfather was willing to let his sons determine the course of the practice. He let them take the lead and do their thing. I'm not sure that he was a visionary who saw the potential in psychiatry. I think he was more focused on the potential he saw in his sons. Karl had the vision for a neurology and psychiatry practice, and he steered the family in that direction.

A significant fact worthy of note is that my grandfather employed an assistant named Mamie Johnson who greeted the patients, helped with records, and did some of the basic lab work for diabetic patients. She was finally phased out in 1922 as the needs became more technical. Her service had been groundbreaking. She was the first Black receptionist in Topeka. This had to be a pretty meaningful arrangement at the time, as essentially all of my grandfather's clientele was white. Mamie reportedly had a very calming presence in the office, keeping my grandfather's hectic practice in order and showing tact when Karl failed to.

The clinic's treatment of psychiatric patients grew quickly, but from the outset had the problem of where to house inpatient cases. Aside from the state hospital, there was no place in Topeka to admit mentally ill patients. The housing of mentally ill patients was forbidden by city ordinance because people complained about having "maniacs" in the neighborhood and hospitalized in close proximity to other patients.

In the early 1920s, Karl was serving part-time at Christ's Hospital, an Episcopal hospital that would eventually become Stormont Vail Hospital. In his role, Karl could slip mentally ill patients into the hospital under various diagnoses. But he and his father knew this arrangement couldn't last. They needed their own facility to house their patients.

While studying on the East Coast, Karl became aware that the best psychiatric facilities provided services and amenities in rural settings that catered to a wealthy clientele. Karl observed the accomplishments at these facilities but believed that type of care needed to be made available to the less wealthy as well. He and my grandfather envisioned a type of therapy that didn't confine the patients to their rooms. They believed early on that interaction and physical activity needed to play a big part in therapy.

By 1925, they knew they had to solve their problem of housing, to get their patients out of Christ's Hospital, and to have a place to thoroughly immerse them in an active, therapeutic setting. They found a farm on what was then the west edge of Topeka, at 3617 SW 6th Street, where no one would protest to the housing of mentally ill patients. The property contained a big house and several other buildings on 12 acres.

The Menningers couldn't afford the property, however. They decided their only option was to go to the community for financial support. My grandfather had by this time earned a great deal of goodwill in Topeka for his benevolence and effective medical care. He was viewed as somewhat of a visionary as well, so people in Topeka were willing to listen to his ideas. At a dinner for 35 Topeka leaders, he and Karl presented the need for a sanitarium. They proposed to form a corporation and sell stock. Several doctors and businessmen agreed to invest in the idea, giving them enough capital to purchase the farm. In September of 1925, they moved 12 patients into the big farmhouse. The other buildings on the property were ultimately converted into offices, workshops, and activity spaces. Of course, my grandfather devoted his spare time to planting and beautifying the property.

This was all happening at the time my father had to decide on his own career path. His education at Cornell Medical School and Bellevue

Hospital in New York had been in internal medicine and surgery. But the clinic was growing so quickly, C.F. and Karl desperately wanted his help immediately. Once his training was completed in December of 1925, Dad returned home with his new bride to become the third Dr. Menninger in Topeka. He subsequently acquired some training at St. Elizabeth's Hospital in Washington, D.C. and at the Hospital of Neurology at Queen Square in London.

With the clinic growing rapidly, my father was installed as the director of the sanitarium at the close of 1925, shortly before the construction of a 25-bed facility on the newly acquired property. That building would later be called the East Lodge. In 1929, they added another building, essentially identical to the first, which was called the West Lodge. West Lodge was finished shortly after the stock market crash in October of 1929, so it sat empty for a while because the East Lodge was rarely full. The Great Depression didn't stop the Menningers, but it did slow them down. Patients in great need who were unable to pay were treated for no charge. Those who promised to pay were often unable to do so.

It wasn't long before the three doctors decided it didn't make sense to keep two offices, so they moved out of the Mulvane Building in downtown Topeka and centralized all their operations at the farm. This was another step toward putting all their emphasis on psychiatry.

It didn't take long for my father to become the instrumental leader of the day-to-day psychiatric care. His assignment to oversee the sanitarium took full advantage of my father's natural talent for organization and leadership. By that time, the clinic employed a small staff of attendants, nurses, and therapists, and my dad was the perfect balance of my grandfather's graciousness and Karl's vision. The staff naturally followed my father's lead.

This arrangement allowed Karl to focus on writing, and his first book, *The Human Mind*, unexpectedly became a hit in 1930. While it was written primarily for students of psychiatry, the book appealed to the general reader in its non-clinical and easy-to-grasp explanation of psychiatric concepts. Karl became somewhat of an overnight celebrity.

The sanitarium employed an original, structured group-therapy method involving everyday activities in a safe, affirming environment they called "milieu therapy." My father's genius exhibited itself in the fleshing

19

out of the theory behind milieu therapy. The routines, the uniformity of responses, and the information-sharing between staff were developed under his intimate care. He was scientific and meticulous. He was steady. He was adept at appealing to recalcitrant patients. Those who resisted the other staff would often respond to my father's warm, patient influence.

My father involved the staff in a way that was unique. He wanted everyone from nurses, activities staff, and attendants to understand the rationale behind everything the clinic did. He believed having everyone pulling on the same end of the rope was the secret to effecting change in the lives of patients. He understood that, while physicians would spend at most an hour a day with a patient, the staff spent the entire day with them.

My father developed *The Abbreviated Guide to Therapeutic Aims*, which was more commonly called *The Guide to the Order Sheet*. It was a thorough plan for all interactions with the patients, ensuring consistency of treatment throughout the program. He wrote in the guide:

> If we are to accomplish the therapeutic aim, it is essential that all persons who come into contact with the patient should maintain a uniform attitude insofar as possible; in other words, one nurse must not be indulgent and another severe, one therapist must not be solicitous and another indifferent.

For this reason, my father convened meetings that brought together everyone on the staff, and he respected the observations of cooks and gardeners along with those of the traditional treatment team. My father was essential to fostering an intimate and friendly community at the sanitarium. They held parties that involved staff and patients. Dad's calm, pleasant demeanor modeled the familial spirit for which the Menninger Hospital became known.

Menninger was one of very few privately-owned psychiatric clinics at the time. Around 1930, just 20 percent of America's 3,500 psychiatrists were in private practice. So, for most people who needed help, there was no other option than institutionalization. Rather than seek help, they hid their issues for fear of being sent to the dreaded "loony bin." The Menningers believed strongly in preventative psychiatry. Institutionalization was a drastic measure only to be taken as a last resort. By addressing mental illness early, their patients could be cured and kept out of the state hospitals.

A distrust in psychiatry and a stigma surrounding institutionalization lingered in America. For that reason, Topeka was significant in the development of the Menninger programs. Unlike the population centers on the East Coast and in big cities, the Menninger Clinic had the full support of the community because everyone knew and trusted C.F. The Menningers were known throughout the community for their involvement in civic activities. Grandfather was involved in many civic organizations. Grandmother conducted a very popular Bible study program. Karl was active in church and was a frequent speaker at professional organizations. Dad connected with the community through the Boy Scouts. Lacking "big city distractions," the staff was fully devoted and worked long hours. And the small community understood and supported the mission. Patients were able to interact with the community. Instead of suspicion and ostracization, they received sympathy from Topekans.

A 1935 *Fortune* magazine article listed the Menninger sanitarium among five exemplary facilities, of which it was the only one not on the East Coast. With an expanding reputation and a large staff, the future was bright.

When Karl became determined to return to Topeka to join C.F.'s practice, his mentor at Boston Psychopathic Hospital, Dr. Southard, told Karl, "Don't forget the children." Thus in 1926, Karl and my grandfather started a home for "abnormal children" called the Southard School. They contracted with Stella Pearson and Lulu Holcomb, two sisters who moved from Oklahoma to start the school named after Karl's mentor, who passed away in 1920 at just 43 years of age.

Southard School stressed the importance of treating the mental health issues of the young. Karl became more and more convinced that the best way to cure mental illness was to prevent it, or to address it at the earliest stage possible. Unfortunately, the school was challenged financially from day one. Parents of mentally ill children were, in most cases, unable to spend money on expensive residential treatment. The school was a drain on the sanitarium for many years and went through many iterations, but the Menninger Children's Division endures to this day.

My grandfather was instrumental in the school throughout its early history. He devoted an hour a week to each individual child, and he proved to be the best of the Menninger men at actually working with children. As a family doctor, he had years of experience with children of all ages, plus he had raised three boys of his own, not to mention all the needy children he temporarily took into his home over the years. His patience and pleasant demeanor appealed to the children.

———•———

Even while having a low number of patients during the Great Depression, the sanitarium grew in stature. In 1931, it gained approval as a nurses' training school, one of the few in the country that offered graduate-level training in psychiatric nursing. Next, in 1933, it was approved for residencies in psychiatry. Young physicians could become psychiatrists under the tutelage of the Menninger doctors. The Menninger sanitarium became one of the best-staffed facilities in the state. Young doctors got training in child psychiatry at the Southard School and learned to treat outpatients who lived in or near Topeka. Nurses often outnumbered the patients.

Part of the attraction to the Menninger residency program was the growing interest in psychoanalytic training in the 1930s. Popularized in Europe by Freud, psychoanalysis had spread only to a few major U.S. cities, mostly in the East. John Stone, business manager and a limited partner in the Menninger programs, was so interested in psychoanalysis he volunteered to go to Chicago to investigate up close the work of analyst Franz Alexander, a protégé of Freud. When he brought back a positive report, Karl committed to the process, which required that he spend a lot of time in Chicago. After a couple of years, Karl received certificate No. 1 from the Chicago Psychoanalytic Institute under Alexander's analysis. This made Karl the first analyst in Topeka and ultimately led to the founding in 1938 of the Topeka Institute for Psychoanalysis—the first such association west of the Mississippi River—as a branch of the Chicago institute. As such organizations were developed as "branches" under the sponsorship of an established institute, the official psychoanalytic institutes in San Francisco and Los Angeles branched out of the Topeka Institute for Psychoanalysis.

Thus, by the late 1930s, the Menninger Clinic began training young doctors in the techniques of psychoanalysis. Part of the attraction was the unusual number of *émigrés* from Europe on staff at Menninger. The *émigrés* were coveted as doctors since there were so few trained psychoanalysts in the U.S. Recruiting veterans of psychoanalytic training to the clinic was beneficial for a variety of reasons. They could better model to the Menninger staff the European version of Freud's methods than could American psychoanalysts. They would also bring prestige and income to the clinic. As psychoanalysis became fashionable in the U.S., affluent patients would pay more for this specialized care than would the typical psychiatric patient. More psychoanalysts on staff meant more wealthy patients willing to pay for specialized treatment. The *émigrés* became even more essential to the Menninger clinic between 1943 and 1945, when many America-born physicians were called to serve in the military.

It's no coincidence that European psychoanalysts were looking to relocate during the mid-1930s. Psychoanalysis was branded by the Nazis as "Jewish science." As the political situation in Europe became more precarious for psychiatrists, particularly the large number of Jews in the profession, Topeka became an attractive new home. It would not be an exaggeration to say that immigration saved the lives of some of these doctors and their families. They were thankful for the opportunity provided by the Menninger Clinic to safely relocate their families and continue in their chosen profession.

———————————

As the Depression loosened its grip, the clinic grew. In the late 1930s, between 100 and 150 patients were admitted per year. About 40 percent of those were classified as psychotic, the rest psychoneurotic. The clinic treated people with a variety of maladies: from epilepsy to alcoholism, schizophrenia to eating disorders.

While the Menninger Clinic was embraced by Topeka, it rose in prominence nationwide. Karl wrote monthly columns about mental health for *Ladies' Home Journal* and *Household Magazine*. He published a second well-received book called *Man Against Himself*. And in 1936, *The Bulletin of the Menninger Clinic* was launched. This bi-monthly journal began as a vehicle for Menninger doctors and residents to publish their research. Soon, other psychiatrists were submitting their papers for publication in *The Bulletin of the Menninger Clinic,* further enhancing its standing in the psychiatric community.

As treatment flourished and the reputation of the Menninger programs spread, money remained tight. While providing care at a reduced rate, or in some cases free of charge, the Menninger men invested much of their profits into the expansion of operations. As a for-profit business, they were unable to solicit grants from philanthropies and to tap the wealthy believers in their programs for support. Additional programs in education and expansion of the facilities required extra funds. To achieve the means to accomplish that work, they established a not-for-profit entity—the Menninger Foundation for Psychiatric Education and Research—in February 1941 to receive charitable donations for tax benefit. The need for funds increased exponentially after World War II as the foundation had a greater commitment to education and research. After the Menninger Foundation was created, my grandfather, father, and uncle all donated their stock in the entity to the foundation and thus gave away whatever "fortune" they might have otherwise amassed.

But Grandfather certainly wasn't concerned about the money. His vision had come to fruition: a father and two sons working together in a practice that was rapidly becoming the psychiatric equivalent of the Mayo Clinic. The Menninger sanitarium had the support of Topeka and was training future psychiatrists during the 1930s.

During that decade, my father may have had at least some inkling that he was raising two future psychiatrists at home as well.

-3-

Growing Up a Menninger

I am the third-born son of a third-born son. Roy was the first of Will and Catharine's children, born in 1926. Next came Philip in 1928. And I made my appearance in this world on October 23, 1931.

My first name is actually William. My father went by "Will" or "Bill," and my older brother was Phil. To avoid confusion, my parents called me by my middle name, "Walter," the name of the doctor who delivered me. I always joked that there were too many "ills" in our family. Though I never went by William, I'm proud to have my father's name. So proud, in fact, I passed it on to my own third son.

After a few years in a house at 1276 Duane (now Medford) Street, my father and mother purchased a house at 1724 Southwest Collins Avenue in 1935. That was the southwest edge of Topeka at that time, a semi-developed neighborhood with dirt streets connecting us to town. It was the perfect spot for my parents to retreat from work or to host guests, as well as to raise three boys, just as my grandparents had done a few decades before.

The new neighborhood, with houses separated by undeveloped lots, allowed us kids plenty of freedom to roam. Our property had a clay tennis court on one side that we used when the weather was nice. My parents kept birdhouses and planted a variety of trees to cultivate the big lot. We had a shack behind the house that served various purposes over the years from club house to chicken coop to potting shed. My parents added on to the house twice over the years, and it became a scene for social gatherings. Of course, what I remember most is having to mow the spacious lawn.

When I was very young, all three of us boys simultaneously came down with scarlet fever (caused by a germ that today would be readily treated with penicillin), a disease which had nearly claimed my father's life when he was a baby. We had to quarantine for about ten days. I don't remember much about it other than my mother having to scrub everything in the house, ostensibly to control the spread of the disease.

One obstacle marred my childhood. I didn't allow myself to see straight.

That's my personal interpretation anyway.

All three of Will and Catharine's children had some sort of visual defect. Roy had nystagmus, which prevents the smooth movement of the eyes and can affect coordination and balance. It compromised Roy some in his athletics.

Phil had dyslexia, a disability that affects the processing of language. It really affected Phil's academics. He struggled in reading and math.

I had strabismus, a condition in which the eyes do not line up with one another. My eyes crossed at about four years of age. If I attempt to analyze what happened, I surmise that I just didn't want to see things straight.

The Oedipal story would say that I wanted my mother's attention. As a child, I underwent two surgeries to correct the condition. When my mother took me to get those surgeries—one in Topeka and one in Chicago—I got her all to myself.

The misalignment of my eyes was such that, at age 19, when I looked at you with my left eye, my right eye deviated 25 degrees. When I looked at you with my right eye, my left eye deviated 40 degrees. We tried one more surgery before I started my senior year of college, improving the condition to some degree. The surgeries, eye exercises, and compensations I learned to make minimized the effect of the condition and made it less noticeable. My saving grace was that when using my left eye—my dominant eye—my right eye isn't that far off. The drooping of my right eyelid conceals somewhat that I'm not looking straight with both eyes.

I have negotiated a life with this condition. My right eye is nearsighted, while my left eye is farsighted. So, I use my left eye for driving or for any long-distance viewing. I read with my right eye. By making accommodations, I've been able to finesse this deficiency.

I was oblivious to how it affected me as a kid. I had good friends and was able to participate in any activity they did. My friends could easily see that my eyes didn't line up, but I never experienced it as any kind of compromise or significant disability.

Every Sunday, we attended First Presbyterian Church on Harrison Street, where without fail we would find my grandparents in their pew. I don't know if they were still renting pews in those days. But regardless, there C.F. and Flo were, in the same place, for every service. Every Sunday after church, we had lunch at The Pennant, a cafeteria on the second floor of a building on Kansas Avenue. In the late afternoon we would drive out to Oakwood, my grandparents' 80-acre farm on the north edge of Topeka.

My grandfather was still working full time at the Menninger Hospital while I was growing up, but Oakwood was his retreat. After Karl and my father got established, grandfather devoted as much time to tending his trees and gardens as his schedule would permit. But the Menninger psychiatric practice depended upon income from my grandfather's general practice throughout most of the 1920s, so he wasn't able to back off much. He was particularly important to the work at the Southard School for children. So, he continued to carry a full load at the Menninger clinic all the way up to his passing in 1953. Regardless, his brilliance as a horticulturalist was on display at the Menninger clinic property, and it was amazing what he could accomplish despite working full-time even in his 80s.

Throughout my childhood, the whole extended family (minus Edwin, who by then was entrenched in Florida) would go out to Oakwood for the Sunday gatherings. Karl and his family—his first wife, Grace, and their children, Julia, Bob, and Martha—would be there to meet Mom and Dad and we three boys. Edwin's son, Eddie, Jr., lived with my grandparents for several years. And a woman named Pearl May Boam, who we called "Aunt Pearl," lived with them as sort of an adopted relative. Additionally, at any given time, there might be other people staying temporarily with my grandparents or with one of our families. So, every Sunday there was a big, vibrant gathering that was exciting for a little boy like me.

Grandmother, Aunt Pearl, Aunt Grace, and my mother would collaborate to make a big evening meal. While they worked in the kitchen, the children were shoved outside to entertain ourselves. I was the runt of the litter, the youngest of my family and much younger than Karl's children. I was a little kid running to catch up. I recall that they had some toy cars and blocks that I played with when I was too young to chase after the bigger kids.

After the kids wore themselves out and the grand meal was consumed, Grandfather would ritually read to everyone from the Bible. Sometimes we would look at pictures through a Stereopticon, which was an old-fashioned slide projector. My grandparents (particularly my grandmother) were serious folks who never let a teachable moment pass. So, most of the discussion and the slide presentations went over my head. We would stay overnight at their farmhouse occasionally. They had one indoor toilet, and you had a urinal that you kept by your bed.

My grandmother would make pounds of candy to give away at Christmas time, so the grandchildren were recruited to crack nuts. I was too little to accomplish much, but I wanted to be part of whatever the bigger kids were doing.

I was too young to remember the actual occasion, but the celebration of my grandparents' 50th anniversary was a pretty noteworthy event in Topeka in 1935. It began with my grandparents dressing up—a rarity for my grandmother—for a party planned by my mother, Grace, and Aunt Pearl. My grandparents drove to Karl's house for dinner, where they were surprised by my family and by the unannounced arrival of Edwin from Florida. It was the first time my grandparents' three sons had been together in 21 years. After the grandkids showered them with our love, my grandparents returned to their home for an open house celebration. More than 200 friends drove out to the Oakwood farm to congratulate them.

Oakwood was a very special retreat for my grandparents that was disrupted by World War II. When gas rationing was imposed, it became problematic for my grandparents to make the trips back and forth from the country, so they moved back into town. But from 1931 until 1942, Sunday afternoons at Oakwood were our ritual.

I didn't realize it as a child, but my grandparents were very important in the eyes of Topekans. Once I became a teenager, I didn't spend much time connecting with them. Therefore, I'm grateful for those times that I spent with them in my first 11 years.

My grandfather was always gentle and gracious to us grandkids. He was also brilliant and had an infinite amount of wisdom to share.

Unfortunately, I never had a significant intellectual conversation with him. I was about 11 when we stopped going to the farm for Sunday afternoons. After the rationing due to World War II ended, I was in high school and was engrossed in my own teenage activities. Then I was off to college, and then medical school.

I regret that I didn't engage my grandfather more. He was a Renaissance man, interested in rocks and minerals and plants and animals, as well as the arts. I guess I wasn't at the intellectual level as a child to recognize what I could learn from him. When our extended family gathered, I was more preoccupied with trying to keep up with my older siblings and cousins. I am trying to not let that happen with my own grandchildren (and great-grandchildren). I make an attempt to really converse with them when the opportunity presents itself.

My grandmother was my grandfather's equal when it came to learning. After moving to Topeka, she sought to join a women's Bible study at First Presbyterian conducted by the pastor's wife. She was rebuffed because the group was for single women only. Flo talked it over with the pastor who suggested that she start her own study for "old married women." She had just moved into the big house at 1251 Topeka Avenue, which would easily permit her to host a large group study. She also had access to some materials from which she could teach.

At first, starting her own study seemed daunting. Looking for a sign of confirmation, Grandmother decided to ask a friend if she would be interested in joining.

"It is just the thing I have wanted to do for years!" the woman replied enthusiastically. There was the sign my grandmother needed. Just three weeks after the birth of my father, she hosted the first Bible study at her home.

Spearheading a Bible study was significant enough, but it was what happened a few years later that really shook things up. In time, she felt she'd exhausted the study materials she was using. She wanted to adopt a more "expository" style, focusing more on the text and essentially letting the Bible teach itself. In 1903, she wrote her first set of lessons. She presented to the leadership at First Presbyterian the idea of charging $5 (to cover printing costs) to participate in what would become the Menninger Bible Lessons. The church leaders voted her down. They didn't feel comfortable with teachers writing their own lessons, and they certainly didn't approve of charging for the lessons.

Not surprisingly, considering her tenacious nature, Grandmother wasn't deterred. She simply went to the local newspapers to announce the launch of her new non-denominational Bible study. Her vision was for a community-wide program, not sponsored by a church.

Word soon spread about the Bible study, and women from other communities began to inquire how they could offer the program as well. Flo began sending the materials out to subscribers. Eventually she was providing Bible teaching to thousands of women.

It's the work she did on the Bible study that I remember most about Grandmother. She was deeply committed, spending time on it pretty much every day. You would find her poring over her notes or preparing packages to mail to her many subscribers. At her house, she had a long set of cubbyholes in the attic, and in each slot was a lesson page. Grandmother drove a battery-operated electric car called a Phaeton to the Bible classes on Tuesdays. The Bible study got so big that in 1923, the YWCA incorporated the program under its management.

Grandmother was always somewhat distant and a bit foreboding to me. You stayed out of her way. She was not the kind of person who sat down and did a lot of socializing. Aunt Pearl was more the one to take care of the children.

I remember well when I was nine years old, I memorized the names of the 66 books of the Bible. Grandmother presented me a set of little books of the Bible for youth, which was her reward for accomplishing the feat. That was her way of showing love and affection. She was a teacher at heart, and she believed the best way to bless others was to help them better themselves. She did not suffer fools. She was busy. She had her projects. Whether it was selling peonies on Memorial Day or writing her Bible studies, she was serious.

But that's not to say my grandparents didn't have fun. They went to the Chautauqua meetings in New York pretty much every year, renting a cabin and interacting with the folks in attendance, many of them friends from previous years. My grandmother was well known in those settings for her Bible study. My grandfather was more likely to keep a low profile, not letting on that he was a significant doctor who oversaw a growing psychiatric practice. My grandparents also frequently went to Florida to visit Edwin. My grandfather took great pleasure in Edwin's effort to promote flowering trees in Florida and was proud that the son who didn't become a psychiatrist was finding success in his own field.

My grandmother wrote an autobiography entitled *Days of My Life*, which was published in 1939. She inscribed my copy of it "To Walter, 'Good words cool more than cold water.' Grandmother, 1940."

Because she was a little hard to feel close to, I look at some of the words in the autobiography for insight into her personality. I can see her faith, wisdom, and dedication, but also her love and care for others:

> Dreams are a common indulgence. Some dreams are fantastic and futile, but others are well founded and become sound ambitions. They urge us to follow our purpose with faith, in the belief that we can do whatever we want to if we think we can. There are many obstacles to be overcome, and many of them we cannot understand, but holding fast to a purpose wins. We can do the thing we want to do if we are earnest enough to make it the first and greatest object in life.
>
> I have never found it hard to believe that there is a God who rules the universe, and that He is the power and strength that man can have if he believes and trusts Him. But how to live according to this belief—that has been my daily problem. How well I have succeeded remains to be told by my own family and by those who have tried to think with me as we have studied our Bibles through together. The whole New Testament tells us about a way of life that cannot fail to help anyone who accepts the pattern. 'I am come that ye might have life, through His name.' Those who have tried this believe it, and by their living help others to a happier life.

―――――――――――

By the time I was born, my father was running the Menninger sanitarium, allowing Karl to focus on writing and promoting new concepts in psychiatry. Dad was almost solely responsible for fostering the family atmosphere at the hospital. With finances still tight for the Menninger programs, he felt pressure to hold down expenses and maximize revenues. And with the sanitarium still developing, he was compelled to personally ensure that each doctor, nurse, and staff member adhered to his *Abbreviated Guide to Therapeutic Aims.*

During the early 1930s, as Karl had a few years earlier, my father underwent psychoanalysis in Chicago, a very time-consuming endeavor. He traveled back and forth, mostly by train, meeting with the same Franz Alexander who did Karl's analysis. Psychoanalysis often requires multiple meetings a week for long stretches, usually over a two-to-three-year period. So, he was away from home frequently during that period of my childhood.

At this same time, my father's stature in the Boy Scouts also continued to grow. He went to the World Jamboree in Hungary in 1933, seizing upon this opportunity to make a grand tour of Europe.

My father showed some remarkable resourcefulness in the late 1920s and early 1930s, devising a Sea Scout program that would allow land-locked kids like those in Topeka to earn their maritime badges. Using an outline of a boat, the *Sea Scout Ship Kansan,* painted on the floor in the basement of the church, Dad taught the boys the skills of navigation.

The Topeka scouts amazed everybody with the skills they could master "cruising" in canoes on the Kansas River and simulating nautical maneuvers in the boat outlined on the church floor. Their record keeping for the *S.S.S. Kansan* won the national award not once, but twice. When they were a shoo-in to win for the third consecutive year, the Boy Scouts presented the Topeka troop an honorary award in order to give someone else a chance.

Dad became a member of the National Sea Scout Committee and wrote a skipper's manual, which was soon adopted by the Boy Scouts of America to serve as their *Handbook for Skippers.* In the late 1930s, he became a member of the National Executive Board of the Boy Scouts and remained a member until his death.

My older brothers, particularly Roy, who is five years my elder, were just old enough to start their involvement in scouting programs prior to World War II. I had to wait, understanding that it was through scouting that we got to engage my father.

When he wasn't occupied with work or the Scouts, my father liked to retreat to the den in our home to work on his stamp collection. That was his escape. He and my mother had desks that faced each other in the den. They would work on their projects, facing each other but engrossed in their own endeavors, enjoying those quiet moments when we three boys weren't disrupting their peace.

My parents loved to travel and in the summer of 1941, they planned a big road trip for the family. Partly as an escape from responsibilities, and partly as a family bonding exercise, Dad and Mom loaded up the three boys in our Buick sedan and headed north from Topeka. We made a pilgrimage to all the great natural wonders of the West: the Black Hills, Yellowstone, the Great Salt Lake, Bryce and Zion National Parks, the Grand Canyon, and Santa Fe.

The three-week trek was one of the golden moments of my childhood. Perhaps it became more meaningful once World War II started and my father spent so much time away from us. Or perhaps it was significant because it was one of our last great adventures before my brothers began leaving for college. For whatever reason, that family vacation meant so much to me, I wanted to share it with my own family. I did, in 1969, in a Winnebago packed with my own six children.

I turned ten in the fall of 1941. Up to then, my childhood had been pretty idyllic. Despite my ocular defect and the lingering effects of the Great Depression, I was a very happy child. We had a nice home, plenty of pets for companionship, and I had good friends. My grandparents were prominent and respected. My mother was attentive and loving. My father was a good role model and leader of the family. He hadn't yet gained the national acclaim that my uncle had.

That was about to change, as were our entire lives.

Dr. Will Goes to War

In the old days, before television, we listened to the radio. We listened to the news, comedic and theatrical programs, and music. It seemed like the radio was nearly always on. So, it was pretty typical when, on the afternoon of Sunday, December 7, 1941, we were listening to the radio in my parents' den before heading off to my grandparents' house for family dinner.

I had just turned ten. I didn't know much at all about world events, much less the politics of Europe and the Far East. But I was mature enough to be impressed by the gravity of the announcements that started coming over the radio. Pearl Harbor had been bombed by the Japanese.

I understood that the world was about to change. But I had no idea how my personal world and the world of the Menninger Clinic were both about to change as well.

After the shock of Pearl Harbor wore off, a wave of patriotism and a grim perception of duty took over. It was sensed that either Dad or Uncle Karl needed to volunteer to serve in the war effort while the other stayed back to run the clinic. Dad was the younger of the two—he was 42 years old when the Japanese bombed Pearl Harbor. So, in early 1942 he went to Washington, D.C. to find out what his options might be.

Karl would take over the responsibility of overseeing all the Menninger programs and finances. Dr. Robert Worthington was designated to supervise the hospital in my father's absence, which was clearly intended to be temporary. My grandfather, now nearly 80 years old, would assist Dr. Worthington on an informal basis.

Of course, the family worried about the future of the Menninger hospital. As was common everywhere, the clinic suffered a manpower shortage during the war. How would they keep staff levels up to provide the quality of care associated with Menninger? For that matter, would enough patients still seek treatment to keep the Menninger doors open?

The family put those worries aside. The war effort came first. There was a fear that if the Allies didn't win the war, nothing else would be left anyway. Children were generally shielded from the specific anxieties parents were experiencing. But air raid drills and flash cards of enemy war planes reminded us of the conflict going on.

The decision for my father to join the Army and for Karl to take over the day-to-day affairs at Menninger had the effect of a role reversal for the two men. Thrust into the world of military, government, and politics, my father would become a reformer on the national scene. Karl would become more focused on the training programs in Topeka, and as was his nature, he saw much more potential than what was being accomplished.

A major problem in the United States came to light as the war effort ramped up: something like 1.5 million prospective soldiers were rejected by the military on the basis of neurological disorders. The country realized that mental health issues were a serious and widespread problem that was not being dealt with adequately.

It was with that fresh realization that the military inducted Dr. Will Menninger in November 1942. He was initially assigned to be the Chief Psychiatric Consultant for the Fourth Service Command. Stationed in Atlanta, he was to go to all the Army installations in the southeast portion of the U.S. to inspect and support their psychiatric services.

That Christmas, after he had been gone a little over one month, Mom and we three boys took our car to Atlanta so that Dad could use it while stationed there. We would take the train back to Topeka after celebrating the holidays with him. Since he didn't have a house for us to stay in, we spent Christmas in a hotel in downtown Atlanta.

My father turned out to be well suited for the assignment. He wasn't the typical "shrink." He knew how to connect with people. He was always able to find something in common with everyone. His warmth, wit, and breadth of knowledge were paired with his serious approach to mental health care. He quickly earned respect in military circles, and his superiors sought his input. Beginning as a lieutenant colonel and neuropsychiatry consultant for the Fourth Service Command, he rose quickly.

One year after my father's induction, Col. Roy Halloran, the chief psychiatric consultant under the Surgeon General, died unexpectedly on

November 10, 1943. When asked about a replacement, Malcolm Farrell, Halloran's assistant director of Neuropsychiatry Division, who was next in line for the position, said, "You don't want me. You want Bill Menninger."

Thus, my father was summoned to Washington, D.C. to take over as Director of the Neuropsychiatric Consultants Division, reporting directly to Surgeon General Norman T. Kirk. By early 1944, he was in charge of all the psychiatry efforts of the Army, ultimately achieving the rank of brigadier general.

My father quickly found himself on a crusade to overcome the military's misunderstandings of psychiatry.

The role he was given at the end of 1943 was a huge responsibility. Once U.S. troops entered the fighting of World War II, about 40 percent of those discharged from the military were sent home for reasons of mental health. The country was about to have a mental health crisis on its hands. My father was well positioned to help with the immediate crisis and to begin to shape the minds of political and military leaders regarding the need for psychiatric health care in the U.S. He fought against the perception in the military that those who showed signs of mental disorders were cowards or undisciplined and lazy. Dad believed that quick intervention was often effective to minimize the effects of the trauma experienced in battle.

My father found the military's approach to mental health and illness was lacking. Screening was cursory at best. The Army had essentially just two categories: "Fit For Duty" or "Sick." It was not prepared to do anything in terms of preventive psychiatry, nor to provide immediate treatment near the front lines. It was really only prepared to remove the disturbed from the ranks. The Army had no common "nosology," i.e., the language of diagnosis. Dad went to work to develop one, consulting with Karl and seeking input from many of the top psychiatrists across the country.

What resulted from my father's work with these other psychiatrists was the *Diagnostic and Statistical Manual of Mental Disorders* in American psychiatry, commonly known as DSM. It was circulated in the military as something called *Medical 203* in 1945. With that unimpressive name, it became the basis of psychiatric classification in postwar America. The DSM is now in its fifth iteration, extensively modernized, but through it my father's impact on psychiatry continues to reverberate throughout the nation.

My father understood that the mental health issues of the military weren't necessarily all caused by combat. In fact, most were not. Of the 850,000 soldiers hospitalized with neuropsychiatric illness, 60 percent of those occurred in the U.S. rather than on the battlefield. This seemed to indicate that it wasn't always the trauma of combat that produced psychotic episodes. Most of these men entered the military with mental health needs, which were detected later.

Prior to the war, psychiatry was largely associated with state hospitals. There weren't a lot of private institutions that were training new psychiatrists. But when the military was faced with so many returning from the war suffering from the effects of trauma—what we now call Post Traumatic Stress Disorder—it had precious little time to respond. My father was at the forefront of the effort to develop a 90-day program to train doctors to deal with this during World War II.

Under my father's guidance, the military's psychiatric services were built essentially from the ground up. In short order, 2,400 physicians were assigned to neuropsychiatric services. When a lot of those doctors came out of that training experience, they had developed an interest in psychiatry and saw the tremendous need for it.

For his work birthing the plan to provide psychiatric care to soldiers, my father quickly emerged from my uncle Karl's shadow. Dad was presented the Lasker Award for outstanding contribution to the mental health of the men and women of the armed forces at the annual meeting of the National Committee for Mental Hygiene in New York on November 9, 1944.

My father's highest honor came after the war, however. He was presented the Distinguished Service Medal in 1946 "for exceptionally meritorious and distinguished services to the Government of the United States, in a duty of great responsibility." A close second would be his inclusion in the French Legion of Honor in 1948 for his wartime contributions to the mental health of the Allied Forces.

When he entered the Army, my father was distressed to find that the lessons learned from treating the neuropsychiatric casualties of World War I had been forgotten. Whether they unknowingly or willfully turned a blind eye to the effects of combat and to the general mental health needs of the men who served in the Great War, the country had failed to take advantage of the opportunity that World War I presented. He was determined to prevent any such learning loss to occur on his watch. Immediately after World War II, my father tried to translate the lessons of the war to the state of mental health care at large in a book entitled *Psychiatry in a Troubled World: Yesterday's War and Today's Challenge*. My father wrote several books, but this was his magnum opus.

One of my most vivid memories of my father's absence during the war occurred in the fall of 1943, and of course, it involved Scouting. Turning 12 was a watershed moment for each of us boys, because it was then that you could earn promotion from Cub Scouts to Boy Scouts. Roy and Phil were several years ahead of me, so they had already become Boy Scouts, and thus had a key connection with my father. By the time my father left for the war, Roy was already an Eagle Scout.

The night I turned 12, I passed my Tenderfoot tests. I called my dad on the phone and told him I got my Tenderfoot badge, the first badge I could get as a Boy Scout. That was one of the most memorable moments of the time that he was away during the war. To be able to call him on the phone to report my accomplishment and get his approval—that was a special moment of emotional connection. I was so proud to tell him about it over the phone, but of course I certainly wished that he had been there to share the moment with me in person.

Dad came home from Washington, D.C. for a short visit at Christmas of 1943. There was some optimism that, with the U.S. now fully involved, the war would end soon. But my parents decided that since Dad would be settled in the nation's capital for at least a couple of years, we should join him there. We finished that school year in Topeka—I was in 7th grade— then moved to D.C. in the summer of 1944. We rented a house at 2260 Cathedral Avenue, right across from Rock Creek Park, which is just north of the heart of the city. Thus, I did my 8th and 9th grade school years there.

Moving to D.C. didn't seem like a hardship to me. It seemed like an adventure. I was happy and had good friends in Topeka, but I wasn't afraid to leave that behind to experience living in another city. We were retaining our house in Topeka and leaving a lot of our things there, so I guess it didn't seem like a permanent move but rather an interlude.

One problem we had when we reached D.C. was that we couldn't find a Boy Scout troop that was a good fit. I had zipped right up to Star—the fourth of seven ranks of the Boy Scouts. But my progress was stymied at that point.

One thing was for sure: if we were going to be stationed on the East Coast, my mother was going to make sure that we saw everything there was to see there. We visited all the monuments and everything of cultural interest. She kept us on the go.

Roy went off to college that year, so he didn't live with us for long in D.C. He packed off to Swarthmore College in Pennsylvania that fall. But Phil and I were back living with Dad under the same roof. Dad commuted each day to his downtown office in the Office of the Surgeon General, just a few blocks from the White House. He was very busy—he made several trips to Europe and the Pacific to visit field hospitals and monitor the programs he put in place—but at least we got to see him on a regular basis.

Phil and I enjoyed riding the buses all over the city, experiencing a new degree of independence in the midst of a vibrant culture. Topeka was all we'd known up to that point, so whether we were seeing the city by ourselves or with my parents, it was a big adventure.

I attended Alice Deal Junior High, which is still in existence today. It was out toward Chevy Chase, Maryland, and didn't really feel much different from the schools I'd attended in Topeka.

The first day, the teacher said, "I'll call you whatever you would like to be called." One of the kids told the teacher that he would like to be called "Hubcap." That impressed me that I could be called something more unique than "Will" or "Walter" or "Walt." Back home, I had been called "Minnie" (short for Menninger, obviously). Inevitably, that nickname evolved into "Minnie Mouse" in my grade school years. In front of the entire class, I shared that suggestion with the Alice Deal Junior High teacher. She didn't call me by that name, but you better believe the other students started calling me "Minnie Mouse." That gave me an immediate identity amongst my new classmates.

My grandparents were so proud of my father's work, they came to visit us in Washington, D.C. Little did we know that my grandmother didn't have a lot of time left. It would be the last time I saw her. She passed away at home in Topeka on the morning of February 9, 1945. In addition to her funeral, a large service organized by the Bible study classes was held in Topeka, to honor her life and recognize her influence. Though the leader passed on, the classes persevered. They are held to this day.

My grandfather visited us a couple more times while we were stationed in D.C. He especially loved the beautifully manicured landscape and the variety of trees and flowers that decorated the city. In Topeka, he continued working as hard as a man in his 80s could to help out at the Menninger Hospital while Dad was away.

Sometimes in life, things that would seem very minor turn out to be very significant in your development. When I was in 8th grade, the Alice Deal Junior High manual arts teacher got drafted. Thus, the school had a hole in its curriculum that it needed to fill. Given a couple of options for a replacement course, I chose Introductory Typing. I know a lot of the boys who wanted to build things and use tools were disappointed, but it turned out to be a boon for me. Learning to type proficiently and compose at the keyboard would pay dividends throughout my life as I wrote countless articles and scholarly papers and even a few books as an adult. I will be forever thankful for the gift of having learned the techniques of touch typing, a skill that was somewhat unappreciated at the time.

Before I could begin writing things for people to read, I brought reading materials to their doorsteps. During my first year in D.C., I started delivering the *Washington Evening Star*, an afternoon newspaper. I soon realized that I could make more money delivering the *Washington Post*, the morning newspaper. My second route consisted of some apartments and residences in our general neighborhood. My brother Phil got a route as well. We would come back from our morning routes and play chess until it was time to go to school.

I learned two things from my newspaper route job. The newspaper company took advantage of kids. You had to pay for the papers, then you had to collect from your customers. So, if you didn't collect from every customer all that they owed, it was money out of your pocket. The other thing I learned was that I could be a pretty good salesman when sufficiently motivated. I earned enough credit from selling new subscriptions to win a ticket to the Washington Senators' opening day game against the Boston Red Sox in 1946. Who should be on the field that day but the great Ted Williams, making his triumphant return from three years of military service. We all cheered when he hit a home run that day.

I suppose a lot of the students at Alice Deal Junior High were children of government employees, but none of us knew what each other's parents did. No one knew who my father was, and no one cared. I got along well with the kids there. I got along with the adults as well, with one glaring exception.

During my 9th grade year, I was with a group of teenagers who had been to see a movie at a theater in our part of the city. After exiting the theater, we gathered in front of a post office branch that was right next door to the theater, pausing to discuss what we should do next. There happened to be a policeman standing against the wall of the post office. "Move along, boys," he said.

I said to one of my friends, loud enough that the policeman apparently heard me, that the officer reminded me of an overly officious administrator at our school who frequently cracked down on us. Now provoked, the policeman started following as we walked down the street to a drug store. As we were about to go into the store, he said to me, "Who do I remind you of?"

I replied, "Oh, a friend from school."

He said, "You know, I could take you in."

We started to go into the drug store, and I guess I must have made some other smart-aleck comment. The policeman waved me back. He said, "Let's go," and he walked me home, about six blocks.

The whole way I was thinking, "Wait until he gets to my house and meets the general." But when we got there, my father opened the door in his civilian clothes and said, "Thank you very much, officer. I appreciate your concern."

All I could think was, *What the hell?!? This ass of a hyper-sensitive police officer thinks I'm some sort of juvenile delinquent.* I wanted him to get reamed out by a general.

But Dad was too smooth.

You can imagine that story went around the school. Minnie Mouse had been hauled off by the cops. What a troublemaker!

———————————

Knowing the kinds of trauma soldiers experienced during the war, my father understood what kinds of needs there would soon be on the home front. By early 1945, the military was sending home about 1,000 soldiers a day from the European Theater. There would be an unprecedented amount, and a unique type, of psychological damage that would need to be dealt with once all the soldiers made it home from Europe and the Pacific. More than 30 percent of the casualties of the war were neuropsychiatric, but just two percent of the doctors in the country were psychiatrists. The country had just 3,000 psychiatrists at the time. My father and Karl estimated that 10,000 psychiatrists would be needed, as well as 1,000 clinics and 5,000 psychiatric social workers. That number of specialized nurses would also be needed.

How would the country ever handle this need, so recently recognized and growing by the day?

In Topeka, Karl was working on that question from the civilian angle, advocating for improved mental health care for all Americans. As the Allies swept across Europe and liberated lands oppressed by the Nazis, Karl was included in a 1944 delegation that viewed war hospital sites and talked with soldiers about the types of treatments they were receiving, as well as the treatments they would need upon returning home. The delegation also toured Buchenwald concentration camp in Germany. Karl was horrified by the physical damage done by the war, the inhumanity of the camp, and the mental toll on both civilians and soldiers. My uncle understood the need for training psychiatrists who could alleviate the crushing need for mental health care following the war. He communicated his commitment to meeting that need in a letter to a friend:

> The instruction of residents—not only physicians,
> but psychologists, nurses and therapists—is the thing that

is closest to my heart. We have felt it so strongly that we have converted our whole institution into a non-profit foundation with its primary aim as education.

After serving as field commander of the invasion of Europe, Gen. Omar Bradley was appointed Veterans Administrator in 1945. He brought with him the chief surgeon for the European Theater, Maj. Gen. Paul Hawley. The two had a desire to drastically improve the VA. They didn't, however, have a clear plan for meeting the crush of mental health casualties.

Working under Bradley, Col. Arthur Marshall would be one of the men making a lot of the decisions regarding VA mental health care. Knowing there was talk of closing Winter General Hospital, an Army hospital located at 2200 Southwest Gage in Topeka, Marshall approached Karl with the idea of turning it into a pilot training center for VA psychiatry services.

Marshall asked if the Menninger training programs could meet the need. Karl's response was "Well, maybe we could train 15 or 20." The largest training program at that point was at Belleview Hospital in New York City, where they trained about 20 over three years.

Marshall responded, "We don't need 15 or 20. We need 100."

The request was audacious. A lot of people, including those on the Menninger staff, doubted it could be done. But Marshall insisted, "There's nothing worse than a modest start—whatever you haven't got, we'll get."

Recognizing the need, Menninger geared up quickly to try to meet the challenge. Out of that necessity was born the Menninger School of Psychiatry. Hawley and Marshall worked with the clinic to establish the training outpost at Winter General Hospital under the umbrella of the school, which I will refer to from this point on as the MSP.

The impact on Topeka was enormous. Imagine a hospital that was about to be closed down—removing from the city those jobs and revenue—increasing to nearly 1,000 employees and more than 1,500 patients to meet an urgent need. At that time, the training program at the clinic was expanded. It attracted hundreds of young doctors, many with families, to the city.

Karl focused on getting Winter General Hospital up to speed. This required a lot of remodeling of the old building, a transition of the inpatient population, and hiring of a lot of staff. It had to be done at a breakneck pace, and it wasn't a flawless process. But the need was so great there was no time to wait.

With Dr. Martin Mayman and Dr. Paul Puyser, Karl wrote *A Manual for Psychiatric Case Study* to guide the students at MSP. He called it "a blueprint for a standard procedure of studying psychiatric patients, recording and organizing clinical data in a purposeful way, and presenting the conclusions and recommendations to which these data have led." It would guide training at Menninger for years to come.

Between January and October of 1946, 108 new residents arrived in Topeka to enroll in the brand-new MSP. That number was more than half of all new psychiatric residents in the VA system and nearly one-third of all residents in the country.

I think Karl assumed that my father wouldn't think twice about any other career options. He planned for Dad to come home to run the hospital again. My father was offered prestigious positions at other institutions around the country. But ultimately, Dad decided Topeka was our home.

The war came to an end right as the 1945-46 school year was about to begin. Dad had to stay and oversee the transition. He was scheduled to muster out in 1946. So, we stayed for another school year. We hadn't had a family vacation since the glorious trip of 1941. Since that trip was to the West, it only made sense that we should see the Northeast before we left D.C. in the summer of 1946. We visited Cape Cod, Bar Harbor, and the New England states. We took a ferry from Buffalo across Lake Erie to Detroit. Then my dad decided, "Let's get home!" So, we drove almost 20 hours straight to get home to Topeka.

My dad left the military in 1946, but he wasn't done fighting. What I didn't really know at that time was that my father was leading a pitched battle over the future of psychiatry.

Many of the young psychiatrists with whom my father worked in the Army experienced a different type of psychiatry than the rest of the world was used to. They learned from my father about preventive psychiatry and about rapid responses to trauma, and they left the Army as a group of "Young Turks," who thought things should be different in the post-war world. They formed the progressive Group for the Advancement of Psychiatry, and they insisted my father serve as their chairman.

The Young Turks were members in the American Psychiatric Association (APA), but they were unhappy with the old ways of psychiatry and pushed for change. This really shook things up at the APA, which was largely controlled by state hospital directors and college professors. Impatient with the old guard, the Young Turks swept through all the major professional organizations like Great Reformers, putting my dad in charge of not just the 4,400-member APA, but also the American Psychoanalytic Association and the Central Neuropsychiatric Association. Suddenly my father was leading a new army—an army of young psychiatrists—that was engaged in a revolution against the old ways of psychiatry.

When he was nominated in 1946 as a candidate for president of the American Psychoanalytic Association, Dad nearly declined. Although he had some strong ideas about changes that needed to be made, he thought the association was ineffective. Ultimately convinced to accept the position, he said in his acceptance speech:

> My impressions of the Association over the last ten years—and they are held by many of us outside the inner circle—is that there has been too much discord about which our critics are delighted to capitalize. One of our first aims must be to develop a uniform front, a spirit of unity towards the enormous jobs to be done. That must eclipse personal differences and sectional disagreements.

He found the organization to be changing, and as he was advocating for changes himself, he decided to join the fight. He believed, in the simplest of terms, that psychoanalysis, while a meaningful discipline, should be merged with psychiatry.

"I am convinced that the psychoanalytically-oriented psychiatrist and not the psychoanalyst per se represents the greatest hope in providing for (present) needs," he said.

My father returned to Topeka in 1946, a national figure involved in important conversations with important people about the future of psychiatry. And he returned to a vastly different set of Menninger programs than the ones he had left four years earlier.

Interestingly, the roles of my father and Karl had flip-flopped during the war. In the 1930s, Karl had been a renowned author and very public figure. He spoke and wrote about issues in mental health but didn't play an overly involved role in the day-to-day activities of the clinic. My father was the one who guided the staff and shaped the treatment programs.

After the war, primarily due to his prominence in the military, it was Dad who was speaking and doing interviews and meeting with dignitaries. Karl ran the booming training programs at the MSP.

Karl's roles continued to evolve in the years following the war. In the first 18 months that the MSP ran the training program at Winter Hospital, it treated more than 12,000 veterans, and he was at the center of everything. Once the MSP was established at the VA hospital, Karl added to his plate another institution that needed even greater reform—Topeka State Hospital. Kansas Governor Frank Carlson asked Karl, "Can you do at the state what you did at the VA?"

Subsequently, my father and my uncle stood as beacons of exemplary mental health treatment. The country looked to see what they were doing so right that others were doing so wrong. Because of Menninger's success at revamping Topeka State Hospital, my father became a resource to other states. Over the next several years, he was called to speak to the state legislatures of 25 states about improving their mental health services. Years later, my brother Roy addressed the legislature of North Carolina on the topic, while I was called to speak to the legislature of Tennessee. It was a proud moment for each of us to walk in our father's footsteps on this mission.

———————————————

In the fall of 1948, a couple of *TIME* magazine writers showed up at our house to meet with my father. He welcomed them in, and my mother provided them drinks as they sat down for an interview/rambling conversation about psychiatry.

What I remember about it was that the *Time* editors really wanted to lambast psychiatry with a negative story. But determined as they were to paint psychiatry in a bad light, Dad won the writers over. After talking for hours (and reviewing Dad's stamp collection) they parted on friendly terms. Those writers went to bat to make sure that the article did not have all of the negative intonations that the editors ostensibly wanted. Sure, they pointed out all the common criticisms of psychiatry. They made a particular point to emphasize the belief that psychiatrists, when they stumble onto success with a patient, don't really know what worked, much less why. They characterized psychiatry as "often experimental and sometimes obscure." And the editors did sprinkle throughout the articles a few cartoons that were not too flattering. But Dad, who they called "psychiatry's U.S. sales manager," was generally pleased by how it turned out.

The article effectively portrayed my father's humble, homespun way of talking. A couple of his witticisms the authors included: "Damage of the same kind can be done by a bullet, bacteria, or a mother-in-law," and "One does not have to know the cause of a fire to put it out."

The cover of *Time*'s October 25, 1948, edition was graced by an artist's portrait of my father partially obscuring a floating, whitish-gray brain with a keyhole in the membrane. Hovering over my father's left shoulder was an elegant, old-fashioned barrel key with a question mark subtly incorporated in the handle.

Below his name on the cover were the words, "Beware of two men in a horse," a subhead that would mean nothing unless you read the article. That sentence was drawn from my father's simple description of the conflict between a person's conscious and unconscious thoughts. My father told the writers that the mind is like the comical horse costume worn by two people—one playing the front end of the horse, and the other, unable to see, playing the back end.

> "The man up front (the Conscious part of the mind) tries to set the direction and make the whole animal behave; but he can never be sure what the man at the rear end of the horse (the Unconscious) is going to do next. If both ends of the horse are going in the same direction, your mental health is all right. If they aren't pulling together, there's likely to be trouble."

The article was even-handed enough to include a box of psychiatric terms, as well as a list of questions my father often used to prompt people to think about their own mental health. While my father was featured in many publications over the years, the *Time* feature would be one of his great calling cards.

-5-

The Trojan Years

My father's work kept him hustling around the country throughout my high school years. On the basis of his effectiveness in the Army, he became the face of American psychiatry.

I wasn't aware of all my father had on his mind at the end of the summer in 1946. I was preoccupied with my own thoughts. Much as I'd enjoyed the adventure of living for two years in the nation's capital, I was happy to get back to Topeka. I never thought twice about leaving Washington, D.C. It was just an interlude; I felt like I was returning home. But I was aware that things had changed in Topeka while I was gone.

Roy no longer lived with us. He was off at Swarthmore College in Pennsylvania. Philip would soon finish high school and enroll at Washburn College. My grandmother had passed away. Some of my friends had moved away from Topeka during the war. And I would be entering Topeka High School as a tenth grader, where I would have to rekindle old friendships, make new ones, and involve myself in new pursuits.

I knew enough people at Topeka High that I didn't feel like a foreigner. But the friends I retained from 7th grade were split up in the big high school. It wasn't like when we were cloistered in a "home room" community like we had been in younger grades. I returned to Topeka for my sophomore year of high school and had the task of finding my place in a social set that had matured a great deal in two years. I had to figure out how my friends had changed during my two-year absence, and what kind of person I would be in this new setting.

———————————✦———————————

One of the first things I set about was going out for the Topeka High Trojan football team. I tried my hand at the center position on the offensive line, but that was short-lived. An event that helped determine my direction as a high schooler was being left off the C Team that traveled to Lawrence for a "sub scrum" football scrimmage my sophomore year. That day in October of 1946, I was forced to come to grips with the reality that I would not be the next Bronco Nagurski. I put the football pads aside and pondered what was next.

With a little more time on my hands, I decided to dedicate myself to work on the *THS World*, the student newspaper managed by teacher Ruth Hunt. I was equipped with a general ability to express myself through writing. Plus, I was one of the few boys who could type well and compose at the keyboard. So, I was a natural fit for the newspaper staff, working my way up to become editor my senior year.

My other great love during high school was theater. Under the guidance of drama teacher Gertrude Wheeler, I joined the Topeka High Thespians, securing roles in a variety of performances. In the theater I made many of my closest friends and developed confidence for being on stage, enunciating, and projecting my voice in that enormous Topeka High auditorium.

I embarked upon these activities while also trying to regain some momentum in the Boy Scouts. During the two years spent in D.C., I had fallen behind on the typical track of a scout. The war, my father's commitments to the Army, and the absence of a scout troop that was conducive to our new life in D.C., had brought my scouting activities to a halt. Again in familiar territory, I got back on track for attaining Eagle Scout status, something that was expected in our home.

Scouting for me was first and foremost a means to connect with my father. He loved the Boy Scouts organization and was involved at a variety of levels. He returned to Topeka busier than ever, called upon to travel about the country for official business. If I wanted to be around him, to garner some of his attention, Scouting was the best way to do it.

My father had experienced the World Scout Jamboree in Hungary in 1933, and he was so impressed by the event that he wanted each of us boys to experience it as well. Held every four years, the routine of the jamboree was interrupted by World War II, so our opportunity to attend the event finally came in the summer of 1947, prior to my senior year of high school. Roy was 20 years old and went as an assistant Scoutmaster. Phil was about to turn 19 and attended as a senior Scout. I joined a group of Scouts for several days of camping at Forest Park in St. Louis that was to orient us for the trip across the ocean for the 6th World Scout Jamboree at Moisson, France, which is just north of Paris. We took the train to New York City, where we spent a couple of days seeing the sights before boarding a troop ship to cross the Atlantic. The trip was highlighted by chess tournaments and other activities.

Docked in Antwerp, Belgium, the ship served as home base for a couple of days of bus trips around Belgium and Holland. On the third day, we joined 24,000 scouts at a campground at Moisson, where we engaged in camping and pioneering activities. A highlight for me was a connection we made with Scouts from New Zealand. The lowlight was the ice-cold showers.

My older brothers got to spend a couple of days visiting Paris. My troop was limited to a single day in the city. The highlight was purchasing a silk scarf for my girlfriend back home.

On the return, the North Atlantic was very rough. We bunked in different parts of the ship with our assigned troops. My quarters were deep in the bowels of the ship while Phil was in the bow. That sounded more glamorous than my accommodation, but Phil got so sick from the rough seas on the trip home, Roy took him to get intravenous fluids.

I had earned my Life badge by that summer. There are some stipulations on how old you can be to earn the Eagle Scout honor. I was considerably off the pace and had a lot of ground to make up. But then, when your father is on the National Board, there are some ways to make things happen. Nonetheless, a lot of my free time during high school was taken up by earning merit badges at a rapid rate to make up for lost time.

Senior year rolled around, and I matriculated to leadership positions in all my activities. I still look back on that year as the most glorious of my life. I was a "big man on campus," a senior in leadership positions and in the spotlight. The highlight of my senior year came when I was cast as Grandpa Vanderhof, a lead role in our school production of *You Can't Take It With You*. To play the elderly Grandpa Vanderhof, I had to be coached on how to move about like an old man. I have no problem doing it now!

After a couple of years in the theater department, I had no fear of being under the bright lights, and I enjoyed playing that role as much as anything I had done in my life to that point. My co-star, playing the role of Alice Sycamore, was Martha Herrick, who later became a beloved drama teacher at Topeka High for several decades. Indeed, she directed several of my own children in Topeka High productions.

Grandpa Vanderhof spoke two prayers in the play. The first prayer ends Act I, and the other ends the play. I've been asked to repeat that final prayer at each Class of 1949 reunion ever since:

> "Well Sir, here we are again. We want to say thanks once more for everything You've done for us. Things seem to be going fine…We've all got our health and as far as anything else is concerned we'll leave that to You. Thank You."

My father had a printed copy of that prayer, displayed with a photo of me from the play, under the glass top covering his desk. That gave me a glimpse of the special place I had in his heart.

As the curtain came down on our performance of *You Can't Take It With You*, we were summoned back to the stage by a standing ovation, the first production under Miss Wheeler that received a curtain call. At the end of that year, Martha and I were named Co-Thespians of the Year.

While Martha found her calling teaching other young thespians like herself, I went on to apply the skills developed in high school theater in a variety of ways: public speaking, appearing live and on camera for interviews, and generally having to "perform" with others watching.

Helping to grow my comfort with public speaking was my experience on the Topeka High debate team during my senior year. I was a novice at the activity and therefore the weak link of the team. But I learned quickly and played my part to the best of my ability, and we won a regional tournament in the spring of 1949.

Journalism, theater, and debate. These three activities honed my ability to communicate and to perform under pressure. In my professional career, I've delivered too many speeches to count. Journalism certainly made me comfortable writing, something I have done every step of the way throughout my career. Writing for the high school newspaper, and later *The Stanford Daily*, propelled me toward later writing accomplishments. I have written columns, books, and a countless number of articles and speeches, not to mention the med school logs and clinical reports I've penned over the years.

Journalism also introduced me to the most important person in my life. But that's a story for a later chapter.

———————————————

While I was immersed in my own world, the Menninger Clinic was experiencing an explosion of growth and responsibility. The Veterans Administration had made Winter General Hospital a major training hospital for psychiatrists and related disciplines under the auspices of the MSP. Now the largest training center for psychiatrists in the world, the MSP was in the process of transforming the state hospital system. When my family left Topeka in 1944, the program for training psychiatrists was a small operation with just a couple of residents. By October of 1946, there were more than 100 psychiatrists-in-training in Topeka.

This development at Menninger changed Topeka. It added a whole new social stratum to the community. All of a sudden, you had 100 new doctors in town—young, highly educated men who were eager to learn, many of them with young families.

Dad was now the preeminent figure in American psychiatry at that time. As was mentioned previously, he was on the cover of *Time* magazine in the fall of 1948—my senior year—as the national spokesperson for mental health. You would think having your father pictured on the cover of *Time* would cause quite a stir, but it didn't enhance my social status much. I don't think many high school students read *Time* magazine.

———————————————

In many respects, my senior year as a Topeka High Trojan was the most glorious year of my life. I felt as though I were on a cloud that whole year—no worries, no cares. Everything came up roses as I remember it.

That was important as I prepared to head out into the adult world. It certainly gave me a sense of confidence that things can go well. They say that you learn from disappointment and from your mistakes. But in terms of just feeling good about life, that year infused me with optimism.

Some children of significant or famous parents struggle with a fear they won't measure up. I didn't have that fear. I guess I never had any doubt that I could achieve in my own right, that I could make my own contribution.

I never really questioned where I would end up. I always felt like life was a little like going on a trip. You plan out the route, and then you start executing the steps. After an unforgettable senior year, I believed I was ready for the next step.

6

From One Trojan to Another

There are few honors I have received of which I am as proud as my induction to the Topeka High School (THS) Hall of Fame in 1996. No matter where you go in your adult life, there's something special about being recognized by your hometown and your school. Receiving this honor is particularly humbling when you consider the many remarkable graduates of THS.

I'm proud to have joined in the ranks of the THS Hall of Fame along with my father, who was inducted in 1991, and my uncle Karl, who was a member of the inaugural class in 1982.

I'm also proud to be enshrined alongside five other members of the class of 1949, the class which claims the most inductees. My graduating class included (in order of induction):

Dean Smith (enshrined in 1983), a basketball coach who led the University of North Carolina to two national championships and the 1976 American squad to an Olympic gold medal. As a coach, he won 879 games, which at the time was the most in NCAA history.

Lt. Gen. Frank E. Petersen (1986), an officer in the U.S. Marine Corps who served in Korea and Vietnam, and at the time of his retirement was the ranking Marine advisor.

Martha Herrick (1993), an educator and actress who was the second head drama coach in the school's history. She taught at the high school for 39 years and directed more than 110 productions.

George Schrader (1999), a public administrator who served as city manager of Dallas.

Dr. Ronald L. Wigington (2001), a technologist and engineer who was engaged in computer research for the National Security Agency and later for the American Chemical Society.

Because of the great history of THS, and because of the many significant graduates of the school, it was a tremendous honor when I was invited in 1992 to deliver the commencement address. It was not just an honor, but an opportunity to reflect on the important role the school played in my own development.

I desired, therefore, to deliver some words of inspiration and relevance to the graduates, as well as all those in attendance. But I also bore in mind the importance of brevity. After all, who remembers any of what's said at a graduation?

In order to try to make the speech relevant, I used a brief questionnaire to sample about one-sixth of the class of 1992 to gain some idea of the concerns on their minds at that time. Below are some excerpts from my Topeka High School Commencement Remarks delivered on May 24, 1992:

> Forty-three years ago, I was sitting where you are—and it was a glorious occasion, the end of an era. As many of you noted, "You're only in high school a short time, and the senior year goes fast."
>
> What now? What does the future hold? You can be sure that there'll be a lot of things you wouldn't suspect as you sit here. When my classmates and I were in your place 43 years ago, I doubt that any of us had any idea that sitting among us was:
>
> - A future Marine Lt. General who would become one of the highest-ranking black officers in the military, and senior ranking aviator in the Marines before his retirement: Frank Petersen.
> - The ninth city manager to be named head of the largest city in this country or the world with a manager/council form of government, Dallas, Texas: George Schrader.
> - The founder and first president of the Airline Stewardesses Union who would have her car bombed and apartment burglarized because of her fighting a takeover of that union by Jimmy Hoffa and the Teamsters Union: Alanna Schenkosky Niles.
> - One of the truly great university basketball coaches of all time: Dean Smith.

- A prime mover and now director of the Head Start program in Topeka: Theresa Byrd Counts.
- The first "First Gentleman" to ever preside over the Kansas Governor's Mansion: Spencer Finney.
- Only the second coach to oversee dramatic productions in all the years of THS: Martha Herrick.

So, look around you. In 43 years, a comparable list of accomplishments will likely be credited to one or another of you, but today you probably couldn't guess who.

Meanwhile, it's evident from the responses to the questionnaires I received that you have lots of concerns about the current state of the world—crime, the preservation of our earth, marriage and family values. Especially, there is concern about so much hate in the world. Let me offer several thoughts to keep in mind as you move forward:

1) Most people have potential for good and bad. We want to be liked and want to do good things; we want to leave the world a better place. But—life is not fair! It never has been and likely never will be. As a result, no one is without pain, and some clearly face more hardship and suffering than others. Because we all have times of hurt and frustration, we get angry, and we want others to hurt like we hurt. We may need to let out some of the anger or rage prompted by the hurt, but you can be certain that if it is directed toward others, hate begets hate! It's a vicious cycle! So, seek safe ways to let off your steam.

2) Try to appreciate what you have, not what you don't have, i.e., look at the half-full part of the glass, instead of the half that's empty. Since our choices in life are often limited by harsh reality, recognize the wisdom that it may be more important to like what you do in life, than to do what you like. And individuals—you and I—can make a difference in this world!

3) Finally, keep your sense of humor. Remember the

wisdom of Murphy's Law: Anything that can go wrong, will go wrong. And its corollaries, including: The light at the end of the tunnel is the headlamp of an oncoming train. The law of life's highway: If everything's coming your way, you're obviously in the wrong lane. The man who can smile when things go wrong has thought of someone he can blame it on. Anything good in life is either illegal, immoral, or fattening. The secret to success is sincerity; once you can fake that, you've got it made. And a final word of advice: Never, never play leapfrog with a unicorn!

Congratulations! And good luck!

7

Me and *You and Psychiatry*

My experiences growing up in Topeka, my family's excursion through Washington, D.C., and my training at Topeka High School were all influential to my personal and professional life. But perhaps the foundation for my career was laid by a book I read in high school.

This was no ordinary book.

It was an at-that-point unpublished manuscript by my father entitled *You and Psychiatry*.

My father returned to Topeka from the Army in 1946 with a book already in the works. When he was not working at the Menninger Clinic or traveling around the country raising money for the Foundation, Dad was likely to be found at the desk in his den. When he wasn't poring over his stamp collection, he was finishing up work from the day or writing. It was in his den that he did much of the work on this book.

I grew up thinking that I wanted to become a psychiatrist like my father, but kids don't normally truly grasp what it is that their parents do. I admit that I didn't really know all that psychiatry entailed. Not until my father came to me one day during my junior year of high school and asked me to read the typed sheets of the manuscript on which he had been laboring.

I don't think he asked me to read the manuscript because he thought it would influence me to become a psychiatrist. As I've mentioned, Dad didn't push me into the field. He may have seen it as a way to connect with his son. But he wasn't trying to teach me or influence me. He wanted to have a young reader test the material. He truly desired my feedback.

I think it was reassuring to him that if a teenager could understand it, he'd done a good job of putting the concepts into easily digestible prose. I don't recall that I gave him any specific edits or recommendations. I didn't impact the book to any real degree. The real impact is what it did for me.

After several years leading psychiatric services in the Army, my father had synthesized many concepts about mental health that he felt would benefit the general public. My father's desire was "to put into simple words and abbreviated form some of this information which applies to all of us in our daily lives."

He stated in the Introduction to *You and Psychiatry* that this was basic stuff everyone should know:

> There are very few adults who have graduated from the public school system of our country who aren't familiar with at least some information on physical hygiene: the necessity of keeping clean, brushing their teeth, getting the right food, fresh air, exercise, and rest. They learned it in terms that they could understand. At the same time, there are many people who have no clear understanding of either mental hygiene or their own personalities.
>
> It would take a pretty hard-boiled citizen to say that there isn't any need for this understanding after taking a quick look around him today. Broken homes, juvenile delinquencies, crime waves, group hatreds, riots, political wranglings, suspicion and fear on all sides are not likely to make a thoughtful man or woman very smug about the state of our individual or collective mental health.
>
> This book is written in the hope that it will make clear to many the fundamentals of the vital part of living that aren't taken care of by food, toothpaste, soap and water, or any amount of money. Don't have any illusions, however; it is no graduate course in psychiatry. No book can solve your personal problems if they are serious. However, it ought to give you a little better understanding of yourself and how you tick. The chances are it will help you know yourself and other people a little better.

My father called *You and Psychiatry* "a war baby." He began the project as a partnership with a man named Munro Leaf, who was working in public relations for the military during the war. Interestingly, Leaf didn't contribute as much to the book as was planned. He was supposed to provide illustrations for the book, but that aspect of the project never materialized. The publisher—Charles Scribner's Sons—decided to leave Leaf's name on the book as a co-author because Leaf contributed to the vision and participated in the planning of the book. Leaving Leaf's name on as a co-author was probably a strategic move as well. Leaf was world famous in the 1930s as the author of the best-selling children's book *The Story of Ferdinand* which was made into a Disney film in 1938. Leaf was a versatile columnist and cartoonist in the 1930s and 1940s whose name was more widely recognized than my father's at the time.

Dad described his collaboration with the PR expert in the Introduction:

> The authors...found their jobs overlapped. The public wanted to know about psychiatry and psychiatry needed public understanding. The terrific loss of manpower in the Army and the Navy from psychiatric casualties started them to thinking that there must be some additional approach to helping the people of our nation understand the basic factors of mental health.
>
> It was their intention to try to put into simple words and pictures for men in the service some of the daily experiences that were common to many men, which made the going 'rugged.' Many believed they were alone in feeling the way they did—about discipline, regimentation, privacy, fear, etc. Most of their attitudes were the result of basic personality factors that existed long before their military service. A realization that they were all in the same boat was reassuring.
>
> Today both feel that there is a much wider need for a better understanding of ourselves which could come from some of the knowledge based on technical findings of psychiatry.

Beginning with the most basic of concepts, Dad provided a definition of psychiatry and what a psychiatrist does. He dispelled the belief that there is a "normal" personality and described how people are generally motivated by two things: 1) aggressive force and 2) the need to love and be loved. He stated that the goal of psychiatry is not to fix people, but to help them gain understanding of themselves in order to grow, to mature, and to improve in their interactions with the world.

He opened the book by describing the makeup of our brains. He then talked about how our personalities are shaped in our early years. He described how we learn to develop relationships and to respond to hardships, and he did so in a very straightforward manner:

> If we are quite honest with ourselves, we cannot always see the reasons for our behavior. After a reaction to a particular situation or person we sometimes find ourselves wondering how we could have been so stupid? So rude? So angry? So passive? So silly? We may even be emotionally upset by our concern over the way we behaved. In other words, all of us have moments when we know that we don't quite understand ourselves.
>
> All of us need some help every now and then. At least some of the knowledge which the psychiatrist uses can be helpful to anyone who understands it.
>
> This is a presentation of what the psychoanalytic psychiatrists believe the personality is, its development, its structure, its mode of action...it is a description of the anatomy and the physiology of the personality.

The *Kansas City Times* praised my father's effort to present psychiatry in an easy-to-understand form in a review on Aug. 27, 1948:

> (*You and Psychitary* makes an important contribution) to the growing body of literature now coming before the people, written by scientists who sincerely desire to give the people knowledge they are crying for. Dr. Menninger's standing is reflected by the honors and the positions to which the psychiatric specialty of the medical profession have elevated him.

I read with fascination the way my father described psychiatry. He did a marvelous job making the material easy to read and understand, because as a junior in high school, I comprehended it.

After high school, I received a fine post-secondary education, as you will read in the next few chapters. But nothing I learned in my next several stops would influence my understanding of the world and of human behavior the way *You and Psychiatry* did. I give special credit, therefore, to my father for how he facilitated my life choice for a career.

I count myself blessed by my father's influence on my life and career by means of the book. Reading it was a significant marker in my life. Not everyone benefits from the same exposure. I realize that things that might make sense to me, others may not have been trained to see.

I'm also blessed that Dad not only sought to explain important concepts about psychiatry, but that he specifically desired to make them relatable to someone like his teenage son. This would not be the only time my dad called upon teenagers to test his material. About that same time, he authored some pamphlets for teenagers—understanding yourself and that sort of thing—and he had me and some of my high school classmates read them and give him feedback.

You and Psychiatry was published in 1948. Would readers today benefit from reading it? Does it stand the test of time?

I believe the answer to those questions is *yes*. It's a book about understanding yourself. It isn't a self-help book as such, but it provides some awareness as to why we react the way we do. As Dad wrote in the preface, having an understanding of what makes us tick, how we function psychologically, can help us make sense of our choices and allow us to better manage some of the aberrations that we experience.

Just as simple and concise as his description of the concepts of psychiatry within the book, my father inscribed the copy he gifted to me at the end of my junior year:

For Walt, with love
Dad
5-20-48

8

Life and Love on The Farm

After my memorable senior year, I felt ready to take on the world. The next step to execute on my journey was to choose a college.

I had already decided to attend Cornell University Medical College in New York, just as my father and brother Roy had done. So, it made sense to look west for my undergraduate experience. Four years on the West Coast. Four years on the East Coast. That was my plan.

But the choice of my specific college was aided by a relationship I made in 7th grade. My best friend was a classmate who lived in our neighborhood named Fritz Fenster. His stepfather was stationed at Winter Army Hospital during the war. Fritz was smart and an extraordinary athlete. He was like a BMOC at our middle school. Everybody wanted to be his friend. He had just moved to Topeka from San Francisco, and we connected and became fast friends. We would play All-Star Baseball for hours—a game in which you put cards on a spinner and simulated a baseball game. Our games always pitted the Menninger All-Stars against the Fenster All-Stars.

At the end of 7th grade, when my family moved to Washington, D.C. to be with my dad, Fritz stayed in Topeka with his family. Then his family moved back to San Francisco before we moved back from D.C. at the end of the war. But though we only attended school together for one year, our friendship endured. We frequently exchanged letters to keep in touch.

In a letter he wrote me in 10th grade, he asked where I was going to college. "What about Stanford?" he asked. I hadn't really thought about college up until then. My only thought about a specific college was of the University of Michigan, just because they had a good football team. But I hadn't really given the topic any serious consideration. When Fritz asked about my plans, he said, "Stanford is a very good school."

He was right. Stanford had been instrumental in equipping young Americans for World War II, booming in mathematics, the sciences, language arts, etc. Following the war, it rose from a regional university to one of great national prestige. Known as "The Farm" because it was situated on rural land donated by Leland Stanford, Stanford was a college on the rise.

I didn't visit Stanford before enrolling as a student in the fall of 1949. I was putting a lot of faith in my friend's recommendation. Fritz knew the campus well and had attended a lot of Stanford sporting events with his parents. His biological father had been concertmaster of the San Francisco Symphony. His mother was also a musician. But after his biological father died, his mother married a physician named George Bernard Robson. During the war, Dr. Robson brought his family to Topeka, where he attained the rank of lieutenant colonel. After the war, they returned to the West Coast for Dr. Robson to become a professor at Stanford and later at the University of California, San Francisco. He went on to serve as epidemiologist for the San Francisco Dept. of Public Health and as Associate Dean of the Stanford School of Medicine.

Fritz was a star athlete from nearby Lowell High School, and Stanford recruited him to play basketball. I went out to California a few days before the fall quarter and stayed with his family. Because I was Fritz's friend, I had a lot of friends immediately. There were probably ten other graduates from his class who attended Stanford.

Fritz remained one of my best friends throughout life. Our oldest son is named after him. After Stanford, Fritz graduated from Harvard Medical School and had a long career, including serving at the Virginia Mason Medical Center in Seattle for many years.

My connection to Fritz helped me make new friends at Stanford, but other than that, I was in fresh territory. I was proud that in high school I earned my accomplishments on my own merit. But in Topeka there was no escaping that I was another one of those Menningers. At Stanford, few of my professors and essentially none of my fellow students had any knowledge of my family. Sure, those with an interest in psychiatry would have known. But for the most part, I was able for the first time in my life to be my own man.

———————•———————

I majored in pre-med and psychology at Stanford, never doubting that I would eventually become a psychiatrist. But during my freshman year, my career got off to an inauspicious start.

The head of the Psychology Department taught the Intro to Psychology course, which was a second-year course. He was preparing to go on a sabbatical the next fall, so I got permission to take the course in the third quarter of my freshman year, which was an extra load of credits. I got a C grade. That was one of the hidden secrets of my collegiate career. At our 25th reunion, I confessed. It became a big joke that "Walt got a C in Introductory Psychology!"

When I went to Stanford, I explored various extracurricular activities. It became clear, however, that in college you can't be a dilettante. You really have to focus on something. I decided to focus on the newspaper as my primary campus activity outside of my pre-med classes. I went to check out *The Stanford Daily* shortly after I arrived on campus and became a cub reporter.

One morning I swung by the *Daily Shack* to check the assignment sheets. On the way, I passed the newspaper's business office, where my eyes fell upon a pert redhead folding newspapers to mail to subscribers. I wasn't exactly a ladies' man, but I felt like I shouldn't pass up the opportunity to meet such a pretty young lady. I stopped in the office, trying to quickly fabricate a reason for being there. I introduced myself and we chatted for a few minutes. *What was something I could say to impress her?*

"My father was recently on the cover of *Time* magazine."

The young lady—Constance "Connie" Arnold Libbey—told me later she thought that was an interesting thing to just bring up. If she was slightly turned off by my claim, at least she was interested enough to try to verify it. She went to the library and found that it was true.

First impression made.

Connie was an economics major, working in the newspaper office to gain some business experience. We had no further interaction that year. When we returned in the fall, I discovered—by a stroke of sheer coincidence—the girl I was dating was Connie's roommate, while my roommate was dating her.

That, however, was about to change.

One weekend early that fall, my three roommates—the rooms in my hall had four beds and four desks for four students—all went away for the weekend. My girlfriend happened to be out of town for the weekend as well. One of my roommates left me the keys to his car and said I could use it for the weekend.

With spare time on my hands for a rare occasion, I drove over to the Russell House to visit Connie. I said, "Since we've been abandoned, would you like to spend the day together?"

As part of her responsibility with *The Stanford Daily*, she had to sell some ads to a merchant in Palo Alto. What a stroke of luck! I had a car! So, we drove to Palo Alto and then ate lunch together in the residence hall cafeteria. To take full advantage of the car, we went driving around again...and ran out of gas. Perhaps because I was unfamiliar with the car or perhaps because I was distracted by my companion, I hadn't checked the gauge. A man came by and asked what was wrong. He said, "Get in. I'll go home, then you can take my car to go get some gas and then bring my car back to me." I doubt anyone would do anything like that today, but that was the nature of the times. It added a sense of adventure to the afternoon Connie and I were sharing.

Once the car's gas tank was refilled, we decided to go out for a nice dinner at a restaurant down the peninsula. So, we both changed clothes and went out on what, looking back, could only be considered a "date." I guess we thought at the time it was innocent enough.

After dinner, we drove back to my dorm in Stanford Village and snuck into my room—no girls were allowed, but we weren't in the mood to let the time together end. There were double bunks in our room, and I had one of the top bunks. Connie hopped up onto my bunk and we started talking. After a while, we suddenly fell into each other's arms. We admitted to each other that we really liked each other. We agreed then and there that we would like to "go together."

Now we had the obvious problem of how to explain this to our roommates. We waited anxiously for them to return from their weekend away. We delicately explained the events of the weekend to our respective partners, and they both accepted it better than we expected. Things remained so amicable in fact, that my roommate, who had been dating Connie, was my best man at our wedding. And as if the world could get any smaller, the girl I had been dating eventually married a Stanford classmate who was from the same area of Massachusetts that Connie came from. He had even taken Connie to his prep school senior prom before any of us ever arrived at Stanford. The coincidences were mind-boggling.

Everyone stayed friends through it all and proved without a doubt that it's essential you treat all people with respect and kindness, because you will most likely cross paths with them again in this world!

———————————◆———————————

I met Connie's parents that spring when they came to visit her at Stanford. Then at the end of the school year, I took Connie to my brother Roy's wedding in New Jersey. She met my whole family there, and my family met Connie's family. Afterwards I went to Cape Cod with her family for several days before I was to report for an internship in Chicago.

I spent the summer after our sophomore year working with Science Research Associates, a publishing house that sold psychological tests and related materials. I lived in a YMCA on Chicago's north side. Every day that summer I wrote a letter to Connie.

One fortunate stroke of luck that summer was that a door opened for me to get back into Scouting. One of the employees at Science Research Associates happened to be involved in Scouting, so he let me tag along on a weekend campout. That allowed me to complete the final few steps to earn my Eagle Scout badge. Normally, all Eagle Scout requirements must be met before age 18. I was 19 and a half. But they made some exceptions for me, I think primarily because my Scouting progress had been interrupted by our years in Washington, D.C. during World War II. The war had disrupted so many things, the Scouts might have been inclined to make exceptions. But the fact that my dad served on the national board probably helped create some wiggle room. At the end of the summer, I returned to Topeka from Chicago, and we had a private ceremony where I was presented my Eagle badge.

Connie and I met back up at Stanford that fall. She remained in Russell House (which no longer exists) for her junior and senior years. For my junior year, I lived with my friend John Menaglia in an on-campus dorm room. Senior year, John's mother bought a house in Palo Alto, and I lived in the "servants' quarters" off the kitchen. Certain we would be married sooner than later, Connie and I bought a car together late in our junior year.

I was continually surprised by just how natural my relationship with Connie seemed. We went to Sunday night movies on campus. We studied together. We attended campus functions together. I joined Alpha Phi

Omega, a service fraternity of former Scouts. The group had various functions that Connie could attend as my date. Connie came home with me by train for Christmas that year. The most memorable thing about riding in the railroad "chair car" was being able to spend 36 hours in each other's arms. That was a luscious time spent together; the trip was the highlight of my junior year.

Connie was a good student, but she was more focused on gaining work experience than she was invested in classwork. We took Adolescent Psychology together and developed a friendship with the professor. We both got B+ grades. I was sure I had done better! I couldn't believe that she did as well as I did. We had some good-natured bickering over it. The professor showed us that we had the exact same number of points.

My senior year brought my first taste of disappointment.

I had steadily risen up the ranks at *The Stanford Daily*, enjoying the diverse experiences and the exposure to campus life outside of the pre-med world. As you moved up the ranks of the Stanford paper, the top positions were editor and managing editor. There were two associate editor positions on the paper, and as a junior I served as one of these associate editors. At the close of each school year, the newspaper staff voted for which of those two associates would become editor. The other became managing editor by default.

The woman who served as the other associate editor our junior year, Dorothy Dodge, was a journalism major. She was gracious. She was solid. She was going to be a journalist. So, it made all the sense in the world that she should be voted editor. Logic said that. But that doesn't mean that I didn't want the position for myself. I was thoroughly enjoying the newspaper experience and recognized that this might be the end of my journalism career. I thought it would be a great honor to conclude my four years at *The Stanford Daily* as editor.

When the votes were tallied, Dorothy had won. She became the first woman elected editor outside of wartime. She was a wonderful person, and she did a good job. She received a master's degree in political science from Columbia University, then returned to California where she worked in journalism for 30 years. She received the Associated Press News

69

Executives Council's California Presidents' Award, the first woman to receive that honor. I was without question defeated by a worthy opponent. But it was the first time in life I didn't get what I wanted. Now, with more than 90 years on this earth, I realize that defeats and disappointments are common. It doesn't seem like a big thing. But it certainly was at the time. I remember being consoled by Connie, which was a first of many times she would be there to support me in times of distress.

Once I put the disappointment behind me, I quickly realized that the managing editor position was better suited to my skills, and more fun than the job of editor. The managing editor's job was more the "journalistic" job, leading the editorial content. The editor marked up each paper after publication, handed out compliments and advice to the staff, and served as the organizational leader of the paper.

The friendly competition between Dorothy and me continued in the fall of my senior year. That was the fall of the presidential race between Dwight Eisenhower and Adlai Stevenson. Dorothy was a Democrat, so she wrote editorials in favor of Stevenson, while I wrote the editorials in favor of Eisenhower. Politics being much more civil back then, Dorothy and I had a lot of fun that fall, battling back and forth, in person and in print. I got glowing letters from alumni admiring my editorials in favor of the Republican. Eisenhower, of course, won the election that November. Though we were both from Kansas, I never met Eisenhower. Although my father was a prominent figure and had served in the Army during the war, I don't think he ever met Eisenhower either.

I was introduced to another enjoyable responsibility during my senior year at Stanford that would continue for several decades. During that time, Stanford needed to raise money, and it hoped to encourage students to support the university financially after graduation. So, they came up with a program called Stanford Today and Tomorrow, for which I was made student chairman. Notable faculty and administrators visited living groups all over campus to talk about the importance of giving to the university. I served as the emcee of these events, introducing the university president and other dignitaries, and developing a relationship with several administrators. After graduation, I remained involved in fundraising for the university. For the next decade or so, I composed letters to solicit funds from my classmates. For the majority of the years that Stanford carried on that campaign, our class led in percentage contributing for our decade, earning me recognition for leading the effort. That work helped perpetuate my relationship with many friends and Stanford administrators for years.

———————————

Psychiatrists have no more insight than anyone else when it comes to falling in love. I've been asked countless times over the years, "How did you know that Connie was the one?" Well, aside from the debate over whether there truly is a "right one" when it comes to marriage—as if we are created with some type of soul mate—I don't have an answer for how I knew I should marry Connie. I just knew. From that glorious day in the fall of 1950 that ended with us in each other's arms, we knew we wanted to be with each other. From that moment on, we totally confided in each other. We were committed from that day forward. I don't think there was ever any question that we would spend the rest of our lives together.

On our third date, Connie asked me, "How many kids do you want?" She might as well not have asked. She knew she wanted six, and what I might have said probably wouldn't have mattered. But having six children became part of our master plan.

We were married on the patio of the Menaglias' home the day after college graduation in the spring of 1953. Connie's parents offered us the option of a small wedding followed by a trip to Europe, but we opted for a larger wedding with friends from Stanford in attendance. My parents and both my brothers were there, as was Connie's family. It was a beautiful California summer day, and we felt like we had the world by the tail.

I had been accepted to Cornell Medical College in New York City for the fall semester, so we had three months for a summer-long honeymoon. We spent our first three days together in Carmel, California. Then Connie had to fulfill a few duties for *The Stanford Daily* before we could depart. With those tasks completed, we began our drive across country—a road trip honeymoon. First stop was Yosemite, where we spent one night on top of the mountain and one at the bottom. We stopped in Salt Lake for a couple of days. Then we arrived in Topeka for a week. That gave Connie an opportunity to meet some of my friends and to become a bit more acclimated to the Menninger extended family. Next, we headed east for a quick stop in Washington, D.C., then stayed in East Orange, New Jersey at my grandmother's house for a few days. From there we commuted into

New York City to find an apartment and to get Connie a job. Once those things were accomplished, we drove up to spend a month on Cape Cod. What a fling for a couple of newlyweds!

My four years as a Californian were in the books. The most important event of my life—meeting and marrying Connie—was a somewhat unexpected benefit to my undergraduate years. Now we were off to experience life as a pair.

9

Becoming a Physician

In 1953, we switched coasts. We left Stanford and moved to New York City so I could attend Cornell University Medical School. I didn't learn until years later that my grandfather had wanted to go to Cornell for medical school but couldn't afford it. Knowing that fact makes me even more appreciative of the opportunity to study there, as my father and my brother Roy had before me. My son, John, also attended Cornell University Medical College in the 1980s.

I probably could have gone to some other med school, but I never even considered it. Cornell had been part of the plan all along.

After our delightful cross-country jaunt that summer, Connie and I finally entered the semi-real world of married life. In the fall of 1953, we settled into our first home together, a one-and-a-half-room "walk-up" on the third floor of a building at First Avenue and 77th Street, which was within walking distance of New York Hospital on East 68th Street.

To help sustain us financially while I was in school, Connie needed to find a job. God bless my father; he had his connections. He knew a vice-president at NBC and put Connie in touch with him. That contact led her to a job with NBC at Radio City as a Program Analyst. She archived scripts and kept records of what was said on live broadcasts. Among other things, she had to keep track of how many Democrats and how many Republicans they had on the news, to keep things balanced.

Hmm…balanced news coverage. Imagine that.

We didn't watch much television at my home growing up in the 1940s, but with Connie in her new position at NBC, she had to be able to watch TV in our apartment. One of our first purchases, therefore, was a television set. There were certain live programs she was assigned to watch and keep a record of. We viewed a lot of television during those years in New York, but of course, we had to watch NBC. Some of the most popular shows on NBC during that era were *Dragnet*, *The Milton Berle Show*, and *The Tonight Show*.

Perhaps the biggest thing to happen in television around that time was on January 1, 1954, NBC broadcast The Tournament of Roses Parade in Pasadena in color—the first coast-to-coast color broadcast. More color breakthroughs followed, and they called it "The Year in Color at NBC." It was an exciting industry with which to be associated.

Connie was assigned to monitor the Army-McCarthy hearings, which dominated the airwaves from April to June of 1954. For a live show like the trial, she had to carefully document what was spoken and shown on the screen as it happened. She did some of that work at our apartment, while I tried to study with the trial playing in the background.

From our apartment, Connie took the bus to her work at Radio City each day. Though we didn't have a lot of spending money, Connie's job (along with some financial support from both our parents) provided enough for us to live comfortably and to enjoy the experience of living in New York.

When I occasionally got out of classes early, I would pick up Connie to attend the first show of the day at Radio City Music Hall. It would be impossible to just show up and gain entrance today, but back then you often could get in spur of the moment. They had a prime movie, then a stage show, and then more movies. Connie and I were both lifelong fans of live theater, and we were blessed by the opportunity to take in an occasional Broadway show. There was a marvelous little French restaurant below the building on 47th Street (on a spot now occupied by a huge skyscraper). After the shows, we often descended the steps into this little restaurant for the quintessential New York City experience.

One highlight of our time in the city was when Connie took me to the set of NBC TV's version of *Peter Pan* with Mary Martin playing Peter, Cyril Ritchard as Capt. Hook, and Kathleen Nolan as Wendy. That was a beautiful thing to witness in person.

All of our getting about the city was by subway, bus, or on foot. We kept our car at my grandmother's house in New Jersey during our years in New York, using it for weekend getaways, to drive to Topeka, or to visit Connie's family's home in Florida.

Our first year in New York City was idyllic, apart from the fact that our apartment was not the greatest accommodation. It was tiny, with a cubby-hole sink and shower, and a pullout sofa bed. We outfitted it with some unfinished furniture segments that we used to divide the room into two living spaces. We hadn't known better when we leased the place, but we quickly found out that it was nearly impossible for two newlyweds to not step all over each other, much less for me to study and for Connie to work simultaneously.

There were six or seven other students in my first-year med school class who were married. One of them lived in the Met Life Insurance housing development called Stuyvesant Town. He suggested, "Why don't you try to get into our community?"

"How do you do that?" I asked.

"Do you know anyone at Met Life?" he replied.

I asked my father that same question. I should have not been the least bit surprised when he responded, "Well, I know the chairman."

So, for the final three years of medical school, we relocated to Stuyvesant Town at 655 E. 14th Street. We had survived the tiny third-floor walk-up. Moving to that second apartment was like moving into a castle. It was two-and-a-half rooms, on the 10th floor, with an elevator—for only $10 a month more!

After four years at Stanford, where the Menninger name was relatively unknown, moving to Cornell put me back in my father's orbit. He knew some of the faculty, and they certainly knew him. When I arrived in 1953, he had recently been recognized as an outstanding alumnus.

Cornell is an excellent medical school, but I must admit I was not overly impressed by much of the psychiatry I learned there. I couldn't help but feel that psychiatry was treated as less rigorous or serious than the other disciplines, which was disappointing. I felt like I learned more psychiatry from reading my father's writings before I even went to college than I did at Cornell.

The most memorable experience of those years was my assignment to monitor a chronic patient. The idea was to provide to the medical student an on-going relationship with a patient. I was assigned a woman with a chronic obstructive pulmonary disease. She was a difficult patient to whom I was expected to listen and respond.

The other outstanding aspect of my medical school experience was the recording of a daily log of my activities for the Columbia University

Bureau of Applied Social Research. I was invited to fill this role because the school had seen some copies of my writings. My years of journalism training in high school and at Stanford made the daily summarizing of my activities, plus reflections and observations about interactions with others in the school, a pleasure. Keeping the logs made me more introspective about the med school experience. Plus, I got paid $1.25 per entry!

One of the benefits of keeping the logs was that I shared them with Connie, and it was a way that she could be aware of what I was experiencing. They were about one typed page per day. I wasn't going to say to her, "This is what I did today." But she read my daily records and knew all I was doing. In a sense, she experienced medical school with me through the logs.

I also shared the logs with my father, which was another tie between us that neither of my siblings had. I typed each entry with two carbons and mailed a set of copies to him every couple of weeks. Dad and I didn't talk about those logs in any consistent way, but occasionally in our conversations he would bring up things that I had written. So, I knew that he was reading them. Three or four times each year, he and my mother would visit New York on fundraising trips. Those occasions gave Connie and me the chance to have dinner with my parents regularly in the city. During our get-togethers, Dad would invariably remark about something he'd read in the logs or ask a question about something I'd written. I don't know that I was ever more proud than when my father would compliment my work or ask for my opinion on some matter.

Connie wanted to have six children, so we had to get started.

We timed it so Connie would give birth to our first child right around the end of the fourth year of medical school. A few months into the pregnancy, she quit work at NBC before Christmas of 1956. That allowed her to spend about a month with her parents in Florida, escaping the cold of New York. When it was time to have the baby, in May 1957, we were blessed by a visit from Fritz Fenster. He was in medical school at Harvard and flew down to stay with us. At 4 a.m. on May 4, Connie went into labor, and later that day our "Fritz," Frederick Prince Menninger, was born. His middle name was taken from Connie's mother's maiden name.

My four years at Cornell came to a close. Our time in New York imbued life with great potential. With our family started and my goal of becoming a psychiatrist in view, we were ready for the next step.

———————•———————

In July of 1957, we packed up our car and moved to Boston, where I had an internship at Boston City Hospital. For Connie, it felt like going home. She had spent most of her childhood and adolescence there, and she was excited to share the city with me. I wanted her to have a year in familiar territory before bringing her to the wild frontier. We got an apartment in Watertown, a short drive from the hospital, where I would serve a year of medical internship under the auspices of Harvard Medical School.

Connie did not work during that year, opting to stay home with infant Fritz. That gave her time to enjoy the city and to pursue some hobbies during her free time. She resumed accordion lessons from her childhood teacher. She read and sewed. Though her parents had relocated to Florida, Connie had a brother and many friends in the city with whom she spent time. Toward the end of my internship, she became pregnant again.

Connie wasn't the only one with family in Boston. My brother Roy was on the staff of the Peter Bent Brigham Hospital. Our professional paths didn't cross, but we visited occasionally.

During internship, there's not a lot of free time. I was on every other night, and on those nights, I slept overnight at the hospital. Because I spent so much of that year at Boston City Hospital, I don't recall a lot of highlights. But I did experience one "lowlight," which served years later to provide me with an unpleasant reminder of my year in Boston.

One Sunday morning in April of 1958, I was scheduled for emergency room duty. Making the pre-dawn drive from Watertown to the hospital, I had to drive across Massachusetts Avenue, something I'd done countless times before. But I failed to realize, as I approached the flashing yellow light, that it was flashing yellow both ways. I entered the intersection thinking I had the right of way. Another car was coming from my right side and banged into my passenger side door. It wasn't a high-speed collision, but I was thrown hard enough into the armrest on my right side to give me a good bruise and a cracked rib.

I made it to the emergency room alright, but as a patient rather than as a doctor. I was checked out and sent home to rest. At the time, the biggest problem was that the car was out of commission for a while.

Once we got the car fixed, I thought the incident was over. But eight years later, in 1966 during a physical examination, the doctor felt my spleen when pressing on my abdomen. Ordinarily you can't feel a spleen. When you can feel it, it's usually not a good sign. More often than not, an enlarged spleen is the result of a malignancy.

The doctor ordered some blood tests, which came back normal. They sent me to a spleen specialist at Washington University in St. Louis who repeated all the tests, looking for some anomaly. He was a specialist in using radioisotopes and determined that the size of my functioning spleen was normal. He performed an intravenous pyelogram—a radioactive dye they put in your bloodstream to assess renal function. The tests showed a big cyst on my spleen. That led them to ask if I had ever had an accident that could have bruised my spleen.

Ah, yes. The "minor" car accident in the early morning in downtown Boston. It all came back to me.

To surgically remove it would be a simple thing today. But at that time, they had to open me up and "deliver" my spleen. It was donated to the pathology lab at the Washington University in St. Louis. That's where my spleen is today.

So, I do still bear the marks of my time in Boston.

10

Menninger School of Psychiatry

Having survived the grueling internship at Boston City Hospital (not to mention the car accident), I was one step closer to my goal of becoming a psychiatrist. My schedule had been too busy for the year in Boston to be an enjoyable experience for me, but Connie was blessed by the time in her hometown. After a year, we were ready to embark on the next leg of the journey—my residency—which would allow me to focus fully on the study of psychiatry.

But where?

Initially I had thought that it might be wise for me to get my psychiatric training at a residency somewhere other than Topeka, in order to bring other perspectives to the Menninger staff. That was our plan.

In the spring of my fourth year at Cornell, Connie and I made the long drive from New York to Topeka. It was during that visit that I started to question our plan. I asked myself, *If my father and uncle have put together the best school of psychiatry there is, why would I consider going anyplace else?* I discussed altering the plan with Connie. Ever the pragmatist, she replied, "One less move."

So, we decided that I would enroll in the Menninger School of Psychiatry. In late June 1958, newly pregnant with our second child, Connie loaded Fritz into a car her parents had recently given us. We made the move from Boston, caravanning in two cars halfway across the country.

In July of 1958, a new Menninger doctor arrived in Topeka.

A lot had changed in the nine years since I'd left my hometown.

Immediately following the war, the Menninger partnership with the VA turned the small Menninger School of Psychiatry into the largest psychiatric training program in the world. In 1948, the Topeka State

Hospital (TSH) was added to the program. Sufficient problems in the state hospital system had come to light that it needed to be overhauled. There hadn't been enough money or staff at the state hospital to provide adequate care. Gov. Frank Carlson appointed a commission to fix the problems. Karl recommended that the state hospital become a teaching hospital. This would attract the staff needed to improve conditions. The MSP would provide the training. At Carlson's request, the Kansas legislature provided the funds—$21 million over two years—to make TSH the third branch of the MSP. Harry Levinson was hired as Director of Education at TSH. The plan reduced the number of patients at TSH while adding the staff necessary to truly provide high-quality care. A grant by the Rockefeller Foundation funded the education program for attendants at the state hospital. The residents at TSH attended MSP courses, just as those at the VA hospital did.

After I left home in 1949, my parents were free to travel for work and pleasure. Between his contacts through the military, Boy Scouts, and the various medical associations, my father quickly became a very effective fundraiser. He had to raise, at minimum, about half a million dollars to keep Menninger in the black. Some years he raised more than $2 million from diverse donors like the Rockefeller Foundation, Schlitz Brewing Company, and the *Readers Digest* Foundation. While he traveled, he wrote. He published several books after the war, most notably *Psychiatry in a Troubled World*.

I had very little interaction with father during my residency. While Dad traveled about two-thirds of the time, raising money, serving in a host of organizations, and speaking about psychiatry all over the country, Karl was the hands-on director of the school. We saw Dad socially on weekends, but it was rare that I interacted with him in any way associated with the hospital.

———————————————

Another thing had changed. Following my departure for college, my grandfather continued to work. He primarily taught courses to the patients at the Menninger clinic. He never stopped learning, and he shared with patients what he had learned: botany and zoology, and his new passion, conchology.

With the passing of my grandmother in 1945, my grandfather didn't slow down, but he needed help. Pearl May Boam, whom we called "Aunt Pearl," stayed by his side. This led to their mutual realization that they were more than friends. It wasn't as surprising as you might expect when they let the family know that they wanted to be married. In 1948, they were wed in a small ceremony at my parents' home. Having relocated to within walking distance of the Menninger offices on 6th Street in Topeka, my grandfather walked to work each day, determined to contribute in some way, even into his nineties.

My grandfather developed a vascular lesion in his brain in 1953. He passed away on November 28 of that year at the age of 91. My father wrote to the Menninger staff, "The greatest honor we could do him is to carry on. His spirit will remain all around the (Menninger Hospital)."

The Menninger School of Psychiatry was a unique collaboration. Karl described it as, "...a new future, a new world, a new kind of medical practice, a new way of helping suffering people in an old, much beat-up world.... Never before have the federal government, a state government, and a private institution combined to set up a teaching machine."

With residents assigned to the VA hospital, the state hospital, and the Menninger Clinic, the MSP provided a very diverse set of experiences. Residents worked a full schedule at one of the three locations, but had time carved out for classroom lectures in an auditorium at the VA.

In the 1950s, the school had post-graduate programs in clinical psychology, social work, nursing, occupational therapy, activity therapy, and music therapy. By the 1960s, a nationwide emphasis on social psychology motivated the MSP to develop a Department of Social Applications, which included Pastoral Care and Counseling, Industrial Mental Health (which worked with corporations), Law and Psychiatry, and School Mental Health.

For my first six months of residency, I was the only doctor assigned to a 59-bed chronic patient ward at TSH. Some patients had been in the hospital for more than 20 years. The patient population was made up primarily of people who were committed to the hospital by a court. They were all profoundly compromised, although some could function very well. Many were non-verbal. Most were docile.

I found that while making rounds in the large day hall, it was possible to make a connection with many of the patients, even if they were non-verbal. I remember one man who, whenever I entered the day hall and started making my way around, would always make his way on the opposite side. He was non-communicating, but very much aware what was going on. We found a connection point with him through his desire to go outside. When a policy change made grounds passes available, we found that he would rise early in the morning so that he could maximize his time outside.

After six months, I was moved to the admissions ward. Six weeks into that new assignment, I was put in charge of the ward. Normally that was the responsibility of a second-year resident. Patients typically spent about four to six weeks in the admissions ward, where their long-term treatment plan was developed.

Throughout the residency, we attended lectures on psychiatric practice. You quickly realize, however, that there's much more to learn on the ward than there is in the classroom. The key aspect of a psychiatric ward is the collective atmosphere maintained by the nurses and aides. If you're smart, you take advantage of their experience. You learn that treatment is really the function of a team. You're using the collective observations and insights and experience of everyone involved to create a therapeutic setting. That's different from general medicine. On a psych ward, there is a lot more interpersonal involvement.

The reality is that the nurses know what's going on. They were there before you arrived, and they'll be there after you're gone. They know all the patients. So, one of the most important lessons you learn is to listen to the people who really know what's happening on the ward. The doctor has to sign the orders, legally. But the nurses and attendants know what you should be writing. They were the real teachers.

I soon learned that my residency would be a crash course in leadership. For graduation from MSP, you had to write a publishable paper. I wrote mine on "The Role of the Ward Physician." One important nugget from the paper was the importance of input from all of the clinical personnel, recognizing that they each contribute a unique and essential perspective. To illustrate this, I used the example of trying to describe a person sitting in the middle of a room. No one seated around the room has the whole picture, but collectively the group could come up with a more accurate picture by sharing their observances from their respective points of view. The most effective treatment plan will take into account the perspectives of each discipline.

Because of the daily staff rotation, it is important that all three shifts are in tune. A significant part of the doctor's responsibility, therefore, is gaining valuable insight from each of the shifts. What you find out is that people tend to neglect the night shift. I realized that some patients really connect with the night shift staff because they find that they get more attention while the majority of the ward is asleep. Patients would actually get up at night to receive more attention from the staff. I started going out each week to spend time with the night shift staff. It was an emphasis I maintained throughout my career. One thing I did in later roles was to pay a visit to the night shift every Christmas Eve, serenading them with a round of "We Wish You a Merry Christmas" and bringing holiday treats.

Because my uncle Karl was Dean of the MSP, I had a significant amount of interaction with him during those three years. He was one of the instructors of our classes, and he hosted a colloquium every Saturday that would feature visiting teachers or dignitaries. The prominence of my father and Karl attracted some famous guest lecturers. Visiting scholars included Margaret Mead, Anna Freud, and Aldous Huxley.

Karl could be an intimidating figure to the residents. I didn't view him with the same degree of anxiety that the other students did, but he could really be a terror. We had to present an eight-page case summary following the format Karl had authored—the *Manual for Psychiatric Case Study*. A resident would have his case summary ready to present, and Karl might stop him after the second sentence to ask, "Why would you say that?" This was so unnerving to some of the residents it might have thrown them off before they could even get started. As my uncle, he wasn't as intimidating to me as to the others, but I did have some of those experiences with him.

That was Karl.

As I mentioned before, a lot had changed at the Menninger Foundation in the nine years I was away from Topeka. The changes continued during my residency. In 1959, the foundation purchased a property on the northwest edge of Topeka that, for about 20 years, had served as a home for the elderly, sick, and orphaned under the management of the Security Benefit Association. The property consisted of a large building with a clock tower in the center modeled after Independence Hall in Philadelphia. The building could accommodate about 200 inpatients. The building had sat empty for several years when the Foundation purchased it.

Now with an East Campus and a West Campus, the Menninger Foundation had 39 buildings, 430 acres, and a staff of more than 1,000. That kept my father on the go, raising funds across the country.

In 1961, the nation got a look into the Menninger hospital and school when CBS newscaster Walter Cronkite came to Topeka to film an installment of the weekly documentary program *Twentieth Century*. The episode was called "Age of Anxiety."

During the late 1950s and early 1960s, Eunice Kennedy Shriver served on the Menninger Board of Directors. My father paid a high-profile visit to her brother during my residency.

During the early years of John F. Kennedy's presidency, there was a push to pass the Community Mental Health Centers Act, which was designed to provide federal funding for community mental health centers and research facilities. Because this piece of legislation was packaged as part of Kennedy's "New Frontier" plan, psychiatrists wanted to have someone connect with the White House to get Kennedy's imprimatur. The president said, "I'll meet with Dr. Menninger." I'm sure that was because his sister was on the board. He certainly was aware of the Menninger Foundation because of her involvement.

My father described his February 9, 1962 meeting with Kennedy in *Psychiatrist for a Troubled World*, a compilation of his selected papers:

> I expressed our warm appreciation—of all of us working in the field of mental illness—for his endorsement and support of the problems of mental deficiency and that I was sure this had brought hope to the hearts of thousands of people...but the whole field of mental illness was woefully neglected—by all odds THE neglected area of all health causes—and what I wanted was his interest and his blessing and insofar as he could

give it, his leadership. I sensed the President's interest in my remarks, and I went on to elaborate that our two greatest needs were trained personnel and more knowledge that could only come from research.

The President was impressed with my enthusiasm and strong feelings, and I felt he was getting enthusiastic about the problem also. I said to him, "We want somebody of your stature who will stand up with us and be counted. So many have been afraid to stand up with us." I then commented, "Mr. President, you are probably going to get your leg pulled because you have been talking to a psychiatrist." He replied, "You are possibly right, but that is all right, I can take it."

The Community Mental Health Act made its way through Congress, and Kennedy signed it into law on October 31, 1963. It was one of the last acts of his presidency before he was killed on November 22 of that year. His loss was a tragedy on many counts, but it was a particularly sad day for the psychiatric community because he and his family seemed to have a genuine concern for the mental health of the country.

As exciting as the developments at the Menninger Foundation were, I was more preoccupied with the developments within my own family. We found a house at 1505 Plass Avenue—just a few blocks from Washburn University and a short walk from my parents' house—that we believed we could remodel to accommodate a large family. Our second child, John Alexander, was born February 22 of 1959. He was named after my close friend from college, John Menaglia. His middle name comes from one of Connie's ancestral names.

Connie was remarkably adaptable. When she visited Topeka for the first time, she said she felt at home there for one odd reason. Connie had lived for four years of her early life in east Texas, where her parents helped run a basket and box factory. She said the Overland Train Station in Topeka—the first thing she saw upon arriving in my hometown as an undergrad in 1952—reminded her of the train station in the small Texas town in which she spent her early childhood. It gave her a sense of familiarity.

Fortunately, Connie was comfortable with my parents, and she was comfortable with the people she met in Topeka. She never seemed daunted by marrying into a family that was prominent in the community. She had enough confidence in her own accomplishments—business manager of *The Stanford Daily*, and employee of NBC—to not feel overshadowed. She harbored no regrets about leaving New York or Boston. Those were just waystations. Topeka was always the ultimate destination.

First Presbyterian Church instantly became a big part of our lives. Connie was a talented musician, and she immediately joined the choir. The theme of the choir Christmas party in 1958 was "Couples who sing together cling together." So, I joined the choir shortly thereafter. It was something we did together for decades.

Connie had many talents besides music. She explored her interests in those early years, getting involved in community organizations while sewing and making fruitcakes at Christmas time. But things remained quite busy in our home. With her vision of six kids always in mind, she got pregnant and gave birth to Eliza Wright on September 13, 1960. She was named after my maternal grandmother, Eliza Wright.

With the Korean War behind us, the world seemed a somewhat sane place in the late 1950s. Little did we know what loomed just around the corner in Cuba and Vietnam. Much as I was eager to settle into my career and family life in Topeka, Uncle Sam still had to be satisfied. In those days, doctors were required to give two years of service to some branch of the military or government, something called the "Doctors Draft." My brother Roy served as a psychiatrist in the Army from 1953 to 1955, following in my father's footsteps. I guess I was always one to go my own way, because I decided on a different direction.

I initially opted for the Air Force. If you wanted to be commissioned, you had to repay two years for your first year. I naively thought, *I'll join the Air Force and see the world for three years as an officer.* When I told my father, who of course had every connection conceivable in the Army, he said, "Why didn't you ask me? The Air Force psychiatry is terrible."

On his advice, I needed to reconsider my options.

At the end of my first year of residency, I became aware of the opportunity to satisfy the Doctors Draft by serving in the United States Public Health Service (USPHS). An alternative to the military was to serve my time in the prison system, and you only had to pay year for year. I applied and was accepted as a commissioned officer in the USPHS in my second year of residency. That meant that my salary would no longer be from the state of Kansas (for whom I was working at TSH), but from the U.S. government. The arrangement gave me some freedom in what I would do for the rest of my residency. I began a rotation of several experiences within the Menninger programs.

First, I was assigned to the TSH adolescent unit for six months. Then I spent three months in the neurology unit. Then, as part of my training through the USPHS, I was allowed three months of travel to visit some federal prisons, to attend a workshop on "mental retardation" in New York state, and to visit a number of psychiatric hospitals in the East.

During that time of training, I was able to spend six weeks at Peter Bent Brigham Hospital in Boston, where my brother Roy was on the staff as a psychiatrist. It was a marvelous opportunity to spend six weeks with my brother. At that time, it seemed like Roy and I would be able to work well enough together when we would eventually join the Menninger staff. But differences in our training came to light.

Roy had gone to Boston State Hospital for his psychiatric residency, where they didn't really have academic courses in psychiatric training. Then he went into the Army to serve his time and was assigned to a hospital in Salzburg, Austria. My brother was really a general physician. He did some psychiatric activity during those years but got limited supervision. Unlike my brother, I was able to defer my service until I completed my residency training, and then was able in the USPHS to operate with a supervisor who practiced psychiatry.

So, my didactic coursework outpaced his. He realized this early on, and it became more of an issue later in our careers. But during those six weeks I spent at Brigham Hospital in Boston, Roy and I enjoyed working together and shared some bonding experiences. We were particularly impacted by one *Aha!* moment. Roy shared with me a case he was working on, and our minds were totally in synch. I thought, *Blood's thicker than water.* As colleagues, we perceived things the same way. That was one very special experience as brothers.

———————————

Upon returning to Topeka from the six-week sojourn, my final year of residency was at the Menninger Hospital. It was during that year I finally became aware of how Menninger Hospital operated and what made it unique in its approach. The "milieu therapy," that was the foundation of Menninger programs, calls for structured group and individual activities in a conditioned environment. It might involve arts and crafts, gardening, athletics, and other activities that are designed to stimulate the body and mind. Each patient had a regular schedule of activities, which might be as basic as sawing wood in a woodpile or as technical as taking a class in ornithology.

The character of psychiatric practice was different at Menninger. You were assigned to work intensively with just six or seven patients. There were probably five or six psych residents from each class working at the Menninger Hospital. The experience drew you close to the other residents. We became great friends.

New patients admitted to the Menninger Hospital had a scheduled conference roughly four to five weeks after intake. During those first few weeks, the psychiatrists prepared a case study which involved information from the social worker, the psychologist, medical assessments, nursing assessments, and activity director. As the physician, you pulled all this information together and then held a diagnostic conference. This thorough and encompassing process was to assess what was necessary or what might be best for each individual patient.

We had the opportunity to really connect with a patient at the Menninger Clinic to help them get a handle on reorganizing their lives. Getting more intensively engaged brought me a much greater understanding of the mental health problems people face. We were trying to help patients reorganize their whole orientation for how to handle life's problems and to enhance their capacity to address their anxieties—to not be so self-destructive. Part of the process is acknowledging the degree to which we can be counterproductive in our lives. Psychiatry asks: "How do we harness our aggressive energies in a positive way that enhances both ourselves and the world around us?"

During my residency, I had one very memorable patient who had worked for the CIA. She had a Mensa-level intelligence. She was extremely perceptive. She subsequently wrote me a letter articulating some perceptions about her experience. She had observed me and wondered why I took interest in the patients. She described the environment of the hospital as one of love. She said, "I realized you love everybody. You really care about your patients." It was an insight into my style, as well as to the principles behind the treatment at the Menninger Clinic.

One of my most valuable experiences during my residency was lecturing to psychiatric nursing trainees. The student nurses rotated through the state hospital every 90 days. In addition to being assigned to work within different wards, they took courses on personality growth and development and psychiatric syndromes. When I began my second year of residency, I was asked to take on the assignment of providing two lectures a week for the nurses' 13-week course. I was fortunate that my father's main commitment in his early years was working with nursing staff. He had developed a series of lectures about the basic principles of psychiatry for nurses.

I handled the lecture responsibility for three rotations before I left for my travel experience. It really compounded my own education. I became most appreciative of the experience when I had to take my specialty board oral exams. I had to respond quickly and fluently to questions by the board. I had already been teaching those concepts for a year, so it was no trouble putting them into words for the board. It proved to me that you learn more as a teacher than as a student.

I would describe my experience at the MSP as a steady accretion of knowledge and experience of something I felt very comfortable being able to master. My residency came to an end in June of 1961.

Upon graduation, I joined a cadre of hundreds of doctors produced by the program. In the 1940s and 1950s, about 15 percent of the trained psychiatrists in the U.S. had part or all of their training at the MSP. Eventually I wound up helping to train others. When you look back on it, it's a blip in history now. MSP graduates are fading out of the field. Other training programs around the country expanded. But it was a remarkable time in history to see the impact one training program had on the entire professional community. When you attended the national gatherings of psychiatrists during the 1960s, a large percentage of them were like your fraternity brothers.

Karl deserves a lot of credit for his commitment to training. Dad was at that point really a public educator, a public spokesman, and a fundraiser. He spoke to lawmakers and government leaders and to the media. He was focused on outreach to the lay people. He wasn't very involved in the teaching and training at the MSP. Karl, meanwhile, was intensely invested in the school.

I didn't experience graduation as much of a landmark event. This was a hurdle I had expected to clear for most of my life. I had known for more than a year that I would be entering active duty in the USPHS upon graduation. So, my feeling was, *We completed this step. We go on to the next one.*

-11-

My Time in Prison

Before I entered medical school in 1953, I knew that I would have to serve some time with Uncle Sam.

When I became aware that my obligation could be met working in the Public Health Service, I decided to exercise that option, committing to serve two years in the federal prison system. That would allow me to complete my last two years of residency without interruption, while collecting the compensation of a commissioned officer. As a USPHS officer, funded through the Bureau of Prisons, I would actually receive double my salary while completing my residency! Upon graduation, I would then serve my two years.

Up until then, like most people, I had little knowledge of the correctional system. My uncle Karl had an interest in corrections and would later write an influential book on the philosophies behind, and the effects of, incarceration. I too, had an interest in the connection between mental health and criminal behavior and thought more exposure to the field would be useful.

My primary motivation, however, was simply to get my two years' obligation fulfilled so that I could get back to my goal of becoming a doctor at the Menninger Hospital. I wasn't aware of the new vista the detour through the USPHS was about to open up to me: psychiatry's relation to corrections and law enforcement.

During the second year of my residency, I was allowed to visit several mental health institutions across the country. Part of that time was dedicated to visiting the Federal Bureau of Prisons in Washington, D.C. and a couple of federal correctional institutions.

While I was researching options for serving my obligation to the government, I was told by an older resident about his positive experience working at the Federal Correctional Institute at Ashland, Kentucky. He was particularly impressed by the superintendent of that facility, Warden John Galvin. I felt that my own experience would be enhanced by working under a warden who was enthusiastic about psychiatry. For that reason, I investigated the opportunity to work under Galvin. During the second year of my residency, I had the opportunity to meet him at Ashland. He was a social worker who fully endorsed psychiatry and he encouraged me to apply to work under him.

The medical director of the Bureau of Prisons was responsive to my request to work under Galvin. But during the time of my application, Galvin took a job as warden at the Federal Reformatory, El Reno, Oklahoma. In order to work under him, I was assigned to that prison as Chief Medical Officer and Psychiatrist.

Immediately upon graduation from the MSP, Connie and I rented our house to an incoming resident. In June of 1961, we packed up four-year-old Fritz, two-year-old John, and nine-month-old Eliza and drove south to become Oklahomans.

El Reno is a small town on Route 66, on the Rock Island railroad. Our first challenge was getting settled in the house provided for us in the federal reservation adjacent to the facility. Soon after we arrived, Connie got pregnant again. Marian Stuart was born on June 30, 1962. Marian was Connie's mother's name, and Stuart was a name in Connie's ancestry.

For the first time, our children began spending part of each day in school. Not one to waste any time, Connie immediately got involved in the community, the library, and in hosting new friends at our home. Once we were settled, we would occasionally drive the 30 miles to Oklahoma City for entertainment.

One of our most significant connections while at El Reno was with Charles Penoi, a Native American who introduced us to the art and history of the Laguna Pueblo tribe. Through our enduring friendship with that man and his family, Connie and I developed a life-long love of Native American painting, sculpture, crafts, and artifacts. We also became much more aware of the Native American affairs in our nation. The friendship sparked a lifelong interest for Connie, and years later she would serve as co-chair of a Native American arts exhibit and competition sponsored by the Kansas University School of Anthropology in partnership with Haskell Indian Nations University in Lawrence, Kansas.

In order to build relationships with the El Reno staff, I took up new hobbies. Soon I was going out to the shooting range and participating in a bowling league. Regrettably, I was a liability to my bowling team.

———————————————

El Reno was a reformatory for young adults, 18- to 26-year-olds, who had violated federal law. For the most part, they were not high-security inmates. The really bad actors were shipped out to the facilities at Terra Haute, Indiana or Leavenworth, Kansas.

My primary responsibility was to oversee the institution's 25-bed infirmary, which had a daily sick call. This accredited hospital had two dentists, both just out of dental school, and a young doctor who had just completed his internship and was going directly into the USPHS prior to residency. So medically, I was their senior. I oversaw the hospital and served as the medical team's liaison to the prison administration.

I regularly met with the six-person management team that included the warden, associate wardens, captain in charge of the correctional officers, chief of classification and parole, and myself. I was responsible for medical services, the psych evaluations of inmates, and communication with judges about sentencing.

The Congressional Youth Corrections Act was about ten years old when I arrived at El Reno. It used the medical model of corrections and aimed to provide specialized treatment to rehabilitate youthful offenders. Under this program, judges gave open-ended sentences. Young offenders were evaluated by a classification team, which included a psychiatric evaluation. Our evaluation would be sent back to the judge, and he would decide, based on our recommendation, what the sentence should be. The evaluation team would then collaborate on a plan for custody level, housing, duties and activities, education, and any treatment needed.

Warden Galvin supported my efforts to bring innovative psychiatric methods to El Reno. For one thing, I started practicing some group therapy with the young offenders. They were, for the most part, misbehaving late-adolescents or young people with an anti-social bent. They were not necessarily mentally ill. It was an exciting new experience to try to apply psychiatric practices in this setting.

After I was there a year, Galvin was promoted to the Federal Bureau of Prisons office in Washington, D.C., and one of the associate wardens was also promoted to another facility. A new warden came in and there was some restructuring. I ended up with more responsibility under that new structure. I was made chairman of a classification unit.

One of my most memorable experiences at El Reno was a research project we conducted to see if some psych medications would be helpful in reducing behavioral incidents. We identified a population of unruly inmates who had misbehaved inside the prison community. Their actions had landed them in more restrictive confinement—the 'jail' within the prison—called the disciplinary cell house. The idea was to see if taking a medication would reduce their propensity to act out.

We monitored three test groups: one given an antipsychotic medication, one given an anxiety relief medication, and one given a placebo. I got authorization from the Bureau of Prisons to pay for the overtime of the medical technical assistants to administer the medication.

One problem that affected our results was that if anyone misbehaved badly enough, they were shipped out to a more restrictive setting. We lost control of the individual we were trying to monitor. But the biggest problem was that the test group was much too small. I had a total of 45 subjects to split between the three groups. You can't get data that is clinically significant from that small a population. I had great participation from the med techs because they got paid overtime. The bureau went along with it. The prison was supportive.

But it wound up being mostly for the education of Walter. It was a tremendous learning experience for me, but I don't think it contributed to the knowledge of the world.

———————————•———————————

I thoroughly enjoyed our time in El Reno. We made good friends in the community, and I enjoyed the camaraderie with the prison staff from top to bottom.

My responsibilities at the prison did permit me time to pursue some endeavors on the side. Perhaps because I had brought a new perspective on mental health to the prison, or perhaps because of my family name, doors seemed to open to me in the community.

I was asked to give some lectures in the town. That led me to be asked to do some professional consultation in the community. To do so, I had to get approval from Warden Galvin. Then I had to get an Oklahoma license to operate a private practice. The Secretary to the Oklahoma Board of Medical Arts lived in El Reno, so I didn't have much trouble getting reciprocity. I was also given a visiting faculty appointment at the University of Oklahoma Medical School's Department of Psychiatry.

The lectures and my small private practice, which amounted just to seeing a handful of patients, provided some extra income for my growing family, and gave me more professional experience.

The two years at the Federal Reformatory, El Reno served as my introduction to law and psychiatry, a field in which I would be involved for the next 40 years. My service to the USPHS thoroughly expanded my worldview. Through conferences I attended and task forces on which I served, I interacted with people from the whole range of the criminal justice system. I really wasn't confined to the reformatory. My relationships extended to corrections at-large.

The El Reno experience was educational when it came to working with a clinical population. It was more beneficial, however, in expanding my ability to apply psychiatric understanding and knowledge of human behavior to my interactions with staff and personnel in the corrections setting.

Through decades of observation of corrections and community mental health services, I developed some awareness of how the two impact each other. The gradual closure of mental hospitals over the years has caused correctional institutions to become primary providers of mental health treatment. Individuals with severe mental health disorders occupy at least 20 percent of America's prison and jail beds. Society's current means of dealing with the mentally ill is to criminalize them. The biggest mental hospitals in America are jails and prisons.

That was not the case in 1961, and it wasn't that way for most of our nation's history. In the early 1800s, we realized that putting people with mental illness in prison was cruel and inhumane. So, the U.S. developed public psychiatric hospitals. In 1880, there were 75 of these. The 1880 census reported that less than one percent of people in prison were considered "insane."

But a movement began in the 1960s to "deinstitutionalize" those with mental disorders, thinking it would be better to let them receive services in the general population. In theory, it sounds like a better idea than locking them up as though they were undesirable lunatics. But without adequate funding for mental health services, those who were previously institutionalized frequently run afoul of the law. The unintended result of deinstitutionalization is we now have a lot of people with mental health issues who are unhoused or incarcerated.

For that reason, I have great appreciation for the professionals serving in corrections. Their task of treating the mentally unhealthy as well as rehabilitating criminal offenders to return to our communities, is monumental, if not impossible. While also fighting for improved community mental health services, I worked hard throughout my career to advocate for funding and support for everyone involved in the criminal justice system, from apprehension to post-incarceration.

Because of the experience I gained and the connections I made at El Reno, I was invited to join a group that reviewed all the medical programs of the U.S. Bureau of Prisons. This fostered a relationship with the bureau that I maintained for the rest of my career. It opened up many opportunities to me. Over the years, I would serve as a consultant to police and to the USPHS and would participate in work groups that dealt with violence, corrections, voting rights, civil rights, and assassination prevention.

So, what I thought would be a two-year sidetrack to satisfy Uncle Sam turned into an exciting and gratifying part of my career for the next 40 years. Next came a decision which took me down another path for the next year, a decision I would have to communicate to my father, who was expecting me back at the Menninger Foundation in the summer of 1963.

12

The Peace Corps

I was a year and a half into my two-year "Doctor's Draft" commitment to the Federal Bureau of Prisons, when in December of 1962, another career detour presented itself.

I was thoroughly enjoying my time at El Reno, but it was merely a governmentally-induced interlude. My plan had always been to provide my service to the government as quickly as possible in order to join the staff at the Menninger Hospital. I was due to be done in summer of 1963.

While on Christmas vacation at my in-laws' home in Florida, I received a phone call that changed the plan, at least temporarily.

The Peace Corps had been established by an executive order of President John F. Kennedy and authorized by the Congressional Peace Corps Act in 1961. Kennedy had presented his vision for the Peace Corps on the campaign trail in 1960 as a way for the U.S. to spread goodwill and promote American leadership during the Cold War. He said the Soviet Union was exerting influence to spread Communism, and the U.S. needed to respond by promulgating the Western values of democracy and liberty.

Kennedy was inspiring hope for the future, and the Peace Corps was one of those hope-inspiring initiatives. The Peace Corps was not his brainchild, however. It had been talked about by numerous leaders throughout the 1950s, including Walter Reuther, president of the United Auto Workers, Senator Hubert Humphrey of Minnesota, and Senator Brien McMahon of Connecticut, who called for a group of young people to work as "missionaries of democracy."

As I mentioned in a previous chapter, President Kennedy's sister, Eunice Kennedy Shriver, served on the Menninger Foundation Board of Directors during the late 1950s and early 1960s. After JFK was elected, her husband, Sargent Shriver, was tasked with bringing the Peace Corps to life.

The Peace Corps was quickly filling out its staff with idealistic young people. To provide psychiatric services to the organization, a young resident from the National Institute of Mental Health (NIMH), Joe English, was selected. When the organization needed a second psychiatrist, an employee of NIMH named Leonard Duhl, who happened to be an MSP graduate, reviewed a list of psychiatrists working for the Public Health Service. Though he was a few years older than me, Duhl and I knew each other. He noticed my name on the list.

"See if you can get Walt Menninger," Duhl told English.

The phone rang at my in-laws' house in Florida that vacation. It was Joe. He described the opportunity and asked if I would like to come join the staff. It sounded interesting, but I was focused on our plan to return to Topeka at the first possible opportunity and told him I would have to decline the offer. When I hung up and told my wife, I thought she would be pleased that I'd said no to something. That didn't happen often.

To my surprise, she responded, "The Peace Corps? Why did you say no?"

Connie always gave wise counsel, and after nearly a decade of marriage I had learned to heed her advice. I thought, *Well, it can't hurt to go talk to them. At least get a free trip to Washington, D.C.* So, I called Joe back and said I would come to visit. When I visited the Peace Corps headquarters in Washington, D.C. in February of 1963, Joe was interviewing some people who were to be joining the overseas staff. He was in the midst of this orientation when I was ushered in, so I just sat and observed. Intermittently there were points where I was able to chime in, and Joe and I were pleasantly surprised to find that we were on the same wavelength. It was a striking connection. I quickly found myself excited about the organization's mission and even more intrigued by the opportunity to work with Joe, who was a couple of years my junior in both age and training.

I continued to visit with Joe for the next couple of days. It was clear he wanted me. When I would say I was leaning toward returning to work at the Menninger Hospital, Joe would contend, "Your father would think this was a good opportunity. This is what your father would do." He was very convincing about that.

While in D.C., I spoke with Connie by telephone throughout the visit, describing the administration of the Peace Corps and my discussions with Joe. She was fully supportive. When I flew home to El Reno, I decided I would do it. I would commit to extend my time with the Public Health Service by a year. I would be one of two full-time psychiatrists with the Medical Program Division of the Peace Corps.

The only thing left was to tell my father.

Mom and Dad were in the den of their Topeka home, sitting opposite each other at their desks, when I called that spring evening. I told them that I had a change of plans. I had decided to extend my commitment to the USPHS by a year to work for the Peace Corps in Washington, D.C. as a consultant.

It was as if the phone line was suddenly cut. There was absolute silence. After what seemed like an eternity, I could hear my mother saying in a hushed tone, "Bill, say something. Say something."

If I ever needed assurance that my father wanted me to come home, that was it. I knew he would be unhappy about my decision, but I didn't dream it would play out so dramatically. From that silence, I could tell how much I meant to him, both personally and professionally. He was distressed that I wasn't going to be coming home in the summer. The potential special satisfaction of having your offspring come home and work with you in a life enterprise that you share was something he wanted, and he made that clear by his silence. Dad would never ask, but he let it be known.

Knowing that I was going against his wishes didn't affect my decision, however. Connie and I felt strongly that going to D.C. for a year with the Peace Corps was the right thing to do and an opportunity that we should not pass up.

———————————•———————————

Connie, Fritz, John, Eliza, Marian, and I (along with our two French Poodles) moved to the nation's capital in June of 1963. For me, it marked a return to the city where I had spent a couple of my middle school years. For the kids, it was a change of environment that would continue to make them brave and flexible. And for Connie, it was another chance to demonstrate her adaptability.

My good friend John Galvin, the former warden at the prison in El Reno, was now Director of Research for the U.S. Bureau of Prisons in Washington, D.C. He identified a house for rent near his in McLean, Virginia. The modern one-story house with a basement was owned by someone who would be doing post-graduate work in Boston for at least as long as we planned to be in town. With several bedrooms and a yard for the children and dogs to play, it was a perfect temporary landing spot.

The Peace Corps headquarters were at the corner of Connecticut and H Street, across the street from Lafayette Square, which faces the White House. The building has since been rebuilt. My 10th floor office window looked out south and east, so I could see the White House, the Lincoln Memorial, the Washington Monument, and the Potomac River from my office.

I joined a carpool from McLean into the city. Who would have thought something as mundane as a ride from home to work could be so interesting? As anyone who has worked inside the D.C. beltway can attest, seemingly everyone is doing something interesting. That is a remarkable aspect of working in D.C.—the caliber of people you interact with. McLean was home to many elected officials, diplomats, and high-ranking government and military officials, partially due to its proximity to the Pentagon, the Central Intelligence Agency, and the many agencies located in Washington, D.C. I carpooled nearly every day during that year with a senior investigator in the World Bank, someone in the Budget Office at the Department of State, and several other high-ranking officials within the government. Creating a network of friends and acquaintances across the federal agencies was an incredible experience. The relationships I made helped me feel connected to the activities of the city, and working in an office situated in the seat of power can be exhilarating.

It happened to be a beautiful fall, and we would commute from McLean across the Potomac River into D.C., driving down George Washington Memorial Parkway with the incredible fall colors all around. To go to work and return home each day in that lovely environment was just a beautiful thing to experience.

The Peace Corps succeeded in spreading a positive image of the U.S.

to the world during the tumultuous 1960s. The ideals of the organization were captured beautifully by Thanat Khoman, Foreign Minister of Thailand, at the presentation to Shriver of an honorary Doctor of Political Science degree from a university in Bangkok, Thailand in 1964:

> It is indeed striking that this important idea, the most important idea in recent times, of a Peace Corps, of youth mingling, living, working with youth, should come from this mightiest nation on earth, the United States. Many of us who did not know about the United States thought of this great nation as a wealthy nation, a powerful nation, endowed with great material strength and many powerful weapons. But how many of us know that in the United States ideas and ideals are also powerful? This is the secret of your greatness, of your might, which is not imposing or crushing people, but is filled with the hope of future goodwill and understanding.

I entered the service of the Peace Corps at approximately the end of its second year of operation. In its first year, it had about 900 volunteers serving in 16 countries around the world. Shriver was the one making Kennedy's dream become reality. He would go on to found not just the Peace Corps, but also the Job Corps, Head Start, and Upward Bound as part of the 1960s War on Poverty. He formed a domestic version of the Peace Corps called Volunteers in Service to America (VISTA) for which I would later do some consulting.

Because Shriver's wife, Eunice Kennedy, had previously been a member of the Menninger Foundation Board of Directors, my name carried weight with him. But I had a very limited amount of interaction with Shriver. The man with whom I worked closely was Joe English.

Although he was still in his 20s, by the time I arrived Joe had established remarkable relationships across the different aspects of the Peace Corps, and particularly with Shriver. Shriver had invited Joe to go with him on his first overseas trip, on which they realized that they were both Catholic in faith, and of the same liberal bent. Joe, ever after, became Shriver's personal doctor, which helped psychiatry have a highly respected status in the Peace Corps.

One of the most remarkable aspects of my Peace Corps experience was the working relationship I had with Joe. From that first encounter when I sat in on an orientation session, it occurred to us that we viewed things professionally and operationally the same way. During the first eight months of my time with the Peace Corps, either Joe or I was out of the office. We crossed paths occasionally at headquarters as one or the other of us was on his way out. So, whoever was in the office had to make the day-to-day decisions. But we never had any disagreement. Whether it was a crisis or something else, the decisions were always easily agreed upon. We approached problem solving the same way. We were simpatico. It was the most extraordinary professional relationship I've ever had. The two of us worked as one.

Joe was committed in his Catholic faith and a principled individual, but he was also diplomatic and open-minded. He knew how to work effectively with a wide range of people. He had political skills that helped him forge coalitions and build consensus everywhere he worked. He went on to hold a variety of government positions, including head of the Health Services and Mental Health Administration in the Department of Health, Education, and Welfare from 1968 to 1970, and president of the New York City Health and Hospitals Corporation. Joe was deeply committed to education and served as chair of psychiatry at St. Vincent Catholic Medical Centers, and professor of psychiatry and associate dean of the College for St. Vincent. Later he was chairman of the Department of Psychiatry and Behavioral Sciences at New York Medical College. We remain friends to this day. Over the years, we enjoyed sharing professional insights and keeping in touch on a personal level. My specific role was as a consultant to various aspects of Peace Corps operations: assessment of applications, designation and orientation of psychiatrists who participated in the organization, training and selection programs throughout the country, and consultation overseas as needed.

The organization was full of creativity, enthusiasm, and idealism. I thoroughly enjoyed meeting the volunteers, who I sensed wanted to enhance their lives through service, and who clearly believed they were capable of impacting the world for good. The task of psychiatry was to screen them, prepare them for their experience, and help them as needed once they were in the field.

Part of my duty was to line up psychiatrists to participate in the selection and training of overseas volunteers. Wherever there were training sites, we had to find psychiatrists in the area to participate. We called colleagues all over the country to assist. Then we had to orient them on what they needed to do.

One of our functions was to assist in times of crisis overseas, when a volunteer needed psychological or emotional support. The volunteers worked under tough conditions, often in isolation from other Americans. We had to evaluate how they were doing and figure out how to help them in times of need. Very few needed to be brought home, but there were some. For those, we had to follow up by getting them hospitalized in the U.S., getting them plugged into a support system, reconnecting them with their families, etc.

On one occasion, an associate director had to call a family to inform them that a volunteer had died in the field. The associate director wanted me to be on the phone call, just to feel reassured. I didn't say anything, but I was there to be a resource if needed.

My first overseas trip—to Nigeria, Sierra Leone, and Senegal— happened to coincide with my 32nd birthday. It was the shortest birthday of my life as I crossed five time zones. I went to Africa for a Completion of Service Conference for one of the very first groups of volunteers to enter the field. That experience engaged me in a sort of "double agent" assignment.

I was sent to surreptitiously evaluate a couple of Peace Corps physicians, one in Sierra Leone and one in Senegal. I went there ostensibly to be oriented to what was going on, but I was asked to assess their functioning without their knowing. I had this unusual role of having to make a judgment of what the issues were.

One was a Caucasian doctor in a mixed-race marriage. Not only was interracial marriage less common in the early 1960s than today, it carried a unique set of undertones in the predominantly Black nation of Sierra Leone. The Peace Corps wanted to make sure the marriage wasn't creating complications. After spending some time there, I didn't see any issue they needed to be concerned about.

In Senegal, I visited a doctor from Georgia who came from a lower socio-economic background and was a little rough around the edges. Because he couldn't get into medical school in the U.S., he had done his training in France. Because he spoke French, he was able to get into the

Peace Corps and was assigned to the French-speaking African nation. But a lot of people in the Peace Corps were middle class to upper-middle class, and they didn't quite know how to take this doctor. He raised goats and some other animals. My job in that case was to reassure the Peace Corps that he was a good doctor. He wasn't as polished as they were used to, but he was competent.

In both cases, I determined there wasn't anything to be concerned about and set the Peace Corps at ease.

My second trip overseas was for a Completion of Service Conference in the Dominican Republic. From there I went to a conference of Peace Corps physicians in Latin America that was held in Lima, Peru. I was asked to stop in Bogota, Columbia to do clinical consultation on a volunteer who they were considering whether or not needed to be sent home. I also attended a conference of Peace Corps physicians in the Ivory Coast, and a Completion of Service Conference on the island of Borneo.

In all, I calculated that I traveled over 80,000 air miles while with the Peace Corps, with trips to South America, the Far East, and Africa. In the Peace Corps, you weren't allowed to stay longer than 24 hours in any place en route. There was to be no appearance that these were vacations. But the Peace Corps travel coordinators in every location were incredible. They would make sure your short stops were memorable. On a layover in Hawaii, a colleague showed me around Oahu in a day before I flew out. I had 20 hours on the island, and he showed me everything time would permit.

After the conference in Borneo, I went to Singapore for 20 hours, then on to Bangkok for 20 hours. In Bangkok, they were having some staff issues, so I got my stay extended for a couple of days to assist them. Coincidentally, a roommate of my wife's father was some form of royalty in Bangkok. During my short layover, that man took me on a behind-the-scenes tour of some incredible sights in Bangkok. From there, I also had a 20-hour stop in Hong Kong. It was a grueling trip, but an extraordinary experience.

As a consultant to an overseas training engagement, I discovered that part of the challenge was to set things up so that the volunteers didn't view seeing the visiting psychiatrist as the "kiss of death." To avoid stirring up apprehensions, I asked to schedule appointments to see six of the top volunteers, six in the mid-range, and the six who were experiencing issues.

That way, no one was automatically identified as the one needing psychiatric intervention. That practice also helped me keep perspective on the nature of the experience and how anyone would do under the circumstances.

The Peace Corps was one of JFK's most well-known and widely-supported initiatives. Most of the people at the top level of the Peace Corps knew the president and his family personally. It was viewed as his program.

As a result, November 22, 1963, when the president was assassinated in Dallas, the headquarters of the Peace Corps felt the blow intensely. I was in the building when the news hit that Friday afternoon. The flagpole for the building was right outside my office. At times the facility staff would come through my office to attend to the flag. When I heard the news, I didn't wait for the facility people to come. I climbed out my window to lower the flag to half-staff. From my window, I could see flags all across Lafayette Square coming down. And finally, I watched as the White House flag came down. It was one of the most powerful moments of my life.

When the news of the assassination reached Peace Corps headquarters, Secret Service immediately picked up Eunice to take her to the Kennedy compound on Cape Cod. Sargent Shriver and Joe went to the White House to work on the funeral arrangements.

The city fell under a pall. The office emptied out. It was very cold that weekend, and we decided that rather than join the hundreds of thousands who went into the city for the ceremonies, we should stay home to watch them on television. The day after the assassination, Lyndon Johnson—the new president—declared Monday a national day of mourning on which only essential emergency personnel would report to work. Rather than try to maneuver through the crowded downtown, we watched from home as Kennedy's body was taken to the Capitol on Sunday, then to St. Matthew's Cathedral, and ultimately to Arlington Cemetery on Monday.

It was difficult to go back to work on Tuesday at the organization to which Kennedy had given so much of his personal attention.

Sad to say, the Kennedy family wasn't the only one to experience heartbreaking tragedy during that time. Shortly after we moved to McLean in June of 1963, we learned that Connie was pregnant. We were excited for the addition of another child to our family that included six-year-old Fritz, four-year-old John, Eliza, who was nearly three, and Marian, who turned one that month.

My first overseas trip—to Nigeria, Sierra Leone, and Senegal that October—was an important one. It would be the first Completion of Service Conference that would not be attended by two staff from the D.C. headquarters; I would be running it alone. I had to get there a few days in advance to train the overseas staff on how to run the conference.

As I prepared to attend this conference, Connie began experiencing complications with her pregnancy. I took her to the Bethesda Naval Hospital to assess the severity of her condition. They did not really grasp our concerns and assured her things were okay.

I was forced to make a difficult decision, to choose between family and my commitment to the Peace Corps. I was the only one who could do this conference and it was essential that I be there. I decided I just had to go, abandoning my wife when she was threatening a miscarriage. I tried to make sure Connie would receive the best of care. Some close Stanford friends came to provide support. But I had to leave and would be gone for three weeks.

Connie spontaneously aborted the child while I was gone. God bless our dear friends who made sure Connie was taken care of.

In the midst of a wonderful experience at the Peace Corps, Connie's miscarriage injected a dose of reality that life is full of disappointments and sadness. My life had gone pretty smoothly to that point. I had felt like I had a lot of control over what happened. But over the next several years, I would learn just how little control we have over our lives.

Interestingly, at a time when Connie and I coped with this personal challenge, I developed an appreciation for how people deal psychologically with change and disappointment, and it came from my observation of Peace Corps volunteers.

I gained a pretty all-encompassing view of the volunteers' mental health because I was screening them in the selection phase and also doing Completion of Service Conferences at the end of their commitments. Along the way, I was doing consultations and evaluations in the field. I was particularly involved with the evaluation and disposition of volunteers who returned from overseas early due to mental and emotional health reasons. I got the flavor of the beginning, the middle, and the end of the volunteer experience.

The Completion of Service Conference was a debriefing of the volunteers before they were to return to the U.S. at the end of their commitments. We understood that they would probably experience a degree of "reverse culture shock" after spending a couple of years giving their all to serve in a foreign, and often impoverished and undeveloped, area of the world. But what we soon found was that we weren't just equipping the volunteers to reassimilate to American life; we were seeing patterns in their experiences and how they processed them. The concepts are simple and somewhat intuitive, but the development of a predictable pattern allowed us to better serve the volunteers.

The Morale Curve, the coalescence of the insights gleaned from the Peace Corps volunteer experience, is a transferable concept with far-reaching applications in preventative psychiatry. Once we identified and studied it, we recognized how helpful it would be for anyone navigating life's changes.

13

The Morale Curve

After two years of service in the field, Peace Corps volunteers participated in a Completion of Service Conference. This debriefing was intended to help them process what they had been through and prepare them for the adjustment back to life in the U.S. In addition to helping the volunteers process their own thoughts and feelings, we wanted to glean all we could from their experiences in order to better prepare future volunteers for what to expect.

At the beginning of the Completion of Service Conference, we asked volunteers to fill out a questionnaire. The staff tabulated the responses to the survey and used the volunteers' responses as the text for the conference. We began the conferences with a discussion of the responses to questions on emotionally neutral topics, gradually leading them to questions that would elicit a more emotional response. We asked what they were going to do after they returned from the two years abroad. We asked them pointed questions about their relationships with co-workers, how they had dealt with obstacles, disappointments, loneliness, etc. One question asked whether they had suffered any "periods of psychological difficulty" during their two years. If so, we asked, "When in the course of service did the period occur?" and, "How long did the period last?"

It was out of the responses to nearly 1,000 questionnaires that we saw a consistent process that volunteers went through during their Peace Corps commitment. We noticed predictable patterns that take place in adapting to a new situation. We began to call this pattern the Morale Curve.

It was only natural to extrapolate this process to other areas of life experience. Each time a person ends a phase of life and enters another, he or she is going to go through this same process. Regardless, whether it's a good experience or bad, whether you start with a high or a low, the pattern fits. Be it a new job, a move, a new school, marriage, divorce, loss of a partner—life change means that patterns by which we have lived will now have to be modified. It involves gains and losses. Major life changes typically affect morale in predictable ways.

The concept of equipping someone ahead of time, emotionally and psychologically, for something they are about to experience is known as "anticipatory guidance." Formulated by Gerald Kaplan, a psychiatrist from Boston, anticipatory guidance is one of the major concepts of preventative psychiatry. We utilized this concept in Peace Corps training.

Looking back, it's not strange that we noticed an identifiable Morale Curve pattern in the lives of Peace Corps volunteers. They tend to enter their two years of service with similar motivations. They made a choice to engage in this activity with an "I-want-to-make-a-difference-in-the-world" attitude. They entered at a high point, with a positive morale.

As we adapt to a life change, we go through a process of figuring out what things are going to be like moving forward. Some initial anxiety is normal. We wonder to ourselves: "What is this going to be?" "Can I master this?"

When people confront their expectations, insofar as their expectations line up with reality, they can feel positive and in command. But if what you encounter is not what you were prepared for, then there is a sense of loss. And the normal response to loss is depression and discouragement.

What we found with these optimistic, ambitious Peace Corps volunteers was that, after the bloom was off the rose and they were faced with unexpected challenges, they were often prone to respond with conscious depression. We saw people getting ill, failing to take precautions, having accidents. Those outcomes were a reflection of the unsettled feelings the volunteers had about their experience. That was what we observed when the new realities of life were fully engaged.

Some volunteers said they went AWOL from their posts and met up with other Peace Corps volunteers who were experiencing similar problems. They were able to share their experiences with each other, learn from each other, and gain new command over their feelings.

We started sharing these insights at Peace Corps orientation and with Peace Corps staff to train them to include it in their curriculum of training. We wanted everyone who might interact with a struggling volunteer to know that these feelings were not out of the ordinary. In fact, they were quite normal and understandable.

Utilizing Kaplan's concepts of anticipatory guidance, we sought to prepare Peace Corps volunteers for any and every scenario. In training, we would ask volunteers, "What are you going to do if…?" or "What are you going to do when…?" This line of questioning gets people thinking about the kinds of dilemmas they are going to face and helps them prepare to deal with them. Peace Corps volunteers might find themselves in a primitive tribal location or in some foreign setting in which some unfamiliar situation might arise. It could be something as simple as: if some tribal leader offers you a drink of something you are not familiar with, what are you going to do?

Anticipatory guidance activities did more than just help Peace Corps volunteers manage sticky situations. It helped them become familiar with the Morale Curve. We taught them that they would experience a predictable process, which we documented across a large number of their predecessors. We were able to alert new volunteers to what to expect emotionally. When a volunteer would get depressed, he or she could remember, *Oh yeah, the doc said I would experience this.*

Possessing this information makes what would have been an unknown more of a known quantity. It's similar to why a medical patient feels more comfortable once they have a diagnosis, even if the diagnosis is bad news. Knowing the situation is helpful.

The Morale Curve we identified in the Peace Corps is a transferable concept that may be applied widely. Understanding this pattern could help people be at greater peace with their circumstances and better able to cope. Regardless of the situation, people can say about their circumstances, "This is an expectable process, and it can be mastered."

The Peace Corps commitment is traditionally for two years. With a period of time that was common to all the people we interviewed, the pattern was easy to identify. We could, with a high degree of accuracy, predict when volunteers would confront each stage of the curve. But we found that the process plays out in the context of the length of the experience. It is very predictable when applied to a time-bound experience like a school year or the typical four-year college course of study. But you can see it in a short-term setting like a week-long seminar, a six-week orientation experience, etc. If you are aware of how the process plays out, you start to notice it as it occurs in your own life and the lives of those around you.

In situations that have an end date, you see how it naturally fits the time frame. Be it a school semester or a military commitment, or even a medical treatment plan, the known time frame forces the pattern to play out in a more or less predictable schedule. The pattern is comparable in an experience that has no end date, like the loss of a loved one, a divorce, or a move to a new town. In those types of ordeals, we noted that the curve typically plays out over a two-year period.

In one of my most widely-circulated presentations, entitled *Adaptation and Morale: Predictable Responses to Change*, I outlined the process as follows:

> From the moment of birth until the moment of death, everyone faces a continuing challenge to cope with change. Sometimes change results from a conscious decision or voluntary action. More often, change is imposed on us by natural events, or the actions of others.
>
> Change always tests our adaptive capacities because it forces us to compare new situations with previous life experiences, to synthesize new relationships to the outside world, and in the process to evolve a new sense of personal self-identity, concept, esteem. The new sense of self may simply be an affirmed self who has successfully mastered a new situation, or it may manifest symptoms that reflect persisting difficulties in adaptation.
>
> Although morale is not a concept discussed frequently by psychiatrists, it is a useful indicator of mental health because it is a reflection of the sense of self going through the process of change.
>
> ...Dr. David Perk identified morale as "the barometer of the individual's and the community's capacity for suitable response to the call of duty and of the fortitude and tenacity displayed in the response." He considered morale to be "the state of preparedness of an individual...for appropriate reaction to a challenging situation."
>
> ...several colleagues and I observed an adaptational

process to a new life situation voluntarily undertaken – in Peace Corps and VISTA volunteers. These observations led us to identify some common reaction patterns and predictable periods of psychological crisis. What is most relevant about these observations is the degree to which they identify a common process of adaptation to change in human beings and offer insights about prevention.

Arrival – The Crisis of Entry:

...along with the enthusiasm and excitement and sometimes unrealistic euphoria, the volunteers manifested some degree of apprehension and concern about their ability to meet the challenge. Although the volunteers had extensive advance training, unfamiliar situations and unexpected problems taxed their coping capacity. Some volunteers were overwhelmed with "gangplank fever" or intolerable levels of anxiety.

Engagement – Facing Up to the New Reality:

Morale commonly was at a low ebb, having fallen from the initial high level due to frustrations with and limited supports in the new life situation. Whereas anxiety was the predominant emotional tone in the arrival period, depression was the central feature of this second period. It was a time of acknowledging losses.

Acceptance – Accepting Life As It Is:

Generally, morale had been restored, with increased knowledge and mastery of the new life situation. The emotional tone, however, was often one of activism and anger. Feeling a legitimate part of the situation, volunteers spoke out more freely and pursued changes.

Re-entry – Going Home:

Although this crisis might be viewed as a function of termination, the period was labeled the crisis of reentry because the volunteers adapted both to giving up something now a part of the self and to anticipating the return to the culture of origin. Morale was generally on an even keel, although the volunteers experienced some combination of satisfaction with positive achievements and completing their commitment, depression associated with giving up their new identity and ending new relationships, and apprehension about facing future uncertainties.

Universality of the Morale Curve:

This pattern of crises and the morale curve are not unique to the Peace Corps experience. Rather, they represent a process that all individuals undergo as they enter a new life situation... The timing of the crises depends on the duration of the new life situation.

Life's Unexpected Challenges:

When the new life situation occurs unexpectedly, is unwanted, and involves a significant loss, the initial crisis is marked by low rather than high morale. Such an event reasonably prompts reactions of shock, numbness, disbelief, outcry, and denial—phenomena described by observers of bereavement, death, and dying. These reactions reflect a first phase of the crisis of arrival.

When the initial impact of the new situation can no longer be avoided, the second phase of this critical period is marked by searching, pining, anger and bargaining, denial, and intrusive repetition in thought, emotions, and/or behavior. Paralleling the crisis of engagement when individuals finally come to grips with the reality of their loss are the stages of depression described by the observers of adaptation to other life events.

The crisis of acceptance has been variously identified in these contexts as acceptance, restructuring, resolution, reorganization, and working through to completion.

The Crisis of Arrival:

The struggle for persons in the crisis of arrival is to

keep their bearings, and usually they either deny change at first or desperately look for something familiar to hang onto. The brain strives to find something in the new experience that "computes" with past experience, which is easier when one has had the opportunity to plan for the change and to become familiar with it. When the capacity to master the change is threatened, the emotional response is anxiety.

The crisis of arrival parallels the phenomenon of "culture shock," a term first popularized by anthropologist Kalvero Oberg in 1955. He suggested that culture shock is precipitated by the "anxiety that results from losing all one's familiar cues. These cues include the thousand and one ways in which we orient ourselves to the situations of daily life... All of us depend for our peace of mind and our efficiency on hundreds of cues, most of which we do not carry on a level of conscious awareness."

The Crisis of Engagement:

The crisis of engagement reflects the realization of the extent of losses—both real and imagined—in the new situation. It occurs at a time of isolation, and for various reasons the anger is internalized. The internalized anger, the sense of hopelessness and helplessness, and the pain of what has been lost all contribute to the emotional experience of depression.

The Crisis of Acceptance:

The crisis of acceptance reflects the achievement of a new sense of self, with a restructuring of emotional forces and relationships. For most people, this restructuring represents a new equilibrium, with greater freedom to vent frustrations by words and actions, with improved effectiveness in work and play, and with stable support from family and friends.

The Crisis of Reentry:

The fourth and final crisis occurs only when there is a clear end point to the new situation... The emotional tasks include working through separation from the experience and grieving for what one is giving up.

As a general rule, persons who have a greater sense of control over what occurs in their lives will remain healthier in stressful times of change than do those who feel powerless in the face of external forces. Part of that control is cognitive control, the ability to evaluate, understand, and incorporate life's stressful events into an ongoing life plan.

Weathering Life's Changes:

Individuals can enhance their own abilities to manage and cope with change by becoming familiar with future likelihoods and thus making unknowns known. Increased knowledge improves the human capacity to interpret and appraise events and contributes to a sense of mastery that diminishes the anxiety provoked by the new situation. In this sense, being aware that adaptation to change is associated with a predictable pattern of morale and expectable periods of crisis can increase the tolerance to that process. As a general rule, however, some anxiety is optimal in prompting adaptational behavior, and some depression and grief work are necessary to work through losses prompted by change.

-14-

Coming Home

I so thoroughly enjoyed working for the Peace Corps that I seriously considered extending my commitment for another year. But as the one-year mark of our time in Washington, D.C. passed in June of 1964, I knew that we really needed to return to Topeka. It was time to get back on course after this detour, to return to our primary plan.

Practically speaking, there were three things that made August of 1964 the right time to return to Topeka. First, the owners of the home we were renting were returning. We would be forced to move into another house if we were to stay in D.C. Second, I really wanted to get back on track for my career with the clinic. Never did I view my time with the Peace Corps as anything other than a detour. And third, I really wanted to raise our children in Topeka. They had spent three years of their childhood away from what I wanted to be our true home, away from their grandparents and extended family.

During those D.C. years, Connie focused on our family while I was preoccupied with the Peace Corps. I knew that as our children grew up, they would need more of my time than I had been able to give. I believed that getting back to Topeka would allow me to devote more time to family. We had a house in Topeka, as well as a church community that we longed to be a part of. We had connections and friends in Topeka that we wanted to rejoin.

Surprisingly, the exciting life in D.C. with its proximity to power and prestige was not that hard for me to leave behind. I enjoyed returning to Topeka, where I was able to jump in the car and dash to work in just seven minutes. Our older children were within walking distance of their school.

What was difficult to leave was the Peace Corps, with its special people and unifying, inspiring purpose. I had such tremendous respect for Joe English and Sargent Shriver and all of the D.C. staff, as well as deep appreciation for the selfless volunteers that I regretted leaving after just 14 months. Fortunately, after I officially resigned from my position in the

Peace Corps, I remained involved as a consultant. I was asked to provide a psychiatric perspective for a week of training in Ghana. While there, I got to travel with some volunteers to view the work being done in that country.

In future years, I became involved in the training of volunteers in another program championed by John F. Kennedy, Volunteers in Service to America (VISTA). Shortly after Kennedy's death, VISTA was officially launched by Lyndon Johnson as part of his Economic Opportunity Act of 1964. The program is the domestic version of the Peace Corps. Volunteers provide enriching educational programs and vocational training for underserved and impoverished communities.

I was primarily involved in VISTA training in 1966 and 1967. In the early days of VISTA, West Virginia wanted to use VISTA volunteers in its mental health service programs in hospitals. They were seeking a location where they could train people for that purpose, and they approached the Menninger School of Psychiatry to be the trainers. At that time, the head of mental health services in West Virginia was a Menninger school graduate. We set up a training program at the State Hospital at Osawatomie, Kansas, a town near Topeka, to train staff specifically for West Virginia. Training VISTA volunteers was fun. Training courses were six-week sessions, and they proved to be perfect laboratories to observe the Morale Curve.

As I mentioned in the previous chapter, the Morale Curve can be observed over varying time periods. It can be detected in a short-term setting like the six-week VISTA training program. If you recognize how the process plays out, you start to notice it in every experience.

What was fascinating in this case was that I saw the Morale Curve played out in that training program in both the experiences of the prospective volunteers and the trainers. The volunteers went through the phases of the Morale Curve, first thinking things like: *Why are we training in Kansas, and in this place?* then later thinking, *Why are they sending us to West Virginia? They need us here!* The faculty, meanwhile, went through the same process, thinking things like: *What is this group doing here? They're never going to cut it!* then later wondering, *Why do we have to send them to West Virginia? We could use them here!*

117

I had been away from Topeka for more than three years, and I was ready to fully devote myself to work at the Menninger Hospital and to my growing family. Having fulfilled my duties with the Peace Corps, we packed up and drove to Topeka. We moved back into our home on Plass Avenue with plans to remodel it and add two more children to the family.

With my return, there were now five Dr.'s Menninger in Topeka. My brother, Roy, had returned to the Menninger staff during my final year of residency. Because I left for my commitment to the USPHS about the time he arrived, we never worked together in any capacity before my departure in 1961. By the time I returned, Roy had moved out of the Menninger Hospital to develop a program related to schools. Our paths didn't cross a lot after I returned in 1964. I was moving in one orbit, and he was moving in another.

My father was always on the go as a preeminent voice of psychiatry in the U.S. and chief fundraiser of the Menninger Foundation in the mid-1960s. Karl remained involved in teaching at the USPHS and overseeing the Menninger Foundation as Chief of Staff.

My cousin Robert—Karl's son—had joined the Menninger Hospital staff in the mid-1950s. Nine years my senior, Robert earned his medical degree from the University of Rochester (New York) School of Medicine and was a graduate of the MSP that his father had founded.

I came back as a junior psychiatrist, caring for inpatients at the hospital. I would handle a little bit of outpatient care as well. Peter Fleming was the hospital director during that era. The structure of the hospital was that there were four section directors with psychiatrists under them. So, there were about 25 or so doctors on staff. I was on the fourth row down of the org chart.

Three years out of residency, I was now an experienced physician. With the Peace Corps, I was more involved in recruiting and training of staff and consulting on problems than I was in direct clinical work. The opportunity to be involved in an individual case over time presents a special view into a person's innermost life and their experiences. To be effective requires long-term, consistent commitment. It's not conducive to traveling since this disrupts the flow of treatment. I was eager to commit to that task.

Once we were resettled into our Topeka home, we found opportunities to reintegrate into the community and to invest in new interests. My brother Phil and I increased our involvement with the local Boy Scout programs. I made time in my schedule to join Connie in the First Presbyterian Church choir and I was made choir president in due time.

Connie was always passionate about improving the larger community in which our children would grow up. She had been an ice-skating enthusiast as a child, and she worked to drum up interest in developing a place for Topekans to enjoy that activity. She also got us involved in Topeka Civic Theater, a wonderful volunteer community program with a long history. Although I had enjoyed acting as a high school student, I didn't have the time to commit to playing roles in TCT productions. We began supporting TCT with both our enthusiasm and our donations. Connie also became interested in the Junior Great Books program in schools. Her involvement began with meeting with 5th grade students on a regular basis to help them gain an appreciation for classic literature. She soon became coordinator of the program for the Topeka Public Schools. She somehow kept all this up while sewing and baking for not just our family but also others in the community.

My interests in criminal justice and the corrections system carried over from my experience at the Federal Reformatory, El Reno. I was asked to fill a role as the primary psychiatric consultant to the Topeka Police Department. The 14 months in Washington, D.C. with the Peace Corps produced numerous contacts that led to interesting opportunities. I was appointed to a group tasked with reviewing the medical programs within the federal prison system, as well as to an advisory committee of the Office of Law Enforcement Assistance in the U.S. Department of Justice.

Though we moved away from Washington, D.C. in 1964, I maintained a role in the capital city for several years. In 1966, I was appointed to a four-year term on the National Advisory Health Council by the surgeon general at the time, William H. Stewart. The 12-citizen advisory council provided guidance on various public policies at meetings in Washington, D.C. I was the only psychiatrist on the council.

Our move to Washington, D.C. and subsequent return to Topeka affirmed my belief that I could commit to a life plan and execute it. It was our decision to commit to the Peace Corps, and it was our decision to leave it. The pieces were in place for a long career with the Menninger Foundation, learning from my father, growing my family, and building my role as a consultant on matters of mental health.

But the poet Robert Burns knew back in 1785 that life has a way of disrupting plans. He wrote about the plowed-over nest of a field mouse:

> *But Mouse, you are not alone,*
> *In proving foresight may be vain:*
> *The best-laid schemes of mice and men Go oft awry,*
> *And leave us nothing but grief and pain,*
> *For promised joy!*

Major trials, heartbreaks, and detours were lurking just around the corner as we entered 1965.

15

Claire

Connie and I returned to Topeka in the fall of 1964 feeling as though we had the world by the tail. Our four children were healthy and developing. I had just completed successful stints with the Federal Bureau of Prisons and with the Peace Corps. Those two ventures helped me forge many relationships and earn credibility that went beyond my family name. I returned to Topeka ready to go forward with my professional career and to continue to grow my family. Connie was pregnant when we moved back to our home in Topeka.

We had already decided upon names for three boys and three girls. This would be the third girl who we were going to name Sarah after Connie's best friend. But a relative of ours had a daughter just before Connie's due date, and they named their daughter Sarah. We knew there couldn't be two Sarah Menningers of the same age in the same school system. So, we were in a quandary. We struggled to come up with another girl's name all the way up to when Connie went into labor the night of a big dinner celebrating my father's 65th birthday.

Connie gave birth that night, October 27, 1964, to a baby girl.

Perhaps because we were attending the party in my father's honor, we recalled the story of how he received his name. My grandmother was hoping for a girl after having two boys. She planned to name her third child Clara Louise. When she gave birth to a third son, they named him William Claire, and my father went by Claire up until high school. That is, until one day he received a letter addressed to "Miss Claire Menninger." After that, he went by Bill, or eventually, Dr. Will. My mother always called him Bill, but to grandmother my father had been Claire. Karl frequently called my father Claire as well.

We named our little girl Claire Arnold, the middle name being Connie's mother's middle name.

From the start, we worried about Claire's health because we thought Connie might have had German measles in the first trimester of her pregnancy. At birth, Claire seemed healthy enough. But she did not develop as readily as had our earlier children. Her eyes tended to cross more, and she was a fussier infant.

On the afternoon of February 20, 1965, Claire seemed a little ill, but not serious. She had a hoarse cry and a slight fever. We called the pediatrician, and he prescribed an antibiotic. Claire ate and nursed well and seemed to be peaceful. In fact, that was the first time she ever fell asleep in my arms. At midnight, we noted nothing unusual when we checked her before going to bed.

In the morning, when we awoke, we were aware that Claire hadn't aroused us during the night for feeding, one of the few times that had happened. And then, to our horror, we discovered why. I'll never forget the anguished shriek from Connie when she lifted our lifeless four-month-old from her crib.

Rather than try to describe retrospectively what we felt, I will include the letter we sent to friends and family following Claire's tragic death:

> "But oh! fell death's untimely frost, that nipped my flower sae early!"
>
> The words of Robert Burns echo our feelings of the passing of our infant Claire Arnold, who left us so suddenly now more than a month ago. Yet her passing has called to our attention so many aspects of life, not the least of which have been the compassion and warmth and thoughtfulness conveyed by so many friends. While these expressions might seem little things, they do add up.
>
> In our relatively brief stay on earth, Connie and I have known little profound sadness. We have been blessed with much, and for that we are extremely grateful. But no one can be prepared for such an event, and we are most appreciative of the thoughts and prayers and actions of those who came to our sides.
>
> The mystery of Claire's illness persists. The events surrounding her passing fit the classical pattern of sudden death in infants…We knew that she was ill, but not so

seriously. She had a hoarse cry and a slight fever the afternoon before. But she ate and nursed well and seemed to be peaceful and nap easily in the evening. She showed no unusual behavior one way or the other at midnight... And in the morning, when we awoke, she was still and lifeless in the crib.

The autopsy showed evidence of a pneumonia and an early meningitis, presumably of viral origin. But the laboratories have been unable to identify any virus. Our friend and associate in New Haven (Connecticut), virologist Dr. David Miller, reports that they have repeatedly been unable to isolate any virus in similar cases there.

So, we are left with a mystery, and a reminder that our lives are in the hands of a greater Power. And we gain our sustenance from faith in Him and in His many other gifts to us, as manifested in the hopeful faces of our children, and strong support of so many good friends.

Among the many notes, some of the most poignant words were quoted to us by some friends who in the past sustained the loss of their son, Dr. and Mrs. John Bright. These words, from Theodosia Garrison's "Transients" convey much of our feeling:

> *The loveliest of lovely things*
> *They never come to stay.*
> *Seeing beauty is the wings*
> *That carry them away.*
> *Though we light lanterns in our hearts*
> *And make the crystal shine*
> *The well-beloved guest departs*
> *While yet we pour the wine.*
> *A heart-beat here – a lifetime gone,*
> *Yet richer life therefor*
> *Remembering the wings that shone*
> *Their moment at our door.*

Connie was devastated. As painful as the loss of a four-month-old is to a father, it pales in comparison to the grief experienced by a mother. That baby is not four months old to her. To her, that is a part of her that has been nurtured within, and then at her breast, for 13 months. No father can say that he has any awareness of what a mother has experienced. Empathy is a critical facet, but so is recognition that the degree of empathy may be limited. With Connie, I realized, "I can't really appreciate what you've experienced."

Prior to Claire's death, I had felt that, somehow, as Connie's husband, I needed to meet her every need. But this was something I couldn't help. I remember experiencing a desperate, helpless realization that I could not assuage all of Connie's remorse and meet all of her needs. She really needed professional assistance to come to grips with the loss. We were blessed by the counseling Connie was provided by Dr. Bernard Hall, a wonderful psychiatrist on the staff of the Menninger Clinic.

When you deal with such adversity, how do you resolve the hurt? Do you blame your partner? It's often said that a death of a child can either drive parents closer together or apart. Fortunately, it didn't drive Connie and me apart. We were always a close pair. The most intimate relationships are hopefully able to express and absorb those feelings.

As we worked through the pain of the loss of Claire, Connie and I experienced heightened fear for the health and well-being of our other children. That kind of response to the loss of a child is not uncommon. We fought to keep this natural concern from producing irrational responses. We realize that there are limits to how much parents can protect their children. We do our best to help them attain a level of function to deal with life's adversities. We try to equip children with the mechanisms needed to come to grip with hardships.

The 1960s were a tumultuous time, with the United States' involvement in Vietnam expanding and domestic issues making the daily news troubling. Inevitably, Connie and I viewed Claire's death in a larger context as part of a cruel and unpredictable world. With several months to process Claire's death, I put into our 1965 Christmas letter some additional thoughts, as well as some more detail about what we'd learned regarding the cause of Claire's death:

> This has been a year of soul searching and many thoughts for us. It has been a year of sudden despair, and hope, and worry and reconstruction. It leaves us more somber, more experienced, more concerned about what we hope for in our lifetimes.
>
> (Claire was) a victim of an acute, overwhelming infection which was presumably viral in origin; she was only hoarse when put to bed and in the morning, lifeless in her crib.
>
> Our hope is in our other children and their growth and maturation... Our worry is the worry of all in the turbulent world; and as parents who suffer with their children and have realized the tenuous quality of our existence, we experience anxiety at each severe scrape and genuine concern with serious accidents.

Interestingly, particularly from the perspective of the psychoanalyst, the impact of Claire's short life and untimely death on our other children was deep and long-lasting.

Our second son, John, was six at the time of Claire's passing. Once he got older, he dated a number of different young ladies. But the relationship that finally clicked, during his psychiatric residency in Colorado, was with a girl named Claire. In 1990, John's marriage brought a Claire back into our lives.

It isn't a coincidence that once in medical school, Marian—age two-and-a-half when Claire died—chose a different path from her Menninger-family predecessors. She would have become a fine psychiatrist if she'd so chosen. But instead of following in the footsteps of her grandfather William and great uncle Karl, and of her father and of her uncle Roy, and of her older siblings John and Eliza, Marian chose a different specialty. She went into neonatology, where she pursued research in sudden infant death syndrome. She devoted herself to keeping other little babies safe, so that they wouldn't suffer the same tragedy as her baby sister, Claire.

Marian may be surprised that I see her choice through a psychiatrist's lens. John may see his marriage to a woman named Claire as sheer chance.

But to a psychiatrist, these things don't happen purely by chance. These are imprints from early life experience. We may assume that most of these experiences are forgotten, but they are not without impact. We may have no conscious memory of experiences in our early childhood, but they are stamped somewhere in the deep recesses of our brains.

The letter informing our friends of Claire's passing was one of the most emotionally painful things I've ever had to do. I have written a lot of heavy stuff in my career, but that was the most difficult to put on paper. How do you make the heavy stuff digestible? How do you articulate these concepts in a way that people can really grasp and apply them?

The psychiatrist is taught not to bring his personal experiences into his clinical diagnosis and treatment. But Claire's passing was an experience that gave me a great deal of sympathy for other parents who lost children. Years later, in a nationally syndicated column, I responded to a letter from a mother who was struggling to cope with the death of a child. She wrote:

> I just wanted to let you know that I faced (the death of a child) a few weeks ago. My son would have been seventeen this month.
>
> I don't know how other parents face this. I am just going crazy. It is just awful to have a kid all those years, get him almost grown, and then lose him.
>
> I feel sorry for anyone who has lost a child. Now I know how it is. I have talked to a priest, but that didn't help. Now I don't know what to do.
>
> I can't sleep or eat properly…I feel at this time that I will never be truly happy since I lost my child.
>
> Can you please tell me what to do about all this? I don't know what to do next to keep my mind.

Here are excerpts from my response:

> A letter like yours always leaves me at a loss for words, because the pain resonates within me. What can

anyone say to relieve your pain? Not much, really.

You have become a member in a special club—parents who have lost a child. My wife and I are members, though our loss was an infant...We found in the time of our grief that there were many others around us who had a similar experience. And they shared how they gradually came to grips with the loss and again found happiness.

Depression is the result of feelings about a loss which cannot easily be expressed—feelings of resentment and anger which are turned inwardly. Thus, you feel down in the dumps, discouraged, hopeless, unhappy.

What's to be done? First, accept the fact that you have been injured seriously, much the same as if you experienced an amputation. A part of you has been ripped away. After such an injury, you must allow some time for healing. This, too, shall pass. Beware of ruminations of guilt or feelings that you somehow did not do all the things you should have done for your son.

If you have a religious commitment, you may find your faith is an important sustaining force. Death is never easy to deal with because it seems beyond any reason to explain. Faith in a Higher Power overlooking our earthly lives can be reassuring.

Having the benefit of years of hindsight allowed me to write that response, but the pain never went away entirely for me or Connie or for any of our four oldest children.

———————————

One of the advantages of our living in Topeka at the time of Claire's death was the access to the support of my parents. Connie and I were at a total loss for what to do. Mom took the lead in making sure all the details were addressed while we grieved. Mom and Dad were always there if we needed anything. They were the rock in all our lives. This was the time of our greatest need. I had a great relationship with my mother. She was so supportive of me, and she was essential in Connie's healing.

Claire's passing keenly reminded us that our lives are in the hands of a greater power. And we found sustenance from a faith in Him and in His many other gifts to us, reflected in our other children and in the wonderful support of our friends, and our church. First Presbyterian Church members prayed for us, expressed their condolences, and offered support in many ways. For Connie and me personally, the church played an integral role in allowing us to deal with crises, losses, and disappointments in a structured environment. It provided support and sympathy. The fellowship found in a religious body is sustaining in our times of crisis, just as having my parents' support at the time of Claire's death was helpful.

Experiencing the death of a loved one inevitably causes us to ponder the existence of a higher power and the control such a power wields in our lives. These questions are important ones to be dealt with in psychiatry because they are so deeply rooted in the human mind. While I don't claim to possess all the answers to questions of a religious nature, I have included in the following chapter some thoughts on the topic I delivered in a talk entitled "Religion and Mental Health" at a church in Ohio in 1978.

16

Religion and Mental Health

The death of our daughter Claire in 1965 did more than just cause our family pain and disappointment. It forced upon me, for the first time in my life, the occasion to really feel what everyone feels at some point in life—the pain that comes from the loss of a loved one.

As adults, we know that death is real. But we can't truly know how it feels to grieve a death until we actually experience it.

In psychiatry, we study what people feel and hope to help them sustain mental health through life's experiences. But to actually experience such a loss personally produces a new type of empathy.

Claire's death was illustrative of how people deal with losses and tragedies in their lives. How do we deal with our hurt? Do we blame God, or some higher power? Do we lash out or withdraw?

We talk in the field of psychiatry about adaptive mechanisms, mental mechanisms for coping. Some of those mechanisms are "immature." Denial, pretending something didn't exist or happen, blaming self or others, escaping efforts like drowning the pain with substances, etc., are all examples of immature adaptive mechanisms.

When we get to the point where we're dealing with these types of trauma with "mature" coping mechanisms, we experience success in overcoming the trauma. A mature response acknowledges the reality and finds solutions.

From the perspective of a psychiatrist, how does religious belief fit into the healing process? In the realm of psychiatry, we see it as a way of coming to grips with life's challenges. Psychiatrists have a wide range of attitudes toward religion. It's generally viewed as a "mature" mental mechanism. Most psychiatrists view religion as a healthy outlet and a way to find answers. Others are more concerned that religion can become, as mentioned above, an "immature" means of dealing with life's issues. There can obviously be some pitfalls if it slips into a process of blaming or turning religion into superstition.

While I am well aware of the potential for abuse of religion, I believe religious institutions help us to deal with crises, losses, and disappointments in a structured environment. They provide support and sympathy. The fellowship found in a religious body is sustaining in times of crisis, just as having my parents' support at the time of Claire's death was helpful.

My father explained how psychiatry and faith can work hand in hand in his interview with *Time* magazine in 1948:

> The psychiatrist deals with unconscious difficulties. To do this, he must often try to remove a sense of guilt. But, remember, neurotic guilt is not the same thing as real guilt. The minister...deals with...a real guilt over transgressing explicit moral laws, not the irrational guilt of the emotionally disturbed.
>
> Psychiatrists think that the unconscious material dredged up in psychoanalysis may become a religious problem once it has been brought in the conscious mind. But while it remains repressed – or unconscious – the clergyman, unless he happens also to be a psychiatrist, cannot get at it. Says Dr. Will, a Presbyterian: there are some emotional crises in which a "religious mentor may be able to provide more important support than a psychiatrist."

———————————•———————————

In 1978, I had the honor of delivering the keynote address at a gathering for the Lenten Lecture Series of Broad Street Presbyterian Church in Columbus, Ohio. Excerpts from my address, "Religion and Mental Health," provide some of my perceptions on the topic:

> I feel reasonably competent to discuss mental health, but less so to discuss religion, which is not my area of expertise.
>
> Not that I am without my share of religious experience—having been raised in a family where there was a substantial commitment to the church: my Grandmother Menninger was a deeply devout woman

who developed a Bible study course...and who was honored by a rose window in the chancel of our First Presbyterian Church in Topeka.

My father and mother met at a Presbyterian retreat in New York, and originally planned to be missionaries, until a number of circumstances prompted them to devote their missionary zeal to a life in the Midwest, and to the cause of mental illness and health.

I had my share of squirming in the church pew during the Sunday sermon, intermittently doodling on the Sunday morning order of service sheet, before becoming president of the high school Sunday evening fellowship group, and for the past 20 years, with my wife, a member of our chancel choir, along with serving in miscellaneous activities, teaching classes, etc.

I have no doubt that my participation in and with the church in these religious activities has played an important role in my mental health, and in that of my wife. This shows up in different ways.

On a typical Thursday, I start the day with a 7 a.m. patient, and continue with a full schedule, often until 6 p.m. Then I dash home for a quick bite before going with my wife to choir practice. Often, I am very much bushed, and I really don't look forward to the demanding hour and a half practice with the choir director putting us through our paces. He usually throws in a fair number of tough and challenging pieces, along with a smattering of familiar numbers.

Yet, by 9 o'clock, when the practice is over, I will feel invigorated and refreshed. And I can only speculate the reasons why—the fellowship, the participation in producing something of beauty, being part of something holy and bigger than all of us, and being able to express feelings in a constructive way.

There is a wide range of emotional health and illness, with feelings, behavior, and/or thinking affected. While we may speak of an ideal state of perfect 'mental health,' we are never in any such static state. We will fluctuate, attempting to maintain what Dr. Karl Menninger has characterized as a 'vital balance,' much as we maintain a balance as we walk.

In going through life, there are inevitably moments which threaten our emotional vital balance—a process which has been eloquently described in a metaphor which opens Dr. Karl's first book, *The Human Mind*:

> When a trout, rising to a fly, gets hooked on a line and finds itself unable to swim about freely, he begins to fight which results in struggles and splashes, and sometimes an escape. Often, of course, the situation is too tough for him.

> In the same way, the human being struggles with his environment and with the hooks that catch him. Sometimes he masters his difficulties; sometimes they are too much for him. His struggles are all that the world sees and it usually misunderstands them. It is hard for a free fish to understand what is happening to a hooked one.

> Sooner or later, however, most of us get hooked. How much of a fight we have on our hands then depends upon the hook, and, of course, on us. If the struggle gets too violent, if it throws us out of the water, if we run afoul of other strugglers, we become 'cases' in need of help and understanding.

Every time I drive west across Kansas on my way to the Colorado mountains, I once again appreciate why living on the plains encouraged a strong faith and became a "Bible belt."

Out in that country where there are not many trees and the sky becomes 90 percent of your environment, you are constantly confronted with a sense of the infinite, and your relative smallness and impotence. As you watch the clouds build up into a storm, all you can do is pray and trust in God that you will survive.

If hail comes and wipes out your crop, if floods come and overrun your land, you can only pick up and start over again. And as you search for some explanation as to *Why me?*, you are left with few alternatives. You can be paranoid and figure everything and everyone is against you and has conspired with God to destroy you.

Or you can take sustenance in religious faith that God is not an evil God or a vengeful God, and you will be rewarded for your dedicated efforts.

Such faith can be extremely important for you to maintain good mental health.

Religion can be incorporated by persons who are struggling with emotional pressures in a number of ways. Sometimes it can contribute to a healthy resolution; sometimes it becomes a part of the emotional disturbance, with a distortion of some sort.

Throughout life, we are all faced with the challenge of coping with some powerful emotional drives—drives of love and hate which are constantly striving for expression. The open expression of these emotions is easily seen and generally tolerated in the small child... As we grow up, we have to put the lid on these feelings. We become aware of the potential conflict of their expression toward persons or objects which are inappropriate in one way or another. Nevertheless, we all do commit an occasional 'thoughtcrime' (in the words of George Orwell).

And we can feel guilty because of our lust or envy or angry thoughts. This guilt is itself a powerful motivating force in life.

How do we expiate our guilt? How can we continue to live with ourselves in the face of such persistent 'thoughtcrimes?' Again, we call upon religion to help us out, to offer forgiveness of such sins, to assure us that we are still acceptable in His eyes.

Religion, therefore, can help us come to grips with the badness within us, and let the goodness prevail.

Coming to grips with the fact that there is both goodness and badness in us is a task that takes a long time to master…and some people never do. Rather they must totally deny the badness within, put the lid on it. They can never express anger. They can never be mussed up.

Most of us do keep our badness to ourselves, although there are those persons who present a special problem to society because of their behavior. We try to reserve our badness to private places…but we don't always succeed, and therefore religion can help us be absolved of that badness, and give us hope.

Much as we may try to rationalize why we do what we do in life, it's clear that the emotional underpinnings are potent. It is as if, no matter how much we think we are following the dictates of reason and logic, the heart of religion is emotional. The powerful sermons are those that touch some powerful emotion, and thus it is only logical that religion and mental health should be closely tied together.

-17-

In the Eye of the Storm

When dealing with a tragic loss like the passing of our daughter Claire, you long for life to resume some sense of normalcy. But that would not be the case for me or for my family, nor for the Menninger Foundation.

Storms were looming on the horizon.

Upon returning to Topeka from the Peace Corps, I had begun work as a psychiatrist in one of the sections of the Menninger Hospital. Dad traveled the country advocating for mental health awareness and raising funds for the Menninger Foundation. My uncle Karl served as the Chief Executive of the foundation, overseeing the hospital and the Menninger School of Psychiatry. My brother Roy, meanwhile, worked on outreach projects on the periphery of the organization.

Just a few weeks after Claire's passing in February of 1965, a conflict rocked the Menninger Foundation to its core.

Uncle Karl, who could be impulsive at times in his administrative decisions, let it be known that he wanted to hire an outsider to take on some role within the administrative staff. The Chief Administrator of the hospital, Les Roach, said, "We don't need another administrator. If you hire (this outsider), I'll quit."

This conflict set off a much bigger reaction. The department directors of the foundation, all of whom Karl had appointed, went to my father and told him, "You have to take over."

Some have termed the events of the spring of 1965 "The Palace Revolt." The department directors were fed up and finally took action. This conflict over hiring an additional administrator was the straw that broke the camel's back for the directors. They asked my father to assume executive leadership. All their frustration built up to the point where, faced with a decision between Karl and Les Roach, they chose Les Roach.

For the directors, it was a professional matter. But for Dad, this was obviously intensely personal.

Over the years, clearly there had been disagreements between Dad and Karl. Without their father, the wise C.F. Menninger, around to play mediator, the brothers often clashed in their opinions of how things should be run. They operated in separate orbits for two decades following World War II because Dad's people skills were necessary for the fundraising that ensured the survival of the foundation. But that doesn't mean he didn't harbor a desire to be more involved in the day-to-day leadership.

The crisis of the spring of 1965 was a much more profound challenge than they had faced previously. Dad felt that he was forced to decide between his loyalty to his brother and his loyalty to the institution.

Though deeply troubled, he ultimately chose the institution.

My father's decision to assume leadership of the Menninger Foundation made a lot of sense from a pragmatic standpoint. Dad was a better administrator than Karl. He was a much more diplomatic and practical leader who was beloved by the staff. While he thrived as a speaker and fundraiser, Dad had always longed to have five years as the primary director of the foundation, to shape the institution the way he saw fit. He appreciated Karl's intellect but understood that Karl was not a good manager of people. Karl lacked some of the basic administrative judgment that my father naturally possessed.

Regardless, whether it made sense pragmatically or not, this split led to a period of considerable difficulty for the Menninger trustees, not to mention awkwardness in the family. Dad's relationship with Karl was always tense. This made it worse than ever. Their brother, Uncle Edwin, came to Topeka to see if he could get Dad and Karl to come together and resolve their differences. He found that to be impossible.

The ultimate result was that the board sided with Dad. Karl was bumped up in an honorary way to Chairman of the Board of Trustees of the Menninger Foundation. His leadership roles, however, were stripped from him. He was cut out of all administrative activity.

Karl was a figure of national prominence, so he wouldn't be relegated to irrelevance. He soon began working as senior consultant with the Stone-Brandel Center of Chicago, spending quite a bit of time there. The Stone-Brandel Center was an effort to create a large community medical complex with 22 specialty units, one of which was psychiatry. Karl worked at that endeavor throughout the late 1960s.

For my father to take over as Chief Executive of the Menninger Foundation, he would need to relinquish some of his other responsibilities. Not only was he traveling extensively as a leading national figure in the field of psychiatry, but he bore all of the responsibility for raising financial support for the foundation. He asked me to help with fundraising.

For me, this new responsibility represented more than just a way to benefit the organization. It presented an opportunity to work closely with my father.

I had always fantasized about engaging in clinical discussions with Dad. A few of those special moments did arise when I was in medical school in New York and we would discuss something clinical, either over the phone or during one of his many fundraising visits to the city. He read my journals, so he was aware of what I was learning and experiencing, and he occasionally engaged me in discussions of theoretical concepts and practical applications.

When I returned from the Peace Corps, however, the clinical conferences about patients at the Menninger Hospital were conducted by Karl. I don't recall my father ever being involved in those meetings. I longed to work by his side during those years. I wanted to be able to partake of my father's wisdom, but that wasn't happening in the collegial setting like I had anticipated. The opportunity I longed for presented itself in the role of fundraiser.

At that time, Dad was raising more than a million dollars a year to support the Menninger Foundation programs, and there was pressure to maintain that level of funding. I had the capacity to help. The Menninger name opened doors, and my personality was suited to the task. I found pleasure in meeting with people in order to promote the work of the clinic.

The obvious drawback was that it would impede my work as a hospital psychiatrist. When you are establishing a psycho-therapeutic relationship, you must be there totally. You can't be interrupting it frequently with trips. The progress isn't just halted, it's derailed every time you interrupt it. Moving into a fundraising position where my time at the hospital was going to be interrupted by trips would cause my day-to-day function at the hospital to change.

I knew getting involved in fundraising would be another disruption to my plan to become a practicing psychiatrist. I wasn't reluctant to make the move, however. I recognized the organization's financial needs. I understood that the important work being done at the hospital depended upon the funds raised. Over the years, my father had impacted the lives of many patients, not by meeting with them as a psychiatrist, but by ensuring that the clinic could continue to thrive. By assisting Dad in fundraising, I had the opportunity to make a similar impact.

I was several rungs down the organizational chart at the Menninger Hospital and thus was far removed from the decisions that stripped Karl of administrative duties and put my father in charge. I had only been back at the institution for about ten months. I was still trying to get established in my career and had my own personal issues to deal with.

Despite the loss of our youngest child, Connie and I were determined to add two more children to our family, and for that we needed space. Our beloved home on Plass Avenue was getting pretty tight. We felt the time was right to remodel the house. We found an architect who did a great job coming up with creative ways of expanding and making use of the space. Our house was on a lot and a half, and he said, "Don't add on to the front or the back. Add on to the side." To make the renovation possible, we moved into my parents' big house just a few blocks away in the fall of 1965. We packed all our furniture into three rooms of our house, thus allowing the construction crews to gut everything and expand the space.

It was interesting to move with my wife and our children into the home where I grew up. Taking in four children who play musical instruments and are otherwise active and energetic was a lot to ask of my parents. My parents' home was a large one, but cramming six more people and their pets into that house was a chore. My parents traveled a lot for work and for pleasure, but still it was quite gracious of them to put up with the overcrowding. I kept up a busy work schedule, so the challenge was much greater for Connie in terms of managing the kids away from our home base.

As if we weren't already enough of a crowd for my parents to take into their home, Connie was pregnant at the time. She gave birth to our fifth child, William Libbey, in March of 1966. He was so named because he was the third son of a third son named William. His middle name is Connie's maiden name.

My first fundraising trip with my father was to be in December of 1965. We booked a trip to New York to pay visits to a number of big donors over several days. I viewed this as an opportunity to learn from him. But the trip did not go as planned.

My father and I were to arrive in New York on separate flights and meet at a hotel before beginning a busy schedule of appointments. I arrived at the hotel to learn that he had been physically unable to make the flight. He would arrive a day late. It was up to me to go solo on the first day's appointments with financial supporters and potential donors.

Dad had been experiencing a number of health problems—chronic bronchitis and emphysema in particular—so I wasn't surprised when he had to delay his flight. But I certainly was taken aback to have to go it alone on my first foray into fundraising. I admit, I was intimidated, going to meet with people at various businesses and organizations on Wall Street. These were people of considerable substance and high position, and here I was having to do it without my dad, the man they were all so eager to see.

I survived that first day of appointments, and Dad arrived that evening. After a few days of meetings, we returned from the fundraising trip to face Dad's health problems. Two days before Christmas, an X-ray revealed a large mass in one of his lungs. The holiday was a somber affair.

I flew with my parents to the Mayo Clinic in Rochester, Minnesota, the day after Christmas and accompanied Dad to his appointments. The second week at the clinic, shortly after New Year's Day, exploratory surgery revealed an inoperable tumor on his lung. He was diagnosed with oat cell lung carcinoma and put on radiation therapy for several weeks. He was sharp mentally the whole time, but the radiation sapped him of his strength. It was painful to watch him deteriorate physically from the treatment.

While at Mayo, Dad received a flood of correspondence from all over the country. He was indeed loved by people who knew him through the Foundation, the Army, the Boy Scouts, and various professional organizations. They all wished him a speedy recovery and expressed their appreciation for what he meant to them professionally and personally.

In March of 1966, Dad was able to return home, and for a time, he was healthy enough to resume some of his activity. He had suffered damage to his voice and spoke in a whisper, but with the use of an amplifying device, he was able to make himself heard. His voice gradually returned, and he picked back up some of his work as CEO of the Menninger Foundation. In May, he even attended the meeting of the American College of Physicians in New York. I accompanied him on that trip, and we met with some donors. Instead of Dad going to visit these donors, they came to see him at the hotel. Some made special donations at that time, obviously due in part to the status of his health. They wanted to demonstrate their appreciation for his work.

Although he was trying to soldier on, Dad was in a lot of pain. Complicating his recovery, Dad contracted shingles in his weakened state. Because we were living with my parents at the time, a couple of my children contracted chicken pox. One of the most challenging experiences for me while we were living with my parents was having to give Dad analgesic injections. I never liked giving anyone shots, and it was particularly hard getting up in the middle of the night to administer the shots to help him get through the night.

My life felt like a whirlwind during that phase. The storms of life, however, continued to increase in their intensity.

———————————————

We stayed with my parents for essentially the entire school year of 1965-1966, moving back into our home on Plass Avenue on May 30, 1966.

If you know anything about Topeka history, you know what happened next.

On the afternoon of June 8, I had heard that there might be bad weather in the area, and I stopped by my parents' house to check in on them. I was there when neighborhood sirens went off, alerting us that a tornado had been spotted in the area. I dashed out of my parents' home to head to my house as quickly as possible.

Prior to that moment, the sky hadn't been markedly overcast, but it was very humid. When I stepped outside my parents' house, however, I noticed the sky had turned an ominous green color, growing darker by the second.

By the time I drove the few blocks to my home, Connie had already rounded everyone up in the basement.

When I say "everyone," I mean our pets and five children, plus two more. It so happened that, during that window of time, we were caring for twin four-year-olds from Nigeria. Their father was serving as an aide at the Menninger Hospital while working toward a degree from Washburn University. He brought his wife and twin daughters with him from Nigeria. Shortly before the day I'm describing, the twins' mother, Janet, was involved in an automobile accident and was hospitalized in traction with a broken leg. The father needed someone to care for the twins, so they moved in with us for a few weeks just shortly after we had relocated back to our Plass Avenue house. Thus, when I rushed to the top of the stairs and peered down into the basement of our home, I saw not just the faces of my five children, my anxious wife, two confused French Poodles and some oblivious gerbils, but two beautiful little black faces peering up at me from the bottom of the stairs.

We had a television in the basement that allowed us to follow the news—like nearly everyone in Topeka, we heard newscaster Bill Kurtis utter his famous admonition—"For God's sake, take cover!"—until the power went out. The house fell silent, and the thundering outside grew in intensity. Fearing the worst, we huddled the group into the little storage space beneath the basement stairs. I watched the tornado through a basement window. I could see debris flying around. It sounded as though a train was roaring right over our heads.

I feared for our safety, of course, but I couldn't help but think, *Thank God I increased the insurance on my house.* It's funny what you think in such moments.

At about 7:30 p.m., the tornado passed by 20th Street and Plass Avenue, about five blocks to the south of our house. It marched diagonally across the nearby Washburn campus, moving from 21st Street and MacVicar Avenue, to 17th Street and Washburn Avenue. Every building on the campus was damaged, if not destroyed.

When after several minutes everything went silent, we asked, "Is it really over?" We cautiously exited the storage room and went upstairs, unsure of what we would find when we reached the front door. Up and down the street, people emerged from their homes, looking about and talking to their neighbors. There were tree limbs and insulation paper all over each yard, but no real physical damage to the houses within sight of our front porch.

What struck so many Topekans as bizarre was the surprising calmness that greeted us when we emerged from our homes. The sun shone brightly, and the air was pleasant. The stifling humidity was gone. It was as if the storm just swept away the gloom.

Despite the pleasant view from our front porch, I knew there had to be some serious injuries that would need to be dealt with. I grabbed my medical bag and, after checking on my parents, headed to the Veterans Administration Hospital. One of the numerous injured people who were brought to the VA died that night. This compounded my gratefulness for the safety of our family and the preservation of our home.

Way too many Topekans were not so fortunate. The storm killed 16, injured more than 500, and caused over $200 million worth of damage. It was the most damage in terms of dollars caused by a tornado in U.S. history at that time. About 800 homes across Topeka were completely destroyed, with nearly 3,000 more suffering some type of damage.

Interestingly, the storm and Topeka's recovery was something my nephew Bonar Menninger—Roy's son and an accomplished journalist—wrote a book about entitled *And Death Followed With It,* in which he recorded the accounts of dozens of survivors.

Like many Topekans, our house was plunged into darkness following the storm. Fortunately, the water was still working, but we had no electricity. We packed up all the food in our freezer and transported it to my parents' house, which, though just a few blocks away, still had power. But we decided to stay overnight in our own home.

While our thoughts and prayers were with the less fortunate, we tried to make the best of being without electricity. In such a situation, the first night is an adventure, particularly for children. You impulsively turn on switches and don't get the expected effect. Once the sun goes down, you try to muddle through with the light from a couple of candles, but that isn't conducive to a lot of activity. There isn't a lot you can do but go to bed.

That change of routine adds to the sense of adventure.

The second night, it's still interesting and challenging and somewhat quaint. By the third night, however, it gets old. We went to my parents' house for dinner each night. We couldn't read or engage in our hobbies. Obviously, there could be no watching television or listening to the radio. All of our routines were disrupted, and we still had nothing to do but go to bed in the early evening.

Early on the third night, I was awakened by a buzzing sound. I got up to investigate. It was Connie's electric toothbrush. "Eureka!" I said to myself, "The power is back on!"

We only had to endure 54 hours of this. Many people went through so much worse. Some Topekans were weeks without power. You certainly felt guilty if you were to complain. How could you grumble about an inconvenience when others had lost their homes, when lives had been lost?

Going through a tornado is a threat to one's very existence; a powerful experience. Something like that reminds us of our infinitesimal presence. And it leaves a scar on a community, like trauma does on an individual. One can't help but be struck by how unfair it seems. How do you understand such a calamity that affected some so greatly, but spared others?

The tornado occurred on a Wednesday evening. The next day's Rotary Club meeting—held each Thursday—was canceled. I happened to be scheduled to give the invocation for the next upcoming meeting, eight days after the tornado. Intent on capturing the sentiment and sharing some encouraging words, I prepared a prayer for the occasion. I certainly didn't intend to make any sort of statement. I just wanted to share some words of reflection that might help.

Something about my prayer struck a nerve. First it was printed in the *Topeka Capital-Journal*. Next it was entered into the Congressional Record. Then it was included in a publication called the *Journal of Pastoral Care*.

On June 16, 1966, I prayed:

Praise God from whom all blessings flow.

But, Lord, it's hard for us to readily accept adversity, to tolerate profound pain and to understand why Fate seems so capricious, why some of us were devastated and others untouched. We couldn't help but be reminded of our relative impotence and our helplessness in the face of this Greater Power.

Most of us are again carrying on our 'business as usual,' yet, in the middle of this busy day, we interrupt our personal pursuits and pause. And we ponder. And we ask You...

What should we have learned from Your Infinite Wisdom? Are we fully open in our understanding? Or are we nearsighted and missing Your communication?

Did You mean to remind us of our one-ness as human beings struggling to survive, of the fallacy of being self-centered and too contented, of your proverb that 'Pride goeth before destruction and an haughty spirit before a fall,' of the necessity to think beyond ourselves and our immediate interests?

And in those brilliant, still moments after the storm had passed, did you mean to remind us of the brightness and glory that can follow adversity? Did you intend us to realize how we must help one another to achieve that goal and understand the thought behind a Nigerian proverb which says, 'When the right hand washes the left hand, the right hand becomes clean also.'

As we consider these imponderables, will you please help us to understand how to accept and deal with the plight of those who have suffered and who are angry and resentful at being devastated or hurt. And assist us all in our responsibilities to lead others to bring forth new hope from our calamity.

We ask this, in Jesus' name. Amen.

These questions resonated with Topekans following the devastating tornado of 1966. They would gain even greater weight with me later that year. The tornado that struck Topeka mercifully relented, but the

Menninger family and the Menninger Foundation were still in the midst of another storm.

————————————

In late June—just a few weeks after the tornado—Dad went for a follow-up appointment at Mayo. While he was there, he took a turn for the worse. At the end of a week of treatment, the Mayo doctors didn't think he would survive that weekend. My two brothers and I took a charter plane to Rochester on that Friday night and rushed directly to the hospital, thinking it might be the last time we would see him alive. Mom was there at the hospital, supporting him every step of the way.

Interestingly enough, from the time of our arriving in his room, Dad's health turned. Perhaps his spirits were lifted by our presence. But his recovery was short-lived. It was apparent that he had little time left. In early August of 1966, Dad was airlifted back to Topeka, where a hospital bed was set up for him in the den of my parents' house. From that point on, it was mostly people coming to the house to say goodbye. Dad was no longer physically capable of work. He tired easily and wasn't able to entertain many guests. What energy he had was focused on communicating his wishes for the future of the Menninger Foundation.

Dad passed away on September 6, 1966, just a few weeks shy of his 67th birthday. My brothers and I and our spouses were there with Mom when he slipped away.

There was a remarkable outpouring of love and sympathy for our family and support for the Menninger Foundation. We received cards and letters, telegrams and mementos from countless friends. The national media recounted his impact on mental health care. His passing was covered by all the major networks and the biggest newspapers across the country.

About 1,400 attended my father's funeral at Topeka's First Presbyterian Church three days after his passing. Menninger Clinic Chaplain Thomas Klink remembered my father by saying:

> He was a man of dignity and deep feeling.
> He was a husband in a creative partnership.
> He was a father of high expectations.

He was a faithful brother.

He was a physician of compassion, a citizen of unfailing responsibility, a scientist, and evangelist for holy causes, a leader and an infinitely responsive friend.

The Rev. Klink penned "An Address to this Occasion," which was widely published after it was read at the funeral. In it, he addressed the loss felt by the Menninger staff:

> There is still darkness, and he helped to bring us light; there is still despair, and he helped to bring us hope; there is still human treasure of undirected wealth and talent, and he helped us bring purpose. So, working, we have honored and we will grieve.
>
> On such an occasion we do not seek easy comfort. We ask only for the stubborn strength to endure and, enduring, the companionship of those who feel as strongly as we.

A memorial for my father was held at the New York Academy of Medicine on December 14, 1966. A touching program consisted of presentations by several dear colleagues. Both the funeral in Topeka and the memorial were attended by a number of dignitaries, which the famed newspaperman William Allan White noted in his column about the Topeka ceremony. Here are excerpts from White's column:

> People living in Kansas do not realize that (the Menningers) and they alone have put us on the national map. When you think of Michigan, you think Henry Ford. When you think of California, it is Hollywood. Washington, D.C., is the White House. Delaware, the duPonts. Florida, Lincoln Road. Minnesota, Mayo's. And Kansas (if you do not come from here), the Menninger Brothers.
>
> At Mayo's there was Dr. Will and Dr. Charlie. So, at the Topeka Clinic—Dr. Karl and Dr. Will—two men who, single handed, have made a national institution...

Two truly great men who, working as a team, have made Kansas known around the world... And all because of this smart and kindly team of brothers who cared nothing for this fame, except that it might be used to restore more souls to the living from the agony of insanity.

So peace to Will Menninger, who in his life brought peace to so many others.

———————————

I felt a little like I was moving through a fog during that period. My memories are not at all vivid. It could be that the stress I endured clouded the memories. We all could see there would be a void in the leadership of the Menninger Foundation that would not be easily filled. I understood that I was about to shoulder much of the burden for fundraising. I knew that my mother would be a widow after more than 40 years of marriage. I was concerned for my children who would grieve the loss of their grandfather. And I wrestled with the emotions of my own personal loss.

I couldn't help but reflect on the decision I made three years earlier to extend my time with the Public Health Service. By accepting the position with the Peace Corps in the summer of 1963, I had postponed moving home for 14 months. We finally moved to Topeka in the fall of 1964, giving me just two years to live in the same city and work in the same organization as my father.

Did I feel deprived of the chance to work closely with him? I don't think I really felt that way at the time. I wasn't the only one pained by his death. The entire staff of the Menninger Foundation felt deprived of working with him. He was not just a figurehead to them; he was an inspirational leader and a guiding force.

Karl addressed the sense of loss felt by the entire organization in a message entitled *A Tribute from Dr. Karl*:

> We are deeply preoccupied these days with the great emptiness left by my brother Will's departure. A different world surrounds us, a sense of hesitation and brooding sadness pervades our hearts.
>
> But this is not in the spirit of Dr. Will's life. His life,

not his death, is what we must think of. He was so assiduous and untiring in his role of psychiatric evangelist and ambassador to the world for the Menninger Foundation that perhaps we tended to think of him as a permanent world fixture. And in one sense he is.

State legislatures can never again be blind to the needs of their people as they were before Will's ringing address to 27 of them. Many men of wealth and organizations and power who never gave a thought to mental illness except as a rare and far-removed misfortune have come to see it as a part of their social responsibility, demanding support of all effort toward better mental health. May we think that military leaders, senators and even presidents of the United States will always remember now that there is a psychiatric side to the nation's problems?

All this change can be said to have come about in large part because William Claire Menninger, with his friendly voice and his irresistible smile and his great earnestness, sat down with these leaders and talked with them about mental health as a national goal.

No one ever approached my brother either in the skill with which he carried the message or in the indefatigability with which he pursued his goals. He did not realize, I am sure, how far his voice carried. He thought he was helping to balance the budget of the Menninger Foundation through the solicitation of grants and donations, the making of friends "for the cause." But he did far more than this.

For in asking the help of the people for the people, Dr. Will taught the world. He made converts of thousands of non-believers, well-meaning, intelligent people who nevertheless had little realization of the potentialities of a psychiatric program, and had no sense of personal concern or responsibility for it. Sad and affectionate messages have come from hundreds of these men to his mourners here in Topeka attesting to his great influence.

In psychiatry, where his colleagues repeatedly demonstrated their regard for him as a leader by electing him president or chairman, his greatest clinical achievement was, I think, his implementation of milieu therapy and the cultivation of an *esprit de corps* in the hospital team. These experiences, also, he put into a manual, which, while not published, was long used in our own hospital and elsewhere almost unchanged, and which continues to be used in many places with such modifications as time and experience have seemed to make useful.

Dr. Will supported me stoutly and loyally when I engaged in organizing the Menninger School of Psychiatry. He taught in it occasionally, less frequently than the men would have liked because he was away from Topeka so much in those years. But in his personal contacts with students and alumni, he got across to them his kindly personal interest, making nearly everyone he talked to feel that he, Dr. Will, was interested in what they were doing and how they're getting along and that he commended it and approved it. He did not pursue theories or issues or new projects; he just gave us his blessing and his smile.

In his kindness and gentleness and his friendliness and hopefulness, Dr. Will exemplified a mental healthiness which goes beyond all the definitions which he or anyone else ever wrote. Of the team of father, Will, and myself, no one of us could have developed The Menninger Foundation without the others. The realization that our purposes are now expressed in hundreds of places by those of you who are reading these lines would have been of the greatest joy to Dr. Will, and the fact that it is true is perhaps the greatest memorial to his life.

18

The Genius of Doctor Will

When my father passed away in 1966, he was a person of national prominence.

As happens with just about anyone who becomes widely known, however, he gradually faded into history. My uncle Karl, whose name was connected to some widely-read books and who lived for another 24 years after his brother's passing, was destined to be a bit more widely remembered than my father.

I am extremely proud of the accomplishments of both these men. I feel a desire to make sure that their attributes and contributions to the world are not forgotten. Particularly those of my father. It's been more than 50 years since his passing. The Menninger Foundation has since moved from Topeka. My parents' two living sons are getting up there in age. My father's name is becoming something you come across in a history book or on a website.

In recent years, therefore, I've taken opportunities to shine a little more light on my father and his considerable accomplishments. One such opportunity arose recently at the Kansas State Historical Society (KSHS).

The KSHS has been important to the Menninger family for many years. Some of my connection to KSHS will be described later in this book. But in short, the archives at KSHS became the repository of all the files and records of the Menninger Foundation prior to its move from Kansas. It is where all my personal files will also ultimately reside. And it was also a place of employment for Connie for many years—more on that later.

In my retirement, I have served on the Board of Directors of KSHS. Recently I stepped into the succession of president-elect, president, and past president, each a year in length.

As each president concludes the year in that position, he or she is asked to provide a message at the annual meeting of the society. I decided to give a talk on what I consider the "genius" of my father, which I believe was his capacity to conceptualize a total treatment program in a psychiatric hospital in a time when there were not all the modern psychotropic medications that exist today. My father's ability to bring his vision to reality is part of what made the Menninger Sanitarium unique.

I don't herald my father's accomplishments simply to bring vain glory to the Menninger family. I think the lessons my father taught to the military and to the mental health care profession decades ago are still important and need to be remembered.

The following are excerpts from my address to the KSHS Annual Meeting on November 4, 2022, entitled "The Genius of Doctor Will."

> Today, I wish to highlight a most extraordinary Kansan, my father, William Claire Menninger... I attribute the term "genius" to him for several reasons: (1) His professional skills. (2) His leadership skills. (3) His relationship ("people") skills.

> **Professional skills:**

> In 1932, long before the advent of modern psychotropic medications, Will wrote (in the *Bulletin of the Menninger Clinic*):

>> A patient comes to the hospital not with symptoms, but with problems. What can be done for him? It is not sufficient that he be made physically comfortable; rest and freedom from responsibility alone will not satisfy his psychologic needs. His problems need to be studied intensively, interpreted and a solution attempted.

> Dr. Will proceeded to formulate a "Guide to the Order Sheet"—a treatment guide outlining what a problem-oriented hospital should contain: environment, scientifically controlled friendship, the daily schedule, recreation, reading, occupational therapy, music, special activities, psychotherapy, and physical therapy.

Dr. Will wrote:

> Psychiatric hospital care should afford specific and continuous treatment; specific in that it is directed toward meeting the conflict of the individual, and continuous in that every contact that the patient makes throughout every day should guide him toward the same therapeutic goal.

The Menninger "Guide to the Order Sheet" was an extraordinary document that was at the heart of what led to the success and renown of the Menninger Sanitarium in the 1930s. Each patient's treatment plan was collectively formulated according to this guide and implemented by the whole treatment team: doctor, nurses, adjunctive therapists, etc.

A colleague, Lewis Robbins, who trained at Menninger in the early 1940s, described it this way: Dr. Will "drew heavily upon his knowledge of psychoanalysis, with particular attention to the ego's adaptive as well as maladaptive operations, to develop a therapeutic approach which would involve all aspects of a patient's life in the hospital, and all personnel with whom the patient came in contact.

"The treatment plan was seen not only as useful for the patient while in the hospital, but was seen as helpful to him in developing new and more effective patterns of living, which along with the insight he might acquire from his psychotherapy, would insure a better and more enduring result."

Although the "Guide to the Order Sheet" formulation is no longer utilized per se, Dr. Will's conceptualization of the therapeutic environment is still relevant in the treatment of mentally ill patients whose symptoms necessitate hospitalization.

Leadership Skills:

His leadership skills were especially evident in three areas: Scouting, World War II, and professional organizations.

(a) Scouting

As the Boy Scouts movement began in 1910, Will became involved, and he sustained his interest in Scouting all his life. After he returned to Topeka and entered his professional practice, he became the Scoutmaster of Boy Scout Troop 2 at the First Presbyterian Church. In due course, under his leadership, a substantial number of boys in that troop achieved the Eagle rank, the highest rank in scouting.

His skills were noted early by the national organization of the Boy Scouts of America (BSA) with his election to the Executive Board of the BSA. For many years, he served as the chairman of the national health and safety committee of the BSA.

(b) World War II

While his leadership skills were evident in his work at the Menninger Clinic, they became most relevant in his response to the challenges of World War II.

Dr. Henry Brosin, a colleague of Dr. Will, noted (in the *Bulletin of the Menninger Clinic*):

> Mobilizing and training over 8,000,000 men created problems in human relations no less serious than those of supply and transportation, but with relatively little opportunity to correct them. While [Dr. Will's] predecessors worked ably and valiantly to promote understanding of the human variables in the military setting, it was his efforts that brought this work to an unprecedented fruition.

Joining the Army in 1942, Dr. Will (called Bill by his colleagues) was initially assigned as the Psychiatric Consultant for the Army's Fourth Service Command, the southeastern United States. In the words of Malcolm Farrell, M.D., then deputy chief consultant neuropsychiatry, office of the Surgeon General of the Army in WW II: "I had the wonderful opportunity of observing Bill in action, improving the status and image of psychiatry in the Army, in spite of overt hostility on the part of some of the regular commanding officers of Army hospitals. Within a few hours, he would win the confidence and respect of the other medical personnel, thus improving the status of the local psychiatrists. In many of the hospitals in his command, he was able to elevate psychiatry to the level of a Service, whereas previously it had been a branch under the Medical Service."

Following the untimely death of Roy Halloran, the Chief Psychiatric Consultant to the Surgeon General of the Army, in 1943, Dr. Will was promoted to that position, in which he faced numerous challenges.

Although psychiatrists assigned to and working with combat troops proved to be valuable in World War I, it was not until nearly the end of the second year of WWII that such positions were again created.

Initially, it was assumed neuropsychiatric casualties could be taken care of in the general hospitals. Immediately after the American forces engaged in combat in the Mediterranean theater, it was found that not more than five per cent of such casualties were returned to combat duty.

As a consequence, improvised measures were created in the forward areas to provide early and immediate treatment... (As a result) an average of sixty percent of soldiers with neuropsychiatric disorders developing in combat were returned for further combat duty. An additional thirty percent were salvaged for noncombat duty.

Establishing a psychiatric presence at a divisional level, near the front lines, so that psychiatric casualties could be treated and returned to active duty instead of being evacuated, was bitterly opposed by the Army Ground Forces.

Because the office of the Surgeon General had no jurisdiction over the Army Ground Forces, the decision had to be carried to the General Staff level, where the decision was finally approved. Observed Farrell: "It was a most gratifying experience to observe Bill in action before the top generals of the Army."

Farrell also noted, "When Bill went to the Surgeon General's office, a neuropsychiatric diagnosis usually meant a discharge as soon as possible, without any attempt at treatment. Bill immediately initiated a treatment and rehabilitation program which salvaged many for return to duty or return to useful civilian careers."

In his summary of the World War II experience, Dr Will wrote:

> The psychiatric casualty is no less and no more expendable than any other individual, and whether a man has a gunshot wound in the arm or a neuropsychiatric condition, if he can give more service, it is the medical officer's responsibility to return him to duty.

It is noteworthy that these lessons have been incorporated in the teaching of military combat psychiatry, articulated as the principles of proximity, immediacy, simplicity, expectancy, and centrality. That is, treatment of the psychiatric casualty in a safe place, close to the battle scene; as soon as possible; initially with simple measures such as rest, food, and a shower; with the clear expectation that the casualty is not ill and will return to his unit; and the casualty will be screened at a central facility by skilled personnel to eliminate inappropriate evacuation on a psychiatric basis.

In 1942, the nomenclature of psychiatric disorders in use by the American Psychiatric Association was not satisfactory for use in the military service. Dr. Will and his associates developed a nomenclature which was not only successful in meeting military needs, but much of it was later adopted by the American Psychiatric Association.

Serving as Dr. Will's deputy in the Office of the Surgeon General, Farrell wrote in the *Memorial for William C. Menninger*:

> At no time did Bill operate a 'one-man show.' All of his decisions were discussed with his associates, who were encouraged to present their own ideas; and he was quick to recognize their assistance publicly. ...His good humor and dedication to duty...were an inspiration to all of us... He was a leader in every sense of the word.

Ultimately promoted to the rank of Brigadier General, the highest rank awarded to anyone other than career officers, he was awarded the U.S. Army's Distinguished Service Medal, as well as the French Legion of Honor Award.

Dr. Will was released from his responsibility as the chief psychiatric consultant to the Surgeon General of the Army in the summer of 1946. At that time and subsequently, he wrote extensively of the lessons learned, with the goal that this nation would not have to relearn the lessons that had earlier been learned and then forgotten after World War I. His most thorough documentation is *Psychiatry in a Troubled World: Yesterday's War and Today's Challenge*, published in 1948.

(c) Professional Organizations

Following the war, he assumed a leadership role for the psychiatric profession. Frustrated during WWII by the lack of effective assistance from the American Psychiatric Association, Dr. Will and a number of wartime colleagues became active as "Young Turks," creating a Group for the Advancement of Psychiatry (GAP).

Colleague Leo Bartemeier noted in the *Memorial for William C. Menninger* that Bill Menninger "always spoke the language of the common man… He behaved as though he had no intention of being persuasive, but by spelling out the facts as he saw them, he exerted tremendous pressure to further advance the aims and objectives of his organization. Bill never knew how truly great he was."

In the late 1940s, Dr. Will was simultaneously chairman of GAP, president of the American Psychiatric Association, and president of the American Psychoanalytic Association. He became a pre-eminent spokesman for the profession and for mental health.

Under his leadership the professional organizations became more proactive in addressing issues of mental health and mental illness. In the fall of 1948, he was featured on the cover of *Time* magazine (October 25), addressing those issues. Over the next decade, he addressed state legislatures or legislators assembled in half of these United States, urging increased funding and enhancement of mental health services provided by the state.

On February 8, 1962, he visited with President John F. Kennedy at the White House, encouraging his support for federal funding for community mental health services. Colleague Leo Bartemeier observed in the *Memorial for William C. Menninger*, "That interview was, I think, directly responsible for President Kennedy's subsequent address on the mental health needs of our country, the first president in our history to have ever taken up our cause."

Relationship Skills:

Perhaps the greatest reflection of Dr. Will's genius was in his capacity to connect with people where they were. Norm Brill, a military colleague, described it this way: Dr. Will gained respect by being "one of the fellows," with "frequent visits after hours with the directors of other services, responding to their concerns."

Further he had social talents such as an ability to play all the old songs by ear on the piano, where he would be joined on the piano bench by the Surgeon General who loved to sing all those old songs. Dr. Will also had the capacity to relate to others with a repertoire of jokes and limericks that were appropriate to break the ice in whatever situation he found himself.

His effectiveness as a fund raiser for the Menninger Foundation stemmed from his ability to establish relationships with individuals in all walks of life. What made him special, as shared with me by the president of a major life insurance company: "When you were with (Dr. Will), you were the only person in the world."

Closing Thoughts:

At a memorial gathering of Dr. Will's colleagues in December 1966, Henry Brosin observed:

"Very few men have had the good fortune to make contributions to psychiatry and humanity of the magnitude of those made by William Claire Menninger... These were made possible by the combination of his own superlative skill as a clinician, scholar, and public expositor in times of swift, dramatic change...

"He saw clearly and felt deeply the needs and aspirations of men and women in the industrial and post-industrial world, ...and understood the nature of the disorder which characterized our culture, what needed to be done to improve it, and most importantly, devised ways in which he himself could actively participate in making this a better world to live in."

19

The Passing of the Torch

At the end of Chapter 17, I included the moving words my uncle Karl shared at my father's memorial. Karl's message was particularly gracious when you consider the events of the previous year, when he was forced out of leadership at the Menninger Foundation. Obviously, among the crowd who listened to his kind words were those same directors who had forced his exile.

The timing of the transition of leadership at the Menninger Foundation was interesting. My father's health issues were concerning, but perhaps everyone thought he had many years to guide the organization. Certainly, he hoped to have several years at the helm.

That all changed in December of 1965. But I believe his fate was determined eight months earlier.

The Palace Revolt which forced my father to side with the institution over Karl happened in April of 1965. A text on surgical pathology that I reviewed upon receiving my father's diagnosis noted that oat cell carcinoma characteristically begins eight months before it is diagnosed. Eight months prior to his diagnosis, my father was in the midst of tumultuous conflict. That lead me to presume that my father's cancer was prompted by the split at the foundation.

Dad always wanted the opportunity to head the Menninger Foundation. But I don't think he could live with having to choose between the institution and his brother.

Certainly, Dad had the susceptibility for lung cancer from years of heavy smoking. He had exhibited symptoms in November. But it's my belief that the stress of the split with his brother brought on his illness.

In January of 1966, he was confronted with the fact that there was not going to be time for him to make the changes he so longed to make at Menninger. The future leadership of the foundation weighed heavily on him during his final months.

Had his time not run out, I believe he would have successfully guided the foundation to great success. He was loved by everybody, and he had the proper sense to get people to work together. After Dad's death, there would be the reaction of the senior staff who had grown up practicing under a certain style. Taking over direction of the organization would be challenging to any leader. Dad knew this, and therefore he worried a lot about the transition that would occur after his death.

After Dad passed away in September of 1966, a search committee considered who should succeed him as president and CEO of the Menninger Foundation. They pondered whether an outside director should be brought in to provide new perspective. Or should it be a Menninger?

It was clear that Karl wanted to resume the role that he'd been moved out of a year and a half earlier, but the board was resolute on that. The search committee came up with a short list of candidates which included Roy and Karl's son Robert.

There were things that pointed to Robert as a likely candidate. He had been working at Menninger since 1952, returning after serving four years in the Army during the war, earning a bachelor's degree from the University of Kansas, and his medical degree from the University of Rochester (N.Y.) School of Medicine. Robert had received his residency training in psychiatry from the Menninger School of Psychiatry and graduated from the Topeka Institute of Psychoanalysis. He had filled the roles of section chief and day-hospital director and was a member of the Menninger Board of Directors. In 1965, he was named director of Outpatient Diagnostic Services. Robert was several years older than Roy and had a lot more clinical experience under his belt.

Robert was a hail-fellow-well-met kind of person. He was an effective Section Director. He did a good job heading the Community Service office. But he never manifested the leadership skills needed at the top. He wasn't a striver. My sense is that he derived much more satisfaction from his personal life than he did from pouring himself into work. For whatever reason, the board did not select him for the position.

In the years leading up to my father's passing, Roy had been working outside of the Menninger Clinic. Focused on outreach programs, Roy had devoted a lot of time developing a program that could be used in relation to schools. He had some psychotherapy patients, but he was not practicing in the hospital. We spent a lot of time together at my father's bedside, comforting my mother, and honoring my father's memory after his passing. But because we were working in different worlds, we didn't interact professionally during the period prior to Dad's death.

Roy hadn't really grown up within the Menninger system, so he was to a degree an outsider to the factions that had turned on Karl in the spring of 1965. Roy had not had any significant administrative experience. He'd only been back in Topeka for six years. He had spent three years in the hospital and the rest on his projects. Additionally, working at Menninger was unlike his clinical experience and training in Boston.

The committee discussed bringing in an older president on a temporary basis to train Roy. One candidate that was strongly considered was James McCain, president of Kansas State University. Another was John Sutherland, a well-known psychiatrist who served as a consultant to the Menninger Foundation.

After weighing their options, Roy was elected president and CEO of Menninger in 1967. One trustee said that Roy would encounter one of the toughest "on-the-job" training experiences imaginable.

Roy had the unenviable task of filling my father's shoes. It would have been an enormous undertaking for anyone, but Roy bore an additional weight.

Roy had longed for Dad to ask him to come back and join Menninger. But Dad didn't ask. You had to understand it without him saying it. That bothered my brother. He was distressed that Dad never directly asked him to come work in Topeka. It was Karl who finally said to Roy, "Come home."

I didn't need that invitation. There was never any doubt in my mind that my father wanted me to become a part of the Menninger organization. I knew Dad wanted me to come home.

I think Roy spent much of his professional life searching for the "good father." He hoped Karl would play that role for him, but that was never part of their relationship. I think Roy felt very alone as he assumed the role of president.

I wanted to help Roy, but he kept me at a distance. As he was setting up his management team, despite the fact that I was nominally in charge of development, he excluded me from the team. I guess I was always a threat to my brother. He saw me as nipping at his heels. He told me, "Walt, you passed me up a long time ago."

I always assumed that we could work together. But I didn't appreciate how much of a threat he perceived me to be. When he was thrust into the position of leadership in 1967, he took steps to keep me at a distance.

———————————•———————————

The one area where Roy relied upon me was fundraising. In my father's absence, I had become the primary fundraiser for the Menninger Foundation. I focused on developing relationships in New York and Los Angeles while another Menninger psychiatrist named Bill Simpson covered Chicago. I would fly on average once a month to New York and LA, usually for five days at a time, to sustain the support network my father had built and to solicit funds.

Roy related well to people, but he hated to ask for money. The biggest contribution Menninger ever got was from a woman in Los Angeles. Roy had a relationship with her, but when he heard of her death, Roy lamented, "I never asked her for that $5,000 gift." Little did he know that she was leaving $40 million to the foundation! He didn't like to talk about money with prospective donors.

I, on the other hand, never had a problem asking. I felt like I wasn't asking for money for the Menningers. I saw it as soliciting funds that would help people. I felt I was offering generous and well-meaning people an opportunity to invest in the work of the foundation. That wasn't a hard thing for me.

We didn't pursue donations from former patients, obviously, because of the ethical conflict. But we had several former patients over the years who reached out to us to support the clinic financially. A number of former patients were quite generous in their donations.

In the late 1960s, the Menninger Foundation employed about 900 staff and had a budget upwards of $10 million, requiring that about $2 million in donations be raised each year. I was the one primarily charged with raising that money. I wasn't looking at the books, so I didn't necessarily feel pressure to reach specific fund-raising goals. I just went out and did the work to raise the money.

It was a heady experience to suddenly be thrust into meeting with people in a totally different social strata, whether it was business and industry, political or medical. I got to peek into their world and savor some of that realm. It certainly expanded my awareness of society.

The job of the fundraiser was ostensibly to keep up those relationships, but the important thing was to ask. I remember on one of my first solo fundraising trips I was meeting with the CEO of a major paint company, and I took a while to get around to finally saying, "Do you think you could contribute to our cause?" The man smiled graciously and said, "A man after my heart. He makes the ask."

Why, you might wonder, when there are so many needs and so many worthy causes in the world, were individuals and big companies willing to donate to the Menninger Foundation?

There was, in the 1950s and 1960s, a great growth in the interest in psychiatry. People were coming to really understand the need for mental health services in our country. My father played a huge role in promoting that cause. People recognized that the Menninger Clinic was training more new psychiatrists in Topeka than at any other place in the nation. But I think a lot of the willingness to donate to our cause was based on the relationships we built. We gave evidence of the worthiness of the cause and presented it in a way that made sense. What we were doing was truly making a difference.

The culminating stage in my professional education began in the spring of 1965 when I was accepted by the Topeka Psychoanalytic Institute for a personal psychoanalysis with Dr. Ishak Ramzy, a respected psychoanalyst at the Menninger Clinic. In addition to developing my professional skills of analysis, looking deeply into my own psyche helped me order my private world. Dr. Ramzy's influence was enormous as I coped with the loss of my father in the fall of 1966.

Meanwhile in the late 1960s, I was offered numerous opportunities for professional growth. The relationships I'd developed in the Federal Bureau of Prisons and the Peace Corps gave me outlets that were stimulating.

In 1967, both Roy and I were made Fellows in the American College of Physicians (ACP). This was of particular significance because our father took such an interest in the organization. Although Dad gained great renown as a psychiatrist, he was always an internist at heart. He had a medical and surgical internship, and he took a keen interest in the ACP, which is largely made up of doctors of internal medicine and related specialties. It was important to Dad that we be involved in the organization as well. Both Roy and I became Fellows at a meeting in San Francisco shortly after Dad died. It seemed significant that we earned that recognition, essentially to honor him.

My personal life was equally fulfilling.

Connie and I added the last child to our family on January 26, 1968. The addition of David Henry to our family gave us four sons to go with two daughters. His first name was prompted by two close friends who will be described later. Henry was the first name of Connie's father.

There were actually two "deliveries" that occurred—the delivery of my spleen noted earlier in Chapter 9, and the delivery of our son David. As described earlier, I had a cyst on my spleen that specialists determined needed to be removed in an elective surgery. Connie was near term when I entered for the surgery on Tuesday, January 23. I was to be hospitalized for several days, and for the first couple of days I was "out of it." We assumed we had several days before Connie would deliver David. But while I was recovering, she came into my room and said, "I think I may be going to have this baby." She was examined by the obstetrician there on the surgery floor and said, "Yes, we need to get you down to labor and delivery right away."

We all went down to the delivery room where they were all more worried about me—being three days removed from surgery—than they were about Connie. David came quickly. But in those days, women typically were hospitalized for several days—even up to a week—after giving birth. So, while our other five children were being looked after by my mother, Connie and I had a luscious week in the hospital convalescing together.

With six children spread out from infant to age ten, we had a lot of work on our hands. Connie was wonderful at keeping the group clothed, fed, and well-educated. But she did much more than that, including the

Topeka Public Schools Junior Great Books program, involvement with Topeka Civic Theater, and the board of the Mulvane Art Center at Washburn University.

In 1969, Connie embarked on a new endeavor which would bring her notoriety and increase her influence on the community. She ran for and won a position on the local school board. With all that was going on in the world in the late 1960s, you can imagine it was a heady time to be involved in school politics. Though Connie was not a "political" person, per se, she was very passionate about education and had a great influence on the board. She was soon added to a Kansas Association of School Boards committee on sex education. She was also involved in teacher evaluations and race relations for the Topeka Public Schools.

I didn't have a lot of free time during those years, but a family highlight of the late 1960s was when we purchased a Winnebago motor home. In the summer of 1969, we piled everyone into the 24-foot-long house on wheels and traveled west. We put 6,500 miles on it on a trip through Colorado, Utah, California, and Oregon.

My family and my personal endeavors brought me joy following those challenging times in the mid-1960s that saw us lose our daughter Claire, then my father. And they softened the blow of being excluded from leadership of the Menninger Foundation.

It was during that phase that I enjoyed one of the most interesting and challenging experiences of my career. It came as a result of the social turmoil of the late 60s and the assassination of a candidate for president.

20

The Violence Commission

The assassination of Robert Kennedy in June of 1968 shook up Washington, D.C.

Just two months prior, Martin Luther King had been shot to death in Memphis. Kennedy's older brother had been assassinated less than five years earlier.

The murders of King and Bobby Kennedy in 1968 occurred at a time when the nation was roiled by political and racial unrest. There were instances of inner-city riots, university campus demonstrations, and violent anti-war protests all over the country. The 1960s were becoming more turbulent by the minute.

Shortly after the Kennedy assassination, President Lyndon Johnson went on television to announce that he was appointing a National Commission on the Causes and Prevention of Violence, chaired by Milton Eisenhower. Johnson listed ten initial members of the commission. The group was a collection of highly qualified and diverse individuals, carefully constructed to try to bring bipartisan solutions to the problems of violence plaguing America.

By sheer coincidence, I was in Washington, D.C. for a meeting scheduled just a few days after the assassination of Bobby Kennedy. I had been in D.C. in 1963 when JFK was laid to rest, and now in a strange coincidence, I was back in the capital city when the younger Kennedy was being memorialized. A somber cloud lingered over the city.

LBJ made his initial announcement of the commission shortly before I arrived in D.C. for a meeting with Bill Crook, head of the Job Corps. Crook was also ambassador-designee to Australia. Joe English, my associate from the Peace Corps, had moved over to work at the new Office of Economic Opportunity headed by Sargent Shriver. It was Joe who had set up the meeting between Crook and myself.

Crook and I talked about a variety of things during our meeting. The assassination of Bobby Kennedy was fresh on everyone's minds. During the course of our conversation, Crook asked me, "How are we going to eliminate prejudice?"

"We aren't," I answered. "It's too deeply ingrained in our development."

Crook was intrigued by my response and probed a little about my views as a psychiatrist regarding violent impulses and behavior. At some point, the topic of the Violence Commission came up.

Now I knew Crook was from LBJ's home state of Texas. And I knew he was an ambassador-designee. He obviously had ties to the White House.

"Would you be willing to talk to the president?" Crook asked.

When you get asked a question like that, there's the infantile impulse to blurt out, "Lead me to him!" I kept my composure enough to respond, "Look, lots of people know more about this topic than I do." But I added, "If you think it would be helpful in any way, certainly."

I didn't know it at the time, but Johnson planned to add a few more members to the commission. Crook may have been privy to that information. I'm not sure. Regardless, something I'd said during our conversation made him think I might have something to contribute to the commission.

My experiences in the field of corrections were not insignificant. On top of having worked at the Federal Reformatory, El Reno, I had been part of a study group that reviewed the medical program of the Federal Prison System, and I had sat on an advisory committee of the Office of Law Enforcement Assistance in the U.S. Department of Justice. At the time, I was also the primary psychiatric consultant to the Topeka Police Department.

Those experiences acquainted me with crime and corrections. But this wasn't really an issue of crime. Of course, there are issues of human development and mental health involved in crime and violence, and certainly when it comes to assassinations. But I'm not sure what I had said in the course of the conversation that made Crook think I would be an asset to the commission.

Regardless, he thought I should be considered. I was flattered but not sure it would lead to anything.

I returned to Topeka at the end of the weekend. The following Wednesday night, Crook called me at home and said, "You'll be getting a call from the White House." He obviously had talked to people involved with the commission and urged them to reach out to me.

"They surely don't want me," I responded. "They want my uncle." Karl had two years earlier published a book called *The Crime of Punishment*, in which he shared some notably strong opinions about incarceration.

"They're not calling you for a suggestion," Crook responded. "They'll be calling you in the morning."

One of the most exhilarating moments in my life was when I walked into my office the next day and informed the receptionist, "I'm expecting a call from the White House." There aren't many days when you can make an impression on the staff quite like that. The call I received that morning was from Joe Califano, Johnson's Special Assistant.

That phone conversation kicked off one of the most interesting days of my life.

———————————+———————————

Accepting a spot on the commission wasn't something I could just commit to on a whim. The commission was going to take a lot of time and require numerous trips to D.C. I was a salaried staff member at Menninger and would need my employer's approval. Fortunately, I had talked to Connie the night before, and she had assured me that our family could make it work. But there were many hoops left to jump through.

The day was June 20, 1968, two weeks to the day following the assassination of Bobby Kennedy. The call came in at 9 a.m. I was surprised by the tone of the conversation. It wasn't so much that he was inviting me to participate in the commission. It was more like he was telling me that I would be appointed. I told Califano that I would need some time to get all the appropriate approvals.

His response: "Well, we're making the announcement at 4 p.m. Eastern Time. So, we have to know before then."

I was undergoing psychoanalysis with Dr. Ishak Ramzy during that period, and at 10 a.m., in my psychoanalytic session I told him that I had this opportunity that would disrupt my entire schedule, including my psychoanalytic appointments. Ramzy responded, "How can you say no to the president?" So, I had his approval.

Next was my uncle Karl. My uncle was mostly at the Stone-Brandel Center in Chicago during this time. But he happened to be at his office at the Menninger West Campus that day. I went out to see him at 11 a.m. His was basically the same response: "How can you say no to the president?"

At noon, I met with my brother Roy, who was then CEO of the Menninger Foundation, and all the department directors of the clinic and the foundation. I told them about the opportunity and explained how it would affect my schedule.

It was very interesting that the person who was most miffed by my appointment happened to be the head of the division of Law and Psychiatry at Menninger. He thought if anyone from Menninger should be appointed, it should have been him.

The rest of the group, however, approved of my accepting the appointment.

The last person I needed to touch base with was Joe English, the person I most trusted on all issues in Washington, D.C.

"Joe, does this make sense? Is there anything I should be wary of?" I asked. He knew a lot of the people involved and without hesitation he encouraged me to do it. Joe was an idealistic person who believed in the need for the commission, and having a relationship with the Kennedy family, he was deeply affected by the recent assassination.

With full approval registered in short order, I called Califano back and said I was pleased to accept the appointment. They made the public announcement of additions to the commission that afternoon. With two other appointees, I was officially added to the commission by Executive Order on June 21.

Looking at the roster of the National Commission on the Causes and Prevention of Violence is like looking at a Who's Who list from the late 1960s. At 36 years old, I was the youngest member. I couldn't help but be impressed and a little awed by the group of prominent figures I'd be joining.

Heading the project was a Kansan, Milton Eisenhower. Although he will always be known as the younger brother of President Dwight Eisenhower, Milton Eisenhower had an impressive resume of his own. At the time of the formation of the commission, he had recently resigned his position as president of Johns Hopkins University. Prior to that, he was president of Kansas State University, then Penn State University. Before entering college administration, he had been a prominent figure in the U.S. Department of Agriculture and in the U.S. Office of War Information. Although Eisenhower never earned a doctorate, he was called "Dr. Eisenhower" by just about everyone. He was a strong, competent leader, but also a kind and considerate man.

The members of the commission were, in alphabetical order:

Hale Boggs, a Democrat congressman from Louisiana who had been appointed by LBJ to the Warren Commission that investigated the JFK assassination. Boggs was serving as the House Majority Whip at the time.

Terence Cooke, Archbishop of New York. Cooke officiated the funeral for Bobby Kennedy at St. Patrick's Cathedral just two days before the creation of the commission. Shortly after being named to the commission, Cooke would be elevated to Cardinal.

Patricia Harris, who was serving as the Ambassador to Luxembourg at the time. She was the first African American woman to represent the U.S. as an ambassador. Harris was a woman who achieved many "firsts." After the commission, she became the first African American woman to be dean of a law school and the first to sit on the board of a Fortune 500 company. Later she became the first African American woman to serve in a presidential cabinet, and the first to enter the line of succession to the presidency.

Phil Hart, a highly respected Democrat senator from Michigan at the time. He had previously served two terms as Lieutenant Governor of Michigan.

Leon Higginbotham, Judge of the U.S. District Court for the Eastern District of Pennsylvania and an advisor to LBJ. Higginbotham had been nominated to the bench by JFK in 1963, just the seventh African American to be appointed to a district court judgeship. In previous positions, Higginbotham had worked with Bobby Kennedy.

Eric Hoffer, a manual laborer, author, and philosopher from California. He was considered to be representative of the "common man," but there was nothing common about him.

Roman Hruska, a Republican senator from Nebraska who was known as a skillful negotiator able to work amicably with members of both parties.

Leon Jaworski, an attorney who had been involved in some high-profile military and World War II war crimes trials. His greatest fame would come shortly after the commission, when he served as Special Prosecutor of the Watergate trial. Jaworski was one of the two commissioners appointed with me several days after the first group of members was announced.

Albert Jenner, another attorney who had been involved in several crime commissions, including the Warren Commission. His father had been a Chicago police officer.

William McCulloch, a Republican congressman from Ohio. He had previously been appointed by LBJ to the National Advisory Commission on Civil Disorders known as the Kerner Commission. McCulloch had been a leading voice in the civil rights movement, pressuring JFK to produce the Civil Rights Act.

Ernest McFarland, a former Democratic senator, and governor of Arizona, who was serving as Chief Justice of the Arizona Supreme Court at the time of the commission. He had gained fame as the "Father of the G.I. Bill." With Jaworski, McFarland and I were added to the commission after the initial announcement.

I was an outsider on the commission. Many of these people knew each other and had worked together previously. They accepted me, but I didn't have the immediate familiarity that many of them had. An interesting note about the members of the commission is that I was the only one who had no previous relationship with LBJ. I had seen him in a few meetings but had never met him. Everyone else knew the president personally.

As I mentioned, I was just 36 years old, and it's likely they thought I could bring a younger perspective to the commission. It wasn't my age that caused Jaworski to disrespect my contribution; it was my occupation. At one point well into the tenure of the commission, he told me, "As a lawyer, I've encountered a number of psychiatrists. Whenever I find one who has a particular view, if I search, I can find one of the opposite view. So, I don't have to pay attention to what you think. I could find someone who thinks the opposite." It was quite demeaning and adversarial.

I got along with everyone else for the most part. The two commissioners with whom I most closely connected were Hart and Higgenbothem,

Senator Hart was gracious and respectful to any contribution anyone had to make. He was solicitous of my views and was the most encouraging member of the commission to me personally. He was widely respected throughout Washington by those of all political persuasions, so it wasn't surprising that he was a pleasure to work with. It was equally unsurprising when, in 1976, the Senate voted to name one of its buildings after him. Hart was diagnosed with melanoma while in office, and his peers voted to name a building after him still under construction—the Hart Senate Office Building—the first time a federal government building was named after someone still living.

Higgenbothem was a prince of a gentleman. He was one of the first black students at Purdue University, where he wasn't permitted housing on campus, so he lived in a cold-water flat and endured a lot to work his way up the ladder. He was a magnificent human being, and you could see it when we had a major split in the commission. He was so elegant in expressing his views against the opposition. He and I had many invigorating discussions during the commission's breaks.

One of the commission's most newsworthy members at the time was Cooke. He had just been in the world spotlight when he officiated Bobby Kennedy's funeral. Then in January—about six months into the commission—he delivered the benediction at the inauguration of President Richard Nixon. Later that spring he was named Cardinal by Pope Paul VI.

I had the opportunity to talk with him about the process, asking what that experience was like. I remember him telling me that people would come up and say, "Your Eminence," and he would look around to see who they were talking to. He hadn't quite wrapped his mind around what was happening.

The commission offered many fun opportunities to peek behind the curtain of the lives of all these interesting, well-known, and powerful individuals. I recall once sitting at a table in the Senate dining room with Senator Hart when up walked Senator Hruska. They began discussing the events of the Senate—Hruska was working as floor manager for the confirmation hearings of Nixon's pick to the U.S. Supreme Court. I listened as these two powerful men from opposing parties talked over this business, which of course was a matter of national interest. When Hruska walked away, Hart looked at me with a twinkle in his eye and said, "He knows he's got a clunker."

Interacting with such a prominent group of people was a heady experience for a 36-year-old from Topeka. Though the commission was bipartisan and very civil, there was no avoiding the reality of partisanship. For someone not involved in politics, it was intriguing to be in the middle of that type of political tug of war.

To a degree, my experiences with the Peace Corps and the Bureau of Prisons and fundraising for the Menninger Foundation had prepared me for these types of interactions. Though I had made connections with high-ranking political and corporate leaders, I'd experienced nothing like this. It was impressed upon me through my interactions on the commission that people are people. They all have the same struggles. They may spend their lives in a different stratum of civilized activity. Some are more privileged or insulated than others. They may live in a grander style. But in terms of struggles or life challenges, I saw more than ever that people are all the same.

———————————

The Executive Order that on June 10, 1968, created the National Commission on the Causes and Prevention of Violence, said the functions of the commission were to "investigate and make recommendations with respect to: (a) the causes and prevention of lawless acts of violence in our society, including assassination, murder and assault; and (b) the causes and prevention of disrespect for law and order, of disrespect for public officials, and of violent disruptions of public order by individuals and groups."

While the commissioners got all the press, the driving force was administrative director Lloyd Cutler and his staff. A prominent Washington attorney, Cutler pulled together a group representing the full political spectrum to work with Dr. Eisenhower. The staff did a lot of the behind-the-scenes work that made it a powerful experience. They researched the various topics to provide us mountains of information, and they lined up speakers and panels to provide expert analysis.

The staff had quite a schedule planned. We began with organizational meetings. Then they had a series of hearings in a Senate office building—Wednesday through Friday—for eight consecutive weeks, each week devoted to a different topic. All our expenses were covered, but this was an uncompensated commitment. It was essential that each commissioner have the full support of his or her employer in order to devote that kind of time.

The commission was appointed at a heady time in American history. Not only had the country been rocked by the recent assassinations of the Kennedys and MLK, it was torn by the Vietnam War and racial turmoil. There had been a rash of riots and demonstrations that turned ugly. Shortly after the commission got up and running, a highly visible riot occurred at the 1968 Democratic National Convention in Chicago. That incident hung like a dark cloud over the commission and was an issue when its findings were ultimately released.

Also affecting the work of the commission was the recently concluded National Advisory Commission on Civil Disorders, often referred to as the Kerner Commission because it was chaired by Otto Kerner, governor of Illinois. That report concluded that lack of employment and educational opportunities were really crippling inner city neighborhoods. It pointed an accusatory finger at policies it deemed racist.

People who had worked on the Kerner Commission warned us to get our funding lined up before we did anything. The Kerner Commission met a lot of political resistance for some of its controversial conclusions. Some leaders felt it was biased and unfair, while others felt it did nothing to fix the problems it highlighted. LBJ didn't like it because he felt it gave no credit to his efforts. Because of the problems the Kerner Commission had faced, we were told pointedly, "Get your money right off the bat." It certainly didn't hurt to have four influential members of Congress on the Violence Commission. They made sure the funding was tacked onto an important Juvenile Justice bill and was approved.

The Violence Commission established task forces to study the following:

- Violence in America
- Law and Order Reconsidered
- Crimes of Violence
- Firearms and Violence in American Life
- The Politics of Protest
- Assassination and Political Violence
- Mass Media and Violence

Experts were lined up to testify on each of these topics, and a Student Support Panel was appointed to provide the perspective of young people. Violence and protests on college campuses was one of the hot topics of the time, and we spent a lot of time talking about the attitudes of college students.

———————————

At the second hearing of the commission, the topic was youth unrest. A member of the Students for a Democratic Society was scheduled to address the commission, but it was nearly noon and time was running short before we were to break for lunch. Chairman Eisenhower asked that we each limit ourselves to just one question of the young man.

"Mr. Chairman, I must protest," I responded. "Up to now, all we've heard are voices of the establishment. This is the first person we're hearing from who doesn't represent the establishment, and I would hope we would not cut short from hearing all that he has to say."

There was a little bluster in the room, and I learned later that the chief press officer had remarked, "Here's this young whippersnapper challenging the leadership of the chairman. That's going to be the lead on the 6 o'clock news."

Dr. Eisenhower responded calmly. He asked the young man if he would be willing to return to the commission after lunch for more questioning. The young man agreed, and we broke for lunch.

As we went down to the cafeteria in the basement of the Senate office building, I felt compelled to articulate why I raised the issue. But when I tried to explain myself, Dr. Eisenhower snapped, "If you want to be chairman of this commission…" He was seething. The temper that Dwight Eisenhower was known for obviously ran in the family.

All during lunch, I was tormented with the thought, *He can't apologize to me. I've got to apologize to him.* So, after we finished eating, I cautiously approached when I could speak to him quietly and said, "Dr. Eisenhower, I want to say I'm sorry…" He just cut me off, saying it was nothing and that I shouldn't worry any more about it. To him, it was water under the bridge. But I had seen firsthand what happens when you poke the bear.

Despite that one incident, Dr. Eisenhower gave me total respect throughout the duration of the commission. (I'm sure that incident cost me what little respect I might have received from Jaworski, but his opinion of psychiatrists was apparently sufficiently low already.) Dr. Eisenhower was a good chairman. He was always gracious, apart from that one blowup. He was thoughtful and conscientious, and very solid in his work with the staff. We wound up having a good relationship.

Early on, I was involved in one other misunderstanding with a member of the commission. On one of the very first days, Higgenbothem and I were discussing instances that provoke widespread unrest like the riots that had been so prevalent. We weren't justifying violence, simply discussing the types of injustice and disenfranchisement that sometimes spark violent reactions. Justice McFarland overheard us and snapped, "If this commission is going to approve of violence, I'm going to resign right now." That was how he interpreted what we were saying, and it stoked his already cemented notions. We were able to explain our positions just well enough to maintain cordial relations with the Justice.

I wasn't the only one to ruffle some feathers. When you work together as long as we did on complex political topics like these, there are bound to be some conflicts.

Hoffer was a unique participant in the commission. In one discussion about Black/white relations in America, Hoffer made some observations which were challenged by Higgenbothem, one of two African Americans on the commission. Right after that session, Hoffer submitted his resignation.

Eisenhower thought, "We can't have resignations from the committee. That just won't look good. He has to stay." So, there was a concerted effort by all the members of the commission to say to Hoffer, "Don't resign. Stay with it. We need you." He was convinced to stay and turned out to be a very interesting man to get to know.

For one of the hearings, my wife went with me to D.C. She sat in the commission room, knitting caps for school children while the meetings went on. After one meeting, Hoffer asked her, "What were you working on?" They struck up a conversation that led Connie and me to develop a friendship with him. Subsequently, on a vacation to San Francisco, we had occasion to visit Hoffer at his home, where we had dinner with him and a female friend of his. This opened up some marvelous vistas into his life.

A lot of Hoffer's life was undocumented and mysterious.

The child of German immigrants, Hoffer claimed to have lost his sight as a child when he and his mother fell down a flight of stairs. He said she died from her injuries shortly thereafter. Despite his lack of sight, he spoke German and English fluently and demonstrated great aptitude for learning. He claimed that, when at age 15 his vision inexplicably returned, he quickly learned to read and devoured as many books as possible fearing he might lose his sight again.

When Hoffer was still young, his father died. Hoffer began to wander aimlessly around the country, working sporadically and subsisting on next to nothing. He wound up working at the one career with which he was generally associated: longshoreman.

Hoffer had taken up writing about his views on life. Without higher learning, his writing earned him teaching opportunities at universities, most significantly the University of California, Berkeley. He was seen as a philosopher and a representative of the common man.

He obviously possessed a brilliant mind. He reportedly would show up for teaching gigs without a prepared presentation, but rather would just rely upon handwritten notes on cards. He would interact with students on a whole host of topics. Among other books, Hoffer published *The True Believer* in 1951, which earned him acclaim from both the academic community and casual readers.

Connie and I enjoyed getting to know such a unique and fascinating person. But then it seemed everyone involved with the commission was brilliant, interesting, and gracious.

-21-

To Insure Domestic Tranquility

No one had any way of knowing that just about a month after we kicked off the weekly meetings of the commission, thousands of Vietnam War protesters would flood the Chicago streets while the Democratic National Convention convened. The city promised to maintain order.

The Democratic Party was split regarding how to proceed in Vietnam. President Lyndon Johnson had announced he would not run for re-election, so the void of leadership sparked some heated interaction and fistfights inside the convention. Outside, protestors faced off with the police.

On the night of August 28, 1968, the simmering pot boiled over. A riot, known as the "Battle of Michigan Avenue," was caught on television. The riots had a strange effect on our work. They were a separate issue from what we had planned to study, but they couldn't be ignored. We had held some preliminary orientation sessions prior to the riots but had not yet started our topical task force work. Chairman Milton Eisenhower and Administrative Director Lloyd Cutler put together a task force on the Chicago riots. To do so made sense—the riot was of great significance. But the timing of the hearings and the political ramifications upset LBJ, who had decided not to run for another term.

In November of 1968, the Republican candidate, Richard Nixon, was elected, but he would not be inaugurated until the following January. LBJ would remain in office for a couple of months. Although Nixon later extended the commission to continue into 1969, we were to make an interim report on our progress to LBJ. The events that followed were a pretty fascinating thing to observe.

The interim report was drafted, and the commission reviewed and edited it. That interim report was published in December of 1968 without issue. But the commission's sidebar study of the Chicago riots was not appreciated by LBJ. There was heavy pressure for Eisenhower and Cutler to go public with the report on the riots, but because of the political ramifications, LBJ didn't want that damning information out. When it came time for the report on the riots entitled *Rights in Conflict* to be printed, he tried to prevent the report produced by the commission's Chicago Study Team from getting out.

That was when Cutler asserted some autonomy. He had a deputy on the staff who worked at the Air Force office at the Pentagon. The deputy arranged for the Air Force press office to print *Rights in Conflict*. It's the only one of the ten reports not printed by the Federal Government Printing Office. When they had a draft of *Rights in Conflict* ready for review, a courier carried it in a locked briefcase to each commissioner. The courier came to Topeka and arrived at my house on a Sunday after church. He sat in my living room while I read the draft version to give it my approval. *Rights in Conflict* needed seven votes to be approved. The manner they went about getting our approval seemed like the type of cloak-and-dagger stuff you would see in a movie.

Once he took office, Nixon reappointed the commission. We undertook the task of releasing the finalized report to the media. Once again showing his cunning and creativity, Cutler used a clever maneuver to bring attention to our work. Typically, when these commissions do their work, they hold a press conference to announce the release of the report. Boom! The report is out. And then in three days, it's forgotten.

Cutler, however, arranged to release the Violence Commission's full report—*To Establish Justice, To Insure Domestic Tranquility*—one chapter at a time with the commissioners gathered at a press conference for the release of each chapter. Cutler brilliantly ordered for each chapter the composition of a summary running approximately the length of one page in *The New York Times*. Thanks to his PR tactic, the work of the Violence Commission remained in the news for a year!

Over the following months, we released the chapters on the different topics studied by the commission. Ultimately, we wound up with 12 chapters, which differed slightly from the task force's initial plans:

- Violence in American History

- Violent Crime: Homicide, Assault, Rape, Robbery
- Group Violence
- Civil Disobedience
- Assassination
- Violence and Law Enforcement
- Firearms and Violence
- Violence in Television Entertainment Programs
- Campus Disorder
- Challenging Our Youth
- The Strengths of America
- Religion and the Problem of Violence

Eisenhower and Cutler saved until last the two chapters that were not unanimously approved by the committee, maintaining a sense of intrigue that kept the media's attention.

One report that split the group was Firearms and Violence in American Life. The commission recommended the adoption of a national firearms policy that would limit the general availability of handguns. Ernest McFarland, Leon Jaworsky, Hale Boggs, and Roman Hruska were all in dissent of that recommendation. They felt like the differences in states across the country made it impossible for one body to come up with a policy that would work in each state.

Gun violence remains a heavy issue for which there is no simple solution. At the time of the commission, we had just seen several instances in which weapons were used to take the lives of political or social leaders—JFK, Malcolm X, Martin Luther King, and Bobby Kennedy—all in a span of less than five years. We knew gun violence was a commonplace problem in communities, but our attention was certainly drawn to the use of guns as a political weapon.

Personally, I felt from the evidence presented that something needed to be done to reduce gun violence, and I thought some commonsense measures were not out of the question. I voted in favor of the commission's recommendations to that end.

———————————————

The other report that was not approved unanimously by the

commission was the one on Civil Disobedience. The split in the commission reflects the controversy within our society as to the feasibility of civil disobedience as a technique of effecting social change.

The vote on the Civil Disobedience report was 7-6. Opposing the report were Cardinal Cooke, Patricia Harris, Phil Hart, Leon Higginbothem, Dr. Eisenhower, and myself. It was the only time I found myself in the minority.

I didn't write a demurral that was published in the report, but subsequently I wrote and spoke quite a bit on the topic. I summed up the split as such:

> In the majority were commissioners who might be identified as the more conservative voices of the commission, including all but one of the members over the age of 60, and only one commissioner under age 60. It included both Southern members of the commission and only one of the non-lawyers, Eric Hoffer. The minority, in contrast, included chairman Dr. Eisenhower, as the one minority commissioner over the age 60. Indeed, Dr. Eisenhower was strongly opposed to the majority statement, although he did not issue a separate public statement. The rest of the minority included both blacks on the commission, Harris and Higginbothem, the one cleric, Cooke, and the one social scientist, myself. Senator Hart was the only non-black lawyer on the commission to reject the majority. And the age differential of the two groups might well come close to a generation gap. The average age of the seven majority members was 65. The average age of the six minority members was just under 50.

Civil disobedience is understandably controversial. There have been some examples of it in American history which are unanimously approved. The signing of the Declaration of Independence itself could be termed an act of civil disobedience. The Underground Railroad is an example heralded as heroic. But the burning of flags and draft cards received far less universal approval.

I was intrigued by the topic and subsequently composed a presentation that gained quite a bit of interest at the time. For a symposium at Wichita State University, I wrote *Civil Disobedience: High Risk, High Gain?* Following this chapter are some excerpts from that presentation.

As I noted previously, of particular interest to the Violence Commission was student unrest at colleges (and to a lesser degree, high schools) over the Vietnam War. The commission believed that giving a legitimate voice to college-age people, as opposed to their just staging protests, would be an empowering change. Thus, the one concrete result to come from the commission was to finally introduce the constitutional amendment to extend voting rights to 18-year-olds.

On February 16, 1970, I addressed the U.S. Senate Committee on the Judiciary in favor of lowering the voting age. Congress seemed unable to find a politically expedient way to make it happen. Hart orchestrated scheduling me to testify before the committee. I wasn't exactly speaking on behalf of the Violence Commission, but I could speak with authority on what the commission had recommended.

I told the committee that day:

> The reluctance of so many people to express openly their distress with enfranchisement of 18-year-olds points to underlying emotional issues as profoundly affecting people's attitudes… There may be a fear of facing our own inadequacies, acknowledging our discomfort that we, too, have not yet created the 'perfect' world. Having struggled to achieve a 'place in the sun,' the older generation is reluctant to pass the torch and give way to youth. Most of us don't like to be challenged, especially by our juniors. It is always hard to accept change, and the rising tide of youth forces change upon us. Youth remind us of our own unfulfilled ambitions.

At that hearing, some argued that media portrayals of young people as unruly and disruptive (or even downright un-American) were deterring states from extending voting rights to those under 21. That charge was made in particular by Birch Bayh, Indiana Democrat, and Marlow W. Cook, Kentucky Republican. Cook could point to the experience in his state, which had lowered the voting age to 18, as a positive example.

At the hearing, one of the proponents was quoted as saying, "The brunt of fighting and dying in a prolonged and unpopular war falls with particular force on those between the ages of 18 and 21." He followed that comment by stating, "If taxation without representation was tyranny, then conscription without representation is slavery."

As for my own testimony, here are highlights that made *The New York Times*:

> Dr. Menninger, the psychiatrist, who was there in his capacity as a member of the National Commission on the Causes and Prevention of Violence, told the subcommittee: "Today's youth are capable of exercising the right to vote. Statistically, they constitute the most highly educated group in our society."
>
> He accused adults of treating young people as immature and thus provoking self-fulfilling prophecies. He called this "infantilization" and said the motives were rooted in adult fears and jealousies of the younger generation.
>
> He insisted that it was important to "keep this population in perspective, since the attention of the news media on disruptive elements tends to obscure the character of the vast majority of these youth."

After procedural jockeying to pass the voting age legislation in various ways, Congress ultimately proposed the 26th Amendment in March of 1971. The states then voted to ratify the amendment over the next several months. I believe this was a positive change in our country. I am pleased that the commission sought to empower 18-to-21-year-olds to participate in the political process and proud to have played a part.

The violence of the 1960s was wearing on the general public. When JFK was assassinated in 1963, I think it was such a shock partly because a sense of innocence and optimism had belied the many problems simmering below the surface in the U.S. Once JFK was killed and the Vietnam War spun out of control, we started seeing on the nightly news more and more troubling images. Other assassinations and high-profile murders followed. War protests, civil rights advocacy, and other movements unsettled the status quo, while poverty and drug abuse increased in big cities.

All these images flooded our living rooms on the nightly news. From that point on, it seems news media has delivered us a steady stream of negativity. I am impressed by how much emphasis on the negative we receive from outside sources. It is quite upsetting.

I'm not sure it needs to be this way.

History is replete with war and chaos. Yet current issues seem like the worst—the world always feels like it's going to hell. But civilization continues to progress. The body of knowledge and the insight into humanity, along with the capability to do good, continues to grow. Rather than focus solely on the negative news around us, we need to see the good that far exceeds the bad.

During the Violence Commission, a study was done reviewing the police reports of youth arrested in Philadelphia for various crimes. They discovered that about 95 percent of violent offenses were committed by four to six percent of the people in the youth cohort they studied. Those numbers revealed the saving grace of society. The overwhelming percentage of the population is law-abiding, conscientious citizens who are doing good things.

The challenge of society is dealing with that "difficult-to-manage," rebellious four to six percent.

Violence in the United States has risen to alarmingly high levels. Whether one considers assassination, group violence, or individual acts of violence, the decade of the 1960s was considerably more violent than the several decades preceding it and ranks among the most violent in

185

our history. The United States is the clear leader among modern, stable democratic nations in its rates of homicide, assault, rape, and robbery, and it is at least among the highest in incidence of group violence and assassination.

This high level of violence is dangerous to our society. It is disfiguring our society—making fortresses of portions of our cities and dividing people into armed camps. It is jeopardizing some of our most precious institutions, among them our schools and universities— poisoning the spirit of trust and cooperation that is essential to their proper functioning. It is corroding the central political processes of our democratic society— substituting force and fear for argument and accomodation.

We have endured and survived other cycles of violence in our history. Today, however, we are more vulnerable to violence than ever before. Two-thirds of our people live in urban areas, where violence especially thrives. Individual and group specializations have intensified our dependence on one another. Men are no longer capable of solitary living and individual self-defense; men must live together and depend upon one another to observe the laws and keep the peace.

The American people know the threat. They demand that violence be brought to a halt. Violence must be brought under control – to safeguard life and property, and to make possible the creation of the understanding and cooperation needed to remedy underlying causes. No society can remain free, much less deal effectively with its fundamental problems, if its people live in fear of their fellow citizens; it is ancient wisdom that a house divided against itself cannot stand.

Those words from the Final Report of the National Commission on the Causes and Prevention of Violence, published in December of 1969, ring true today. It was my great pleasure to participate in a commission dedicated to the reduction of violence. But I was not then, and will not ever be, of the belief that violence can be eradicated. Violence is an innate biological impulse. It is the belief of the psychiatrist that we must learn to understand and manage our impulses, but we will never be rid of them.

Sigmund Freud and my uncle Karl wrote a lot about the drive for life, the aggressive drive to compete, to achieve, to possess, to master. We're born with those drives. Further, we are prone to react to frustration when we're denied what we want. This is readily apparent in children. What saves us is that most children cannot do anything about the rage they feel. (As we all know, there's nothing like the rage of an infant.) Because they don't have any power, children must learn to manage that frustration as they develop. Hopefully, by the time they are grown, they've learned to cope with their energy and channel it in a positive direction. This is a natural process of human development, but it doesn't just stop when we become adults. The eternal challenge is how do we master our aggressive energies and focus them on constructive, rather than destructive, urges?

First, one must recognize the challenge for what it is. Then he or she has to find ways to deal with it that are socially acceptable and constructive. The way to diminish violence, theoretically, is to help people enhance their capacity to recognize and manage their drives and frustrations by increasing their mastery. The concept of milieu therapy was to find alternative ways for people to work out their frustrations. If they're angry, they need to direct that energy to something positive. Instead of hitting a wall (or a person), try hitting a punching bag to release that energy.

One of the best sports we found for directing violent impulse for good was volleyball. First, the separation of the opponents is maintained by a net. Instead of hitting a person, you are hitting an object in a physically aggressive way. It's not a contact sport where you beat up another person. You direct your aggression to the ball.

Another activity we found to be effective was ceramics. We gave our patients a big ball of clay. Before they could do anything productive with it, they had to "prepare" it. You have to take the air out of the clay, and you do this by what's called "wedging." Wedging involves taking that hunk of clay and slamming it down numerous times on a hard surface. Once the slamming is done, there is still hard physical work involved in molding the clay into a general shape. Then comes the more delicate work. In the end, you graduate from aggressive activity to delicate handling, ultimately forming something with your aggressive energy that is beautiful and/or useful.

The Violence Commission sought ways to direct people's energy toward positive outlets. Voting was a tangible way of involving a young person in decision making. You can have a student burn down his school, or you can give him a student council where he participates in the direction of that school.

The Violence Commission dealt with a set of issues in 1968 that are still with us today: gun violence, police violence, riots and civil unrest, the portrayal of violence in media and video games… We did our best at the time to understand the causes of violence. But I was under no misapprehension that we could bring an end to all violence. Violence goes hand-in-hand with the American heritage of advancement, mastery over the frontier, etc. The history of our country is replete with violence.

Wars have been fought throughout history as groups of people took what they wanted from each other or imposed their will on each other. Part of the improvement in our ability to work out our differences, ironically, has come from the realization that we now have the power to destroy the world. With the increasing capacity for mass destruction, enough people said, "Wait a minute. We've got to do something besides fight because this could destroy everything."

———————————◆———————————

Each of the members of the commission received a framed certificate of appointment from President Johnson. The inscription on the document is significant. It explains what was expected of the commissioners. We weren't appointed because of our expertise. The commendation states that we were appointed because of our "integrity and ability" to assess the information presented. Research staff were paid to study the various issues and then present to the commissioners for our education. Our role was that of judge, rather than advocate.

An incredible amount of material was studied—16 volumes of information were published from the commission. How much impact that learning had on the country is hard to say.

Politicians, for the most part, don't read; they are preoccupied by other things. So, it's hard to say who the commission influenced. There was a lot of research done, whether it was on guns, or on media, or on any range of areas, but this research had no big effect on public policy. Looking back, while it was a gratifying experience, I'm not aware of any tangible change except for the lowering of the voting age to 18.

I am not discouraged by that lack of impact. I don't think it was an ineffective endeavor. Obviously, the people who worked on the commission were in influential positions, and I'm sure the experience informed their decisions.

But the impact of the work done in 1968 was not long lasting. I have come to believe that each generation has to learn these difficult lessons for itself.

22

Civil Disobedience: High Risk, High Gain

The National Commission on the Causes and Prevention of Violence produced a plethora of reports which I described at the time as "penetrating and seminal." Taking information from research staff and testimony from experts, we studied a diverse set of issues, many of which related to demonstrations and protests of a political nature. While the 13 commissioners reached consensus on nearly all of the themes studied, one topic over which it was split was civil disobedience.

You couldn't open your eyes without seeing a public display of opposition to some law or policy or perceived injustice in the late 1960s and early 1970s. America was divided on a host of issues. With the country's constitutional guarantee of freedom of speech and expression, people felt empowered to oppose things they disagreed with.

The question became in what form were they allowed to express that opposition. Where could protestors gather? Were they allowed to express their views at their places of employment? Were they allowed to burn symbols such as flags and draft cards?

The issue which divided the commission reflects the controversy within our society as to the feasibility of civil disobedience as a technique of effecting social change. For many individuals, the high risk associated with civil disobedience is that violence will occur and ultimately our system of legal justice will be placed in jeopardy. The opposing view is that constitutional rights and privileges are denied many citizens by the rigidity of our governmental and social institutions and by local majority view which condones or supports the violation of constitutionally guaranteed rights. In their view, such conditions justify the use of civil disobedience as a means of achieving the legal rights of all citizens.

I was so intrigued by this debate that, following the conclusion of the commission, I studied and wrote on the topic of civil disobedience. On October 2, 1971, I was asked to speak in a series of annual presentations on civil disobedience and non-violence given before the Library

Associates of Wichita State University. Here is an excerpted version of that presentation.

> The concept of civil disobedience may be presented as a moral issue, but in another, basic sense, it is a legal issue. In recent times, the term "civil disobedience" has been applied to a wide range of events—activities in support of blacks gaining civil rights, activities challenging this country's participation in the Vietnam conflict, sit-ins, marches, picketing, etc.
>
> For a definition of civil disobedience, let me quote that formulated by one of its leading proponents, Professor Morris Keeton of Texas:
>
>> By an act of civil disobedience (is meant) an act of deliberate and open violation of law with the intent, within the framework of the prevailing form of government, to protest a wrong or to accomplish some betterment in the society.
>>
>> ...civil disobedience differs from evasion of law in that the violator does not attempt to conceal his violation; on the contrary, he makes a point of being visibly in violation of the law. Generally, if not always, the very openness of the violation is part of the strategy of civil disobedience.
>
> One of my legal colleagues has noted that civil disobedience has traditionally taken two forms. One is the violation of a law which is in itself believed to be unjust, a circumstance elucidated in Dr. Martin Luther King's "Letter from a Birmingham Jail," written in April 1963. Dr. King wrote:
>
>> ...A just law is a man-made code that squares with the moral law or the law of God.
>>
>> ...An unjust law is a code that a numerical

or power majority compels a minority group to
obey but does not make binding on itself…a just
law is a code that a majority compels a minority
to follow and that it is willing to follow itself…

The second form of civil disobedience is the
violation of a law, not in itself believed to be unjust, for
the purpose of drawing attention to grievances not directly
connected with the law violated. Thus, one might have a
public street demonstration advocating the cessation of
the military draft, while actually only violating an
ordinance which forbids the obstruction of traffic.

Historical Perspective:

Various public demonstrations in recent years have
called our attention to civil disobedience as a powerful
political instrument to prompt change. But this is no new
problem. The origins of civil disobedience can be traced
back to philosophical issues discussed in Sophocles'
Greek tragedy "Antigone." In the play, Antigone
attempted to provide for a decent burial for her brother
despite an edict from King Creon that the brother should
rot in the fields as a traitor, having fought against the king.
Subsequently, there is the following dialogue between
Antigone and Creon:

Creon: Now tell me thou – not in many
words but briefly – knewest thou that an edict
had forbidden this?

Antigone: I knew it: could I help it? It was
public.

Creon: And thou didst indeed dare to
transgress that law?

Antigone: Yes; for it was not Zeus that had
published me that edict; not such are the laws
set among men by the Justice who dwells with
the gods below; nor deemed I that thy decrees

were of such force that a mortal could override the unwritten and unfailing statutes of heaven. For their life is not of today or yesterday, but from all time, and no man knows when they were first put forth.

...prior to (Henry David) Thoreau, most writers considering the right of the citizens to disobey unjust laws did so on the basis of satisfying the conscience of the disobedient individual. Thoreau appeared to advocate the use of the doctrine as a technique for legal change to alleviate a protested law or condition. Indeed, to show his nonsupport and to protest the tacit government sanction of slavery and the participation of the United States in the Mexican War, Thoreau refused to pay his taxes. He made no pretext of first finding taxes unjust per se. Rather, in this action, he introduced the concept of violating a statute, not of itself unjust, to call attention to a condition or injustice existing in society.

It was Gandhi who refined civil disobedience and developed it as a viable and active force for social and legal change. And Gandhi emphasized particularly nonviolence as a critical element in the Satyagraha doctrine of civil disobedience, to raise the deliberate suffering of a man of outraged conscience to the status of a moral sanction that would compel respect and secure results.

Regrettably, in some of his early efforts in India, Gandhi was not able to keep his followers from becoming violent. Indeed, he became increasingly concerned in subsequent efforts to assure a leadership that would maintain control and nonviolence. At the same time, the response of the police and law enforcement authorities to nonviolent protestors has often been quite violent!

The reality that violence has been associated with civil disobedience on many occasions, whether in the form of protesters losing control, or in the form of a violent police response, brought the subject into the scope of the Violence Commission.

The Violence Commission:

The membership of the commission (13 members) was predominantly from the legal profession. There were nine lawyers: four legislators...two judges...a law professor...and two attorneys in private practice.

With an awareness of the legal orientation of the majority of the commission, one can appreciate the special concern that was given the subject of disobedience to law. The majority of the commission were by profession committed to the support of the rule of law, and a concept which proposes disobedience might well be expected to provoke considerable debate.

The majority...held that, "In our democratic society, lawlessness cannot be justified on grounds of individual belief... If personal or group selectivity of laws to be obeyed is to be the yardstick, we shall face nationwide disobedience of many laws, and thus anarchy."

The majority implied that any civil disobedience is equivalent to disrespect and disloyalty for our government. Ms. Pat Harris countered in her minority statement: "Willingness to incur the wrath and punishment of government can represent the highest loyalty and respect for a democratic society. Such respect and self-sacrifice may well prevent, rather than cause, violence."

The critical issue which then split the Violence Commission was a matter of degree, with the majority holding close to an extreme position condemning all nonviolent civil disobedience, and the minority holding acceptable disobedience which was nonviolent, as long as the protestors stood ready to accept the penalty that the disobedience would visit upon them.

...The majority did state, however, that their concern

with civil disobedience was not that it might involve acts of violence per se. They acknowledged that most civil disobedience does not. Rather, their concern was that erosion of the law is an inevitable consequence of widespread civil disobedience.

Most eloquent, however, is the rebuttal of Judge (Leon) Higginbotham:

> Of course, it is always easier to blame the failures of our society on those who protest than it is to accept our responsibility to create a just society.

Is nonviolent civil disobedience, as the majority suggests, the major factor to single out as leading inevitably to the erosion of law and the onset of violence? It was not nonviolent civil disobedience which caused the death of the Kennedys and Dr. King. It is not nonviolent civil disobedience which causes millions to go to bed ill-housed, ill-fed, and too often with too little hope.

High Risk, High Gain:

The title of these remarks incorporates the ideas of risk and gain as matters to be considered when one discusses civil disobedience. There is a consensus of opinion that civil disobedience does represent some risk to a society governed by the Rule of Law.

The unanswered question is, "How high is the risk?" The majority members of the Violence Commission perceived the risk as too high, with anxiety about the contagion of disobedience and the erosion of law. And yet does recent experience or common sense really confirm that expectation? We are all aware of unrealistic and unenforceable laws which are held in slight regard... To what degree does the disrespect for these laws lessen our respect for other laws? Certainly some, but most people can and do distinguish between such laws and laws against serious offenses. And no data developed by, or presented to, the Violence Commission showed a significant relationship between civil disobedience based on conscience and violence.

Life is a constant process of adaptation, a process of achieving that which Dr. Karl Menninger has referred to as *The Vital Balance*. In the process of achieving a balance between conflicting forces, internal and external, the extreme position is rarely tenable. The human tendency is to view controversy in terms of extremes, right and wrong, good and bad, black and white... But life isn't really that way; with close scrutiny of almost any issue, we find the distinctions fade into shades of gray.

The concept of civil disobedience is no less subject to these distinctions. If we really had achieved the perfect utopia of governmental operations, then perhaps we could take an absolute stand against any challenge to that system. While we have devised what we believe to be the best possible governmental system, we certainly have not achieved perfection. It behooves us all to therefore keep open to challenges of the system and to tolerate reasonable challenges.

I could not and cannot agree with my fellow commissioners who took the majority position on this issue that our governmental system is so fragile that the challenge of nonviolent civil disobedience will prompt its collapse. I concur with Senator (Phil) Hart who noted, "My faith in the flexibility of the American democratic system just will not allow me to get terribly 'up tight' about the prospect of massive disobedience." I have faith that the truth "will out"; and while it may present a high risk, the potential high gain justifies a place for nonviolent civil disobedience in our society.

23

Making the World Safe

The Violence Commission sought to address issues of violence in the United States during a turbulent time in the nation's history. It took a close look at many serious issues in hopes of reducing violence.

Inevitably the question is, "Just how safe can the world be made?" We understood, realistically, that there will always be violence in the world. Yet we hoped that by looking at the issues we might better understand some of the underlying causes of violence.

Shortly after the conclusion of the Violence Commission, I was asked to speak at the Quarterly Staff Meeting of the Divisions of Psychiatry at Cedars-Sinai Medical Center in Los Angeles. Recognizing the 1960s had been a decade of both hopefulness and unrest, for this talk I chose the enormous topic of "Making the World Safe." The talk addressed the human tendency to hope, and to despair, over the condition of the world.

Following are excerpts from that talk, delivered on Jan. 27, 1971:

It is a hazardous world, and for a long time, man has faced the eternal challenge to make the world safe. We have sought comfort, security, freedom from pain and anxiety, protection from threatening elements, and safety for us as individuals and for those close to us.

As physicians, we have a major commitment to help people in their struggle with the environment to alleviate pain and suffering and to protect from illness, from germs, and public health hazards. An increasing amount of attention is given to preventative medicine and public health to make the world safe. However, my experience of working 18 months as a member of the National Commission on the Causes and Prevention of Violence, as well as my clinical work in law enforcement and corrections has prompted a focus on a different aspect of problems of public and private safety. It is some thoughts about these problems that I would like to share with you.

From whence cometh our anxieties? Obviously, there is no simple answer for that question. Many of our anxieties have their roots in our childhood, when we begin life in the land of the giants and experience the helplessness and limited physical power of the child. No matter how protective and reassuring were our parents, we inevitably encountered situations provoking great fright and insecurity. Of course, the character of the care and concern given us by our parents shaped our sense of trust and security, or distrust and insecurity. And the cold, cruel world, with its predatory features and real dangers must also bias our anxiety titer—the reaction to the sirens signaling a tornado alert in Topeka, Kansas today is far more serious and respectful than prior to June 8, 1966, when we finally experienced a devastating tornado in our community. And youngsters growing up in the ghetto with its 'subculture of violence' must inevitably have a biased attitude and practice toward violence.

Our reaction may also stem from the sensitivity of one who has experienced a loss, and recalls the intense pain of that loss, thus being hypersensitive to any renewed threat of loss. If we went through the Depression with some awareness of the deprivation of those times, we may be ever sensitive thereafter to being threatened with a comparable loss. The 'have-nots,' who have never had anything and have nothing to lose and who make demands on us, may represent an extra threat to we who have.

When we talk about making the world safe, and we refer to 'haves' and 'have-nots,' we must think about the problem of Who is the Enemy? Who represents the greatest threat to our safety? Whenever we experience disaster at the hands of others, we struggle for explanations. We search for the enemy, and often we come up with the conspiracy theory—that there are those who are organized to destroy us.

While it is unlikely that the scope or extent of conspiracy is as great as some would have us believe, or as we might like to believe ourselves, there clearly are some real enemies to our safety. There are the rebels, the unsocialized individuals, the criminals, the misfits. There are those people around us, small in number and yet significant in the potential of their destructive action, motivated by extreme philosophies, intent on destroying the world as we know it. Inevitably, our society will have to invest a disproportionate amount of energy and money in containing or trying to deal with these misfits, in the legal process from law enforcement to prison systems, and in hospitals.

The enemy is ubiquitous and is not always easily identified. We seek safety and security in developing a government of laws to provide some order and maintain civilized behavior. In a government of law, one is inevitably troubled when people blatantly disregard the laws or feel they shouldn't suffer any consequences when they disobey laws with which they disagree. One is troubled when a public official, sworn to uphold the laws and to uphold the Constitution of the United States, refuses to do so... Such persons are no less a significant threat to our safety as provided by the rule of law.

As we continue to study who is the 'enemy,' beyond the ravaging forces of nature, beyond the actions of other people about us, we must finally come back to look at ourselves. Dr. Karl Menninger presents the idea this way in his book on *Man Against Himself*:

> One would expect that in the face of the overwhelming blows at the hands of fate or nature, man would oppose himself steadfastly to death and destruction in a universal brotherhood of beleaguered humanity. But this is not the case. Whoever studies the behavior of human beings cannot escape the conclusion that

we must reckon with an enemy within the lines. It becomes increasingly evident that some of the destruction that curses the earth is self-destruction; the extraordinary propensity of the human being to join hands with external forces in an attack upon his own existence.

It is indeed interesting to observe the ways that people explain their accidents as the result of fate and disclaim any responsibility for their own injury. Frequently, we can identify quite clearly the way that individuals contribute to their own injury and undermine their own safety. Sometimes this is a subconscious process, sometimes extremely obvious… Petulant, self-injurious or self-destructive behavior is frequently apparent in children. How often the youngster, frustrated and enraged, takes something of special value and throws it down, tears it up, or otherwise destroys that which he really treasures.

In our eternal search for safety, there is the constant tendency to look for the simple solution, to find the one elixir to solve everything. Throughout history people have sought to escape discomfort by simple means, and physicians, wittingly or unwittingly, have been allies in the escape through the use of some kind of drug. Whatever may be the careful medical use of analgesics, people have been ever ready to abuse drugs, to find oblivion as a substitute for safety, with the help of alcohol, or marijuana, or opium, or some other substance to alter one's state of consciousness.

For some, ignorance has provided an escape. But increasingly in our highly educated, modern, complex world, we can no longer experience the bliss of ignorance… We aren't able to blind ourselves so easily, although we still will attempt to deny some obvious threats.

Another approach to providing safety is practiced in

some societies—simply repress any deviance, any difference of opinion. Prohibition was one search for safety by enforcing conformity and restruction; totalitarianism is another. It is quite evident that in a number of totalitarian regimes, there is no less crime and violence than in our free society. The 'overkill' response of those governments significantly represses deviation. But this approach in the search for safety is not compatible with the freedoms cherished by our traditions.

As we talk about the question of how can we be safe, we have to again acknowledge that we will always have a special problem with those in the extreme. Society will always have those who don't abide by the rules or who erupt with episodic destruction. Society has to be prepared to contain the damage that those extremists threaten, and to acknowledge that there will be a cost to control these people.

The larger society has to continue to seek the most economic way to try to contain the threats of these individuals, at the same time adhering to humane standards. It is therefore important for us to be aware of the job being done by the correctional systems and the mental hospitals in working with these individuals. All too often, we end up being penny-wise and pound foolish, operating a penal system in a penurious way, failing to recognize the greater costs to society when the failures at rehabilitation are inevitably released from the prison to return to a pattern of criminal behavior practiced to the detriment of the larger society.

What can we do as individuals to make the world safe? We have to acknowledge our limitations; yet there are a number of things we can consider. First, we have to recognize the need for compromises, and avoid the trap of the all-or-nothing stance. We have to recognize that you can't have your cake and eat it too. You can't have the freedom and mobility provided by an automobile without exposing yourself to the risk of an automobile accident.

You can't have the security and freedom for everybody to have a gun without acknowledging that the more guns that are available, the more guns will be used in crime and violence, and the more fatalities there will be from firearms. All too often, people get in the stance of seeing these issues as all or none. Either extreme, of total permissiveness or complete prohibition and rigid repression, is undesirable. We have to acknowledge the importance and necessity of compromise.

Secondly, a vital challenge is to get the facts about the threats we face, and to recognize the degree to which our emotions distort our judgment and interfere with the reasonable solution of problems. We must avoid the prejudiced response of "Don't confuse me with the facts. My mind's made up!" We also need to recognize the role of the self-fulfilling prophecy, the degree to which our expectations can lead us to approach people in a way to make our expectations come true. This is true in confrontations of adversaries in the same way that it is true in the subtle interaction between a research investigator and his experimental subjects. The most dramatic example of this self-fulfilling prophecy was demonstrated in the study of *Pygmalion in the Classroom* (a 1968 book by Robert Rosenthal and Lenore Jacobson), where teachers were led to believe certain students had a potential for academic improvement. Despite the fact that there was no real indication for such potential, the teachers, biased by the input of psychologists saying there was such a potential, approached the marked children differently; and these students did respond in later testing with significant academic and intellectual advancement.

These are times when we have a special need for exemplary individuals to restore the sense of hope that individuals can make a difference in what happens in the world. There is a desperate need for good leadership from individuals exemplary in character and quality, who will show the way toward constructive solutions, whose actions match their words. There has to be a willingness to work with others, for it is obvious that no one profession or individual has *the* answer to our problems. All of the disciplines will need to work together. Indeed, we must counteract and reject the tendency to polarization and the focus on differences among people which some politicians have appeared to emphasize.

Some differences are inevitable, and our pluralism in this nation has been very much to our advantage. But we have to agree at times to disagree, and to disagree without respecting one another any less, without forgetting some basic life experiences and some basic hopes and fears that we all have in common. Let me again quote Dr. Karl Menninger (from his 1942 book *Love Against Hate*):

> The world is made up of people, but the people of the world forget this. It is hard to believe that, like ourselves, other people are born of women, reared by parents, teased by brothers, adored and importuned by sisters, solicited and threatened by playmates, exhorted and reproved by teachers, courted by lovers, consoled by (spouses), worried by children, flattered by grandchildren, and buried by parsons and priests with the blessings of the church and the tears of those left behind. It is hard to believe that there are not some supermen and some arch fiends who manipulate the rest of us and guide our destiny. It is easier to speak of fate, and destiny, and waves of the future, than to consider the ways we determine our own fate, right now, and in the immediate past and future.

A basic step for all of us is to look at ourselves and to deal understandingly with the problems and conflicts we have with others. It is always easier to blame others and see the threats to our world as being due to others. But we must look inward as well as outward to the causes and prevention of violence, and to make the world safe.

Let me close with one of our conclusions as stated in the Violence Commission's report, *To Establish Justice, To Insure Domestic Tranquility*:

> When in man's long history other great civilizations fell, it was less often from external assault than from internal decay. Our own civilization has shown a remarkable capacity for responding to crises, and for emerging to higher pinnacles of power and achievement. But our most serious challenges to date have been external – the kind this strong and resourceful country could unite against. While serious external danger remains, the graver threats today are internal; haphazard urbanization, racial discrimination, disfiguring of the environment, unprecedented interdependence, the dislocation of human identity, and motivation created by an affluent society – all resulting in a rising tide of individual and group violence.
>
> The greatness and durability of most civilizations have been finally determined by how they have responded to these challenges from within. Ours will be no exception.

24

The Topeka State Hospital Years

I t's more important in life to like what you do than to do what you like."
That sage advice, given to me by Dr. Felix Wroblewski when I was a second-year medical student at Cornell, became a guiding principle in my life. Dr. Wroblewski had a profound influence that would be important to me in the phase of my life that followed my work on the Violence Commission in the late 1960s. I was so impressed by Dr. Wroblewski's advice that I wrote about it years later:

> He was a living example of that observation. He had
> not originally wanted to go into medicine. He had wanted
> to be like his father, a chemist. But his father insisted that
> he go to medical school. So he did, reluctantly, hating it
> all the way. Only after he was drafted into the Army and
> given responsibility for general medical care for some
> soldiers and their dependents at a camp in New Jersey did
> he find enjoyment in the practice of medicine.

After returning home from the Peace Corps, I was doing what I liked. I had envisioned since my youth being a psychiatrist on the staff of the Menninger Clinic. Although I'd had several side-trips along the way, my goal remained the same. I was a junior psychiatrist with several inpatients in my care, as well as a few outpatients from time to time. I was making money for the Menninger Clinic as one of 15 or so physicians at the hospital.

Following Dad's death, I took on the challenge of raising funds for the Menninger Foundation, which involved a change in my role, but my mission was still the same.

I traveled a great deal in the late 1960s. The Violence Commission alone required that I take 26 trips to Washington, D.C. in 1968 and 1969. I averaged one trip a month to Los Angeles or New York raising funds for the Menninger Foundation. So, it was not abnormal for me to be out of the office.

I returned from one of my many fundraising trips to unsettling news.

A recent departure of one of the supervising psychiatrists at Topeka State Hospital had created an opening there that needed to be filled. While I was gone, Roy "volunteered" me to fill the void. I was to immediately assume responsibility for a 75-bed unit and direct supervision of four residents.

I didn't want to leave Menninger, but I felt I had no choice.

While supervising psychiatrist at TSH was an important position, it felt like I had been exiled. I had not been asked or consulted about the transfer. My brother made this decision without my input. I didn't feel any pride or excitement about taking the position. I felt that I'd been manipulated.

I changed jobs and responsibilities many times throughout my career. Like everyone, I often got what I wanted in terms of positions and promotions, but there were times I didn't. It was in those times when Felix Wrobleski's words were particularly poignant. After I adjusted to the shock of being pushed out of my position at the Menninger Clinic, I realized I could either be unhappy because I wasn't doing what I liked, or I could be content by choosing *to like what I was doing*. I determined to focus on making lemonade out of lemons.

That doesn't mean I was happy with the turn of events. I didn't want to be held at arm's length at the Foundation. I didn't like being manipulated. But I decided to make the most out of what I could control.

I would continue raising funds for the Menninger Foundation. I maintained an office for seeing my analytic patients in the Menninger outpatient service. I would continue to teach in the Menninger School of Psychiatry. So, I remained a presence within the Menninger programs, but not to the degree I desired.

———————————

Following on the heels of the deaths of Claire and my father, being pushed aside at the Menninger Clinic was yet another painful and frustrating situation. These experiences certainly taught me a lot about life. A few years later, I wrote the following about coping with disappointment and loss:

> Conceived by others, most of us are shoved into the cold, cruel world with force and intensity at birth. While we may be protected and cared for in infancy and childhood, we can't escape disappointments.
>
> When you can acknowledge that life is full of injustice and there aren't any simple solutions to all the hurts one experiences, you're on the right track... When you can accept the fact that life is just not fair and can proceed on your way without being filled with bitterness or preoccupied with a sense of injustice, you will have achieved no small accomplishment. You are well on the way toward the ultimate ideal of emotional maturity, the criteria for which were formulated by my father:
>
> > Having the ability to deal constructively with reality.
> >
> > Having the capacity to adapt to change.
> >
> > Having a relative freedom from symptoms that are produced by tensions and anxieties.
> >
> > Having the capacity to find more satisfaction in giving than receiving.
> >
> > Having the capacity to relate to other people in a consistent manner with mutual satisfaction and helpfulness.
> >
> > Having the capacity to sublimate, to direct one's instinctive hostile energy into creative and constructive outlets.
> >
> > Having the capacity to love.

Much as I was reluctant, I moved into a new role of teaching and supervision that ultimately proved most rewarding. What was supposed to be a temporary assignment wound up being the next ten years of my career. Once I settled into work at TSH, I enjoyed it. Though my ambition was always to have a full-time role at Menninger, what I was doing was gratifying and satisfying in its own right. I was doing work that needed to be done. I was just doing it under a different roof.

Topeka State Hospital was one of three Kansas hospitals that were publicly funded by the state for the care and treatment of the mentally ill. The others were at Osawatomie and Larned. (For a time, there was actually a fourth near the University of Kansas Medical Center in Kansas City.)

TSH operated for about 120 years before it was closed in 1997. It was located close to the other hospitals in the center of Topeka.

The state hospital was not unfamiliar territory to me. I had spent about 21 months of my residency in various wards of the hospital. A decade had passed, however, since I last worked there. Things at TSH operated much differently than at the Menninger Clinic, creating a bit of a learning curve.

At that time, TSH was directed by a superintendent who reported to the secretary of the State Department of Social and Rehabilitative Services. Under the superintendent were the clinical director and an assistant superintendent over the business operations.

When I returned to TSH in 1969, those in the hospital were mostly there for short stays. It had transitioned from a long-term residential care facility. Now its emphasis was to help patients prepare to go back into the community as soon as appropriate. In 1969, there were three adult sections, which had been reduced in size, as well as an adolescent and children's service unit and outpatient services.

TSH served a very different clientele from the Menninger Hospital, and I perceived this population really needed help. Patients at the state hospital tended to be from a lower socio-economic stratum and they tended to have a less supportive safety net in the form of family and community. A precarious existence often awaited them upon release from the hospital.

I recall a man in the ward who walked around waving his arms like he was brushing something away. When asked what he was doing, he would say he was protecting us from tornados. When it came time to reduce the population of the state hospital, we had to release this man into the community. We told him "You know, you protected Topeka State Hospital from tornados. Now the city needs your help." We managed to find a place for him in the community, and alerted the community that he was no threat to anyone. And he thought he was protecting the city. That was one relatively successful transition of a patient into the community. It was tough to watch people you knew needed help exit those doors. Many who left our inpatient care didn't go out with the best of support structures.

After nine months serving as a supervising psychiatrist, the head of one of the adult sections—the 240-bed Woodsview Section—departed for another job. The superintendent of TSH said I was the logical person to put in charge of the section. Before accepting the promotion, I visited with my brother about the offer. That conversation made it clear that he didn't want me back at Menninger. So, in 1970 I took the promotion, committing to stay at TSH for the indefinite future. The Woodsview Section, with its inpatient and outpatient services and day treatment center, was the primary teaching section of TSH, with more than 20 psychiatric residents.

My rise up the ladder at TSH was rapid. After a year, I was asked to assume responsibility for all the adult services, and also to become director of the TSH residency training program. Then in 1972, I was made clinical director and assistant superintendent of the whole hospital under Supt. Eberhard Burdzik.

When you rise to that level of administration, you aren't seeing many patients. You're supervising the staff and addressing the issues that allow the clinical practice to go forward as it should. I had some patients in individual psychotherapy, but not many. I was mostly occupied with supervising staff, which included eight psychiatric residents-in-training.

When I accepted the position, I inherited the secretary to the previous section director, Mary Donohue. Mary became a very important person in my career.

Born in Greeley, Kansas, near Osawatomie, Mary became a secretary for the Chief of Psychology at the Osawatomie State Hospital in the 1960s. When that doctor came to TSH to work, he convinced her to come with him. Mary had a sister who had preceded her in moving to Topeka and who would become the primary administrative assistant for the Kansas Highway Patrol for more than 30 years. So, Mary made the move in the late 1960s to Topeka, to live with her sister and to work at TSH.

When I first inherited her (or she inherited me!), I noticed she kept a drawer full of paperback novels. Obviously, she had not been fully challenged by work. Her talents were not being utilized. I decided I was going to keep her busy. I immediately began giving her more responsibility and allowed her to tap into her managerial skills.

After a year as section director, I was asked to become head of all adult services and director of residency training, and then clinical director. I asked Mary if she would transfer with me. She told me, "I won't make up my mind until you make up your mind." A week later she told me, "I'm as reluctant to break in a new boss as you are to break in a new secretary." So, we knew we would prefer to stick together. We relocated our office to the main administrative building of TSH in 1972.

Mary was an integral part of my success throughout my years at TSH, and beyond. But more on that later.

While at TSH, it was a constant challenge to get the funding and resources we needed. You will remember that I mentioned in a previous chapter that, prior to the 1940s, state mental health facilities were woefully underfunded. My uncle Karl had been tasked with improving the services at TSH under Kansas Governor Frank Carlson, and great strides had been made. But state agencies are always locked in a battle for funding, and TSH was still challenged in the 1970s. The staff of the state facilities was starved for support and resources. I tried to provide consultation and encouragement to them as best I could despite the limited funds at our disposal. I recall in 1977 writing to friends of the tedium of constantly struggling for adequate funds:

> (I deal with the) eternal and wearying challenges to the hospital programs from one or another part of state government—budget, legislature, courts, etc. You succeed in getting one group educated only to encounter the same questions from another quarter, and it can be quite discouraging.

This struggle continues to the present day. After my retirement, I maintained consulting roles with the state mental health providers for many years. Sadly, I believe that the state has neglected its duty to those in need of psychiatric help over the last several decades.

One joy I discovered during my years at TSH was the impact of being an administrator. I still thoroughly enjoyed working one-on-one with psychiatric patients. I never lost the desire to love and care for them as they worked through their problems. But I soon learned that as an administrator, I wasn't assisting just a handful of patients at a time. Instead, I was overseeing the treatment of hundreds of patients. I could teach, encourage, and advocate for all the doctors and staff at TSH. The position of leadership had a multiplying effect upon my efforts.

I took a lot of pleasure from the supervision of residents at TSH. Some of those residents went on to become leaders in the field of psychiatry. A psychiatric hospital is like a small city—and when operating effectively—a very collegial environment. The doctors, nurses, therapists, and staff should all be helping and educating one another. Knowing that your supervision helped develop influencers in the field of psychiatry is very gratifying.

One resident I oversaw during this period who went on to prominence was Glen Gabbard. Gabbard served on the staff of the Menninger Hospital for many years, including as director from 1989 to 1995. Next, he served as director of the Topeka Institute for Psychoanalysis from 1996 to 2001. In 2001, he became Professor of Psychiatry at the Baylor College of Medicine in Houston. He is a renowned author and editor.

I gained a little bit of insight into the experience of residents at TSH years later in a letter from Steve Wolfe. Dr. Wolfe went on to develop innovative treatment techniques for chronically compromised patients. He proved to be very effective at working with patients who had been incapable of holding a job. His techniques helped them regain their ability to work and to function independently. As a resident, Wolfe was a bit of a rebel; someone who was resistant to too much control. He was an independent sort who liked to think outside the box. While he butted heads with others during his time in Topeka, Wolfe and I got along well. In his letter, Wolfe described many of the experiences of his long career and the influence of training at TSH:

> I began to think of the many people who had a profound impact on my life... I believe another plaque you should get is from the many students such as myself who enjoyed your mentoring... It's always hard for one to know how much you were really taught in such situations, but I'll never question how much you encouraged me and gave me the freedom to learn and

especially to explore.

Support obviously promotes better learning than rigid control, especially with adults. I always felt that support from you. Generally, I tried not to abuse it.

Walt, I hope that in my tale, you cannot only hear my thankfulness, but some examples of your effect on where the rubber meets the road.

Wolfe's letter was very gratifying, because it confirmed I had succeeded in fostering a collegial give-and-take between myself and the residents. I believed in the power of collaboration and the open sharing of ideas and strove to create a learning community at TSH. Wolfe's letter conveyed that he had experienced just that. I took special pleasure in seeing the creativity and individualism of the residents come out as they gained experience at TSH. By encouraging a collegial spirit, I saw residents come up with insights a veteran psychiatrist might not have.

In addition to the fine residents, I worked with many skillful people at TSH. The staff was competent and committed. We understood the immense need and believed in the work we were doing for the state of Kansas.

The position of Clinical Director was a good fit for me in several ways. It allowed me to utilize my administrative strengths, and it also blessed me with a lot of autonomy. Looking back, you could say that moving from the Menninger Clinic to the TSH was a blessing in disguise. Doors opened to me that might not have otherwise, and I had the marvelous freedom to respond to a whole range of opportunities.

I was still doing some fund raising for the Menninger Foundation, and I was also teaching Law and Psychiatry at the Menninger School of Psychiatry. I was able to be active in a number of boards and consultations, including the American Psychiatric Association. It made for a full schedule, that's for sure.

In the early 1970s, aside from advocating for lowering the voting age to 18 and speaking on the topic of civil disobedience, I wrote and spoke on a number of occasions in connection to the Violence Commission. The work we had done over those 18 months in Washington, D.C. provided a wealth of material and a platform from which to speak. Recognizing that violence is a systemic problem, I wrote:

> The first step for all of us is to look at ourselves, and to deal understandingly with the problems and conflicts we have with others. It is easier to blame others and to see violence as being caused by others. But we must look inward as well as outward to the causes and prevention of violence.

In 1971, I was made editor of *Psychiatry Today*, an abstracting publication sent to 22,000 psychiatrists in the U.S. and Canada. This didn't require a lot of work on my part, and therefore didn't provide much by way of compensation. My role was to review and oversee the compilation of the material in each edition. But it did elevate my profile in the publishing world, with more opportunities soon to come.

My ties in Washington, D.C. remained strong and would lead to many more consulting opportunities. In 1972, I was elected to the Institute of Medicine (now the National Academy of Medicine), a new organization formed to work outside of government to provide objective advice on matters of health. My nomination to this, the most prestigious society of American medical scientists, was another perk to the friendship I formed with Joe English while working for the Peace Corps. Now working for the U.S. Department of Health and Human Services, Joe had been inducted as part of the institute's second year class, and he nominated me to be a member of the third year's class. My involvement with the Institute would later produce some exciting moments in my career as I participated in workshops and study groups.

In 1973, I was voted Chair of the Committee on Mental Health Services within the Group for Advancement of Psychiatry (GAP). My father, you will recall, was a founder of that organization when it was formed right after World War II. The Young Turks who spearheaded GAP pushed back against the old-boy network of the American Psychiatric Association. It was an honor to be elected to a leadership position by the same organization that had been so influenced by my father. We worked to identify and respond to needs in the field of psychiatry.

Throughout this period, I continued my psychoanalytic training with Dr. Ramzy. In 1973, I completed that analytic training and was formally certified as a psychoanalyst by the American Psychoanalytic Association.

What goes on in psychoanalysis? Practically speaking, the person being analyzed—the analysand—typically lies on a couch with the analyst seated out of sight. This allows the patient to relax, to speak without reacting to the facial expressions of the analyst. This promotes free expression, tapping into the unconscious mind. The analysand is freed from the compulsion to modify his or her comments based on the analyst's visible response. The analyst does just enough talking to facilitate the sharing of the patient's thoughts.

Analysis facilitates exploring one's motivations and seeks to identify distortions and minimize them in everyday life. Using this technique, if you relax physically and you minimize the environmental elements, your distortions are exposed.

Psychoanalysis is not something many people get, or need, to experience. It's a processing of one's experiences and feelings. I compare it to a coin sorting machine you might find in a bank. You put the coins into a sorter, and the machine gets them all into proper place and in a settled context.

In some ways, it is a self-indulgence to have somebody listen to you talk and not criticize or interrupt to give you feedback. It's a luxury because not everyone can afford to have someone listen to them for an hour a day, whatever it is they want to say.

Psychoanalysis is different from counseling, and it is certainly different from talking informally to a friend, pastor, etc. The processing that occurs in those relationships is essential. Access to an objective second party to help you process your thoughts—to get the noise out of your head—is something everyone could benefit from. We should all have a few people in our lives with whom we can confide and get good feedback.

Psychoanalysis, on the other hand, is not something everyone needs or would benefit greatly from. For most people, their distortions are not extreme or do not compromise their ability to function.

But for some, the ability to process is so affected by their distortions that they need to better understand the cause of those distortions. When you're in the midst of a difficult situation or a personal conflict, the challenge is to dampen down emotions. In the face of emotions, reason gets distorted. When you encounter a problem that you can't solve, you puzzle over it and keep coming back to try to solve it. Psychoanalysis is a process for one to express and to identify distortions that you can then clarify. Getting it out of your head makes it easier for you to see the distortions.

Psychoanalysis intends to help patients identify unhealthy attitudes and behaviors and allow them to be more successful in their relationships. It allows them to identify their own life patterns that are counterproductive and ameliorate them, and to amplify successful life-adjustment strategies.

Psychoanalysis is fascinating from both the side of the analysand and that of the analyst.

From my experience on the couch, I became aware of feelings and attitudes that I hid from myself—things I didn't want to acknowledge. My analysis was an opportunity to discuss life's challenges openly with someone. I was blessed that it came at the point in my life that it did. My analysis began shortly before the crisis at the Menninger Clinic and eight months before the awareness of my father's illness. Part of my analysis was what I call "Learning to become my own father." Then came the conflict with my brother, Roy, at the Menninger Foundation. It was to my benefit to have the opportunity to work with the objective analysis of Dr. Ramzy during that phase of my life. He was instrumental in my processing of many internal challenges during that period.

The analyst has to know how to guide analysands to sort out problems in their own minds. It's not fixing them. It's helping them find answers for themselves. One key is to not let the analysand blame others. The analysand must take responsibility for his or her thoughts and actions. It's particularly important that the analyst not allow the patient to turn things on others, particularly on their spouse. When I would come in complaining about something Connie had done, my analyst would ask, "How did you set that up?" He would never side with me. He would challenge me to deal with conflicts. When I would come home and tell Connie what he had said, she saw him as her ally.

I recall showing up for a meeting with Dr. Ramzy once and describing how I had dreamt that a tornado had wrecked his office. Only half-jokingly, he asked what I was so unhappy with him about that I wanted to destroy him. I protested that I wasn't angry with him. But obviously there was some association in my mind between his office and some of the hard things with which I was dealing.

Analysis is an expensive endeavor, but it was an expense that paid dividends in my life. Once you become a certified psychoanalyst, you can begin to analyze others, even while still in the process of being analyzed yourself. Psychoanalytic training consists of classes, personal analysis, and at least four cases analyzing others under the supervision of a certified analyst. I began meeting with a few analysands in the early 1970s. My schedule wouldn't allow me to meet with four congruently, so they were spread out over the course of a few years.

One of my analysands was so intrigued by the experience that they changed their career to become an analyst. That person would eventually hold an influential position within the American Psychoanalytic Association. Others went on to impactful careers in psychology, social work, and administration. I feel very gratified that each of those individuals took advantage of the therapeutic effort.

Subsequently I was involved with the Association's application of psychoanalytic understanding in the larger community. We looked at how to use what we learned about human behavior to address problematic behavior within communities. For me personally, this took the form of helping police function more effectively. I became involved with the Topeka Police Department in the latter half of the 1960s and continued as a consultant for the rest of my career.

I had my fingers in a lot of pies during the early 1970s, but not many of them earned me substantial income. Due to the arrangement made when I moved to TSH, I continued to draw my salary from the Menninger Clinic, turning over my monthly paycheck from the state to the Menninger Foundation. I began to worry as I watched my children grow: how could I ever afford to provide a quality post-secondary education for them all? The cost of college, while much less than what it is today, was sufficiently high for a family of our means. Our oldest child, Fritz, would graduate in 1975 and the others would be hot on his heels.

An opportunity was presented to me that year—one which I did not seek out—that would solve this dilemma. I began to be paid for my "insights."

25

In-Sights: Sex (and Other Unrelated Topics)

This chapter won't really be about sex, per se. Sorry if that's a disappointment.

It is about an unexpected opportunity to share thoughts about mental health in a format that I hope was helpful to people across the country in the late 1970s and early 1980s.

In an instance that could be described as "out of the blue," I was contacted by the Universal Press Syndicate (UPS) in 1975 about writing a newspaper column.

Advice columns were very popular at that time. I wasn't a particularly avid reader of the popular columns of the day, but it was impossible not to be aware of them. The "Ann Landers" and "Dear Abby" columns were known by everyone. There were advice columns on nearly every topic published in just about every newspaper in the country. There were a few columns about issues of physical health running in newspapers that I was aware of at the time, but nothing devoted specifically to mental health.

Two people came over from Kansas City—one a writer/editor and one a businessman—from UPS to discuss the idea of me writing a column. UPS was known at that time as "the house that Doonesbury built." In addition to some popular comics, UPS syndicated some columnists, and they thought I might be a good candidate to add to their stable.

The idea for my column was to fill a niche of psychological advice. I was intrigued by the idea of trying to educate the general public on issues of mental health in these short snippets. This was going to be a strange bird, but I said I'd give it a try. I wrote ten sample columns and they said, "Let's go for it."

The general purpose of the column was to get people to look beyond the usual explanations for everyday phenomena and to look within themselves for a broader psychological perspective. Connie came up with the title "In-Sights" for the column.

I was giving countless speeches and writing for a variety of purposes during that period of my life, so writing some short columns was not the least bit daunting. The biggest challenge was to condense my thoughts on a topic to just 700 to 1,000 words.

Launching into this new adventure brought back to my mind the joys of high school and college journalism. It's hard to say how my involvement with newspapers in high school and college helped prepare me for this new endeavor. But those experiences certainly taught me to be careful and effective with language. And, of course, one of the many fortuitous events of my life—learning the skill of touch typing in 8th grade—would pay dividends in this new task.

The initial plan was for me to produce two columns every week. I knew the columns needed to address current issues in order for them to be relevant. For that reason, I couldn't write my columns months in advance and keep them "in the can." To keep them timely, I developed the routine of retreating to my den on Sunday evenings in order to fully focus on writing. The kids knew on Sunday nights to not bother Dad—he's writing his columns.

Before 11 p.m. each Sunday night, I would deliver my fresh columns to a distribution center to mail them "Special Delivery" to Kansas City, where they had to arrive by Monday morning. It was a grueling routine.

In order to keep a file full of ideas for my columns, I had the librarian at Menninger ship to me the table of contents page of 15 or so medical journals. I would review those for topics that I thought might make for an article that would be edifying to a reader. If there were some current issues in the media, I would try to seize upon those ideas. And of course, once we got the column out in the public, letters would come in that would be fodder for future columns.

Eventually we expanded to three columns each week. I had to really discipline myself to keep coming up with new ideas and to keep my schedule clear on Sunday evenings to do the writing. Another challenge, obviously, was vacations. Believe it or not, I had to take a typewriter and all the materials I needed to get the job done. It was a labor of love.

———————————•———————————

I never really thought about my writing as having power. I considered myself pretty good at organizing concepts for speeches and professional papers, so I believed I could handle the columns from a technical aspect. I wasn't one of those people who processes thoughts and feelings at the keyboard. But I do feel like I have an ability to articulate and share experiences in a meaningful way. I don't necessarily think of myself as rhetorical, but obviously I have done a lot of writing in my life, whether it was composing the columns, articles, or speeches. There are times when things need to be articulated in a way that others can consider them.

The important thing to me at the time was that writing the columns provided extra income that I could apply directly to the cost of educating my children. I began writing the columns in August of 1975, simultaneous to our oldest son's enrollment in college. Our four oldest children would all be ready for college within the next five years. The cost of sending them all to college would be substantial.

My motivation for accepting the offer from the UPS, therefore, was not self-promotion or egotism. But it really threw Roy and the Menninger leadership a curve which I wasn't aware of. Unbeknownst to me, they had been preparing to do a syndicated feature from the Menninger Foundation. I didn't discuss with them the offer to do it. It honestly never occurred to me to do so. While I was nominally employed by them, I was out of their orbit. I was for all intents and purposes "on leave."

Looking back, I can appreciate how angry Roy was at what I had done. I wasn't aware of his plans or how I undercut them until years later. I never intended to cut the Menninger Foundation out of an opportunity to generate income. I was still loyal to the organization. But the opportunity to write the columns arose at a propitious time for me.

Sometimes in life it seems that when one door closes, another opens. I saw the columns as that sort of opportunity.

I began producing two columns a week in August 1975, and by December more than 50 newspapers across the country carried it. The subscribers' list included some of the biggest newspapers in the nation.

After I had spent about half a year producing the column, the folks at the UPS felt like there was enough good material there to produce a book, utilizing 60 of the best or most popular columns. It wouldn't require any extra work on my part, so I was pleased to accept the offer. The UPS worked with a publishing company called Sheed, Andrews, and McNeel in Mission, Kansas, to put the book together with only minimal input from me.

Looking back, I'm not a big fan of how it came out. The columns were only loosely organized into four sections, without any additional explanation or unifying commentary.

Making matters worse, the title of the book didn't exactly "turn on" prospective readers.

Happiness Without Sex, the title of the compilation of my columns published in 1976, was derived from the book's first section, which began with a letter to me from a divorced woman whose initials were R.J. She wrote to me that she was experiencing contentment in abstinence following her divorce:

> I am a very happy and fulfilled woman. But I am sure, from what I read, that no publisher or writer would ever care to print such an unexciting, unnewsworthy, and dull existence. I guess it's just not sellable material. I would hope that those who really don't have the opportunities to find any sexual fulfillment could realize that life can be still complete without it.

I wasn't at all surprised that R.J.'s letter inspired many others to write to me about their own experience of fulfillment and contentment with abstinence. Several such letters were printed in the book, along with my own take in a column on the subject:

> Many people believe that Sigmund Freud overemphasized sex. What Freud actually emphasized was the fact that the major motivation behind much human behavior is the search for pleasure. And that pleasure is by no means restricted to sexual activity. Many pleasures in life have little to no direct relationship to what is commonly considered sexual behavior.
>
> While most people might not willingly choose it, happiness without sex is quite possible. Happiness without pleasure is inconceivable.

221

There are occasions when one's need for pleasure is adequately satisfied through nonsexual activities. This is achieved through a process which is labeled sublimation—the mental process by which basic sexual drives are unconsciously converted into other socially acceptable endeavors. One thereby achieves substantial and lasting sources of satisfaction in life through work, play, social, and religious activity. In general, the greater one's capacity to sublimate, the better one's emotional health.

The process is evident in exceptionally mature people, whom Abraham Maslow has characterized as 'self-actualizing.' From his studies, Maslow concluded that 'loving at a higher need level makes the lower needs and their frustrations and satisfactions less important, less central, more easily neglected.'

The letter from R.J. and the correspondence that followed made for interesting reading. Those letters and my responses filled about 11 pages of the book. That would have been all well and good, except that the folks at Sheed, Andrews, and McNeel decided to make this the first section of the book. Then, for some reason, they decided that this small section should inspire the title for the book.

Happiness Without Sex. Who in the hell was going to buy a book with that title?

------------------------+------------------------

The title notwithstanding, the book actually contained quite a bit about sex, as well as relationships and family dynamics. The columns contained covered a very wide range of topics that were not easily grouped into sections. Sheed, Andrews, and McNeel decided to organize them into four very loose themes:

1) Happiness Without Sex
2) Your Family, Your Children
3) Social Problems, Personal Solutions
4) The Strain of Coping

The individual selections contained in the book demonstrate just how wide-ranging my newspaper column could be. There were several on smoking (a hot topic in the 1970s), as well as gambling, ageism, homosexuality, rape, race, retirement, sleep, parenting, death…and the list goes on. Naturally they seem dated now, but I felt at the time they were pretty edgy. And I believe there is still some wisdom contained in those columns that rings true today.

I guess it's not entirely inappropriate that the book with "sex" in the title pulls together a broad swath of topics. From a psychiatrist's perspective, the term "sex" can apply to a broad set of feelings. As the 1948 *Time* magazine article about my father stated, "To Freud, the concept of something being 'sexual' encompassed a broad sense of love and pleasure."

One aspect of love is the romantic kind typified by attraction, partnership, and procreation, which also involves a general sense of caring. This calls to mind the concept of "agape love" in my uncle Karl's book *Love Against Hate*. He understood the importance of agape love to health:

> Love is the medicine for our sick old world. If people can learn to give and receive love, they will usually recover from their physical or mental illness.

In Karl's Love vs. Hate concept, the hope is to mobilize the constructive forces within oneself, as opposed to the destructive force. Love is intended to inspire the positive forces. That's a battle going on within everyone. Everyone has impulses of anger and rage and discouragement and depression. They have to possess skills to attenuate those impulses. They have to direct their energies to constructive, creative, and beneficial expressions, to make a better world rather than to destroy it.

But in a person with mental health struggles, they may have blocks or disconnections from positive impulses. They must learn to redirect to those positive internal forces that most people connect with naturally. It's for this reason that the Menninger Clinic put such emphasis on engulfing patients in an "atmosphere of creative love." One of the biggest obstacles to treating the mentally ill patient is to teach them to receive love and to demonstrate love appropriately.

When I graduated from the Menninger School of Psychiatry in 1961, I did so without receiving any real education regarding sexuality. The topic was not addressed in undergraduate programs to speak of, and medical schools dealt with sexuality purely from a physical standpoint. It wasn't dealt with specifically at the MSP. Higher education's lack of focus on the subject didn't really change much over the years.

In the early 1970s, some residents in the MSP attended a presentation on human sexuality in Kansas City, and they came back and asked, "Why aren't we learning about this?"

It was a valid question. Human sexuality, as central as it is to human behavior, has been poorly studied, but that doesn't mean it isn't an important topic to psychiatrists. The numbers bear out how important it is to know how to treat patients in the area of sexuality. Something like one out of every four women will experience some sort of sexual trauma. For men, it's about one out of every six. There are so many people who have been hurt in this area, and that affects their view of themselves and how they relate to others. That's not to mention the number of people who struggle with their gender identity and attraction to the same sex. Add to that the number of those who are unhappy in their romantic relationships for whatever reason, and you see that the mountain of problems in the area of sexuality is overwhelming. Psychiatrists need to know how to help in the area of sexuality if they are to truly make a difference.

In 1973, I undertook trying to remedy this problem in partnership with an esteemed public health physician named Evalyn Gendel.

Dr. Gendel was a physician who had a private practice in Auburn, Kansas, before beginning to work on special projects for the government, particularly in the area of maternal health. She served on the Board of Directors and later as President of the Sex Information Education Council of the United States (SIECUS), the governing council of American School Health Association, and the board of the National Center for Health Education. Later in her career she became Professor of Psychiatry and Director of the Sex Counseling Service and Sex Education Program at the University of California.

SIECUS was encouraged to educate and broaden perspectives on sexuality and gender issues. Dr. Gendel and I began looking around to see if human sexuality was being taught anywhere, and if so, how. We learned that the University of Minnesota had a weekend program for couples to be exposed to a range of teaching about sexuality. Dr. Gendel and I set up one of these weekend programs at the MSP to educate the psychiatry students.

The workshop asked questions like "What is sexual?" and "What is attraction?" It established that sexuality is a broad concept. The course challenged a lot of traditional mindsets. It could be threatening to some people. But the process of de-toxifying sexuality was important for the training of psychiatrists who would then treat patients with issues in the area of sexuality.

So many of our emotional challenges derive from feelings within us—perceptions of attraction or self-esteem—that are not necessarily subject to reason. People get guilt-laden from their feelings. But they need to realize these feelings aren't rational. The course at the MSP asked the provocative questions: "How do we make sure that we are managing our feelings?" "How do we make sure our feelings aren't managing us?" "How do we develop a sense of ourselves, and then relate to others in a healthy manner?"

For several years, Dr. Gendel and I collaborated to teach Human Sexuality at the MSP. We did our best in the 1970s to teach psychiatrists-in-training how to help patients achieve mental health in the area of sexuality.

Looking back 40-plus years later, I'm proud of the effort we put forth, but I am not certain we made much progress. I don't know that the teaching of sexuality at schools of psychiatry has advanced much. It's a taboo subject for some, and a confusing one for all. I know that we didn't have all the answers. But I believe that, at the very least, we were effective at helping the students look at the subject in a new and uninhibited way.

Resident psychiatrists (and those teaching their courses) aren't the only ones troubled by the topic of sex. The following are excerpts from a column I wrote in the mid-1970s describing how perplexing this topic is to everyone:

> Sex is fascinating and mysterious. It's a powerful force in life. Because we sense that power, we are often afraid of it. It attracts us like the candle flame does the

moth, but we wonder if it will destroy us.

The myths surrounding matters sexual are sometimes incredible, but they persist and persist. In part, that's because it's hard to find a reliable and accurate source of information to dispel them. Another reason myths persist is that we get distorted ideas about sex in our childhood when we really don't understand what it's all about.

It's important to acknowledge that sex is a powerful force in life. Knowledge should be our ally in managing that force, so that it doesn't manage us.

26

Caution: Living May Be Hazardous

The Greeks had an illogical practice of killing the messenger who brought bad news. Thank goodness Americans don't apply that approach to psychiatrists, who often are required to tell people things they don't want to hear.

In my public writing and speaking, as in my practice, I felt an obligation to "tell it like it is." The syndicated column "In-Sights" I wrote in the 1970s often touched on political and societal issues controversial at the time. Some of those topics were guns, women's rights, sexuality, death, divorce, body image, addictions…the list goes on and on.

One of the biggest obstacles in psychiatry is breaking down opposition to the truth. The old saying, "Give it to me straight, Doc. I can take it," isn't really true deep down. It's human nature to be so committed to what we want to believe that when reality doesn't match up, we find a million reasons to reject that reality.

As I've mentioned, a set of 60 of my columns had been compiled in my book *Happiness Without Sex*. I wasn't exactly thrilled by how that book turned out. After cranking out a couple hundred more "In-Sights," I had a much clearer idea what I wanted when I was approached by Sheed Andrews and McNeel in 1978 about putting together a second book. After the columns were grouped into four sections of the book, I composed transitional introductions to each section that smoothed out the flow of the book and provided additional information about each section.

Each of the four parts of the book addressed a general theme: Caution, Living, Hazards, and Coping.

The title of my second book, *"Caution: Living May Be Hazardous," Debunking the Happiness Myth* derived from one of the transitional sections, in which I wrote:

> A number of years ago, I came across a cartoon of a
> nurse tending to newborns in a hospital nursery.

Prominently displayed on the wall of the nursery was a sign: "Caution: Living is Hazardous to Your Health."

The general theme of my second book, therefore, was to help people come to terms with life's challenges and to manage their expectations, painful as that might be.

———————+———————

It's interesting to look back on the columns I composed in the 1970s and 1980s with hindsight. I believe I was courageous to take on some of those topics, but it's impossible to know how things will eventually turn out. I see that at times I was prescient, while at other times I was flat out wrong. Some of the issues have shifted and changed with time. Some of the problems I addressed have only become bigger problems. And some of them have been resolved or are just no longer considered problematic.

As I reflect on many of my columns, I hope that the wisdom remains timeless. But what I tend to realize as I review the last 70 or so years, observing the events of the world, is that every generation must learn the same hard lessons the previous generation learned. We encourage ourselves that we mustn't repeat the mistakes of the past. We proclaim the importance of learning from history. Yet it seems to me that each generation needs to figure things out for themselves.

Addressing current affairs has never been more treacherous than it is in the 2020s. Social media, tribalism in the traditional media, and the divisiveness of the political climate has made opening your mouth quite dangerous. But I faced some of the same dangers when composing "In-Sights" more than 40 years ago. A passage from one of my 70s-era columns rings true today:

> How safely can we express our views, when they are an exception or contrary to the prevailing view? Will people tolerate a challenge when 'like it is' isn't like they want it to be? As John Locke commented in *An Essay on Human Understanding*:
>
> > New opinions are always suspected, and usually opposed, without any other reason but because they are not already common.

I'm committed to telling it like it is. I've found it a special challenge to help people face some painful realities. Repeatedly, my patients have shared with me a reluctance to admit some things about themselves."

Because the truism, "The first step to recovery is admitting you have a problem" is ubiquitous, that doesn't make it any easier to apply. It's apparent that we don't lack for people who will "tell it like it is." But we all have a reluctance to "hear it like it is."

Whether it is a wound from our past, an addiction or stubborn habit, a personal bias or a political stance, accepting the truth is no easier today than it was in the 1970s when I wrote the following:

All of us have a struggle with unacceptable feelings in ourselves which we don't want to face—our hates or fears or forbidden desires. Most often we put the lid on these thoughts and feelings, "filing" them in the recesses of our mind, concerned that any expression of these ideas will destroy our world. Hopefully, we can learn to face such things openly and cope with them without being destroyed.

We all have a personal responsibility to do a better job of telling ourselves "like it is" in our own lives. At the same time, we have to confront society with its hypocrisies and challenge people to be fully responsible for their inconsistencies. We must constantly seek to hear it like it is and control our urge to strike out irrationally when like it is isn't what we want it to be.

In this era of advocacy news and internet "echo chambers," it's apparent that people aren't getting better at hearing and accepting things they don't like.

The message of my second book, if boiled down to its most simplistic idea, would be that "life is hard, and happiness is not found in comfort or pleasure."

When we start out in life, we haven't the slightest idea of what we're getting into. The infant can't understand what the world is about. But gradually, the developing baby does come to appreciate two important sensations—pleasure and pain... It doesn't take long for the child to appreciate the difference and to prefer pleasurable states while protesting painful states. The infant thus becomes strongly motivated to operate on the basis of the pleasure principle, that is, to seek pleasure and avoid pain. That motivation persists all through life to influence much of human behavior.

The infant assumes that pleasure is good, because it is a pleasant feeling; and pain is bad, because it is an unpleasant feeling. Yet is that always true? Can we be sure that pleasure is always good for us, and pain is bad? Not necessarily.

...uncomfortable though it may be, pain is not always such a bad thing. Pain is an important signal to the organism to alert it to some kind of injury or disorder. In its absence, one's survival may be threatened.

Further, much as we might prefer to avoid painful circumstances, they are inevitable in life. In order to survive, you have to develop some capacity to tolerate and cope with pain, both physical pain and psychological pain. Coping effectively with painful experiences can strengthen one and contribute to keeping life in a proper perspective.

Unless you can accept the fact that you will experience some grievous hurts in life, you are going to be even more devastated when they occur.

———————————•———————————

I think one of the reasons why people engage in the game of golf is because they are required to manage the obstacles the course presents. I seized upon this theme to introduce the section entitled "Hazards" in my 1978 book:

A golf course has a number of hazards, both natural and artificial—the rough bordering the fairways, streams and ponds between the tee and the hole, and sand traps protecting the greens. These hazards are generally designed so as to make the course more interesting and more challenging to the golfer; on a competitive course, they also serve to separate the good golfers from those who are less talented. While one may emphasize these well-defined physical hazards which affect the game of golf, the actual play of the golfer is influenced as much or more by other factors which are equally hazardous to his successful play. These factors include the character and skill of the golfer himself and the driving forces within him, the state of his physical and mental health, the worries he has about other things going on in his life which he can't put out of his mind.

On the golf course, the physical hazards serve to do more than complicate the golfer's life and increase the difficulty of his play. They may prompt him to improve his skills and sharpen his game more than if he were to play on a course with wide fairways and few bunkers. When your ball lands in a sand trap, it can be most frustrating. But unless you have some experience in that position, you may not develop any skill for getting out of such a jam. In the same way, hazards in life, though frustrating and painful, can have a positive side. A certain amount of stress is necessary to challenge one to grow and develop and increase one's mastery in life. Most educators realize that an optimal amount of anxiety is necessary to stimulate students to learn; and one of the functions of examinations is to force the student to review his material and reinforce the learning process. There is value in being tempered by adversity and by experiencing an optimum of frustration and failure. The key to having such an experience be beneficial is that the stress be sufficient to stimulate growth but not so great as to overwhelm or devastate.

In life, as in the game of golf, the hazards or stresses exist both within the individual player and outside on the "course." Some are natural; some are artificially created. Some are obvious; some are hidden. One may tend to focus on the external hazards since they are usually more obvious than the internal. Further, if our psychological defenses are working effectively, we blind ourselves to some of our inner conflicts and weaknesses. Nonetheless, the inner hazards may be far and away the most significant influences upon one's adjustment in life.

Why in my second book did I focus on this theme of managing hazards, overcoming disappointments, and having realistic expectations about "real life?"

Looking back, I think it's safe to say that, in the mid-1970s, I had spent significant time wrestling with, and eventually resolving, the pain I had experienced over the past decade. After growing up in a loving, protective family, receiving an excellent education, finding a loving partner in Connie, and embarking on an exciting career, I was beset by disappointments in the mid-1960s. Beginning with the death of our baby Claire in 1964, painful experiences continued to crop up. My father passed away in 1966. I was pushed aside at Menninger to work at Topeka State Hospital.

It seems natural then to surmise that my writing was an outpouring of what I was experiencing in my own life. I was telling others of the importance of dealing effectively with adversity because I learned it firsthand.

I introduced the final section of *Caution: Living May Be Hazardous, Debunking the Happiness Myth* with the following thoughts:

Presumably, you have gotten the message by now that a successful adaptation in life requires a realistic perception of those hazards and an assumption of personal responsibility for what happens to you.

There are a number of principles to keep in mind

while grappling with and adjusting to the many hazards in life: Acknowledge the potential for good in people, while respecting the presence of badness; respect and accept the presence of feelings, while not being compelled to act on them; learn the restorative and cleansing value of giving of oneself; develop skills to turn change to your advantage, focusing on the new challenges rather than dwelling on the losses.

In the same way that we must come to grips with pain and disappointment in life, we must also make peace with the seasons of life. All good things must come to an end.

In 1983, after eight years of writing the "In-Sights" column, I was ready to hang it up. The columns had helped me put several of my children through college, but more importantly, they allowed me to educate the general public on issues of psychiatric health in what I hoped were light, enjoyable, and easy-to-read articles. It provided a gratifying opportunity to practice preventative psychiatry on a grand scale.

When I decided it was time to discontinue the project, it was with sadness that I wrote in my final column:

> It is all too easy to get discouraged about the state of affairs in this world and to forget how many good people are working to increase our knowledge and mastery of life... Life is not simple, even though most of us would like it to be. These days it is more complicated than ever. If we are to survive in peace and good health, we must remain open to new understanding, and be slow to blame others for things that go wrong. Remember the wise words of Walt Kelly's Pogo: "We have met the enemy, and they is us."

27

TGIF Syndrome

One of the biggest moments in each doctor's career is when he or she takes board exams to become certified to specialize in a chosen field of medicine.

After I completed my residency at the Menninger School of Psychiatry and gained two years of experience at the prison at El Reno, the time came in December of 1963 for me to take my boards to become a certified psychiatrist. I took the tests at the New York State Psychiatric Institute at the Columbia University Medical School in New York City. Mom and Dad happened to be visiting New York at the time, and I stayed with them at their hotel.

In those days, the boards consisted of six hours of oral exams in basic psychiatry, neurology, and clinical examinations of patients. It can be a grueling ordeal. It's natural to experience nervousness in the anticipation of the event, as well as a lot of stress during the actual test itself.

I had one thing working in my favor. While at the MSP, I had been in charge of teaching a course of basic psychiatry for nurses in training. I realized when it came time to take the boards that the teaching of nurses had really prepared me for the oral exam. Teaching had given me comfort with the concepts.

I got a good night's rest at the hotel. I felt prepared. I don't remember being overly nervous during the administration of the tests. I felt fine throughout most of the day.

But when it was finally over, I lost my voice.

It was the only time in my life that I've ever lost my voice. Why would I manifest a physical condition—one I had never experienced before—*after* the pressure of the event had been relieved?

I didn't realize at the time, but what happened to me was somewhat common. After studying examples of such physical responses to stress, I learned that some people who endure a stressful experience do not just relax and get ready to go again. They get sick.

Physicians are keenly aware of the relationship between stressful events and the onset of illness. Sometimes an illness develops in the midst of the stress. But there is also a pattern of illness where the symptoms develop only after the stressful event is past. It would almost appear that the person does not get sick until it is "safe" to be sick. During the stressful period, the individual rises to the occasion and gives little or no evidence to others that he or she is under such a severe strain.

But when the pressures are removed, the body becomes aware of just how much energy and effort were necessary to meet the demands. The person experiences a sense of exhaustion, accompanied by the development of additional symptoms or a full-blown illness.

My experience following my boards was an example of this. You hold up through the stress. But after the event causing the stress is over, the stress manifests in various ways. When I didn't need to talk anymore, I couldn't talk.

Stress had affected me in another annoying manner in the past. In medical school, when I had studied as much as I could possibly study, when I could physically do no more, I would often develop a mouth ulcer, commonly known as a canker sore. That was my body's signal that I was reaching my limits.

The body has limits. Life can push us past those limits. Somehow our minds have the ability to keep things together when necessary. Our cognitive capacity overrides the danger signals. It can keep one going when needed. But the body manifests this overload in a variety of bizarre ways.

We don't really have a good explanation for how the mind knows to do it. How do you explain a woman of normal stature who can lift a car off her child? You can explain it in the sense that all our muscles are not one solid mass, but thousands of little fibers that activate in a chemical contraction. It's possible to gain increasing control over those types of abilities by training. Or you can, in response to an emergency, do something impulsively that would seem impossible, i.e., the lifting of a car off a child. Clearly, the functional capacities are far beyond what we realize.

Lifting a car to free a child is a happy example of our bodies' ability to respond to stress. But our bodies also may manifest annoying and sometimes debilitating symptoms like losing your voice, developing a canker sore, or much worse.

I experienced something more severe than a canker sore when I endured a stressful event while working as clinical director at the Topeka State Hospital. The superintendent went to a conference in Colorado, along with the state's Secretary of Health and Rehabilitation Services. While the head of TSH was out of town, the psychiatric aides at the hospital threatened to strike.

As clinical director, I was the highest-ranking person available to deal with the situation. I started going to the hospital every shift to check on the aides, trying to head off a full-blown strike and ensure that the patients continued to receive care. I held a series of emergency meetings with all shifts of personnel and forestalled precipitous action by the aides.

We made it through the weekend and got things settled. I prepared a report for the superintendent and the state head of mental health for when they returned from Colorado.

But then, after everything returned to normal, I got sick as a dog—acute upper respiratory infection, fever, sore throat—and had to take three days off. I had pushed past my physical and emotional limits, and my body collapsed after the pressure was off.

I am not unique in experiencing such physical responses, obviously. This phenomenon is quite common. After studying occurrences of such physical reactions in others, I called this pattern the 'TGIF Syndrome.'

———————————————+———————————————

"Thank God it's Friday!" It's what we say when we're ready to plop down in a chair at the end of a hard week and relax from the pressure we've been under. I borrowed that term to discuss the propensity to manifest physical effects after a period of stress.

I wrote a paper that was published in the Journal of the Kansas Medical Society in 1975 entitled "Friday, Already? The TGIF Syndrome – Response to Stress." I presented the concept in a variety of settings over the years. In the paper, I provided a few case illustrations to represent the range of symptoms and illnesses which may be encountered, from "minor symptomatology" to "profound incapacitation."

A dramatic illustration of the TGIF Syndrome was related to me by a World War II Air Force officer who had served as a gunner in a B-17 bomber. In the Air Force, aircraft crew knew that if they completed a certain number of missions, they would receive "R&R," a break from action to recuperate. This particular officer served uneventfully on his allotted bombing missions leading up the last before being granted R&R. Even on that last mission before his scheduled return to the U.S., he was fine.

Fine, that is, until his plane was safely back over friendly territory. At that point, he became violently ill to his stomach. The nausea and vomiting persisted and were of such degree that, after landing, he required medical attention and was incapacitated for four days. That's a pretty clear example of TGIF Syndrome! When the officer finally felt safe and could look forward to a much-anticipated return home, his body let loose of all it had held back.

The TGIF Syndrome is more common than many people might realize, and it serves a number of psychological purposes to the person who experiences it. Generally, we are angry about being put under pressure, and the syndrome can be a way to resolve the anger and resentment felt toward the stress experience. The resentment can't be expressed directly, but by being sick, you can escape continuing demands. You also get some attention and sympathy from others, all without having to feel guilty. After all, you can't be blamed for being sick.

This all happens at a subconscious level, of course. These aren't situations where the person wants to get sick or fakes illness. The manifestation of symptoms is beyond their conscious control.

Specifically significant is the degree to which the TGIF Syndrome signals the limit of an individual. In effect, the symptoms let one know that his or her ultimate limits of coping are being approached. Indeed, if the limits are not acknowledged, then a recurrence of the illness may be predicted in the face of comparable stress. Your body is trying to tell you: *Don't push me this far in the future.* While we can't always control the amount of stress we experience, we can learn to listen to our bodies and take preventative measures.

I found in my own life, when I saw the warning signs, I needed to take time out. It's an acknowledgment of limits. Back off. Regroup. Live to fight another day.

———————————•———————————

One may see some similarities between what I called the TGIF Syndrome and "Post-traumatic stress disorder" (PTSD). But there are some very important differences.

The PTSD phenomenon has been known for a long time. In the past it was called "shell shock," or something to that effect, and was almost exclusively associated with war veterans. But we have come to know that any kind of trauma has residual effects that fit the definition of PTSD.

The difference between PTSD and TGIF Syndrome is that in the TGIF Syndrome, the individual has been taxed to the limit of their capacity, but they have survived. It's at a cost, physically and emotionally. The symptoms are a sign of the psychological toll that's been taken, pointing to the need to take time out and heal.

In PTSD, you've encountered a situation you could not solve. You are overwhelmed by it. The brain works to understand what can't be understood, and it becomes paralyzed because it is so overwhelmed by the stimulus. Unlike the TGIF scenario, even though the situation is over, you continue to process it, over and over, with flashbacks, nightmares, etc., because you did not solve it.

What I was describing in the TGIF Syndrome was a physical reaction to the amount of energy and effort required to meet a demand. In the TGIF scenario, you have completed and solved the situation, but at a cost to the organism. Some degree of exhaustion is perceived, along with the development of additional symptoms which may range across the whole spectrum of illness. After the symptoms manifest themselves, the individual rests and eventually recovers and moves on with life.

Conversely, PTSD is recurring and requires resolution. Rest won't do it. In most cases, the individual needs professional help to break free of the repetition compulsion they are experiencing. This is because in the life situations that often prompt PTSD, there is no logical solution. It's as if the mechanism is still clicking and clicking, trying to solve it. It's like a computer that is caught in a loop it can't escape. But you're not able to solve it, thus you reach no resolution. It's as if you have been physically injured in a way that you can't cure.

To summarize, in the TGIF scenario, there eventually comes a resolution. In PTSD, no resolution is found. Thus, hope is compromised.

———————

I enjoyed presenting on the TGIF Syndrome over the years, and believe the concept is something everyone should consider. We all experience a great deal of stress in our lives. Work, family, relationships, finances—they all crank pressure down on us that we need to handle appropriately in order to minimize the damage stress does to our physical health.

The following are a few excerpts from my 1975 paper on the TGIF Syndrome:

> Stress occurs when an organism is forced into strenuous effort to maintain essential functions at a required level. When an additional load is placed on the organism, in order to maintain adequate functioning, some compensatory efforts must be made. Dr. Karl Menninger has described various levels of compensatory activity or 'special regulatory maneuvers' in his discussion of the vital balance.
>
> The most common manifestation of the TGIF Syndrome is a simple kind of exhaustion, with conscious awareness of the demands to which one has had to respond. Yet, for a considerable number of individuals, there is more clearly an illness response. The classic migraine headache occurs after the stress; and the poorly understood "stress ulcer" after severe trauma characteristically develops 6-14 days after the initial injury.
>
> What actually prompts illness is still unclear, but a number of factors come into play. These include the motivation of the individual, his personality strengths or ego resources, his learned patterns of dealing with or defending against stress, and the resources or supports in the environment. The illness itself may represent an

additional stress; however, in this context it more likely serves a number of other psychological functions. It may represent a resolution for the anger and resentment toward the stress experience; it also is a regression of behavior which allows the individual to get some compensatory attention, to escape from regular responsibilities and have reduced demands upon him, to have a period of dependency which is acceptable and for which he does not have to feel guilty. Sick leave is justifiable leave from work. It allows time for an individual to recuperate and regain a sense of balance from the stress.

In every case, although the physician rarely thinks of illness in such terms, illness represents an instance where the limits of successful adaptation of the individual have been exceeded.

28

Caring

While the Menninger Clinic kept up on technical and philosophical developments in psychiatry over the decades, the hallmark of the clinic was always intentional, genuine care for its patients.

My grandfather, C.F. Menninger, was a naturally warm, attentive man whose bedside manner was from the old school of the "house call" doctor. From his studies, my uncle Karl Menninger understood the importance of genuine interactions with the mentally troubled. His interest in Christian missions translated into care for the hurting. And while he could be gruff with staff and students, he was always caring and kind to patients.

My father had a vision for how to make the concept of caring programmatic. He understood how impactful the everyday interactions of staff were in psychiatric healing. He developed the Menninger Clinic's Guide to the Order Sheet which ensured that every patient felt loved and cared for. More than anyone else, he fostered the "community" of the clinic, modeling the familial spirit for which the hospital became known.

I grasped these principles and endeavored in my practice to always exhibit genuine compassion, patience, and understanding. As the years passed, I felt like some of those concepts, which seemed more common in previous eras of healthcare, were giving way to sterile clinical practices. I didn't feel like this change should occur without at least some effort to remind the medical community of the importance of caring.

While serving as clinical director of the Topeka State Hospital in the mid-1970s, I delivered a talk on the subject of health care quality at the November 1974 meeting of the Institute of Medicine, National Academy of Sciences in Washington, D.C. My paper, published in the *Journal of the American Medical Association* on November 24, 1975, was entitled "'Caring' as Part of Health Care Quality."

While that paper is now nearly half a century old—and draws on observations by Dr. Francis Peabody which are now nearly 100 years old—I believe the need for a return to genuine caring in the medical field remains strong.

The paper follows:

> Most discussions of heath care quality give short shrift to the concept of "caring" itself. Dictionary definitions of "caring" identify it as the action of the verb "care," and "care" has a number of definitions, ranging from a burdensome sense of responsibility to painstaking attention, to loving and liking, and to perfunctory management of custody as "under a physician's care." Yet, caring implies more than perfunctory concern. It implies a broader concern for the whole patient, rather than just for the patient's disease. As Dr. Francis Peabody observed in his classical dissertation (delivered at Harvard Medical School) in 1927:

>> The most common criticism made at present by older practitioners is that young graduates have been taught a great deal about the mechanism of disease, but little about the practice of medicine—or, to put it more bluntly, they are too "scientific" and do not know how to take care of patients.

> Life is a constant adaptational process between the individual and the environment in which he or she exists. There may be myriad outcomes of that process, ranging from successful adaptation to various maladjustments, including illness. Illness may represent a search for care as the patient seeks readjustment, since every individual has an inner wish to be cared for and to be taken care of. This is a permissible and desirable attribute in infancy and childhood, but as we mature, we are expected to find other ways to achieve that desired state. Indeed, one of the determinants of a good marriage is the degree to which it allows a balance of caring and being cared for.

> For all too many individuals, an ideal relationship of

caring and being cared for is not achieved; indeed, for each of us, that relationship and other supporting relationships are at times strained or may even break down temporarily. At such times, we then search for a substitute "caring" person, and with the proper ticket of admission—an illness—we go to a physician.

Every illness has both physical and emotional components, although medical education and practice tend to focus on the physical. Every physical chief complaint is accompanied by a corresponding emotional component or emotional chief complaint, and—as noted by Dr. Ivan C. Berlien—"The (emotional chief complaint) is often either not conscious in the patient or is not given because (of) social custom, cultural mores, or perhaps shyness."

A patient's survival may be primarily a function of resolution of the physical chief complaint. Yet, it is equally likely that the quality of living may be as much or more a function of resolution of the patient's emotional chief complaint. The bleeding ulcer may be stayed, but the underlying, gnawing, internal stress that makes life so uncomfortable may persist. One may treat the physical manifestations of thrombophlebitis with anticoagulation and surgery, but it is clear that the resolution of that illness may require more than just attention to the physical symptoms.

The role of the physician or health care provider in our society is one of a surrogate "care" giver. He is committed to attend to the "dis-eased." He has the power not only to give attention and concern to ill persons, but also the capacity to excuse them from the performance of everyday duties and responsibilities. When we are ill, we are allowed to retreat from the demands of our employer, family, and friends.

However, patients have ambivalent expectations as they seek medical care. The experience of seeking and receiving help is complicated not only by ambivalence and anxiety, but also at times by a sense of shame, inadequacy, failure, humiliation, resentment, worthlessness, and feeling "not OK." It behooves the physician to be sensitive to these feelings in order to meet the patient's total care needs.

For the most part, discussions of health care quality address objective, technical aspects of care, i.e., how much the specific tasks carried out in relation to a given patient are consistent with the latest scientific knowledge and understanding of the disease process and the treatment thereof. There have been occasional apologies for the omission of measuring in some way the subjective "caring" aspect of treatment by getting feedback from patients. In the "quality care" discussions of the November 1974 meetings of the Institute of Medicine, (Dr. Adevis) Donabedian acknowledged that the psychological aspects of care are often just given lip service. At the same time, (AL) Cochrane emphasized that it is important to differentiate "quality of care" from "outcome," and what he perceived to be most important in the quality of care was a poignant personally experienced feeling of being cared for.

Clearly, the patient's emotional response to the health care he or she receives should be respected as a valid aspect of health care quality. Obviously, measurement of this response introduces the inevitable dilemma of "the eye of the beholder," and is subject to distortion in some patients. Nevertheless, it should also help to identify the degree to which treatment matches the expectations of the patient and his or her understanding of what quality care is.

There are numerous examples of physicians who are absolutely superb technicians, with all the latest knowledge and skill, but who approach patients in such a cold manner as to prompt doubt and distress. Members of medical society boards of censors are keenly aware that patients are often so unhappy with that kind of care that they file a formal grievance. In the investigation of such complaints, it becomes clear that, more often than not, the breakdown has been in the "caring" aspect of the physician-patient relationship—not in the quality of technical care and treatment provided.

One may wonder how much physicians and other health care providers should care about their patients, as opposed to what extent they should dispassionately oversee the patient's illness-recovery process. In his training, the physician is taught to maintain some emotional distance from the patient, i.e., to sense the patient's experience empathetically without becoming so involved sympathetically that the physician's rational and effective clinical judgement is impaired by emotional involvement. Yet there is necessarily a degree of application of the Golden Rule of doing unto others as you would have them do unto you. Indeed, it may be advisable for every physician or health care provider to periodically be a patient, to re-experience that role, and to be sensitive to some of the forgotten aspects of that experience.

Caring is an important aspect of health care quality. It is, therefore, a continuing challenge to the medical profession to include some means of assessing this aspect of health care as part of the professional standards review. Certainly, many physicians will resist the idea that they might be graded, in part, for the quality of their "caring;" some won't trust their patients' judgments. Yet more and more, the medical profession is being confronted with consumer feedback that it cannot disregard.

In summation, one cannot improve on Dr. Peabody:

> The good physician knows his patients through and through, and his knowledge is bought dearly. Time, sympathy and under-standing must be lavishly dispensed, but the reward is to be found in the personal bond which forms the greatest satisfaction of the

practice of medicine. One of the essential qualities of the clinician is the interest in humanity, for the secret of the care of the patient is in caring for the patient.

29

Assassins and the Secret Service

W orking for the U.S. Bureau of Prisons in the early 1960s, and serving alongside policymakers and distinguished leaders on the Violence Commission in the late 1960s, provided me some unique insight into issues of crime, corrections, and public safety. For the rest of my career, I continued to be involved in the field of Law and Psychiatry, which drew me into some historically significant legal issues over the years.

My work in corrections got me into the area of forensic psychiatry. Occasionally, I was involved with assessing the capability of persons accused of a crime to stand trial. I performed many such assessments over the years. Regardless of the severity or notoriety of the crime, my job was the same.

One notable assessment, however, was the psychiatric evaluation of a person for their competence to stand trial for an attempt to assassinate a sitting president.

Allow me to explain briefly the role of the psychiatrist in such a case. If someone is delusional and distorted in their understanding of facts, they can't be dealt with in the same way as someone who is fully oriented and understands the nature and extent of the charges against them. If you are mentally compromised, then you cannot be fairly tried. The competence to stand trial is determined first, before the trial which determines guilt or innocence.

I'd performed a range of forensic evaluations of people for legal purposes. I didn't, therefore, think of this particular case as really different from any other evaluation. Of course, this case had national notoriety. The entire country was watching to see what would happen. But to the evaluator, the process is the same for a notorious figure as it is for any other individual for whom there's some question about their mental state.

The Hippocratic Oath prevents me from commenting on evaluations I performed. However, my role in the trial was documented by the media. So, in order to explain my interest in the Secret Service, I will allow the media to tell you a little bit about this story.

I was interviewed by *The New York Times* in November of 1975 about the process of determining competence to stand trial related to this particular case:

> A psychiatrist who participated in the court-ordered mental examination of (the accused) said this week that "the odds are tremendous" against any accused person undergoing such tests being found incompetent to stand trial.
>
> Although he refused to discuss any matters relating directly to the (individual) charged with trying to assassinate President Ford in San Francisco on September 22, Dr. W. Walter Menninger described the pattern of many similar pretrial examinations he has conducted for the courts.
>
> "We have found very few defendants to be so disturbed that they could not be placed on trial," he said in a telephone interview from the Kansas State Hospital, Topeka, where he is director of clinical services.
>
> "The odds are tremendous, actually overwhelming, against a finding of incompetency."
>
> Among 116 persons referred to Dr. Menninger by judges for psychiatric study over a 16-month period, in cases involving homicides and a wide range of other crimes, only about 1 in 10 was committed to an institution for treatment rather than brought to trial.
>
> Of one group of 55 defendants, he said, five were judged to be incapable of understanding the nature of the charges against them or of cooperating with their defense counsel.
>
> Dr. Menninger said he thought that excessive use was being made of pretrial psychiatric studies in the courts, with some judges ordering them as a routine safeguard.
>
> "Competency examinations can be abused, and often are, as a ploy on the part of defense and prosecuting

attorneys," he said. "Either side can use them to stall a case. At other times, such examinations become a means of denying bail."

———————————◆———————————

"If anyone wants to do it, no amount of protection is enough. All a man needs is a willingness to trade his life for mine."

Eerily, President John F. Kennedy uttered those words less than a month before he was shot in Dallas in 1963.

Kennedy understood the limits to physically protect a president in public. What this observation underlines is the importance of the research the Secret Service does to preemptively identify people who would do harm to the president before they act.

In 1980, I was asked to help the Secret Service with that effort.

It all began when H. Stewart Knight, director of the Secret Service, met Dr. David Hamburg, president of the Institute of Medicine (IOM, now the National Academy of Medicine), at a cocktail party. During their discussion, Knight said, "We could use your help."

What resulted was an Institute of Medicine Workshop on Behavioral Research and the Secret Service, which brought the two organizations together to study how the Secret Service could improve its methods. Shortly after that chance meeting between these two men at a cocktail party, I took a call from staff of the IOM asking if I would head the project.

Over the course of several months spanning 1980 and 1981, I worked with research staff to develop a workshop on how the mental health community could better assist the Secret Service. Mental health experts were invited to contribute their expertise because of how many psychotic individuals with an idiosyncratic rationale are a threat to the president. We were under no delusion, however, that we needed to fix the Secret Service. A lot of their agents were better at interviewing than a skilled psychiatrist. We were just trying to help them sharpen their already excellent skills.

The big question was: "How can we mobilize resources from the behavioral health community to help the Secret Service do the work of evaluating potential threats?"

In a subsequent report, Knight noted what he hoped mental health experts could provide the Secret Service:

> We are asking you to tell us whether we are doing the right thing in the right way... We recognize that there is no magic solution. To oversimplify, what we are asking you to do is to help refine our task of trying to predict individual human behavior.

On March 8-10, 1981, the conference was held at the National Academy of Sciences in Washington, D.C. It was a gathering of both clinical and research perspectives, and included psychiatrists, psychologists, lawyers, decision theorists, and criminologists, along with staff from the Secret Service and the IOM.

The activities that March were not broadcast to the public. The Secret Service wanted to keep our findings close to the vest, for obvious reasons. The significance to me was personal—to have had the opportunity to help the Secret Service enhance its capabilities to identify and sort out who are real threats and who are not. The late 1970s and early 1980s were a time of fractious political rhetoric. When the opportunity arose to try to address potential threats to the president, I was pleased to be asked to participate. At the time, I sensed an effort to assassinate the president was a very real possibility and I expressed this concern to the conferees.

Little did I suspect how quickly my fears would be realized.

What happened just three weeks after the conference (and prior to the publication of the summary report) is stranger than fiction and could not have been a better illustration of what the Secret Service is up against.

———————+———————

On March 30, 1981, a man obsessed with gaining the favor of actress Jodie Foster shot a .22 revolver six times in an effort to kill President Ronald Reagan outside the Hilton Hotel in Washington, D.C.

John Hinckley Jr. failed to hit Reagan directly, but the president was struck in the chest by a bullet that ricocheted off the side of his limousine. Three other individuals were hit directly by shots fired by Hinckley. Presidential press secretary James Brady was permanently disabled by a shot to the head. He died in 2014.

Hinckley was reportedly obsessed with the movie *Taxi Driver*, in which Robert DeNiro's character contemplates an attempt on the life of the president. The movie featured a young Foster playing a sex-trafficked 12-year-old. Hinckley made numerous attempts to build a relationship with Foster, writing her songs and poems and calling her on the phone. Shortly before attempting to kill Reagan, he wrote to Foster, "The reason I'm going ahead with this attempt now is because I cannot wait any longer to impress you."

The conference of the Secret Service and the IOM was three weeks before the assassination attempt on Reagan. In the subsequent report, I wrote: "There was a sense of urgency expressed that these were times when the president would be at greater risk and when the Secret Service should get all the help it could from the scientific community. Little did the conferees anticipate that just three weeks later the Secret Service protection would be breached."

Hinckley represented the most dangerous type of threat to the president due to the fact that he seemed to have no distinguishable motive. He was not a paid assassin. He had no ties to a larger threat. He was not motivated by political beliefs or ideologies.

He just wanted to impress a girl.

The most serious threateners are those who have an agenda in their head that follows a logic that you're not able to recognize. They are not people with a specific agenda against the president. They have some sort of distorted rationale that they hope an assassination will achieve. Hinckley was not the first. There had been others before who had a psychotic agenda who attempted to kill a president.

How is the Secret Service supposed to predict someone like Hinckley becoming a threat?

In the official report from the conference, we described (without giving away any sensitive information) the efforts of the 27 behavioral scientists and the members of the Secret Service who gathered. In the Introduction to the report, I wrote:

> No act is more repugnant or more upsetting to a democratic system of government than presidential assassination. During the 205 years of this Republic, one

of every four presidents has been the target of an assassin's bullet. This traumatic event was again experienced by the American people last March 30 with the shooting of President Ronald Reagan as he left a speaking engagement at a Washington hotel.

Charged with the protection of the president, the United States Secret Service has an enormous responsibility, a responsibility that is increasingly difficult to fulfill in our individualistic, mobile, affluent, gun-prevalent society. Ever since the assassination of John F. Kennedy in 1963 and his presidential-candidate brother Robert in 1968, there have been searching studies of the phenomenon of assassination and how to protect presidents and presidential candidates from such attacks. One such study a staff prepared for the National Commission on the Causes and Prevention of Violence, concluded:

> We are as yet unable to comprehend the individual and social forces at work sufficiently to be able to identify potential assassins in advance of their attacks. Characteristics common to assassins are shared by a large number of citizens. It is, however, both impossible at this point and probably undesirable in a democratic political system to attempt to identify and isolate potential assassins on any broad scale, based on present knowledge.

Because of the problems cited by (the Violence) Commission's staff, the Secret Service has invested heavily in assuring the adequate physical protection for the president and minimizing his exposure to risk. At the same time, the Secret Service is constantly confronted with a myriad of threats to the president and other persons whom it is mandated to protect. The Service is obligated to assess and respond both to known threats and unknown dangers to those it protects, as best it can. It fully recognizes a need to increase its capacity to assess and deal with threatening persons.

As evidenced by its wholehearted support and participation, the Secret Service, and particularly its Intelligence Division, clearly wishes to learn from the behavioral science field all it can to improve its capacity to protect the president and others. Primarily action-oriented, the Service devotes most of its resources and energies to its day-to-day operations; it has little opportunity to reflect on, analyze, or evaluate some of its practices regarding the identification, assessment, and management of potential threateners.

At the time of the attempt on Reagan's life, the Secret Service numbered more than 1,500 special agents, up from 389 at the time of the assassination of JFK, according to an April 13, 1981, article in *Time* magazine. It sounds like a formidable army capable of rooting out potential threats.

The problem is, they aren't dealing with an exact science.

It was later learned that Hinckley had plotted to kill President Jimmy Carter months earlier to try to make history. He was even arrested in Nashville, Tennessee on a firearms charge. So, there were behaviors along the way that could have alerted the Secret Service, if they'd known what to look for.

In so many cases, like that of Lee Harvey Oswald, the Secret Service has knowledge of the would-be assassin and yet fails to stop them. The whole focus of the workshop was to enhance and refine their ability to separate the wheat from the chaff.

I don't mean to make this sound in any way easy. The most intuitive and insightful interviewer can get fooled. Psychiatrists don't have any real magic when it comes to reading people's thoughts. You can't know what a disturbed person is thinking unless he or she shares their thoughts with you.

The Institute of Medicine Workshop on Behavioral Research and the

Secret Service looked hard at ways to approach a person in a way that unlocks the lock. Can you connect with them in some way to get past their defenses?

Did the workshop help the Secret Service improve their methods? I am certain they improved their capturing of material and their tracking of data. For a time following the conference, I chaired a formal research committee, following up on specific recommendations from the commission.

I remained a consultant to the Secret Service for more than a decade. Ten years after the formation of the plan for the workshop, we reconvened in Washington, D.C. in 1990. The reward for my service was lunch in the White House mess.

This would be my third visit to the White House on official business. In the late 1960s, I attended a ceremony hosted by President Lyndon Johnson to honor Sargent Shriver. And in 1985, I attended the 75th anniversary ceremony of the Boy Scouts of America. On that occasion, I sat at a table with Barbara Bush, whose husband was then vice president.

George H.W. Bush was president when I made my third visit to the White House in 1990. I didn't sit with anyone famous on that day. But I had the satisfaction of believing I'd played a small role in ensuring the safety of Barbara Bush's husband and son, and subsequent presidents.

30

Cops, Courts, Corrections

My involvement with the Secret Service recounted in the previous chapter came naturally from years of experience in related fields.

After spending two years as Chief Medical Officer and Psychiatrist at the federal prison in El Reno, Oklahoma, I had developed a pretty good knowledge of the justice system, and I had gained some insights into what causes some people to commit crimes, as well as the attitudes of those in prison. Shortly after Connie and I and our kids returned to Topeka in 1964, I became the primary psychiatric consultant to the Topeka Police Department. The consultation involved teaching recruits, interviewing applicants, providing counseling in times of crisis, and meeting regularly with the Police Chief. My nearly 40-year relationship with the Topeka Police force led to a lot of interesting experiences.

A significant part of the job was training new officers. I would spend about 40 hours with each group of recruits. My primary goal in training police officers was to help them understand the psychological reactions of people with whom they might come in contact.

Part of my responsibility in the training was to sharpen the sensitivity of the officers to mental troubles and emotional problems that people might be experiencing. That could include domestic disturbances, sex crimes, people with mental illness, people with dementia or Alzheimer's, etc. The task is to provide law enforcement officers with the kind of mental health resources they need.

Over the years, there has been talk of putting more community resources into mental health crisis responders in order to relieve police of some of the pressure to deal with the mentally ill. My interest in this issue is not political. I have observed the great need for more funding in the area of mental health. But I also understand that we will always need police, and law enforcement officers need to be prepared to deal with emotionally troubled individuals.

Responding to mentally disturbed people can be an enormously difficult task. How do you prepare police to acknowledge and best assist people with psychological issues? How do you then have a second line of social workers trained to work with law enforcement? How do you ensure these equally important entities work well together?

The bottom line is this: the police need help. They need professional assistance in dealing with emotionally troubled people. In recent years, with the closure of many public mental hospitals, jails are serving that purpose. And the disturbed individuals don't get adequate treatment once they are incarcerated. Can police be equipped to work with troubled individuals in such a way that does not have to end in arrest? And when people are arrested, can we get them the help they need so that they don't wind up clashing with police again in the future?

Unfortunately, police are charged with not just preventing crime and catching criminals but with dealing with disturbing behavior that is not criminal. Interacting with people with mental health issues is complicated by the fact that, no matter if the person is innocent or merely committing a minor crime, the situation is likely to become escalated during a confrontation. These are individuals with limited verbal skills in many cases. The incapacity to advocate for themselves or explain themselves clearly is one of the biggest frustrations of the mentally challenged.

In addition to training police officers, I was often called upon to counsel them following traumatic events. I provided assistance when officers dealt with the occasional disturbingly violent crime, intense conflict, or the injury or death of a fellow officer.

Sometimes I was also called upon to help victims deal with horrific experiences.

The most traumatic of these events was, without a doubt, the bombing of the U.S. District Courthouse in Topeka in 1993.

On Thursday, August 5th of that year, a railroad worker named Jack McKnight was due to appear in court for sentencing on weapons and drug charges. Angered by the charges and determined not to be incarcerated, McKnight wrapped his body in explosives and entered the courthouse, reaching the fourth floor before being confronted. He flung pipe bombs and fired semiautomatic pistols, killing a security guard, and injuring four people. A bomb McKnight was wearing on his body detonated. Badly injured, he shot and killed himself.

Police outside didn't know at the time that McKnight was dead, however. Thinking he might be holding hostages, they locked down the courthouse while panic-stricken occupants hid in fear. For several tense hours, a SWAT team slowly searched the building before finally finding his body.

When the pieces of the puzzle all came together, it was learned that McKnight had used his pickup truck to tow his car to the town square of nearby Oskaloosa, Kansas, where he left the pickup behind and drove to Topeka in the car. Shortly thereafter, a bomb in the bed of the pickup exploded, fortunately causing no harm. He also denotated a bomb in the car in the courthouse parking lot.

The 1990s weren't exactly an era of lax security. But still, this type of destruction in a public place just seemed beyond the scope of imagination. The building occupants who endured the attack were understandably traumatized. This type of horror has a similarly deep impact on the police, fire, and ambulance crews who are called to respond.

When the magnitude of the incident became clear, I was called as a liaison to the police department. When, by the end of the day, they had found McKnight's body and determined the crisis was ended, I met with victims and personnel who had been held hostage. We set up emergency psychiatric first aid services to provide immediate support. That weekend, we held a de-briefing for the judges and other courthouse personnel who had been involved.

Meeting with crisis victims initially, then following up with those who need continued counseling, demonstrates the range of interventions one can make. My job was to try to figure out how to attenuate the trauma through first aid, hoping that it would lessen the effect of the trauma later on. I found in working in such a crisis that every situation is different, and every person's response is unique.

Helping victims of crimes deal with their trauma could be downright painful. One of the hardest events I was ever involved with occurred in Topeka in 1989.

On the evening of December 3, a teenage boyfriend and girlfriend burglarized a Topeka home, suffocating the elderly resident, Ida Dougherty. The couple dumped the woman's body in the country, then returned to spend the night in the house and search it for valuables.

Neighbors Lester Haley and Verne Horne became concerned for Dougherty's safety when they noticed her newspaper remained on the sidewalk late into the afternoon of December 4. Using a key Dougherty had given them, Haley and Horne entered the house, surprising the burglars who were still in the house.

Using a handgun, the burglars held the neighbors in the house. Soon, Haley's wife, Nancy, came looking for him, and she was held at gunpoint as well. The male burglar, Tyrone Baker, put the three into a car and drove them to the spot where he had left Dougherty's body the night before.

Baker demonstrated some reluctance to kill the three elderly friends, and they tried to reason with him. In his hesitation, the three were able to escape into a wooded area. Horne made her way to safety, but Baker eventually found and shot the Haleys.

Baker and his girlfriend, Lisa Pfannenstiel, were still high school students. Schoolmates learned of what had happened and alerted the police. By the night of December 5, Baker and Pfannenstiel were arrested without incident at a Topeka hotel.

Verne Horne, the lone survivor of the incident, happened to be the wife of a psychiatric colleague of mine, James Horne. While I was not involved with the subsequent trial, I interviewed Verne about her ordeal. My goal was two-fold: one, to help police officers better understand the trauma experienced by victims of violent crime and to help them be more sensitive and perceptive; and two, to help a friend process her emotions, which ran the gamut from anger to confusion to despair.

A particularly intriguing aspect of Verne's ordeal was her effort to appeal to the mercy of the perpetrator. She convinced him to go check Dougherty's body, that perhaps he hadn't killed her after all, that he might not be guilty of murder.

Unfortunately, Verne continued to demonstrate various aspects of trauma after the event. One result was that, when they put Baker in a lineup, she didn't recognize him. He had cut his hair and altered his appearance somewhat, but the real issue was she was having post-traumatic terror.

At trial, Pfannenstiel agreed to plead guilty to aggravated burglary and conspiracy to commit aggravated burglary, with a sentence of six to 15 years in prison, in return for agreeing to testify against Baker.

Because the crimes occurred in two different counties, there were two trials for Baker. On the witness stand, the young man described mental illnesses with which he claimed to struggle. These included having a "friend" who would at times take over control of his actions. He claimed that when this happened, he wouldn't remember what he had done during those periods. He testified that he didn't remember anything from the events of December 3 and 4.

The legal proceedings continued for several years. Central to the case were the testimonies of competing psychiatrists. It was a classic example of how psychiatrists are called to support the case made by attorneys. An article in the *Topeka Capital-Journal* contained the following paragraphs about the court battle:

> The jury also heard from two Topeka psychiatrists who agreed Baker was a paranoid schizophrenic but disagreed on whether he suffered psychotic episodes in which he lost contact with reality.
>
> Defense psychiatrist Dr. Gilbert Parks found Baker insane and not responsible for his acts. The state's psychiatrist, Dr. Herbert Modlin, said Baker was sane and fully capable of understanding the nature of his acts and that they were prohibited by law.
>
> "What these two trials to me boil down to is a battle of experts," said Suzanne James of Topeka, Nancy Haley's daughter. "Whose expert was more compelling than the other. It seemed very clear to me, but you don't know how it's affecting other people."

While I didn't perform any function in this trial, I include those paragraphs here to demonstrate how psychiatrists are often called upon to support one side or the other in a trial. That's a role I found myself in frequently over the years.

Not every case I dealt with involved heinous criminal acts, per se. Sometimes I was asked to help people following traumatic accidents. And sometimes I was asked to help people avoid liability for such accidents.

I was called to assist in the aftermath of a famous tragedy, the July 17, 1981, collapse of two skywalks at the Hyatt Regency Hotel in Kansas City, Missouri. Such a cataclysm will undoubtedly produce traumatic symptoms in those who endure it. But in this case, it was my job to assess the emotional damages—to determine whether claimants had truly suffered significant and persisting psychological injury.

The 40-story Hyatt Regency building was just a few years old. One of its defining features was its elegant lobby with walkways made of concrete and glass suspended from the ceiling.

Approximately 1,600 people attended a party at the hotel that evening, and large groups gathered on each of the 120-foot skywalks on the second, third, and fourth floors. The walkway on the fourth floor, which was directly above the one on the second floor, fell onto the walkway below it, sending both crashing to the crowded main floor.

Aside from crushing people below, the walkway debris trapped many uninjured in the lobby, causing hysteria.

Rescue efforts, which took several hours, revealed 114 dead. More than 200 people were injured but survived. The aftermath involved both criminal and civil repercussions for the builders, lots of government reforms, and billions of dollars in insurance claims. More than 300 lawsuits sought a cumulative total of $3 billion in damages.

All the defendants went together in an effort to protect themselves from liability. The Hyatt corporation, the builders of the hotel, and the builders of the skywalk, all mounted a unified front to minimize the financial damage. This group hired the Menninger Law and Psychiatry staff to serve as the defendants' psychiatric consultants. We were tasked with examining the plaintiffs who claimed psychological injury to determine the extent of the trauma experienced by each.

Assisting me on the Hyatt consultation was Dr. Herb Modlin, who was mentioned in the *Topeka Capital-Journal* story in the previous section. Modlin had come to Topeka in 1946 to serve as Chief of Psychiatric Services at Winter General Hospital in the early days of the Menninger School of Psychiatry's involvement at the hospital. He then joined the staff at Menninger in 1949, so he was a contemporary of my father and my uncle Karl. Over the years, Modlin had become nationally recognized as a forensic psychiatrist.

In the end, at least $140 million in settlements was awarded to victims and their families. But a few were found not deserving of damages.

Everyone who claimed psychological damage was referred to Modlin or me. Two of these people—a man and a woman—who were among those trapped in the lobby amidst the rubble, were both scheduled to see Modlin. The man protested something or other and was reassigned to me. We subsequently found out that they were "a couple," although each was married to someone else. That explained the man's motivation for seeing a different psychiatrist from the woman. They didn't want to see the same psychiatrist because they feared he would pick up on any inconsistencies in their stories. Otherwise, their stories would have to match perfectly. Modlin and I did not pick up on their relationship at the time.

This couple apparently thought they could capitalize on the tragedy. They both got themselves admitted to a hospital, claiming to have been injured. The man was in the hospital for a week. His discharge diagnosis: hemorrhoids.

Modlin and I didn't immediately identify that this man and woman were dating, nor that they were being untruthful. But subsequently they weren't subtle enough for their ruse to go undetected. The man and his wife soon split, and he and the girlfriend rented a house together where they began hosting large parties. They were apparently convinced a big settlement was coming their way. But lawyers got wind of their relationship and sent some investigators to check out the couple's activities. In due course, Modlin and I reassessed our evaluations, dashing the pair's hopes of a windfall.

It's always shocking and sad when you see how people try to take advantage of tragic events. A stark contrast to this deceitful couple was the case of a man who was truly badly injured, his wife killed in the Hyatt Regency disaster. Injuries left the man unable to work for a period of time, further compounding his plight.

When he came in to see me, the man said, "I don't really want to talk to you. I want to talk to a lawyer. If I were to break your back, and kill your wife, how much would it cost me?" That's how he felt. Everything had been taken from him. How was a financial settlement supposed to help him move forward with his life?

I examined another woman who had suffered a neck injury in the Hyatt catastrophe. The doctors didn't want to immediately try to fix her injury because they didn't want to make it worse. When the plaintiff's attorneys deposed me, I acknowledged, "No question she was damaged." My deposition was then used at her trial. I was subsequently hired by the plaintiffs to testify in a later case.

———————◆———————

Through my involvement with the Federal Bureau of Prisons in the early 1960s, I developed a relationship with the bureau's director, Norman Carlson. Although I only worked officially in corrections while at El Reno in the early 60s, Carlson got me involved in numerous consulting activities.

Two years after I left the bureau, I was named to a committee reviewing the medical program of the bureau. When the bureau created the National Institute of Corrections in 1974, Carlson named me to the institute's advisory board. Subsequently, in 1980, I was elected chair of the 16-member advisory board. That was a special honor. Also on the board was a former classmate at Stanford, a seated Congressman at the time. In my dozen or so years on the board, I met Supreme Court Chief Justice Warren Burger, U.S. Attorney General Elliot Lee Richardson, and a lot of other significant people.

My involvement with the National Institute of Corrections was the perfect example of how a detour in life can open up brand new vistas and opportunities that you never planned to explore.

I never planned, for instance, to venture into architecture and design. Yet in 1971, I was named to a six-member facilities planning panel by the Federal Bureau of Prisons which was beginning a major building program. They were planning a new generation of prison design. I had the unique and enjoyable role of being consulted for new designs for prison facilities. In the 1970s, the Bureau hoped to improve upon the traditional "bars and gates" style of prisons. A group of architects and some facility planners from the Federal Bureau of Prisons even came to Topeka to meet with me about designs. It was intriguing to try to consider improving on what was traditionally done. Having worked in a prison myself and having conversed with numerous prison directors, I had some thoughts about how to better design them. Those architects came up with some interesting departures from the traditional prison design, and I enjoyed working with them on the project.

In 1974, I flew to Pleasanton, California for the dedication of the California Federal Correctional Institution, one of the facilities that incorporated concepts I had discussed with the architects.

The concepts of punishment, incarceration, and rehabilitation as they relate to public safety provoke a lot of opinions. Beyond the issue of capital punishment, which fires up passionate views from just about everyone, we all have beliefs about how best to deal with individuals convicted of crimes.

In the early part of my career, I didn't get too involved with laws and policies. I spent most of my time focused on the mental health of people who commit crimes, and that of the victims of crimes. For my work in the field, I was invited to provide the keynote address to the 1970 National Institute on Crime and Delinquency. I noted in that address:

> For every citizen, there are some personal steps toward making the world safe. A vital challenge is to get the facts, and to recognize the degree to which our emotions may distort our judgment and interfere with the reasonable solution to problems. We have a desperate need for good leadership, from individuals exemplary in character and quality, individuals who will show the way toward constructive solutions, individuals whose actions match their words.

I was honored to be asked to speak on incarceration and rehabilitation to experts in the field. But I was not the only member of my family who took an interest in this topic.

Shortly after I completed my two years at the Federal Reformatory, El Reno, my uncle Karl published a book called *The Crime of Punishment*. That book rankled some who made the overreach of assuming Karl just wanted to let offenders off scot-free. To reach this conclusion, they focus on a couple of his comments like the following:

> I suspect that all the crimes committed by all the jailed criminals do not equal in total social damage that of the crimes committed against them.

And:

> ...there is one crime we all keep committing, over and over. ... We commit the crime of damning some of our fellow citizens with the label 'criminal.' And having done this, we force them through an experience that is soul-searing and dehumanizing.

I don't feel the need to try to defend everything my uncle wrote. He certainly wasn't right on every point he ever made. But I believe the general idea he was making here was to shift cultural thinking from "punishment" to "penalty." He pointed out that, in most cases, offenders have mental health needs. Their deficiencies are often the cause of their anti-social behavior. Treating them as "bad" won't improve their behavior.

Karl and I were not the only Menningers discussing concepts of crime and punishment at that time. In the early 1970s, Connie's wide-ranging interests led her to become a member of the Kansas State Advisory Committee to the U.S. Commission on Civil Rights, which since its creation in 1957, has studied a host of issues. The Kansas committee asked Connie to chair hearings on the state's corrections system. One of the reports released by the group in 1974 was "Inmate Rights and the Kansas State Prison System."

Looking back, it's funny that I don't recall discussing with her the committee's study of this issue. Up to that point, my work in the corrections field had been limited almost entirely to the Federal system. Knowing Connie, I'm certain she did a great job chairing the committee and, like everywhere she went, I'm certain she brought wisdom, compassion, and fairness to the study of inmate rights.

I said earlier that in the 1960s and 1970s I wasn't involved in corrections at the state level. But in the 1980s and 1990s I became very involved in that field. I served on some study groups, most notably the

Advisory Committee on Prison Overcrowding during Governor John Carlin's administration.

Those activities led me into a very interesting and well-publicized endeavor in the 1990s.

In February of 1994, I was appointed to the William I. Koch Commission on Crime Reduction and Prevention, a commission funded entirely by Bill Koch himself and which worked closely with then-Governor Joan Finney. Technically, Finney formed the commission—designated as a two-year commitment—and appointed its members. The commission aimed to bring together a variety of viewpoints on the various crime-related problems facing the state of Kansas at that time.

The Koch Crime Commission gained a lot of notoriety in the 1990s, probably in large part to its connection to a family known for its involvement in philanthropy and politics. Court battles and personal conflicts kept the family in the public eye. Bill Koch was best known at the time as the winner of the America's Cup yacht race in 1992.

The commission wasn't focused on corrections, per se. It was focused on public safety, fighting crime, and reducing recidivism. It billed itself as "the most comprehensive assessment of crime and what to do about it that has been undertaken."

I was honored to be appointed to the Koch Crime Commission in February of 1994. Bill Koch, in turn, was honored with the Karl Menninger Award at the Kansas Correctional Association Conference on October 18 of that year. The award had been initiated a decade earlier to recognize my uncle's 90th birthday. The award was presented annually to an individual who, while not employed in the field of criminal justice, made an important contribution to criminal justice in Kansas consistent with principles advanced by Karl Menninger. A deserving recipient of the award, Bill was making headlines for his funding and leading of the commission.

Some of Bill's interest in the problem of crime derived from a personal experience. He and his seven-year-old son had attended a July Fourth celebration in Wichita in 1993 at which two people were killed in an exchange of gunfire.

The work of the commission was interesting, in part because of the input it received from a broad swath of people. It interviewed gang members, repeat offenders, crime victims, and youth involved with the criminal justice system, as well as judges, prosecutors, corrections professionals, and citizens from the business community. It was the belief of the commission that government cannot solve the crime problem. For that reason, it sought input primarily from people outside of government.

The commission was initially slated to last just two years. But as we explored a wide range of topics, it became clear this would have to be a longer-term project if it was to produce any real impact. After spending two years and $5 million of his own money, in 1996 Bill extended the project for another three years.

Like most Kansans, I was cautiously optimistic that the Koch Crime Commission would produce some solutions to the problems Kansas was facing in the 1990s. While I believe we produced some valuable research and had a significant voice in policymaking during that decade, it made what appears to have been minimal impact.

As a psychiatrist, I unfortunately see too much in the human psyche that leads to criminal behavior. I wish I had better solutions. But I can say without hesitation that it was my great pleasure to work alongside police officers, corrections officials, politicians, educators, mental health professionals, and private citizens throughout my entire career.

Sadly, humans still rage against the world and against themselves. What is that rage? Where does it come from? Can it be controlled?

In 1995 at the height of the commission's work, I formulated some thoughts on *uncontained rage*.

31

Understanding Uncontained Rage

Recent decades have seen scores of shootings in schools, malls, churches, and other public places. Attacks on random, innocent people who just happened to be in the wrong place at the wrong time have become disturbingly common.

Why do people act out in such extreme ways, wreaking destruction and mayhem that seems disproportionate to the amount they are provoked or harmed?

Years of work in law and psychiatry gave me many opportunities to meet people who were accused of violent and destructive acts. Particularly in pre-trial psychiatric evaluations, I had a chance to ask them about their thoughts and motivations.

Insight into the perspectives of these people gave me a lot to reflect upon in 1995, when I composed a lecture for a conference in Berkeley, California. I later adapted that lecture for an article entitled "Uncontained Rage: A Psychoanalytic Perspective on Violence." Below are excerpts from that article, which ran in the spring 2007 *Bulletin of the Menninger Clinic*:

> Explosions of violent behavior have periodically riveted public attention. While such behavior may be associated with a major psychiatric illness, there is a continuing challenge to understand the emotional underpinnings of such behavior, the sources of aggression, hostility, anger, hate, rage, and violence. Analysts from Freud to Karl Menninger…have speculated as to the confluence of psychological and real forces that prompt violent outbursts. Other analysts have explored the manifestations of aggression and rage in infancy and childhood. An instance of a violent outburst is presented, and underlying factors are explored.
>
> Critical elements prompting such behavior include:

(1) an individual perceives a narcissistic injury that is experienced as being profoundly unfair; (2) the individual has no hope for achieving a reasonable resolution to the injury; (3) the individual reaches the decision that the injury cannot be tolerated further and must be responded to with action; (4) the individual has access to weapons to enhance the capacity and potency to respond; and (5) the individual feels a sufficient sense of potency and/or disregard of the consequences to initiate violence.

The extraordinary outburst of rage by Cho Seung-Hui, a senior student at Virginia Tech University on April 6, 2007, prompted a host of observations by pundits and social scientists on the phenomenon of unanticipated, apparently senseless outbursts of destructive behavior. Over the past 41 years, beginning with Charles Whitman at the University of Texas, there have been a number of notorious instances of uncontained rage in the United States that resulted in multiple casualties. In nearly all of these incidents and similar events of less magnitude, the perpetrator (always male) has been killed or has taken his life at some point during the incident. Thus, we have not been in a position to carefully study such persons. It behooves us to understand as well as we can what drives a person to such an extreme violent behavior.

The psychoanalytic perspective of aggression has tended to address it as an instinctual drive or drive derivative, as opposed to a behavioral phenomenon. It was not until 1915, at age 59, that Freud wrote of aggression as a primary drive distinct from sexuality. Subsequently, in his essay on "Civilization and Its Discontents," Freud observed: "Men are not gentle creatures who want to be loved, and who at the most can defend themselves if they are attacked; they are, on the contrary, creatures among whose instinctual endowments is to be reckoned a powerful share of aggressiveness."

Karl Menninger was profoundly impressed with Freud's death instinct concept, and elaborated on it at length in his second book, *Man Against Himself*, which he opened with these observations:

> Try as we may, it is difficult to conceive of our universe in terms of concord; instead we are faced everywhere with the evidences of conflict. Love and hate, production and consumption, creation and destruction—the constant war of opposing tendencies would appear to be the dynamic heart of the world.
>
> One would expect that in the face of...overwhelming blows at the hands of Fate or Nature, man would oppose himself steadfastly to death and destruction in a universal brotherhood of beleaguered humanity. But this is not the case. Whoever studies the behavior of human beings cannot escape the conclusion that we must reckon with an enemy within the lines. It becomes increasingly evident that some of the destruction which curses the earth is self-destruction; the extraordinary propensity of the human being to join hands with external forces in an attack upon his own existence is one of the most remarkable of biological phenomena.

In *The Vital Balance*, Karl Menninger and his colleagues, Martin Mayman and Paul Pruyser, discussed the life process in mental health and illness. They believed the surfacing of aggressive instincts to be a reflection of a profoundly disturbed equilibrium or adjustment. "It is as if the instinctual forces were constantly stirring and striving, restless in their restraints and looking for any opportunity for expressive release." Menninger and his coauthors viewed the phenomenon of "naked aggression" to be a defensive effort on the part of the human psyche to achieve some kind of resolution or accommodation to an internal disequilibrium.

My own perspective is that aggression is bivalent. Clearly, the striving for mastery and control of one's life is a most powerful, motivating force in every individual. In pursuit of autonomy and independent functioning, and in pursuit of full control over ourselves and our destiny, aggression may be manifested in positive and constructive actions as well as in negative and destructive behaviors… When our capacity to be in control of what happens is compromised, we experience trauma. Indeed, the posttraumatic reaction is one that occurs when we are overwhelmed by a life event for which we may or may not be prepared and our capacity to be in control over our life is taken away from us. Posttraumatic symptoms and behaviors reflect efforts of the ego to regain mastery, either by reexperiencing and reprocessing the trauma or distancing from it to regain a sense of integrity and control.

Consistently, the affects associated with the aggression are anger, hostility, hate, and rage.

When the infant is born into this world, his or her capacity to understand or appreciate what is happening is most limited. The immaturity of the brain and central nervous system preclude having the ability to systematically integrate and respond rationally to personal experiences. It is apparent that the infant has no interest in the world except to selfishly gratify or have gratified his or her own cravings. The demand of the instincts at birth is for satisfaction, and that is the infant's only motive in life.

In the early months, the infant gives nothing to anyone else; he or she makes no attempt to please anyone. The infant is interested only in receiving what he or she wants. The infant follows the path of gaining all the pleasure he or she can, and insofar as possible, avoiding all displeasure and pain. This pattern of behavior is governed by the so-called "pleasure principle." Thus, the child is self-centered and seeks immediate and direct gratification of whatever impulse strikes, with no real conception or concern for what may result from his or her action beyond the satisfaction of impulse. The child sees himself or herself as the center of the universe, and everything revolves around the child.

At the same time, the infant/child has a simplistic attitude toward being hurt. Pain is not readily tolerated. When the child suffers pain, he or she wants to let others know about it; indeed, the child wants others to know exactly how he or she hurts. This is the basic source of the "lex talionis," the law of the talion, an eye for an eye. When I am hurt by you, I want you to hurt like I hurt; therefore, if you hit me, I will hit you back. It makes no difference that the hitting back does not resolve the conflict or stop the pain where I was hit. This is not a logical process. This is an insistent emotional reaction, which unchecked may go on unto mutual pain to someone's final destruction, like the feud of the Hatfields and McCoys.

It is the challenge of society that all human beings become oriented to a different principle of operation than the pleasure principle and the lex talionis. We cannot always have immediate gratification of our desires or impulsively strike back at our frustrations. Our behavior must be regulated for the benefit of everyone. Out of the anarchy of self-centered behavior must come some intelligibly organized existence, with respect for other people, and with recognition that some gratifications must be deferred and that some frustrations are inevitable in life. That is, we must come to accept living by the "reality principle." However, while we mature physically and emotionally, this infantile beginning does persist within all of us. The core of the pleasure principle and the impulse to strike back against hurt are powerful motivating forces within us all, albeit covered by a veneer of the reality principle.

One may formulate a sequence of events that

culminates in violence. The initial stimulus is an experience of frustration or an injury, which may be either real or imagined. This stimulus is experienced as a profound narcissistic injury, a threat to the integrity of the individual, prompting varying degrees of anxiety and/or anger and a flight-or-fight stress response. Depending upon the intensity and severity of the injury or threat, and on the integrity of the ego of the individual, the affect response may escalate from anger to rage and then violent behavior.

Naked aggression or a violent outburst is characterized by Karl Menninger et al. as a third order of breakdown or "dyscontrol" of ego function. They concluded:

> When the aggressive drive is expressed directly upon the environment, we have to assume either that the ego was unsuccessful in its efforts to restrain, divert, or neutralize the dangerous impulses, or else that the ego 'came to the conclusion,' as it were, that efforts to control an aggressive act should be suspended in the interests of self-preservation or the total good. Such justifications for the expression of violence—'self-defense,' 'a blow for righteous-ness,' 'the destruction of evil'—are often formulated only after the fact and are apt to smack of self-deceptive rationalization.

Two critical elements contribute to an awful outcome: (1) the availability of weapons that raise the "potency" of the perpetrator to wreak such havoc, and (2) the loss of hope.

There is a desperation, a sense there is no possibility of a reasonable solution to the perceived dilemma, and no possibility that the individual could maintain mastery/control over his life. For an individual to explode with uncontained rage, there must be a substantial sense of hopelessness. (W.F.) Lynch identified (in *Images of Hope: Imagination as Healer of the Hopeless*) three powerful feelings that emerge when hope is absent:

> (1) The sense of the impossible: what a man must do he cannot; no matter what he does it leads to a sense of checkmate; he is in a trap.
> (2) Too-muchness: life is too much for us; there is something there that is too big to be handled.
> (3) Futility: what is the use? There is no goal, no sense, no reason; so I do not hope or wish or will.

> Perpetrators of explosive, violent behavior appear to experience a profound sense of hopelessness, but they are not helpless. Their rage becomes directed, or misdirected, in an explosive manner to protest and gain vengeance for their profound sense of loss. Feeling mistreated, alienated, unacknowledged, deprived of hope, they embark on a course of self-destruction that transfers their pain to others. In nearly all of these instances, the fact that the behaviors consistently end in either self-destruction or destruction of the self by responding authorities points to a recognition of the high probability that the release of the rage would conclude in death of the self. But these individuals are determined to achieve a sense of final control through their actions and a sense of final identity by going out in a blaze of glory.

Although I first delivered this speech nearly 30 years ago, the problem of violent outbursts only grows in its magnitude. In view of the meaningless shootings and other violent acts that seem to occur almost daily, the elements prompting the behavior which I mentioned in the speech bear repeating. The elements include:

1) an individual perceives a narcissistic injury that is experienced as profoundly unfair;

2) the individual has no hope for achieving a reasonable resolution to

the injury;

3) the individual reaches the decision that the injury cannot be tolerated further and must be responded to with action;

4) the individual has access to weapons to enhance the capacity and potency to respond; and

5) the individual feels a sufficient sense of potency and/or disregard of the consequences to initiate violence.

-32-

Defense of an Unsavory Client

O ver the years, I provided consultation and testimony in many trials. I have discussed some of the more noteworthy cases in previous chapters. But one case is worthy of mention for its significance as well as for its unique subject matter.

I was contacted by a defense team employed by some publishers from New York on a case that was to be tried in Wichita. It didn't seem that out of the ordinary—until the lawyers showed up at my house one evening in 1976 after I returned home from church choir practice.

I invited them in, and they explained the case to me—an obscenity and pornography case brought against their clients. The lawyers produced some of the exhibits to be used by the prosecution in the case. You can imagine the surreal turn my evening took: just a few minutes earlier I'd been singing hymns at church, and now I was being shown pornographic photos in my living room.

"These ARE dirty," I told the lawyers.

"They may be dirty, but they're not 'obscene.' Not by the definition of obscenity," the visitors explained, and then proceeded to educate me on laws of obscenity and pornography.

This began my involvement in what became known as the *Screw* and *Smut* Pornography Trial, an important First Amendment case that brought national attention to Kansas.

———————————————

Why was a trial involving New York publishers Al Goldstein and Jim Buckley being held in Wichita?

The answer is that a clever yet simple plot executed by New York Postal Inspector Raphael Lombardi brought this First Amendment issue to Kansas. In 1974, the inspector sent money orders and completed subscription forms to six Kansas postal inspectors. Those officials submitted the orders and payment to Milky Way Productions in New York. When the publishers mailed copies of the magazines *Smut* and *Screw* to Kansas addresses, the local postal inspectors remailed—unopened—the sealed envelopes to Lombardi.

Why Kansas?

The laws about what is obscene and what constitutes pornography are very murky. So those people who wanted to prosecute needed to find a sympathetic jury who would see it their way. They wanted to bring Goldstein and Buckley to the Bible Belt where they presumed there would be strong bias against such materials. The defendants argued that the government's cherry-picking of Kansas as the site of the offenses constituted entrapment. *The New York Times* called it "venue shopping."

And why me?

Dr. Edward Greenwood, a psychiatrist at the Menninger Clinic in the 1960s and 1970s, had participated in the President's Commission on Obscenity and Pornography, initiated by President Lyndon Johnson. That commission wound up producing in 1970 some findings that were not well received by the public. Most objectionable to some people were the commission's statements that they found:

> "...no evidence to date that exposure to explicit sexual materials plays a significant role in the causation of delinquent or criminal behavior among youths or adults," nor "evidence that exposure to explicit sexual materials adversely affects character or moral attitudes regarding sex and sexual conduct."

Among those who disagreed with these statements were President Richard Nixon and some in the government who wanted to bring much stronger restrictions to the availability of pornography.

The attorneys for Goldstein, who faced up to 65 years in prison if convicted, asked Dr. Greenwood to testify on behalf of the defense. Greenwood declined the request, but he recommended me.

These visitors to my home in 1976 told me of the strategies and tactics they anticipated on behalf of the prosecution. I agreed to testify on behalf of the defense if called by the prosecution.

It's worth noting that the sting to get Goldstein may have been, at least in part, politically motivated. *Screw* had been outspoken in its criticism of Nixon. Regardless of the motivation, the publishers were brought to Kansas in October of 1976 for a trial of national importance.

———————————

I was hired by the defense to provide testimony as an expert witness at the trial. My role was to clarify the difference between obscenity and pornography. Providing this type of testimony is a chess game. You know the points your opponents want to make, and your task is to parry those without being inaccurate or misleading. It's an engaging challenge.

One of the issues argued in this case was whether the magazines met the definition of "prurient" which the court used as the litmus test for obscenity. The prosecutors sought to show that the activities portrayed in the magazines were prurient, meaning they incited similar behavior from the average citizen.

I was questioned by a prosecutor about some of Freud's theories, which he tried to claim made some responses automatic and beyond a person's control. The prosecutor threw around the classic Freudian terms "id," "ego," and "superego" in some pretty meaningless ways. These frivolous accusations were easily shot down. He also attempted to misrepresent the findings of the President's Commission on Obscenity and Pornography, which I was able to dispatch in part due to my relationship with Greenwood and others on the Commission.

The prosecution came with a desire to portray the viewing of pornography as directly tied to undesirable behavior. They overplayed their case. Their contentions were not tied to data or accurate representations of basic psychiatry. Because their arguments were not sound, they were easily countered.

Goldstein later said of the prosecutor's questioning me about basic psychiatry: "(The attorney) was like a high school student who thinks that because he has dissected a frog, he can tell a brain surgeon how to operate."

———————————

The conservative jury in Wichita eventually convicted Goldstein.

According to *The New York Times*:

> The jury deliberated for seven hours on Thursday the 17th and Friday the 18th of June, and then handed down a guilty verdict. Out on bail, Al Goldstein went back to New York to await sentencing, feeling that he had been convicted for all the sins of his hometown.

But that was only round one. Goldstein's attorneys got the Wichita ruling overturned on appeal. So, I testified at a second trial, this time in Kansas City. It took another year and a half, but in the end my client paid a fine to end the whole ordeal. On April 16, 1978, *The New York Times* summed up the resolution of the case:

> Al Goldstein, the subject of two Federal obscenity trials in Kansas, pleaded guilty today to obscenity charges filed against his company, Milky Way Productions Inc., and paid a $30,000 fine.
>
> In accepting the guilty plea, the Federal Government agreed to drop personal charges against the magazine publisher and his former associate, James Buckley, thus bringing to an end government prosecution of the much-publicized case that began more than three years ago.
>
> Judge Frank Theis of Wichita ordered Milky Way Productions to pay $30,000 – $5,000 on one count of conspiracy and $5,000 on each of five counts of mailing obscene material into Kansas.
>
> United States Attorney Ben Burgess said that he would drop all charges against Mr. Goldstein and Mr. Buckley upon payment of the fine in full.
>
> Mr. Goldstein, whose first trial, in Wichita, Kan., resulted in a conviction that was later overturned and whose second resulted in a hung jury, said that he was prepared to pay the fine immediately.

Following my appearance at the trial in Kansas City, one of Goldstein's lawyers told me, "You know, I could get you a lot of business, Dr. Menninger, if you didn't charge so much."

I graciously declined. One pornography trial was enough for my taste. Some guys might make this a regular part of their business, but I didn't want that to be my claim to fame.

The Cuckoo's Nest

While I didn't make acting my profession, I have a great love for theater. And dating back to my days playing *You Can't Take It With You's* Grandpa Vanderhof in high school (for which I was named Topeka High School Male Thespian of the Year in 1948-49), I had a few opportunities over the years to perform on stage. One of my joys in life came in 1975, when I played the role of Col. Matterson in the stage adaptation of the 1962 novel *One Flew Over the Cuckoo's Nest* at Topeka Civic Theatre.

I'm proud to say, not only did we perform the play, we won awards for our production! Okay, so it was first prize in a state community theater competition. Not exactly the Tony Awards. But still fun, nonetheless.

My professional obligations made it impossible for me to attend very many of the rehearsals. The funny thing was, because the character of Col. Matterson was confined to a wheelchair, I didn't have to learn any of the blocking. They just moved me around the stage. The greatest affirmation of my performance came when a close friend told me, "I didn't recognize you until after the intermission!"

It's worth noting here that Topeka is blessed to be home of the remarkable Topeka Civic Theatre, one of the oldest continuously running community dinner theatres in the country. Connie and I were as involved in TCT as our schedules permitted us to be. Connie's parents had been supportive of community theater throughout her youth, so once she settled in Topeka, she became connected with TCT and was eventually named to its board of directors. She served on the play selection committee and played many roles behind the scenes.

Over the years, TCT entered numerous competitions. On a few occasions, Connie and I traveled with the entourage to these events. In 1979, we were in attendance when the TCT production of Neil Simon's *The Good Doctor* took first place in the Festival of American Community Theatre competition in Memphis. We reveled with the cast and crew when the award was announced.

With Connie serving in various volunteer roles, our involvement with TCT endured for several decades. One of the highlights came in 1993 when I performed the two-person play *Love Letters* with Maureen "Twink" Lynch, the beloved longtime administrative director of TCT. *Love Letters* is a dramatic reading between a man and a woman sitting at a table, essentially reading the history of their relationship from their correspondence over the years. Twink asked me if I would do it with her. We performed it in the band box theater in the basement of the Topeka Municipal Auditorium, which is now the Topeka Performing Arts Center.

Twink had become a great friend to Connie over the years, and we were also close to her husband John Lynch, an orthopedic surgeon in Topeka. It was a delight to work with her on the production of *Love Letters*.

Interestingly, Connie and I were hardly the only ones connected to Menninger to be deeply involved with TCT. Irv Sheffel, an administrator at Menninger for 40 years, and his wife Beth donated $1 million in 1999 to renovate Topeka's former Gage Elementary School into what is now TCT's current location. Irv's photo hangs in the theatre in honor of this generous lead gift for the campaign.

Dr. Irwin "Irv" Rosen was a talented performer and musician as well as chief psychologist at the Menninger Clinic, and he and his wife Betty were also generous patrons of TCT, as was staff psychiatrist and psychoanalyst Dr. Jerry Katz.

Menninger staff seemed to gravitate to the volunteer theater. Dozens performed on the TCT stage over the years. But it wasn't just the staff who took the stage. Patients were often encouraged to use the theater as a therapeutic outlet for their talents. This was usually a very productive activity for the patients, although it wasn't always without a hitch. *The First 75 Years*, a book commemorating the history of TCT contains the following:

> During the 1972 run of *Fiddler (on the Roof)*, one Menninger patient in the cast relapsed into his severely psychotic behavior and refused to leave his apartment, despite entreaties of Menninger doctors, nurses, and social workers. He finally emerged only when the man

playing the village rabbi appeared and shouted through the door, "As your rabbi, I demand that you come with me to the theater!" They made the curtain.

The most significant of all Menninger employees to participate in amateur theater is undoubtedly Jacques Levy, a staff psychologist in the 1960s. He produced and directed TCT shows in his free time. The only problem was, he was so talented and dedicated to the theater that he finally had to make a choice. He moved back home to New York City so he could attempt to continue to practice psychology while pursuing his true passion. It wasn't long before he became connected to musical greats like Bob Dylan and Roger Guinn, writing music and conducting shows on Broadway.

The play version of *One Flew Over the Cuckoo's Nest* was a big deal in the 1960s and early 1970s. Big enough that stars like Kirk Douglas, Joan Tetzel, and Gene Wilder appeared in the Broadway production. Unfortunately, the stage production has been overshadowed by the 1975 movie version starring Jack Nicholson.

The movie failed to capture some of the most compelling intrigue of the novel and play, particularly the power struggle between the patient who was the main character, and the head nurse over the psychiatric ward.

But even worse, the movie painted a disturbing picture of those who suffer mental illness, and a vile picture of those charged with caring for them. That Hollywood would paint an unrealistic picture of psychiatric treatment is not surprising. The truth is my father and uncle entered a field of health care that has been greatly misunderstood throughout history.

Interestingly, the movie had an impact on the mental health community despite its inaccuracies. The antagonist Nurse Ratched sends patients who cause trouble for electroshock treatment or psychosurgery. People came to the defense of mental health providers, while simultaneously calling for improved funding and needed reforms in the industry.

Shortly after the release of the movie version of *One Flew Over the Cuckoo's Nest* in 1975, I wrote one of my "In-Sights" columns about my perception of the film. Following are a few excerpts from that column:

> Who's really crazy in this world? The folks who are sent to the mental hospitals? Or maybe the people who work there?
>
> As a clinical director in a public mental hospital, I...wanted to see how the film production handled the psychiatric hospital scenes.
>
> The author is clearly critical of psychiatry, so in the story the quality of the psychiatrists and psychiatric treatment is less than adequate. I suspect therefore that the average movie-goer will not realize that the image of state hospital treatment in the movie is not the way it is in many settings today.
>
> How much does this mirror the current psychiatric scene? Little, if at all. Regrettably there still are many public mental hospitals in older buildings...unable to meet the standards of the Joint Commission on the Accreditation of Hospitals (JCAH).
>
> In the Topeka State Hospital, which I know best and which is JCAH accredited, the patients are all housed in modern, one-story buildings with nearly all one- or two-bedrooms. The facilities are much like a modern college dormitory. Electroshock treatment is rarely practiced and psychosurgery not at all.
>
> As a portrayal of a provocative power struggle and as a commentary on mental hospitals twenty-five years ago, *Cuckoo's Nest* is a good drama. It should not be taken to represent current psychiatric practice in most state hospitals.

To the uninformed, psychiatry and mental health care can seem mysterious. Many books and movies touch on the treatment of the mentally ill. By taking great liberties with the truth, media have created compelling and often terrifying stories like *One Flew Over the Cuckoo's*

Nest. In one of my columns, I decided to try to combat the effect of one television portrayal I feared was particularly harmful:

> Mental illness is still much misunderstood and often frightening to people. Many are so unsettled by the subject that they stay as far away from it as they can. Thus, public education is very much needed in this field.
>
> At times over the years, the media have played an important role in education about mental illness and the care provided by public mental health facilities. Some television shows have been sensitive and constructive in their approach to the topic.
>
> This is not always true, as evidenced by a recent...television show, which was particularly unfortunate. In an atmosphere of anger and condemnation, that show portrayed what might best be labeled half-truths. It pictured some of the worst treatment for mental illness, without keeping it in full perspective.
>
> In years past, the care of the mentally ill in most state hospitals has left much to be desired. In many states, that care still falls short of the ideal. And you can find places where it is really bad. But to imply that treatment in *all* public mental hospitals is harmful, inhuman, and barbaric is unconscionable!

I wrote those words about 50 years ago. I am pleased with the progress made regarding the portrayal of mental health, but there are still many examples in media and popular culture which do not help the cause. Aside from progress in the media, I am pleased by the amount of concern, empathy, and understanding I see in the general populace when it comes to mental health. The stigma of mental health care is nothing compared to what it was in the past. Depression, anxiety, trauma, suicidal thoughts—these are topics now discussed with compassion and transparency. I applaud the efforts of all who have moved the perception of mental health care in a positive direction.

The same year I performed the role of the crippled colonel in *One Flew Over the Cuckoo's Nest*, I played a more familiar character in the musical *Fifty-Grand*, a locally-written work celebrating the anniversary of the formal incorporation of the Menninger Sanitarium Corporation in 1925.

Irv Rosen and Jerry Katz—those multi-talented Menninger senior staff who were so involved with Topeka Civic Theatre—put new lyrics to standard songs to tell the Menninger history. Their delightful production was performed at the Top of the Tower Club in the downtown Topeka Tower Building.

Remember a few chapters back when I learned in psychoanalysis to be my own father? My role in the *Fifty-Grand* production: to play the part of Dr. Will.

I didn't put a lot of time into reflecting on any deep meaning or transcendental experience in "being my own father" in the musical. It was just good-natured fun with friends and colleagues. I didn't exactly try to get into character or "channel" my father. I just performed it the way I would normally act. I'm sure there are some similarities between my father and me, which I suppose were recognized by all who knew both of us.

———————————

Enjoyable as those shows were, they were small productions seen only by the local community. That would not be true of a project for which I was consulted in the 2000s.

I will let the *Topeka Capital-Journal* tell that story through the following excerpts from May 10, 2013:

> Topekans who stay to watch all of the credits of "The Great Gatsby," the just-opened film adaptation of the F. Scott Fitzgerald novel of the same name, will see a familiar name acknowledged on the big screen: W. Walter Menninger, M.D.
>
> Baz Luhrmann, director, producer, and co-writer of the movie, which is playing nationwide, including the Regal Hollywood Stadium 14 theaters in Topeka, said Menninger was crucial in helping provide a bookending

device that allowed the tale's narrator, Nick Carraway (Tobey Maguire), to be more than "a disembodied voiceover."

The movie opens and closes in a fictional institution, the Perkins Sanatorium... modeled after the Menninger Clinic, which was founded in 1919 in Topeka... Luhrmann consulted with the 81-year-old Menninger, the retired leader of the Menninger Foundation founded by his grandfather, C.F. Menninger; father, Will Menninger; and uncle, Karl Menninger.

Luhrmann said: "We were very lucky to engage with Dr. Menninger, whose family were some of the earliest advocates of progressive psychoanalysis techniques in the States, as far back as the 1920s, and it was an explosive moment for us when Dr. Menninger explained that it was very reasonable to think that patients would have been encouraged to come to terms with their experiences through self-expression, writing for example."

As another nod to W. Walter Menninger's help, the character of the psychiatrist who runs Perkins Sanitorium and suggests Carraway write down his Gatsby story was given the name Dr. Walter Perkins by the screenwriters.

In F. Scott Fitzgerald's *The Great Gatsby* novel—which was published in 1925—there is no mention of Carraway being in a mental institution. For the 2013 film, Luhrmann wanted to do something creative with the method of narration provided by the Carraway character. The director thought, *Okay he's come back to the Midwest. He's depressed. Perhaps his parents sent him off somewhere to get help.*

The story is set in 1922. Technically, my uncle Karl returned to work with his father in 1919, so the Menninger psychiatric practice was indeed established prior to 1922. But the Menningers didn't purchase the sanitarium property at 3617 SW 6th Street in Topeka until 1925. The facility portrayed in the movie—The Perkins Sanitarium—is fictional, so the timeline of Menninger is immaterial. Regardless of the timing, Luhrmann patterned his Perkins Sanitorium after Menninger.

The *Capital-Journal* failed to describe in detail the interaction I had with the director, as well as with actor Tobey Maguire at a couple of meetings in New York.

It began when Luhrmann's assistant called the Menninger Clinic in Houston to try to connect with someone who might be able to provide some consultation. The clinic in Houston referred them to me. Luhrmann called me from New York City, where they were preparing and rehearsing much of the movie in a loft in Lower Manhattan. After talking for a bit, I told Luhrmann that I would be in New York in a couple of weeks and would be willing to meet in person if he would like to talk at greater length.

We met at the loft, where we talked in detail about the creative license he was considering taking with the story, to intersperse throughout the movie scenes of dialogue between a psychiatrist and the narrator. He wanted to create a scenario in which the lead character, Nick Carraway, would be writing the story. This was indeed plausible, considering that writing is one strategy for helping emotionally disturbed people process their thoughts.

After visiting with the director for a bit on that trip to New York, Luhrmann asked me if I would come back to the city to meet with Maguire about his portrayal of Carraway in the fictitious sanitarium. I said, "Sure."

In case you're unfamiliar with Maguire's career, it's been a mighty successful one. He's best known for playing Spider-Man in several movies, but he also received Oscar nominations for his roles in *Cider House Rules* and *Seabiscuit*.

Sworn to secrecy about the project by Luhrmann, I flew back to New York several weeks later to meet with Maguire. Luhrmann and his co-writer were there, and they videotaped the interaction between Maguire and me. They told me to try to role play a psychiatric session with Maguire acting in the character of Carraway. They asked how I would approach the Carraway character. Maguire, who is very friendly and outgoing, played the part of Carraway as reserved, depressed, and reticent to talk.

In our ad-libbed psychotherapy rehearsal, I said, "I understand, a thing like this might be a little hard to talk about. If you don't want to talk about it, maybe when you're back in your room, you could write down some of your thoughts and feelings about it and we could discuss it later," or something to that effect.

I left New York after that meeting curious how the injection of a mental health aspect would be portrayed in Luhrmann's movie, and hopeful I had been of some assistance.

———————•———————

The 2013 film *The Great Gatsby* begins with an exterior shot of a castle-like building that appears to be surrounded by a moat. The sign outside the building reads "The Perkins Sanitorium." Inside a study, lined with bookcases and warmed by a roaring fire, a psychiatrist with white hair and beard, wearing glasses and a white overcoat, talks with a lucid and talkative Carraway. The young man lays the groundwork for the story through flashbacks he describes. A few scenes of dialogue in the psychiatrists' office slowly reveal the memories with which Carraway wrestles. Then, about 15 minutes into the movie, Carraway suddenly resists discussing specific events with the psychiatrist.

"Then write about it," Dr. Perkins suggests. To the patient's mild objection, Perkins reminds Carraway that he himself said writing has brought him solace in the past. The doctor assures the patient that no one need ever read his writings.

When Carraway asks what he should write about, the doctor responds "Anything. Whatever brings you ease. A memory. A thought. A place. Write it down."

It was in this way that Luhrmann revealed to the audience that the events of the story are in fact Carraway's composed memories.

———————•———————

Several months later, I flew to New York for the big premier of the 2013 release of *The Great Gatsby*. My daughter Eliza, who lived in Boston, met me for the Hollywood-style affair. At the intermission of the showing, Eliza remarked just how much the actor playing Dr. Perkins—Australian Jack Thompson—favored me. I didn't pick up on the resemblance, but my daughter Eliza insisted, "He looks just like you!" During the intermission, when I happened to catch a glimpse of myself in a mirror in the theater hallway, I suddenly realized she was right. Luhrmann had made Thompson look very much like me!

After the showing, we went over to a big 1920s-themed bash at the Palace Hotel. I saw Luhrmann at the party, and he gave me a hug. For a few minutes, we celebrated how well the movie had come together.

It was a fascinating experience, to get a glimpse at the creative process, to contribute a small bit of knowledge to the development, and then be there to watch movie makers celebrate their accomplishment.

-34-

How, On Earth, Have We Survived So Far?

The collapse of the skywalk in the Hyatt Regency. The bombing of the federal courthouse in Topeka. Riots. Murders. Violence. Criminal and civil trials. Incarceration.

I have witnessed a lot in my life. I was often struck by the damage people wrought upon themselves and others. I shared those thoughts in our 1991 Christmas letter:

> Our perspective is always limited, but we seem to be living in a most remarkable period of history—a period of incredibly rapid change, of incomparable intellectual achievement, of extraordinary technological capacity. Yet we are ever vulnerable to the vicissitudes of emotional eruptions and violence—individual and group. Newspaper headlines and television news soundbites emphasize the dissonance in our lives... Can we master all this change and conflict? Not if we continue to be self-oriented. We—especially people in leadership roles, locally, nationally, and internationally—must look beyond ourselves. There is hope in the desire of most people to be good and do good, and to join together to make the world a better place than we found it. Not over-zealously, but thoughtfully and reasonably.

Those thoughts were a small encapsulation of some of the writing and speaking I did during that phase of my life. We survived those years, and the world keeps turning. But still, we can't help but wonder, how have we survived it all?

Below are excerpts from a talk I gave to the Southern Conference of World Futures Society in April of 1989 that reflect that sentiment entitled "How, On Earth, Have We Survived So Far?"

We do live in a hazardous world. Throughout history, we have sought safety, and throughout history we have experienced violence, particularly at the hands of our fellow human beings... How do we place these negative events in perspective?

How, on earth, have we survived so far? We have a clearly demonstrated capacity for insensitive wastefulness and fouling of our planet, whether in oil polluted oceans or chemically polluted drinking water or smog-polluted atmosphere. But we have also achieved great technological advances which have allowed us to master our environment.

Critical to our survival and environmental mastery has been the combination of the opposable thumb and our extraordinary forebrain. The capacity to walk upright and use our hands has facilitated our mastery of the environment. But equally or more important has been the incredible computer housed within our skull—permitting us to take life experiences, translate them into symbols we call language, share them with others, record them permanently in ways that will cross space and time, and allow us to explore a wide range of events and phenomena through thought and calculation rather than trial and error actions.

At the same time, a factor which has limited the effectiveness of our intellect and our facile hands has been the influence of our emotions. Shortly after the outbreak of World War I, Sigmund Freud observed in his essay "Thoughts for the Times on War and Death: The Disillusionment of the War":

> Students of human nature and philosophers have long taught us that we are mistaken in regarding our intelligence as an independent force and in overlooking its dependence on emotional life. Our intellect, they teach us, can function reliably only when it is removed from

the influences of strong emotional impulses; otherwise it behaves merely as an instrument of the will and delivers the inference which the will requires.

...the shrewdest people will all of a sudden behave without insight, like imbeciles, as soon as the necessary insight is confronted by an emotional response.

Freud was pointing to a phenomenon we repeatedly observe; namely the Archie Bunkers of this world whose minds are biased by various emotional factors and who protest, "Don't confuse me with the facts; my mind's made up!" We generally do not like to acknowledge that we are, indeed, emotional animals as much or more than intellectual animals. Our emotions, powerfully motivating forces within us, are not always rational. Often we explain to ourselves why we think we do what we do, though our explanations may be transparently false. We may not really know why we have the prejudices we do.

Toward what do our emotions prompt us? One observes in children, and also in adults, that one primary goal is to find pleasure and avoid pain. We seek happiness. We want to become happy and remain so, eliminating pain and discomfort, perpetually searching for as much pleasure as we can.

The pursuit of pleasure is something evident from the beginning of life; when the infant is born into the world, he doesn't really understand what is happening. His responses are instinctual. He has no capacity to rationally or logically assess what is going on; his central nervous system is not yet mature, so he is unable to systematically integrate his experiences, much less perceive them in much order. The infant is a biological organism and his interest in life can be formulated simply: to gain as much satisfaction and to find relief for any discomfort which he perceives. This is a self-centered orientation, with no appreciation for the outside world.

When the infant is, as he must inevitably be, frustrated or hurt, the response is likewise simplistic. He wants to let others know he hurts, and he expresses his frustrations and rage accordingly. This is the basic source of the lex talionis—the law of the talion or "an eye for an eye." "When I am hurt by you, I want you to hurt like I hurt; therefore, if you hit me, I will hit you back." It makes no difference that the hitting back does not resolve, but only may prolong the conflict. This is not a logical or rational process; it is an insistent, impulsive, emotional reaction to being hurt.

Society is challenged to modify this infantile orientation to life and to inculcate in this individual a different principle of operation than the pleasure principle and the lex talionis. We can't always have what we want when we want it. We can't always strike back at our frustrations. Out of the anarchy of self-centered behavior has to come some intelligently organized existence, with respect for other people and the recognition that some frustrations are inevitable in life and some gratification must be deferred. This principle of operation we call the "reality principle." While living by the reality principle is the ultimate, mature lifestyle, it is important to recognize that while we may mature physically and emotionally in life, the infantile beginning persists within all of us.

The consequences of a self-centered orientation and the rage response of the lex talionis have limited consequences as long as these forces are primarily manifested in young children, the overall population is small relative to the space on earth, and the tools for expression of the destructive impulses are limited. However, when the infantile orientation persists in an adult individual, the population increases and crowds the earth, and the destructive capacity evolves to semi-automatic weapons, plastique explosives or nuclear warheads, the survival of the species becomes more tenuous. The survival is further compromised when the search for pleasure leads to the unbridled use and abuse of substances to achieve artificial highs—alcohol, marijuana, heroin, cocaine.

Where's the Hope?

Throughout history, humankind has seen some extraordinary builders and toilers whose contributions have facilitated our survival in the face of much adversity. Perhaps most consequential in their impact have been religious and spiritual leaders—Christ, St. Paul, Muhammad, Buddha, Confucius, Moses, St. Augustine, Martin Luther. Powerfully significant have been scientists and inventors—Isaac Newton, Galileo Galilei, Johannes Gutenberg, Louis Pasteur, Charles Darwin, Albert Einstein. Explorers, philosophers, political leaders, artists and literary figures have likewise played meaningful roles in the extraordinary tangible and intangible achievements of our present-day world.

As a species, we are remarkably adaptable and resilient. And there is within us, for the most part, a powerful force for growth and development, and a great desire to love and be loved.

Anyone who has studied human nature recognizes that there is a potential goodness and badness in everyone. For some, the bad seems to prevail, presumably because of some powerful negative experiences early in life which shape and reinforce an inability to trust others. In recent years, we have come to recognize the incidence of family violence and sexual abuse to be far greater than most generally assumed; and these experiences certainly contribute to a lack of basic trust and an accumulation of rage toward the world. Overall, the incidence of "bad" persons is relatively small, although the rest of society must necessarily devote a disproportional amount of energy and resources to contain the damage of this group.

Most people maintain some degree of commitment and responsiveness to being good and having a positive sense of themselves. Given the opportunity to do something positive, most will opt for the chance to do so. The phenomenon of "goodness" is evident in nearly every tragedy, when one finds an out-pouring of concern and assistance from volunteers giving of themselves and their goods.

In George E. Vaillant's survey of the mechanisms of adaptation described in his 1977 book *Adaptation to Life*, he felt the healthy ones were effective because they helped integrate four sometimes conflicting aspects of human behavior—conscience, reality, interpersonal relations, and instincts. Earlier, I made reference to anticipation as one of these mechanisms. Another is altruism, which Webster defines as "uncalculated consideration of, regard for, or devotion to others' interests, sometimes in accordance with an ethical principle." Vaillant defines altruism as "getting pleasure from giving to others what you yourself would like to receive." Part of the psychological significance stems from the personal gain from being allied with a cause or activity which enhances one's sense of self.

What Lies Ahead?

And now the thought comes to me: What will the result of our labors look like (at the end of human history)? Will it be lost in the dreadful scene of destruction? Or will it appear, if only for a second, as a bright flash of light, illuminating and guiding and spreading? Will it grow, or will be extinguished...?

Will there be...enough men and women here and there in the surging mass—enough men and women with courage and idealism and vision to stem the tides of destructiveness, to oppose not only the ravages of nature but the evil within man himself, and turn defeat into victory?

We have so little time left—and so much to do. We can only do it together.

35

Return to Menninger

It's interesting that, considering all that I accomplished in the 1960s and 1970s, I still hadn't achieved the one goal I'd had before me the entire time. I had held rewarding positions with prestigious and important organizations and had been involved with numerous significant endeavors. But the one thing I most wanted had thus far eluded me.

I had not been involved in a significant way in the leadership of the Menninger Foundation.

Technically speaking, I never left the Menninger Foundation. For the 11 years that I was on staff at Topeka State Hospital, I collected a salary from Menninger. I turned my checks from TSH over to Menninger.

Additionally, I was on the teaching staff of the Menninger School of Psychiatry. As director of residency training at TSH, I supervised 12 MSP residents. As part of the bigger training program, I was a member of the faculty and on the governing board of the MSP and taught a variety of courses at MSP.

I also carried on fundraising responsibilities for the Menninger Foundation throughout the decade of the 1970s.

But during that period, I didn't officially hold a position and wasn't involved in any of the decision making at Menninger. I watched from the sidelines as others, led by my brother Roy, guided the organization.

As I watched Roy lead the Menninger Foundation, I perceived the growing pains he experienced in his role as CEO. He himself admitted that he found the role intimidating at first as he still perceived himself as a young and inexperienced psychiatrist. Suddenly, he was forced into what must have been a no-win situation. He felt like he was replacing not just one but two legendary figures—our deceased father and our uncle Karl.

Admittedly, I was frustrated throughout the 1970s by my banishment to TSH. But over time, my sympathy for Roy, and my appreciation for his predicament, grew.

Roy's training had been so different from what he found upon joining the Menninger staff in 1961 that he experienced a learning curve. Among other differences, he found that patients at Menninger were treated with more dignity and positive personal attention than they were at Boston Psychopathic Hospital.

Roy's formal education in Boston was interrupted by service in the Army, and he experienced a similar attitude toward patients while stationed in Austria. Soldiers with mental health struggles were criticized. They were seen as weak and lazy malingerers. The important thing—the only thing—was to get them shaped up for service. Some of the stories he recounted from his time in the Army were heartrending. He longed to truly help the people he encountered but felt limited in what he could do by the rigid structure and uncaring commanding officers.

When he arrived at Menninger in 1961, Roy encountered a new approach to treating patients. For the first time, he experienced a great deal of collaboration and interaction with staff. He was impressed that at Menninger there was greater professional equality and less interdisciplinary competition. He called the treatment program "patient-centered," much more empathetic and supportive than what he'd experienced previously.

Roy was going through a lot of personal growth and development during the early 1960s. As long as Karl was in charge and my father was a supportive influence, Roy was safe in his role to learn and adapt to this new way of thinking. But unfortunately, the security that permitted personal growth was stripped away when Dad died. He was thrust into leadership of the Menninger organization under precarious circumstances.

It's only natural that the employees in an organization should fear change and doubt the capability of a new leader. What Roy walked into was what he called a "triple threat." He feared the staff would perceive him as too young, having insufficient training, and likely the beneficiary of a purely nepotistic hire.

On top of his own fears, Roy faced the insecurities and territorialism the Menninger staff had developed. It took time, but he gradually succeeded in uniting the staff. One of his best moves was to take small groups of staff to training seminars at the AK Rice Institute for the Study of Social Systems. These seminars helped these small groups gain insight and better understand what makes for a healthy organization.

You could call this era "The Education of Roy Menninger." To his great credit, my brother grew as a person and as a leader.

Throughout all this, I longed to be involved and make some contribution. I was motivated by my own ego and desire for control, certainly. And I desired to ensure that what my father left behind would flourish. But I also felt love and sympathy for my brother and wanted to help him succeed.

Unfortunately, that was not possible in the 1970s. It's not that it wasn't considered. At one point during the decade, I was nominated to the Menninger board of trustees. I suspect that it was Uncle Karl who nominated me. My election to the board would put me in a position to help make some decisions about the direction of the organization. It was obviously a situation rife with complications. The trustees tasked Roy with telling me about my addition to the board.

When he approached me with the news, it was perfectly clear that he was unhappy about it. I decided, *I'm not going to put him in such a difficult position.* I declined the position at that time and continued to wait on the sidelines.

You might wonder if there was something that I could have done to alleviate the pressure I apparently exerted on Roy. I really don't think I could have done anything differently. I realized once Roy volunteered me at TSH that the best thing I could do was stay out of his hair. And so, for ten years, I did.

Roy changed over that decade. He grew in his confidence to lead and in his security within the organization. He settled into the role of CEO, and gradually he perceived me as less of a threat. Yet, I remained at TSH until Roy was nudged by outsiders to reconsider my role at Menninger.

In his position as head of Menninger, Roy was approached by a couple of institutions about my availability. Because I was still employed by Menninger, those institutions asked Roy if they could interview me for a variety of roles.

The matter became serious when, in the late 1970s, the Institute of

Pennsylvania Hospital in Philadelphia was searching for a new chief of staff and asked Roy about interviewing me for the job. Connie and I did go to Philadelphia for an interview.

Ultimately, I wasn't offered the job, but the experience got Connie and me thinking that we would have to go someplace else if I was to progress in my career. Though we really didn't want to leave Topeka, we tried to have an open mind. At that point I seriously questioned whether I would ever go back to work at Menninger.

But the interest other employers showed in me may have been the push that was needed. As Roy observed that other institutions valued my abilities and experience, he determined to work out a solution. When he was finally comfortable with bringing me back to work at Menninger, the issue became finding the right fit—a position that fit my qualifications yet wouldn't threaten Roy's leadership.

In the late 1970s, I was put forth as a candidate for a section director at the Menninger Hospital. When the hospital director put it up to a vote, I was deemed overqualified.

Next, Menninger searched for a new chief of staff for the Menninger Clinic. It was a position for which I was qualified. But when it came time for the hiring committee to make its decision I was passed over for that role.

One of my colleagues said, "Walt, if your name weren't Menninger, there wouldn't be any question." It was painful. I realized that the only way I could go back was in a position that didn't threaten anyone. That right opportunity just hadn't arisen yet.

———————————•———————————

Throughout the 1970s, I focused on the words of my mentor, Dr. Felix Wroblewski, who told me, "It's more important in life to like what you do than to do what you like." But I never lost focus on my goal, to participate in the leadership of the Menninger Foundation.

That door finally opened in 1980. That's when the head of Law and Psychiatry at Menninger departed.

As I recounted in previous chapters, I had done extensive work in the realm of crime and courts. With specialty board certification in both administrative psychiatry and law and psychiatry, I was sufficiently qualified to teach on the subject. Helping to make everyone comfortable with the fit was the fact that the only person who might perceive me as a threat to his position was Herb Modlin, the primary forensic psychiatrist at Menninger. I had worked with Modlin on projects previously, and we had a great rapport. He was an older man and a respected expert in law and psychiatry himself. He was solidly established in his practice and comfortable with his own reputation. He wasn't at all threatened by me.

The opportunity finally seemed right. It was a face-saving way to bring me back without threatening anyone.

The Menninger Foundation door had actually swung partially open to me earlier in 1980. I was renominated to the Menninger board of trustees, and this time I accepted. It was apparent that Roy was working to bring me back in some capacity. I was elected at the annual meeting in April of 1980, which coincided with a groundbreaking ceremony for a major building program at the Menninger West Campus.

When the Law and Psychiatry position opened up, everyone seemed to believe it was time for me to rejoin the Menninger staff. So, I announced my resignation from TSH that fall and planned to assume my new role on January 6, 1981.

My tenure at TSH was 11 and a half years. My departure was certainly cause for reflection.

While going to the state hospital wasn't what I wanted in 1969, my time there brought me a great deal of pleasure. There were many fine people on the staff, and I made many friends. My roles at TSH permitted me a great deal of flexibility and opportunity to expand my professional reach. During those years I did a great deal of speaking, writing, consulting, and engaging in professional organizations.

And, of course, it was gratifying to know that at TSH we were providing a much-needed service to the state. As a Kansan, I take satisfaction that that part of my life was dedicated to helping my fellow Kansans. As I have recounted in previous chapters, state-run mental institutions did not enjoy the best of reputations at that time. I was proud to help ensure Kansans had access to quality care.

I had chosen during those years to make lemonade out of lemons, and in the end it all worked out very well. Dr. Wroblewski's advice had proven wise in my experience.

With the new year, I bid my colleagues at TSH farewell, minus one. Being so important to my organization and efficiency, I really wanted my secretary, Mary Donohue, to come with me when I made the transition to Menninger. Her assistance was crucial to my success through each of the roles I held at the state hospital. We had developed a great rapport, and she was a tremendous asset. The only sticking point was that Mary had served the state for 20 years and thus had accumulated considerable sick leave. When I asked her to come with me, we worked out the issues so that she wouldn't leave those benefits behind.

In January of 1981, Mary and I set up my office at Menninger's West Campus. The Menninger Foundation was in the midst of a complete consolidation of both campuses at the West Campus, a project for which I had helped raise $27 million in the later part of the 1970s. Although I was moving to a new location, I felt like I was finally coming home.

With my new position at Menninger came some new opportunities and responsibilities. Along with the increased teaching role came opportunities to speak on a variety of topics and contribute to a variety of projects.

In 1980, I was elected chair of the 16-member Advisory Board of the National Institute of Corrections. That was special. I had continued to have a relationship with the Federal Bureau of Prisons after I left the organization in 1963. Two years after I left the bureau, I was named to a committee reviewing the medical program of the bureau. That appointment led to decades of gratifying work in the area of corrections. It culminated with my election to chair of the advisory board.

As I mentioned earlier, I also spent twelve months working with the Secret Service to improve the protection of the U.S. president, culminating with a March 1981 conference in Washington, D.C. I oversaw the report from the conference—"Behavioral Science and the Secret Service: Toward the Prevention of Assassination"—which was published by the National Academy of Sciences Press.

In 1982, I was appointed by Governor John Carlin to the Kansas

Governor's Advisory Committee on Mental Health, Retardation, and Community Mental Health Services.

The year 1983 was a whirlwind of professional activity. I addressed the Association of State Chief Justices and participated in the Brookings Institute Seminar on "The Administration of Justice" in Williamsburg, which was convened by the U.S. Supreme Court Chief Justice, the U.S. Attorney General, and the U.S. House and Senate Judiciary Committees.

As I recounted earlier, it was that year that I worked with Herb Modlin evaluating the victims of the Hyatt Hotel Skywalk collapse.

We called 1983 "The Year of Education" at the Menninger household, as every member of our family was involved in some sort of college study. Though still in high school, our two youngest children— Will and David—participated in some college courses at Washburn University that year. For my part, I taught Forensic Psychology to grad students as part of a Wichita State University outreach program.

In 1983, in order to accommodate my many commitments, I called it quits on my "In-Sights" column after eight years. In reality, the column had run its course. The market was changing. Newspapers were slimming down. "In-Sights" was an atypical column from the beginning. There were advice columns and there were medical columns. Mine didn't really fit either category. So, the publishers found that demand for my column was dwindling by the early 1980s. It was really a mutual decision to discontinue the column, and I wasn't unhappy to see it end. It had become sort of a drag. There was always that pressure to get the columns written. Frankly, I don't know how I kept up that grind for eight years.

My return to Menninger was a landmark in my professional life. My personal life, meanwhile, held many joys as well. By the early 1980s, our children were all in high school or college. Connie and I saw our roles evolve from caregiver to guide and cheerleader as our children discovered their own personalities and talents. While our children became more self-sufficient, Connie and I found opportunities to pursue some of our own passions.

At the start of the new decade, I received a special opportunity to follow in my father's footsteps. Prior to his death, my father had been an influential leader in the Boy Scouts of America for about 40 years. It was an interest he passed on to his children, and it was a way for us to connect with him. Even after his passing, I kept up my involvement with the organization.

In 1980, I was appointed to the National Executive board of the Boy Scouts of America and was named National Health and Safety Committee Chairman. Both of those positions had been held by my father. I had been added to the Health and Safety Committee shortly after Dad's death in the 1960s.

The Health and Safety Committee was a good group at that time, consisting of 15 to 20 doctors and experts in health and safety, all of whom were specialists in wilderness medicine and scouting. They always had a doctor as chairman of the committee. In the 1970s, they brought in a contractor to hold the position, and he asked me to be his vice chair. At the conclusion of his term, he nominated me, and I was elected to the executive board as the new chairman of the committee.

It gave me immense internal satisfaction to be active and engaged in the role my father had held in the Boy Scouts. It was so important in his life. He was the first chairman of the Health and Safety Committee, and he remained chair until his death—a tenure of nearly 30 years.

Over the years, the Health and Safety Committee became a powerful entity due to the liability the organization faced. The committee reviewed all deaths and serious incidents that occurred within the organization. One fourth of the deaths we reviewed were due to adult leader heart attacks. A fourth of the deaths were from drownings, so we were particularly concerned with water safety. Auto accidents made up a similar percentage, and we got a lot done in terms of promoting driver safety.

But the most significant thing we did during those years was to ban smoking in all scouting activities. We felt it was time, under my leadership, to address the issue of smoking. It's no coincidence that I had a father whose death was caused by lung cancer. We believed we needed to send the message to young, impressionable scouts that smoking was a harmful habit. We decided it was time to ban it in the organization.

Interestingly, when we brought forth the proposal to ban smoking, the president said, "Walt, hold that until I give you the word." On the board at that time happened to be a very important donor from North Carolina. When that man went off the executive committee, the president said,

"Walt, you can bring that proposal now."

———————————•———————————

Honors continued to come in for the Menninger Foundation and the men who made it. In 1981, my uncle Karl became the first psychiatrist to be awarded the Medal of Freedom, the nation's highest civilian decoration. At a ceremony on January 16, 1981, President Jimmy Carter presented the medal to a group of individuals that included, among others, newscaster Walter Cronkite, actor Kirk Douglas, politician Edmund Muskie, and Supreme Court Justice Earl Warren. (On a side note, President Carter's wife, First Lady Rosalyn Carter, served on the Menninger board of trustees and established a task force to study mental health care during her husband's presidency.)

Because Karl was unable to attend the ceremony, my brother accepted the medal from Carter. The President's comments at the ceremony were:

> Dr. Menninger, as you may have anticipated, is busy enhancing the mental treatment qualities of this nation. He's on the West Coast, and, honored by this award, of course, he still asked that he be excused so he could continue his work uninterrupted. A not-so-valuable nephew, Dr. Roy Menninger—[laughter]—has volunteered to come forward to accept the award for his uncle. And I would like to read the award now.

> *THE PRESIDENT OF THE UNITED STATES OF AMERICA AWARDS THIS PRESIDENTIAL MEDAL OF FREEDOM TO KARL MENNINGER*

> > Karl Menninger has taught us much about ourselves and our behavior. An acute observer and social critic, he has put into action what he has put onto paper. As an author and doctor, his works range from popular, written accounts of psychiatry to studies done in his own hospital, from creating homes for parentless children to

reforming the penal system. With the wisdom of his years, he truly does represent the ideas of another generation—one of the future, rather than of the past.

All of those in this room who have been interested in improving the quality of mental health of this nation have heard the name Karl Menninger since many years ago. He has been a pioneer, but as the closing phrase of this citation reminds us, he has never looked backward. He has always looked forward. His entire family has made the Menninger Clinic what it stands for, a powerful factor for a better life for Americans, not just in its own neighborhood but throughout the world. And with his research and with his writing, with his lecturing, with his training of other doctors, psychiatrists, psychologists, and others, he has literally transformed the mental health care attitudes of our great nation.

To Dr. Roy Menninger, I want to express my deep thanks for accepting this award on behalf of his uncle and express my thanks also to the entire Menninger family. It's with a great deal of pleasure that I present this award to Dr. Roy Menninger for Dr. Karl Menninger.

This is one of those, people would say, "Why wasn't it done long ago?"

Better late than never, Mr. President.

36

Assuming Leadership

After 11-½ long years on the sidelines, I returned to the Menninger team in 1981 as the head of the Law and Psychiatry department. Once I was back, Roy and I gradually discovered our ability to complement each other.

After such a long wait, things started to happen pretty fast. Within just a couple of years, I began to be given additional responsibilities.

In February of 1984, I was asked to take over direction of the entire Department of Education for the Menninger School of Psychiatry and Mental Health Sciences. This was a special honor. Not only would I be continuing the program my uncle Karl and my father took to such tremendous heights following World War II, but I would become dean of the school that had produced so many noteworthy practitioners in the field of psychiatry. The MSP became a sort of fraternity as it churned out hundreds of psychiatrists over the decades. Meetings of the various professional organizations felt a bit like alumni gatherings for the MSP graduates. That's not to mention all the psychologists, social workers, nurses, adjunctive therapists, and clergy who graduated from the school over the decades.

That opportunity was an honor that I was excited to accept. But it was just the beginning.

In September of that same year, after an exhaustive search by the Menninger Foundation Board of Directors, the board authorized Roy to offer the position of Executive Vice President and Chief of Staff of the Menninger Foundation to me. This position would make me head of all of Menninger's professional staff. I would remain the dean of the MSP and the head of Law and Psychiatry in addition to this new post.

This was a substantial challenge. It was essentially three different jobs. But I knew I could make it work. The circumstances finally allowed me to assume these various responsibilities, and I was determined to have the opportunity I had desired for so long.

When Roy offered me the position, he said (partly in jest but with grave implication), "If this doesn't work, we're both out of here."

I understood what my brother meant. Everything was riding on our ability to navigate the rapidly changing world of health care. The future of the Menninger Foundation would be in the hands of two brothers, just as it had been in the 1950s and 1960s. Karl's impetuosity had led to an emotional split and challenging adjustments in the direction of the organization in 1965.

It was crucial that we not repeat that history. We needed to work well together, to lead effectively in this new era.

There were a lot of great things happening at Menninger in the 1980s. By the mid-1980s, the $35 million building project at the West Campus was complete. The old Security Benefit Association hospital, orphanage, and home for elderly—purchased by the Menninger Foundation in 1959— was now fully modernized and adapted to the needs of the foundation. The old hospital building—modeled after Independence Hall in Philadelphia and visible across much of Topeka—remained the aesthetic centerpiece of the 28-building, 350-acre campus. The modernization consisted of several new or renovated buildings, a power plant, and a swimming pool.

With more than a decade of experience as CEO under his belt, Roy had grown in his understanding of, and ability to meet, the needs of the organization. He had developed a campaign to bring favorable media attention to Menninger. His efforts paid off. In the first half of the 1980s, *Family Circle*, *Good Housekeeping* and *Town & Country* each named Menninger the top psychiatric hospital in the United States. These were each great honors that helped bring new sources of revenue, as well as stimulated giving from donors.

One of my great pleasures during the 1980s was my assumption in 1984 of directorship of the annual Menninger Winter Psychiatry Conferences. These annual events, which began in the late 1970s, gathered psychiatrists from across the country for professional development in Vail, Colorado. Those who wished could hit the slopes during the day, then participate in high-quality training sessions led by prominent teachers and speakers in the mornings and evenings.

After hosting the conference in Vail the first year, we decided to move the event to a new location. We chose Park City, Utah.

Not being skiers, Connie and I enjoyed the breaks in the schedule by getting to know all the wonderful shops and galleries in the artsy little town. Connie and I fell so in love with Park City, in fact, that we decided, since we were spending time there each year, we should invest in a timeshare in the town. Thus, in the 1980s, Park City became more than just a work destination. It became a vacation home, a place we could visit with friends or gather with family. Our children and grandchildren took to it as a place for holidays. We delighted in visiting shop owners and artists with whom we built decades-long friendships. We continue to gather there every third year for a Menninger family reunion.

The conferences provided great material for publication in the *Bulletin of the Menninger Clinic*. The Menninger founders started publishing scholarly papers in the bulletin in 1936 in order to share what they learned, as well as to give others a forum to do the same. The quarterly "peer-review publication" continues to this day. As head of the Winter Psychiatry Conference, I was responsible for the content of the event, which was then published in one of the quarterly bulletins.

Unfortunately, during this era, Menninger faced new financial challenges, and thus new sources of funds were greatly needed. Insurance companies were paying less for long-term mental health services. To make up for loss of revenue, we were crisscrossing the country raising funds from donations and grants. The reality, however, was clear. The need for transition and diversification was imperative.

One of the Menninger Foundation's strategies during the mid- to late-80s was to branch out to other areas of the country. First, we collaborated with hospitals in Kansas City, St. Louis, and Albuquerque. Next, in 1987, we established the Menninger Services at St. Joseph's Hospital and Medical Center in Phoenix. In 1989, we established similar psychiatric services at hospitals in Burlingame, California, and Tampa, Florida. These ventures were intended to develop a network of Menninger treatment programs that would grow both the influence and the revenue of the foundation. We hoped this model would be an effective adaptation to the health care industry's shift toward outpatient and short-term hospitalization.

In the late 1980s, the financial challenges facing the Menninger

Foundation continued to mount, however. Issues of cost containment, quality assurance, and accreditation preoccupied me in my role as Chief of Staff.

I was well prepared to deal with a lack of resources from my years at the Topeka State Hospital. But the obvious difference was what could be done about it at the two different organizations. At the state hospital, it was a constant battle to petition for more funds when elected officials wanted to keep taxes as low as possible. The hospital administration was required to demonstrate its needs to governors and legislators in a manner that compelled them to provide adequate funding.

At Menninger, the battle to generate adequate funds to provide high-quality care involved a multi-pronged approach. You had to find the balance between cutting costs, increasing fees, and procuring grants and donations.

Wealthy individuals who donate large amounts to a business are often referred to as "angel investors." Menninger benefited in the mid-1980s from what seemed like divine intervention from one such angel.

Roy had developed a fundraising relationship with an oil heiress from Los Angeles named Liliore Green Rains. She was a bit of a recluse who didn't reveal a lot about what she intended to do with her $250 million after her death. Roy didn't like to ask for money. And as I mentioned in a previous chapter, my brother, therefore, didn't have any idea of her plans for the money and instead was disappointed he hadn't asked for "that $5,000 gift."

Needless to say, Roy undershot his expectation from Ms. Rains. After her death, she bequeathed $240 million to six different recipients, a list on which, quite unexpectedly, we were included. Four California colleges (including Stanford), the Los Angeles Hospital of the Good Shepherd, and the Menninger Foundation were each gifted $40 million. The stipulation placed on the two hospitals was that they spend only the interest made off the investments.

It was an incredible windfall. It did not, however, put Menninger on Easy Street. It forestalled some of our challenges, but it didn't fix them. The stress showed in my 1989 Christmas letter when we wrote to friends:

> A number of factors have contributed to this being
> one of Walt's most difficult years since assuming

responsibility as Chief of Staff for Menninger. It has been a time of "pruning" because of decreasing support for ╵long-term psychiatric treatment, a lower hospital census, reduced governmental support for education and research, and increasing regulation by government as well the Joint Commission on the Accreditation of Healthcare Organizations.

It's often said that there's no such thing as bad publicity. That might be true, I guess, but sometimes it's painful to have your dirty laundry aired in front of the world.

In 1988, *U.S. News & World Report* reached out to us for inclusion in a feature entitled "Amazing Families" that would consider the question, "Why do certain gifted parents produce gifted children?" The Menningers would be one of several families featured in short sketches.

Sounds flattering, right?

The writers of the two-page feature of our family chose to focus on the conflict between my uncle Karl and my father that ultimately caused the 1966 split at the foundation. At the time of the *U.S. News & World Report* feature, Roy was CEO, while I was Chief of Staff. The feature concluded with a few paragraphs about my ability (or lack thereof) to mesh with Roy:

> When Roy's youngest brother, Walt, also a psychiatrist, applied for the job of chief of staff, many feared the next generation would repeat the turmoil of the first. After all, Roy is even tempered like his father. Walt is quicker to anger and more intellectually driven, like Uncle Karl. It took years to persuade the trustees that their partnership could succeed. But at a meeting in 1984, the two publicly worked out their differences, and Walt moved into the office down the hall from Roy.
>
> So far there has been peace. Walt still feels like the younger brother, "Waiting for his turn on the swing." Roy senses that his sibling is always striving to surpass him.

> But they are able to talk in ways that Karl and Will, men
> of a less introspective generation, could not.

It was sad that, alongside the favorable features of several other prominent families, *U.S. News & World Report* chose to focus on the interpersonal conflicts experienced by our family. Undoubtedly, those conflicts were a part of our story. But they aren't the whole story. Roy and I were working well together in our respective leadership roles in the late 1980s. We were navigating very tumultuous times in health care nationwide and doing so amicably.

While *U.S. News & World Report* chose to focus on the Menninger family's internal rivalries, there were wonderful new developments taking place in my own home. Connie and I entered a new phase of life as, one by one, our children left home and began making their ways in the world.

Connie and I passed some significant milestones in the mid-80s. In 1985, Marian was the first of our children to marry, and in 1986 she gave birth to our first grandchild. At 55, I was old enough to be a grandfather, but I couldn't help but experience a bit of shock thinking of us as grandparents.

Because of the gap in our children's ages, we barely got our last child graduated from high school before we became grandparents. David graduated from Topeka High School in May of 1986. That was a significant milestone in and of itself. For 14 years, Connie and I had at least one child enrolled at the school from which my father, my two brothers, and I had all graduated.

In the fall of 1986, Connie and I delivered David to Stanford University. This was another significant milestone, about which I wrote in that year's Christmas card:

> We returned home to have the house to ourselves and
> be together alone for the first time in 29+ years. We're
> free to go places impulsively. When we put books or
> papers down, they stay where we leave them. The
> downstairs bathroom hand towels last for weeks. The

kitchen stays neat. The laundry is done with dispatch. Hooray for the empty nest!

Our children each found their careers and callings in their own time. More on that in an upcoming chapter. But an event of note during that phase of our lives was our son John's decision in 1984 to become a psychiatrist. That meant a third generation of Menningers would enter the field. John became the first fourth-generation Dr. Menninger in 1985 (there would eventually be others).

John's career decision led to a joyous occasion in 1987 when he and I attended the annual meeting of the Group for the Advancement of Psychiatry (GAP). There we were, father and son, participating in the organization my own father had helped form and served as its first president. I had attended my first GAP conference with my father in 1959.

While Roy and I struggled to move the Menninger Foundation forward in the 1980s, our uncle Karl remained the most celebrated of the Menningers.

In 1983, we dedicated a sculpture entitled "The Vital Balance" in Karl's honor on the Menninger Hospital's original location. Kansas artist John Whitfield's metal structure—standing 21 feet tall and weighing more than 3,000 pounds—took its name from a book published by my uncle in 1963. Whitfield attempted to portray in this beautiful sculpture "balance without symmetry."

In 1986, we celebrated the 40th anniversary of what was renamed in his honor the "Karl Menninger School of Psychiatry and Mental Health Sciences," of which I was then dean. At the time, the school had trained more than 2,000 mental health professionals, including about five percent of all psychiatrists in the country. It was a wonderful opportunity to celebrate the influence of a man who, for the past 20 years, had been on the fringe of the Menninger Foundation.

Karl had involved himself in other areas after he was removed from the lead role at Menninger. He started The Villages, a series of group homes for neglected children, and invested a lot of time and energy in that worthy cause.

He also continued to write influential books. After being displaced at the Foundation, he published *The Crime of Punishment* in 1968 and *Whatever Became of Sin* in 1973.

Even in his 90s, Uncle Karl was a force to be reckoned with. He was serving as chairman of the trustees of the Menninger Foundation in the 1980s, and in that role, he continuously tried to interject himself in the direction of the organization. But at that point, he wasn't really a helpful voice or guide.

His stature required that he be dealt with carefully. He was sort of a mythical figure by that point. He had been the professor to so many who respected and honored him. But to Roy, he was more of a challenge than a help.

The 1988 article in *U.S. News & World Report* described the challenges Karl posed to Roy.

> Will's oldest son, Roy, was elected foundation president in 1967 over objections of his uncle Karl, still chairman of the trustees. The patriarch has found it hard to forgive his nephew for taking the position he felt belonged to himself, or perhaps to his own son, Bob. "Karl felt that Roy never came to him for advice," says a longtime associate. "Roy would have liked advice but felt it was never forthcoming."

Certainly, the way that he was removed only to see the leadership of the Menninger Foundation shortly transferred to his much younger nephew was a bitter pill for our uncle. Karl's involvement in the foundation was a source of consternation for Roy. My brother, therefore, often asked me to run interference with Karl for him. He would ask me to talk to our uncle about sensitive subjects or to play sounding board for Karl's suggestions. Karl always had ideas of what the Menninger Foundation ought to be doing differently, and it was tough for Roy to tell him no.

Dr. Karl Menninger passed away on July 18, 1990, just four days short of his 97th birthday.

Like my father's death in 1966, my uncle's passing was an event of national interest. Here are some excerpts from his *New York Times* obituary:

> One of the first physicians in the United States to receive psychoanalytic training, he held certificate No. 1 from the Chicago Psychoanalytic Institute. But his views sometimes ran counter to accepted Freudian wisdom.
>
> While Dr. Menninger emphasized creating a humane environment for patients to live in, Freud limited treatment to the therapy session itself.
>
> Dr. Menninger took it as an article of faith that psychiatric treatment, in the proper circumstances, was helpful for virtually every emotionally disturbed individual. Dr. Menninger felt that an absence of parental love accounted for much individual destructiveness and mental illness. He carried this concept into a study of crime, in which he contended that most crime was a stage of mental or emotional sickness and should be treated as such. He felt that imprisonment without such treatment was virtually useless in curbing antisocial behavior.
>
> With patients and in his books, Dr. Menninger conveyed the impression of being a father figure, but a benevolent rather than an authoritarian one. He seemed to hold out hope that the afflicted could learn to cope with themselves and surmount their problems.
>
> This, combined with his emphasis on society's role in emotional illness, gave him a wide reputation as a humanist. In the opinion of many colleagues, Dr. Menninger had the distinction of seeing patients as human beings with mistaken ideas about how to live and to treat them accordingly.
>
> One of Dr. Menninger's accomplishments was explaining psychiatry to the public. Although the chief hypotheses of Freud were more than a quarter-century old when Dr. Menninger began to expound them, knowledge of them was confined to a small group of Americans. To

the general public, the mentally ill or emotionally disturbed were often "lunatic" to be confined in insane asylums.

Dr. Menninger had a hand in changing those conceptions through his papers, articles, and books, some of which became bestsellers. His success as an expounder was unintentional. His first book, "The Human Mind," was written for medical students. But when it was published in 1930, it caught the attention of thousands of lay readers, to whom it explained psychiatry as a relatively uncomplicated method of helping the disturbed.

Although Dr. Karl liked to say that he was "more Freudian than Freud," he was very elastic in his approach. He was the clinic's chief of staff for many years, while Dr. Will, before his death in 1966, was responsible for the clinic's organization. Dr. Karl often emphasized that in the treatment of patients there was no commitment to any one form of therapy. There was constant examination and re-examination of successes and failures, with Dr. Karl asking at staff conferences: "What do we know? How can we be sure?"

It was in this spirit that he was disinclined to classify patients on rigid diagnostic lines. Instead, he believed that virtually any emotional disturbance would yield to a loving, caring environment. Summing up these views a couple of years ago, Dr. Francis J. Braceland, a fellow psychiatrist, wrote that Karl Menninger saw "patients not as bearers of bizarre diseases, but rather as human beings, somewhat isolated from their fellow men, harassed by faulty techniques of living and making awkward maneuvers to keep themselves emotionally intact."

In another divergence from Freud, who felt emotional illness chiefly resulted from conflicts in the mind, Dr. Menninger argued that such illness was often induced by society. "It should be a help," he said over and over, "for any people to be getting three square meals a day and to know that there is opportunity ahead – things to be done, land to be turned, things to build." But he never spoke of cures or panaceas, but rather of helping patients to find "a caring environment" in which to work out their potential for creativity.

Dr. Menninger's interests were as wide-ranging and as eclectic as his psychiatry. At one time he belonged to a number of sociology organizations, the American Indian Defense Association, the Kansas State Historical Society, the American League to Abolish Capital Punishment, the Planned Parenthood Federation, and the Council on Freedom From Censorship.

"Nothing of human concern is really outside psychiatry," he remarked, "so, in one sense, I have no hobbies; they are all part of my work."

He is survived by his wife; their daughter, Rosemary, of Topeka; three children by his first marriage. Dr. Robert of Topeka, Martha Nichols of Cheyenne, Wyo., and Julia Gottesman of Sierra Madre, Calif.; a brother, Edwin, of Lillington, N.C., and nine grandchildren.

———————————————

Growing up observing an individual in personal settings, living and working closely to him for many years, you are permitted to see both his admirable character traits and his foibles. Between work and family interactions, I had an intimate view of my uncle Karl for more than 50 years. My recollections in this memoir about my uncle may have seemed a bit rough at times. It's certainly not my intention to demean the legacy or impugn the character of the great psychiatrist.

There's no question, Dr. Karl was one of the most important people in the world of mental health care—indeed in all of medicine—in history. For that matter, he is one of the most noteworthy Americans of the twentieth century. His contributions were immeasurable.

The people who knew him understood that he could be acerbic. He had a temper. Intentionally or accidentally, he could leave people feeling wounded by his words. But those same people knew he cared deeply for the hurting and disenfranchised, particularly the mentally challenged. He helped so many people, not just through his teaching, writing, and counseling, but through his community activism and promotion of social causes.

I have been known to say of my uncle Karl that "when he was good, he was very good. But when he was bad, he was awful." I say that about his interpersonal skills. When it comes to his insight and ability to communicate mental health concepts, he was not just good. He was brilliant.

I will conclude my observations of my uncle with perhaps his most famous and astute depiction of the mental health struggle, from his 1930 book *The Human Mind*:

> When a trout rising to a fly gets hooked on a line and finds himself unable to swim about freely, he begins with a fight which results in struggles and splashes and sometimes an escape. Often, of course, the situation is too tough for him.
>
> In the same way, the human being struggles with his environment and with the hooks that catch him.
>
> Sometimes he masters his difficulties; sometimes they are too much for him.
>
> His struggles are all that the world sees and it naturally misunderstands them. It is hard for a free fish to understand what is happening to a hooked one.

———————————•———————————

Although Karl's influence on the Menninger Foundation had been minimal for nearly 25 years, his death was nonetheless monumental in the history of the organization. At that time, a document surfaced that was authored in 1953 by the three founders of the Menninger Clinic—C.F., Will and Karl—just prior to the passing of my grandfather. It was sealed until "the death of all three of us."

The existence of the theretofore unopened letter hadn't exactly been forgotten to the Foundation. But no one had paid it much thought over the 37 years since its composition. When it was brought to me, still unopened, on the day of Karl's passing, I was surprised. I had no knowledge of it. It had been in the safe in the business office. Roy was away on business when someone showed up at my office with the envelope.

Instantly upon reading the letter, I recognized its significance. The letter was a rededication of the organization to its mission. The eloquent 22-page statement was no less relevant than when it was written:

> It has been our belief and practice since the inception of the Menninger Clinic that only scientific medicine of the highest standard should be practiced in this Clinic... The general idea that doctors should confer with each other, that two heads are better than one, and perhaps three better than two, that teamwork was essential to the best practice of the complicated science of medicine— this we have believed in and we believe in still...
>
> Our work has been and we believe always should be "patient-centered." By this we mean that the physician's chief responsibility is to help the individual who comes to us needing help. The work of the Foundation in terms of education and research is very important, but they are in essence by-products of our physicians' responsibility to help the patient in the most effective way...
>
> A certain spirit develops in an organization, and this spirit has a kind of immortality of its own. Dedication to the relief of human suffering does not appeal to little people. The kind of workers that walked under the trees and sat in the rooms of this institution have long since been infected with an idealism and purpose which will carry on long after all of us have fallen asleep.

Though the text bore Karl's writing style, the letter conveyed the passion of my grandfather for personal attention and empathy for the patient. It certainly was consistent with my father's dedication to collaboration and the familial spirit of the organization. It was like a letter from the grave, bearing the passions and wisdom of each great doctor. Recognizing the significance of this message, we printed copies and circulated the message widely as a recommitment of the Menninger Foundation to the mission of its founders.

While my load at the Menninger Foundation increased dramatically throughout the 1980s, I still found time for some "extracurriculars."

In 1987, I co-chaired a committee of the American Psychiatric Association on the chronically mentally ill. We hosted a conference in Topeka at which some fine research was presented. This material was subsequently published by the American Psychiatric Press in a book I co-edited entitled *The Chronic Mental Patient*.

I somehow made time for several organizational involvements, including: Chair of the Committee on Mental Health Services of the Group for the Advancement of Psychiatry; Chair of the Committee on Psychoanalysis, Community and Society of the American Psychoanalytic Association; and Chair of the Research Advisory Committee of the U.S. Secret Service. My work in the field of criminal justice continued as well. I chaired the Kansas Governor's Criminal Justice Advisory Commission and served on an ad hoc committee under the Federal Sentencing Commission to research alternatives to imprisonment.

For a ten-year stretch beginning in 1989, I served as Distinguished Visiting Professor for the Wilford Hall Air Force Medical Center at San Antonio, Texas. I would spend a week each year consulting with the psychiatric staff at Wilford Hall about their programs. I always find it humorous when I think about my father's remarks when I told him I planned to join the Air Force, "Why didn't you ask me? Air Force psychiatry is terrible." I didn't find it to be that in 1989. Quite to the contrary, I was greatly impressed with their programs, and I enjoyed all my interactions with Air Force medical staff.

It just so happened that my service in this role coincided with the Gulf War. I was pleased to assist in the readiness of the U.S. military for casualties of this modern war. It was so unlike the war in which my father engaged in the 1940s, but yet I took pride knowing I was making small strides in his enormous footsteps.

I wrote at the time, "With all the anxiety in anticipation of the war in the Gulf, it was impressive to review, with the psychiatric residents and staff, the still relevant insights from writings by my father about lessons learned by psychiatry during WWII."

And the family involvement in the field of psychiatry continued in the early 1990s. I mentioned my pleasure in being joined by my son John at a 1987 convention of psychiatrists. That joy was increased exponentially at the 1991 convention of the American Psychiatric Association, which was attended by not just John but his wife Claire (who was resident representative of the Colorado Psychiatric Society Executive Committee), and my daughter Eliza, who completed her psychiatric residency at McLean Hospital in Massachusetts that year. The Menningers were in full force at that convention as it was attended by Roy and his son Brent as well as by Karl's son Bob.

In 1992, I was presented the American Psychiatric Association's Administrative Psychiatry Award at that organization's meeting in Washington, D.C. I delivered the award lecture "Hope & Morale: Critical Elements in Organizational Function."

The previous year, I received a special recognition from the Menninger School of Psychiatry which seemed to cement my standing within the Menninger Foundation. I was honored at the commencement of the MSP with the school's Distinguished Alumnus Award. It was one more wonderful event in my return to the Menninger organization a decade earlier.

Happy as I was to be so involved in the Menninger organization in the early 1990s, there were even brighter lights, and darker clouds, looming on the horizon.

37

CEO

That letter written in 1953 by my grandfather C.F. Menninger and his sons Karl and Will, opened upon Karl's death in 1990, reaffirmed the mission of the Menninger Foundation: "To be a national resource providing psychiatric care and treatment of the highest standard, searching for new knowledge and better understanding of mental illness and human behavior, teaching what we know and what we learn, and applying this knowledge in useful ways to promote individual growth and better mental health."

The statement noted that the organization had, due in part to necessity, evolved over time: "The relative emphasis on various aspects of our work (had) changed several times." The message stated that more change would be inevitable and, indeed, necessary if the foundation were to continue as a leader in the field of mental health. The three patriarchs wrote: "We are more than willing to leave it in the hands of those whom we have taught and counseled and guided the best we could to use their discretion, dignity, sincerity, and idealism in formulating the expansion after we are no longer here to influence it."

In whose hands was the organization at the time of Karl's death? Who would be in the positions of leadership, having been taught, counseled, and guided by the patriarchs, to guide it into this new era?

None other than my brother Roy and me.

Our goal was clearly articulated by our predecessors—to be a premier provider of psychiatric services with an international reputation for quality. Our values were established: caring, service, integrity, initiative, and hope.

The structure was built. Now fully consolidated at the 310-acre West Campus in Topeka, Menninger had 1,050 employees and a $58 million annual budget in 1990.

The problem, unfortunately, was that the times were changing. The Menninger Foundation faced considerable challenges as it entered the

1990s.

In the 1980s, tremendous inflation in the costs of health care prompted a focus on containing or reducing the most expensive part of care—hospitalization. The across-the-board emphasis on reduction in length of hospitalizations applied to psychiatric care. This was particularly challenging to the Menninger Hospital, which specialized in treating patients who had not responded to treatment elsewhere by engaging them for extended periods of hospitalization. By the end of the decade, in spite of a significant increase in hospital admissions, Menninger was experiencing a substantial reduction in the patient average length of stay and total hospital days. This resulted in a serious economic challenge.

In the early 1990s, we tried to adapt to the changing economic environment by discontinuing or reducing services for which there was no reimbursement. Unfunded research was reduced. We tried innovative programs which we marketed to organizations, businesses, and individuals with a capacity to self-pay. Partnerships were developed with providers in cities across the country. We also managed behavioral healthcare services and provided employee assistance across the country through a program called Menninger Care Systems. The Menninger School of Psychiatry, over which I served as dean, continued to be a preeminent training center.

We did all we could to procure donations and grants to supplement the organization's income. But still, our economic challenges persisted. I turned 60 in 1991. At a time when many men are contemplating retirements full of vacations, golf, and grandchildren, I was in the fight for the survival of Menninger. The stakes would be raised even further in 1993.

I had spent the last quarter of a century looking forward to "my turn on the swing."

That turn came in the spring of 1993. The Associated Press announced on May 3:

> Dr. W. Walter Menninger will succeed his brother,
> Dr. Roy W. Menninger, as president and chief executive
> officer of Menninger on July 1, the organization

announced Saturday.

Walter Menninger will become the fifth CEO in the 68-year history of Menninger, the internationally known psychiatric center for treatment, education, and prevention of mental illness.

Walter Menninger, 61, was elected by the trustee board of directors of The Menninger Foundation to replace Roy Menninger, 66, who will remain chairman of the trustees after 26 years as president and CEO.

"This transition assures the continuation of our tradition of strong leadership to provide the highest quality psychiatric care and support for our mission" said Thomas Clevenger, chairman of the Menninger Foundation board.

I know Roy was not happy about this decision by the trustees. He would have liked to remain the organizational head for life. I'm not sure what all went into the decision, but they requested he step down.

As mentioned in the Associated Press article, Roy was 66 at the time of the decision by the trustees. I don't think their decision was based on his age. Roy was still relatively energetic and healthy. I think it had more to do with the new types of challenges facing the organization and the need for fresh ideas. I believe it may have been a function of how long he'd held the post. The optimal tenure of a CEO is eight to 11 years. In 11 years, you're going to do what you can do. After that amount of time, you need to step aside and let new blood come in and move forward.

The trustees knew me. They had observed my work. They believed I was ready. I became the fifth Menninger to head the organization.

I've mentioned numerous times in this book that my brother perceived me as a threat and therefore maneuvered to have me work elsewhere. I've mentioned my desire to put my own stamp on the organization. But there are two things I don't want to suggest: 1) convey the idea that Roy was an ineffective CEO, and 2) give the impression that Roy and I didn't work together effectively or relate well to each other as brothers.

Roy is to be credited as CEO for healing the divisions within the organization and winning people over to his leadership. When Roy took over as CEO in 1967, there was a lot of distrust, competition, and fear within the ranks. He had to convince the staff that he could provide guidance and vision without Karl's impetuosity. He stepped in at a very precarious time in the history of the organization and smoothed the waters, earning the respect of the staff in due time. He deserves great credit for making the organization run effectively for a quarter of a century. He was always a patient and gracious leader who was loved and appreciated by the staff of Menninger.

During the 11 years that I worked at Topeka State Hospital, I remained connected to Menninger as a supervisor of MSP residents, an instructor at the school, and fundraiser for the foundation. Understanding the delicacy of the situation, I never overplayed my hand or asserted influence. I let the situation run its course. Once I was brought back to Menninger in 1981, I continued to "stay in my lane," never wanting to cause Roy to feel challenged. Our personal relationship never wavered. As I gradually took over more responsibility, first as Director of Education and then as Chief of Staff, we kept a healthy balance as colleagues and brothers.

Finally, the opportunity which I'd desired for so long had arrived. It wasn't that I wanted to shove my brother aside. We had, in fact, worked together surprisingly well for the past 12 years, including nine years in which I served directly under him as the clinic Chief of Staff. We'd gotten along particularly well when you consider the financial pressure we'd been under.

I was no Pollyanna. There was no hiding from the facts. The impact of the dramatic change in hospital occupancy had forced a 17 percent reduction in Menninger personnel—realized through early retirements and job elimination—over an 18-month period spanning 1992 and 1993. That's the situation I inherited as the new CEO.

I put together a management team of leaders I trusted and set to work. Determined to improve the foundation's finances, we acted aggressively.

We sought to develop new alliances and to strengthen some programs while discontinuing others that were no longer relevant or economically viable. We beat the bushes in expanded fundraising efforts. And we cut expenses everywhere possible.

I loved the work. I can honestly say that, despite the challenges we faced, I woke up every day excited to face them. I felt confident in my ability. And even more than that, I felt confident in the abilities of the people who worked at Menninger. The people were marvelous, deeply committed, ethical, competent, even brilliant. I'd watched the management styles of both Karl and my father and tried to glean strengths from them both. The most important thing I could do was be humble and listen. I believed that if I just trusted people and gave them the space they needed, they could do their jobs effectively.

Of course, some oversight is required in every organization. I learned a tough lesson about assessing those who report to you. Something I misjudged was the accuracy of assessment you have of a direct report. In one case, I discovered that a key director would make decisions and set things in motion, then backtrack, leaving the people beneath him in the lurch. I only discovered the degree to which this was happening after the fact from the people who reported to him. It illustrated to me the importance of getting honest and accurate information when something isn't right. It's one of the greatest challenges that face CEOs.

I was blessed in my new position to have the continued assistance of my longtime secretary Mary Donohue. Having made each transition with me—from the state hospital throughout the 1970s to each step up the ladder at Menninger in the 1980s and 1990s—she understood how to help me succeed. She kept my calendar and maximized my time, organized my files, and kept me on top of paperwork, and generally made sure I was paying attention to the right things at the right times. I couldn't have accomplished what I did without her help. She was aware of organizational priorities, and she also helped when personal matters required my attention while at work.

One of the biggest differences between Roy and me was that he hated to make decisions. He wanted the group to make decisions. But groups don't make decisions. I felt like I could make some of the tough choices that a head of an organization must make. That would allow us to pivot more efficiently and to do some things that weren't necessarily popular but needed to be done. I was never bothered by the pressure of making decisions, and I think I acted diplomatically and communicated effectively when I had to make a decision that some people didn't like.

I wasn't ever bothered by any crisis that came up. To me, it was never that big a deal. Issues came up, and we just used good judgement to address them. I was not paralyzed by crisis. To be able to keep things going smoothly and respond to issues was actually quite enjoyable.

That's not to imply I was a flawless leader. Quite the opposite. The things you remember are when you put your foot in your mouth. I recall an instance when a Menninger psychoanalyst made a statement, and I made a critical comment in response. I realized that what I had said came across as arrogant and dismissive. I went to apologize to him for my impetuous observation. I remember being irritated at myself, realizing, *You can't do things like that. These are people with pride that you have to respect.* Fortunately, those instances were few and far between, but they did happen.

Conversely, the fun part of the job was making people feel good about their work, recognizing their efforts, and giving them credit. As head of the organization, I was often given credit for other people's great work. I tried at every turn to remind the public that the organization was a collection of talented and well-meaning individuals. And I enjoyed being a conduit for the praise and thanks that was rightfully due the staff. It gave me great pleasure to bring to the staff those messages of appreciation from the public.

The Menninger Foundation faced some stiff challenges, but we addressed them as best we knew how. Our efforts were not without effect.

A confirmation of our success was received in 1996 when the Menninger Hospital was ranked first among psychiatric institutions in that year's *US News & World Report* survey of top hospitals. We had previously been ranked second behind McLean Hospital in Massachusetts. It was a gratifying acknowledgement of not just Menninger's great tradition of quality care but an affirmation that we were keeping up with the times, adapting to changes in health care. We were making significant improvement in the bottom line by re-engineering our methods, enacting a regional strategic plan, and growing our endowment. I crisscrossed the country meeting with donors.

Two significant anniversaries were recognized in 1996.

In June, the MSP celebrated its 50th anniversary. We held a celebration complete with speeches and dedications in honor of the occasion. Jon G. Allen, at the time senior staff psychologist at the Menninger Clinic, wrote a tribute to the MSP tradition:

> There was an uncommon intellectual kindling that has left a lasting mark on psychiatry and more broadly, on all the mental health disciplines. This golden anniversary provided an opportunity for rekindling memories of a "golden age" that has become history. But the golden anniversary also provided an opportunity for reaffirmation of values that grow more precious in the current climate of cost cutting, downsizing, hospital closings, brief treatment, and increasingly depersonalized practice.

It was a milepost for the organization. The MSP was credited with training about seven percent of psychiatrists in the U.S. over the past five decades, not to mention the scores of psychologists, therapists, nurses, and other clinicians it produced. The school was born out of necessity when the country faced a crisis of health care following World War II. The Menninger Foundation had responded in the time of need, expanding overnight from a small, somewhat informal training program, to a well-structured, innovative program capable of training exponentially more mental health professionals than any other program in the world.

It was an equally meaningful recognition of the MSP's continued relevance. The school continued to train mental health professionals capable of serving in the new world of care. Allen wrote of recent graduates:

> ...these scholars and clinicians continue to pursue agendas for mental health that were first being forged a half-century ago in the KMSP. All have left The Menninger Clinic for distinguished careers elsewhere.

A few months later, I passed a significant mile marker in my own life. I turned 65 that October. I didn't feel old or ready to retire. I felt like I was just hitting my stride, three years into my tenure as CEO of the Menninger Foundation. Perhaps having children under my roof into my late 50s helped me feel young. Maybe Connie and I were just too busy to think about getting old.

But I think my energy and ambition were fueled by my responsibilities at Menninger. I felt as though I was finally doing what I had longed for so many years to do. For years I had lived by that profound advice given by my medical professor, Dr. Felix Wroblewski, "It's more important in life to like what you do than to do what you like." But now, in my 60s, I was finally doing what I liked, what I had so long desired the opportunity to do. There were always problems to solve, issues to consider, and new challenges to conquer. It was invigorating.

But turning 65 didn't happen without some acknowledgment of my mortality. Long range planning was essential. We hired staff that we hoped would provide a bridge to the future. Recalling the letter penned by my grandfather, father, and uncle which we opened in 1990, I hoped to place Menninger "in the hands of those whom we have taught and counseled and guided the best we could to use their discretion, dignity, sincerity, and idealism in formulating the expansion after we are no longer here to influence it."

———————————•———————————

Some of the extra-curricular activity that I'd so enjoyed over the years was reduced out of necessity in the 1990s. My focus as CEO had to be almost entirely on the Menninger Foundation.

By the latter half of the decade, our children were scattered all over the U.S. and the majority of our vacation time was spent traveling to see them. Throughout the decade we turned trips to Stanford, California, Park City, Utah, and other interesting sites into short working vacations. We splurged on one great excursion in August of 1997, when Connie and I enjoyed a marvelous Trans-Canada rail journey from Vancouver to Montreal on the American Orient Express, preceded by visits to Seattle and Victoria, British Columbia.

One professional commitment that was also a personal thrill was an opportunity to lecture at medical schools in Saudi Arabia, Qatar, and the United Arab Emirates in 1996 and 1997. Some members of Saudi royal families had come to Menninger for treatment over the years. As we were looking for opportunities to expand, we thought it made sense to try to explore further relationships with the Saudis in the Middle East. I made my first trip to lecture in Riyadh and in eastern Saudi Arabia, and to connect with people with whom we'd already built relationships. The things you imagine about the wealth of the Saudi royalty are true. There is a lot of royalty there and I was treated like royalty myself.

I made a second trip to Qatar and the United Arab Emirates the next year. Unfortunately, we were never able to work out an arrangement that made financial sense. It was like all our other outside ventures. They inevitably meant spending more money than we made. We had to abandon the goal of a presence in the Middle East, but not without plenty of effort to explore the possibility.

I received a couple of honors in the late 1990s that were particularly gratifying. First, in 1996, I was elected to the Topeka High School Hall of Fame, joining my father and Uncle Karl. It's interesting. No matter what accolades one receives in life, recognition from one's childhood friends and adolescent peers seems particularly sweet. I bore such happy memories from my youth and held my school and classmates in such high regard, it was especially humbling and gratifying to receive such an honor. Topeka High hosted an "Ultimate Reunion" in October of 1997 to celebrate the school's 125th year. In remarks at a Hall of Fame luncheon, I read from articles in the student newspaper from when I served as editor in 1948.

In 1997, I received a commendation from the Topeka Police Department for 30 years of service. Over those three decades, I had helped the police force by interviewing applicants, teaching recruits, educating the staff in various matters of psychology, and responding to emergency calls after critical incidents. My service to the Topeka police would continue for several more years. Of all my volunteer efforts over the years, my work with the Topeka police was particularly rewarding.

In 1998, harkening back to my work three decades earlier with the Violence Commission, I chaired and presented at the Symposium on Violence and Mental Illness at the American Psychiatric Association Institute on Psychiatric Services. Problems of violence hadn't improved much in 30 years, and psychiatrists continued to grapple with this issue. The next year, at the invitation of Dr. Rod Munoz, president of the APA, I delivered the William C. Menninger lecture at the Convocation of Fellows during the association's annual meeting in Washington, D.C. in late May.

At the close of the decade, the Shawnee County Medical Society surprised me with a recognition for "Outstanding Achievement." This was another opportunity to reflect not just on my own life, but my family history. My grandfather had moved to Shawnee County from nearby Holton in 1889—about 110 years earlier—to begin his Topeka-based medical practice. My uncle and my father helped him develop a world-renowned psychiatric clinic, effectively turning Topeka into the "Psychiatric Capital of the United States."

I hoped I had done a worthy job of adding to that legacy.

———————•———————

The final few years of the 1990s looked to have the Menninger Foundation heading in a good direction. The hospital served more patients in 1997 than it had in the previous six years. We launched the Menninger Corporation, which was a taxable subsidiary engaging in mental health related projects of employee assistance and managed behavioral healthcare in the for-profit arena.

We understood clearly the challenge facing all mental healthcare providers at that time—seeing more patients for shorter periods of time while receiving less compensation for those services. By the end of the decade, we had seen a fourfold increase in admissions, but a sevenfold decrease in length of stay—a reduction from five months to just two to three weeks on average. This resulted in a 39 percent reduction in total hospital days and a sixfold increase in contractual adjustments (which reduced income). During this same period, there was a 173 percent increase in employee salaries.

It was time to make some aggressive moves in response to those challenges. In 1998, the Menninger trustees endorsed a plan developed by management to reconfigure our operations in Topeka and reduce overhead expenses. We would continue specialized treatment programs for professionals in crisis and difficult treatment problems on the Topeka campus. We intended to expand our regional presence and remain committed to excellence in our programs of education and research.

As CEO, I balanced administration, trustee relations, fund raising, clinical consultation, teaching, and clinical research as best I could.

I finally had my dream job. But the conditions were hardly a thing of dreams. Reality forced many painful decisions.

I remember thinking in the mid-1990s that while others our age were taking life easier, I was working harder than ever. I continued to absorb responsibilities as one by one my peers at Menninger retired. I felt, as Lewis Carroll wrote, that "the hurrier I go, the behinder I get."

Thankfully, I had a wonderful family, great friends, and the perfect partner to lean on.

-38-

The Love of My Life

An African proverb states "If you want to go fast, go alone. If you want to go far, go together."

How sad it would be to scale a great height or complete a long race, only to discover that you had no one there to share it with. As I reflect on the trials and triumphs of my life, the best thing I can say is that I was never alone.

In this book, there is, unfortunately, not nearly enough room to mention all the people who have made my life interesting and enjoyable. Teachers, classmates, co-workers, and friends have always been the spice of life, as well as my support in times of need.

Certainly, I am grateful to have had loving and supportive parents. I grew up in a happy home with two older brothers to look up to. And my own children and familial relatives are particularly dear. I am blessed beyond measure by my burgeoning brood of descendants.

But there has always been, without a doubt, only one true "love of my life."

As I described early in this memoir, I was taken instantly by the attractive, self-confident, and driven young woman I encountered in the business office of *The Stanford Daily* in the spring of 1950. As freshmen at college, Connie and I were both in relationships at the time, but the spark of attraction inevitably developed into a flame. Finally, one evening, we fell into each other's arms and confessed our mutual affection. From that moment, we were inseparable. We spent three glorious years as a couple at Stanford before tying the knot and embarking on a great adventure together. Connie was always my support, my counterbalance, and my best friend. She encouraged my endeavors and provided sound advice. She was always honest with me and knew how to gently redirect me when necessary. We shared many interests, so we never tired of each other's company.

Our relationship wasn't without challenges and hardships, but there was never a question in my mind that Connie was my soulmate.

———————————————

Born in Newton, Massachusetts on November 20, 1931, Connie was less than a month younger than I. Her youth in the Boston suburbs was interrupted prior to entering elementary school when she moved with her family to Pittsburg, Texas, where her parents assumed the management of a family-owned box and basket making factory. She spent just a few years of her youth in Texas, but that experience was not without effect. I believe it showed Connie that the world was much bigger than the plush Boston suburbs. She learned to love the outdoors, animals, and physical activity. Connie had a pony and loved to ride horses. After returning to Massachusetts, Connie learned to play the piano and the accordion. She learned to cook and sew and loved just about any type of activity that got her hands dirty.

My wife's red hair was a declaration of her fiery disposition. Connie had a passion for justice and fairness and wasn't afraid to stand up for her beliefs. She was an independent thinker from day one, which often led her to divert from the pack. Connie was much more about substance than style. She always chose as her friends those people who were doing something. When the day came for her to be celebrated with the other young debutantes of suburban Boston, she chose instead to attend a Red Sox game with a few friends.

She wasn't the least bit afraid to leave her comfortable life in the Northeast for college on the West Coast. She jumped right into activity on campus at Stanford. As a business major, she saw an opportunity for hands-on experience in the business office of *The Stanford Daily*. That is where we first crossed paths, where our love story began.

———————————————

You may have noted that, in the recounting of memories of my life, I stopped describing Connie's activities around 1970. That was a purposeful decision. I felt it would do her greater justice if I described her activities and accomplishments in a more seamless manner, rather than sprinkling them amongst the accounts of my experiences.

Connie was, above all else, a devoted wife and mother. We married in an era when it was common for women to stay at home when their children were small, rather than working outside the home. So, my description of our family life during the 1960s portrays Connie as the classic homemaker, and indeed she was that. Even despite our several moves during the early 1960s, she made sure our home was full of love and comfort. Connie took great joy in her children. Her delightful laugh could descend to red-faced snorting and coughing when playing with the kids and relishing their antics.

Connie was a woman of many talents. In addition to cooking, cleaning, sewing, and educating our children, she was a leader and an organizer of people. Those skills were displayed in the 1960s when she oversaw the remodeling of our house, helped lead the Cub Scouts, and made efforts (sadly unrealized) to develop an ice-skating rink in Topeka.

Those activities were precursors of greater things to come. The people who knew her during the early 1960s were aware that, in due time, Connie's talents would be applied to the greater community. But while our children were young, she focused her efforts on those closest to her. Connie had a natural gift for teaching, so she engaged in making sure our kids got the most out of their educational opportunities. She ensured that they had all the extra-curricular enrichment available—music and dance lessons, horse riding, and Scouting, for example.

A proud and protective mother to a fault, Connie was never afraid to pick up the phone and lodge a complaint or concern when it came to her children. God bless the Topeka school teachers and administrators who fielded calls from my wife. She more than made up for any headaches she caused with her volunteerism at the kids' schools, most notably Randolph Elementary. We served as co-presidents of the school's Parent Teacher Association and rallied parents to support improvements to the facility.

Tyra Manning, a teacher and later an administrator, would say that Connie showed her willingness to serve by saying, "How can I be of help?" "What may I do for your students?" and "I am here for you." That type of dedication to Topeka Public Schools would only continue to flourish in later years.

We weren't a wealthy family, so Connie cooked and sewed not just out of enjoyment, but as a way to provide. She might have been best known for her skills as a seamstress. Her inspiration for clothing items often came from popular catalogues. Particularly with our daughters, she would shuffle through the pages, asking, "Which ones do you like?" Then she would fashion by hand replicas of the most popular and stylish of items. She made clothes suitable for highly formal events like prom and college dances. The kids' Halloween costumes were always delightfully creative. Connie eventually would alter her own wedding dress (which her mother had previously worn in the 1920s) for our two daughters and one daughter-in-law to wear at their own weddings.

Our house was full of items Connie made—curtains, sofa cushion covers, redecorated couches. Seeing her practicality and creativity displayed throughout the house gave it warmth. Likewise, the homes of our children featured Connie's creative and practical handiwork. Connie's temper was on full display when she discovered while making draperies for one of the kids' homes that the tape measure she'd used had been stretched, resulting in uneven-length window coverings. Determined to exact some revenge, she cut the measuring tape into little bits.

If Connie had any talent that exceeded her sewing skill, it might be her culinary ability. Cooking for a family of eight wasn't the least bit daunting to her. On the contrary, our dinner table was a welcome place for guests. Any friend of our children who visited was invited to stay for dinner. For decades, Connie prepared a meal every Thursday for soloists in the church choir. High school students who attended science seminar lectures at Washburn University in the evenings frequently joined us for dinner during the 1970s and 1980s. And that's not to mention all the parties and meals provided for guests connected to work and our numerous community involvements.

Connie had a passion for baking breads, pastries, and pies. She was known for her Joe Frogger cookies, a type of cookie popular in New England flavored with molasses, rum, and spices, most notably ginger. Connie was also distinguished for the dozens of fruitcakes we mailed to friends across the country. I say "we," because the fruitcakes were a project that involved the entire family. Making them required an assembly line—we were all involved in cutting up candied fruit, chopping nuts, stirring vats of dough, and cutting pan liners from grocery bags.

Connie also called upon the children to help with making plum jam, a project that might have involved condoning petty theft by the kids. Connie's plum jam was in high demand. When the tree in our yard didn't produce enough plums, Connie sent the children foraging in other people's yards and on the Washburn University campus for more fruit. There were never any criminal charges brought against us. Perhaps Connie was rewarding the offended parties with some of the final product.

Aside from what the kids pilfered from the neighborhood, a large portion of the ingredients in Connie's cooking was raised under her watchful eye. She grew vegetables in our garden, giving the food an especially fresh taste. Connie also nurtured a dazzling array of flowers—marigolds, violets, lilacs, daffodils, crocuses, hyacinths, geraniums, and tulips. The children's tradition of making May Day baskets displayed their mother's green thumb.

As if six two-legged children weren't enough, Connie raised several four-legged babies. She was fond of French Poodles and honed the skill of clipping them in the classic style.

Connie was an active, committed woman focused on developing the community while raising her own children. She worked tirelessly to make Topeka a good place for them to grow up.

Connie's first foray into community activism saw her advocate for a community ice skating rink. Having grown up in Boston, she loved skating and wanted her children, as well as other Topekans, to have the chance to enjoy that activity. That goal was not achieved while our children were young, but Connie was undaunted. She enjoyed meeting people in the community and working toward a goal. That was just the start.

Connie's community leadership skills were fully tapped for the first time in 1967 when she volunteered for the Junior Great Books program in the Topeka Public Schools. Begun in the 1940s, the Great Books Program spawned a Junior Great Books program in the early 1960s to teach students in grades five through nine about high-quality literature. The program relied in part upon volunteers to engage students in activities fostering comprehension, critical thinking, speaking, listening, and writing skills. After an 18-hour training seminar, Connie began guiding students through the program, introducing them to the works of Homer, Aristotle, Swift, Thoreau, and many more. She loved the program's creative approach to interpreting the books.

Connie's leadership qualities soon led her to become coordinator of the program for all of Topeka's schools. She recruited, trained, and organized the volunteers. Her involvement in this program led her to build relationships with school leaders and volunteers across the community.

In 1968, Connie's passion for art led her to a new activity. She joined the board of the Mulvane Art Center at Washburn University.

These activities demonstrated that Connie could "bloom where she was planted." We already knew this was true because of how she thrived in her stint as a program analyst for NBC while I was in medical school in New York, made friends and integrated into the community while I worked for the Federal Bureau of prisons in El Reno, and navigated the unique social climate of Washington, D.C. when I worked there with the Peace Corps. Once she had her feet on the ground in Topeka, it was only a matter of time before she would become a force for good in the community.

I was aware of just how much Connie did to nurture our children and keep the family running while I focused on my responsibilities and travel for work. By the late 1960s, I was pleased to reciprocate. I gradually took on a supportive role in our home to allow Connie to become more engaged outside it. Our last child, David, was born in January of 1968. The other kids were becoming more self-sufficient, clearing the way for Connie to become more involved in the community later that year.

Her involvement in our kids' schools and her leadership of the Great Books Program made her a natural candidate to step in when a spot on the Topeka Public School Board of Education was unexpectedly vacated. Connie agreed not only to fill the seat temporarily, but to run for the vacancy in the November election. "Vote Menninger" signs suddenly appeared around the neighborhood.

Connie won the election, becoming the first woman in 20 years voted to the board. She attacked the new role with the same vigor that she applied in our home. She set out to visit all 50 schools in the district, in short order meeting as many people and learning as much about the district as possible.

It's interesting how often the issues I worked on and those that involved Connie were similar. She joined the school board at about the time I was finishing up my service to the Violence Commission. Soon Connie was looking at civil rights, education, and poverty issues similar to those that we dealt with on the commission. Next, Connie was appointed to a Kansas Association of School Boards' committee on sex education, a topic I taught at the Menninger School of Psychiatry in the early 1970s. A little later, Connie would engage in a study of civil rights in corrections (more on that in a minute), which was of course an area of focus throughout my career.

The overlap in our interests would indicate that not only were those hot topics of the time, but that Connie and I were generally of the same mind. But contrary to what you might expect, we rarely discussed these issues at home. We didn't share what we were learning with each other, and we never debated our opinions on the issues. Home was all about family.

Opportunities did present themselves for both of us to observe the other from the sideline. And sometimes the lines blurred a little. One of the most interesting of such occasions occurred when I was invited to speak to school board associations in a number of states, including Illinois.

While on the Topeka board, Connie was designated Regional Vice President for the Kansas Association of School Boards for 1972-73. In 1973, she traveled with me to Chicago, where I was to address a gathering of Illinois education leaders. Among the several thousand attendees was none other than Richard Daley, the longtime mayor of Chicago and one of the most prominent politicians in the country at the time. The title of my speech for the gathering at the Palmer House in downtown Chicago contained a mild profanity. I asked the people running the conference if that was a concern considering the mayor's attendance.

"Oh, don't worry about it. He never stays for the whole thing," they assured me.

Well, he did stay, and he was seated prominently for my talk. But my speech wasn't of much importance to him. His interest in me quickly vanished when he learned that I was accompanied by a member of the Topeka School Board. Never one to miss a chance to engage another elected official, Daley shifted his attention instantly to Connie. I was a nobody. She was the celebrity that night in his eyes.

Two of Connie's passions connected while she served on the school board—children and sewing. Connie became particularly involved in the local Head Start program, which provides free learning and development services to children ages birth to five from low-income families. It came to her attention that many of the children in the program did not have adequate winter clothing. Connie went to work mobilizing local knitters to meet the need. She started a personal tradition that continued for many years of recruiting knitters, providing them yarn and patterns, managing donations, and handling publicity for the annual mitten drives.

The mitten project is just one of many examples where Connie identified a need and rallied others to help meet it. She could be diplomatic or assertive as the situation demanded. To paraphrase a comment about Connie by Kansas education leader Susan Garlinghouse: "She always desired to lock arms rather than lock horns."

———————◆———————

Much as Connie desired to build bridges and bring people together, a clash in Topeka brought her time on the board of education to an end after just one term.

As everywhere, racial tensions ran high in Topeka in the 1960s and early 1970s. An NAACP survey of Black students in Topeka revealed that they perceived discrimination was limiting their opportunities to, among other things, win election to student government positions, the cheer squad, and drill team at their schools. The survey indicated that the students believed prejudice was demonstrated in classrooms as well. Observations of Black Culture Week in April of 1970 brought to a head some of their frustrations.

On that April 16, frustrated by a meeting with the principal of their school, Black students at Highland Park High School gathered in the school auditorium and set fire to the stage curtains. Theater sets, the stage floor, a grand piano, and theatrical equipment were also destroyed. The total damage was estimated at about $27,000. Those involved were suspended from school.

Subsequently, about 100 Black students walked out of the three Topeka high schools, boycotting classes. They demanded the reinstatement of the students responsible for the damage to the auditorium. They also sought the firing of 20 allegedly prejudiced teachers and administrators and the hiring of more Black educators. They demanded a review of school rules and policies.

The city that brought desegregation of schools to the nation via *Brown v. Board of Education* in 1954 was in turmoil. In hopes of calming the uproar, the school board agreed to suspend classes for several days. Black students and white students staged protests over their concerns, prompting the mayor of the city to publicly address disruption of the education environment.

Three days after the fire, nearly 1,000 people attended a chaotic meeting of the school board, which was moved at the last minute to the Topeka High auditorium to accommodate the crowd. Heated debate over school policies and students' right to protest ensued. As a member of the board, Connie watched as the board's president had his gavel stolen, then broken by angry attendees. Throughout the evening, he banged his name plate on the table, attempting to maintain some semblance of order.

Among the concerns brought forth by Black students was their perceived lack of programming in the school regarding issues of importance to them. They requested that some extra school assemblies be planned to address these topics. In an effort to foster positive dialogue, Connie met with some parents of Black students and assured them she would advocate for additional programs. She helped craft compromises that she hoped would appease both sides.

Connie's efforts were not well received. Her predominantly white district didn't agree with some of the policies in the compromise. She worked hard to regain the confidence of voters, but she was defeated in the November 1972 election.

Connie was understandably wounded by the voters' response. She believed she had done her best in response to a very difficult situation. She was disappointed, but her passion for education and for serving the community was not diminished.

When I experienced disappointments in my career, I usually found that other opportunities arose. Similarly, when Connie was voted off the Topeka Public School Board of Education, she found she had time to invest in other things. She remained active at church, serving as a ruling elder, holding a seat on the religious arts committee, and continuing to participate in choir. She led a summer choir camp. She devoted more time to volunteering at Topeka Civic Theater.

Two new opportunities arose in the mid-1970s. First, she became involved in the Topeka Community Resources Council, an entity that focuses on community planning of social services, legislation, public education, and welfare. It identifies gaps in available services and makes sure that various organizations are working toward the same goal. After serving as a board member of the organization from 1969-71, Connie rejoined the council in 1973. She was subsequently voted its president-elect for 1974-75, president for 1975-76, and treasurer for 1976-77.

In 1973, Connie was appointed to chair the Kansas State Advisory Committee to the U.S. Commission on Civil Rights. At the conclusion of her two-year term, she was reappointed as chairperson for two more years. This was a great honor and a special opportunity for Connie to participate in policy research. The group dug into two issues in particular during her time on the committee: women's rights and prisoner rights.

First, she held hearings that produced the "Inmate Rights and the Kansas Prison System" report in 1974, presenting the findings of the committee to state legislators. As I mentioned earlier, despite my background in the field of corrections, Connie and I didn't engage in a lot of discussion about the work of the committee. We left those things at work. When I came home, it was to be "Dad." She learned the issues of the Kansas prison system for herself and fought to ensure that inmates were treated justly and served effectively.

Next, the civil rights committee held hearings and issued a report on "The Availability of Credit to Kansas Women" in 1975. Amazingly, a Kansas woman couldn't receive her own credit card in the mid-1970s. Connie testified before legislative committees upon request for this topic as well.

Connie took on another women's rights issue in the late 1970s. She was appointed to the Defense Department Advisory Committee on Women in the Services (DACOWITS) in 1979. She served a three-year term on the committee, during which she visited McConnell Air Force Base and Fort Riley Army Base, both in Kansas, and the Air Force Academy in Colorado. The group studied various problems faced by women in the military. Connie was proud of the accomplishments during her term. Among many other things, DACOWITS furthered options for women in the military who wanted to develop skills besides traditional roles such as nursing, technical, and desk work.

I was proud to support Connie during these exciting experiences. So many times over the previous couple of decades, Connie had stood by my side, or covered home base, while I engaged in public activities. I enjoyed going to events and ceremonies as her companion, providing silent support.

Volunteerism wasn't Connie's sole occupation in the 1970s. The maturation of our children permitted Connie more time and freedom. She felt ready to accept her first full-time job in 20 years, should the right opportunity present itself.

As leaders of the choir at First Presbyterian Church, we hosted weekly meals for the members. One of the regulars at these gatherings was organist Dr. Robert Jacoby, a singer in the choir and a medical practitioner in Topeka. Jacoby had received a Robert Wood Johnson Foundation grant in 1975 to develop a family practice group, and he needed a grant administrator and office manager to get organized. Organization was one of Connie's strengths. Jacoby asked Connie if she would like to help him. We decided that the position was a good fit for Connie and for our family.

For five years, Connie helped Jacoby build his family practice group. She aided in the recruitment of new doctors, dealt with hospitals and grant administrators, and oversaw the office. Jacoby built a successful practice and would eventually be honored as Kansas Family Physician of the Year by the Kansas Academy of Family Physicians.

The diversity of Connie's experiences during that era included another foray into the medical field. She was named to the newly established board of overseers for the development of a medical school at Morehouse College in Atlanta. One of her colleagues on the board was Barbara Bush, whose husband, future president George H.W. Bush, was then director of the CIA.

Jacoby was a good friend and Connie enjoyed working for him. But by 1980, she was ready for a change. With kids in college and others looking to attend college soon, we decided to take a risk. We invested in a

Burger King franchise. Connie would help with marketing responsibilities for the restaurant. It was not one of our shining moments. The restaurant went bankrupt in 1981. We did the best we could to protect our family finances from the bankruptcy, but we couldn't avoid the damage entirely. Our attorney told us, "You're not rich enough for it not to affect you, but you have too much wealth to just disregard it." We had to make some tough decisions to settle the business expenses and put it behind us. We lost a fair amount of money. A few years earlier, we had purchased some rural property near Lake Perry, just northeast of Topeka. We had to sell that property to pay off the debt.

Some of the disappointments she experienced during the 1970s helped lead Connie to a turning point. The moment just so happened to come in a hospital.

39

Connie Menninger: Archivist, Historian

O n her 50th birthday, in November of 1981, Connie found herself hospitalized with cervical nerve root syndrome, a spinal condition that can produce pain, muscle weakness. and numbness in the shoulders and arms.

Our lives were complicated enough at that moment. Connie's father—a widower since 1974—had recently moved in with us. Our kids ranged from college to late grade school. We were still recovering from the failed Burger King experiment. I was pleased to have recently returned to work at Menninger, but my new job was keeping me very busy, and I was trying my best to step up inside the house to support Connie's work outside of it.

There's nothing like turning 50 in a hospital bed to make you think about life. Connie looked at me and said, "You may know what you want to do, but I don't know what I want to do."

Connie had dedicated herself to being a great wife, mother, and volunteer to numerous organizations. She found those activities to be fulfilling. But you can't blame her for wanting a career of her own. Her jobs at the medical clinic and at Burger King hadn't exactly scratched where she itched. Understandably, she desired something different in this new phase of her life. She was a smart, talented woman who wanted to make sure her skills were fully utilized in the years she had left.

Though she didn't know exactly what job she wanted, Connie did have some idea what she enjoyed. Connie loved history and had a passion for preserving it and passing it on. She also had a knack for organization. She had recently begun volunteering at the Shawnee County Historical Society and was serving on its board of trustees. That experience really piqued her interest. She believed it was a passion worth pursuing further. She decided to go back to school to get a master's degree in historical archives. It just so happened that the University of Kansas had recently developed a Masters in Historical Administration and Museum Studies

(MHAMS) program. She decided to apply.

From the first moment she made this decision, Connie had her eye on one particular project. The Menninger archives were in sorry shape. No professional attention had ever been applied to them. The director over the materials was not a trained archivist. When that person resigned in mid-1983, Connie saw an opportunity. She knew the history and the people of the organization. She was a natural fit for this project. She believed some technical training in archival research and preservation would prepare her for it. She enrolled in the program at Kansas University in 1983, hopeful that she would be allowed to take over the Menninger archives in due time.

It was not lost on her children that the acronym for the program— MHAMS—was homonymous with "mom's." She received quite a bit of ribbing around the house for being enrolled in the "moms" master's degree program.

While in the program, Connie interned at the Kansas State Historical Society (KSHS). She built strong friendships with the staff of the historical society and became one of their most valued volunteers. She also continued her volunteer work with the Shawnee County Historical Society.

As part of her studies, Connie made two presentations to the Midwest Archives Conference in October of 1984: a discussion of professional development opportunities for archivists and a presentation on the potential for railroad records. She created aids for research of the Arthur Capper senatorial papers, and for the history of Catholic education in Topeka. She created an oral history of a groundbreaking female railroad executive named Margaret Hauke, a fellow Kansan.

In 1985, Connie became the first graduate of the MHAMS program at KU. We were so proud of her for reinventing herself as a trained archivist at 54 years of age. She barely edged out our children for a graduate degree. Our son John graduated medical school at Cornell the same weekend in May. Being the ever-faithful mother, Connie was willing to forego her own graduation exercises at KU to be at the Cornell ceremony at Carnegie Hall.

One sad note: neither of Connie's parents lived to see her receive her graduate degree. Having lived with us for about three years, Connie's father passed away in 1984. In addition to all her hard work in the graduate program and her dedication to our children and our home, Connie ensured that the final years of his life were rich. She took good care of him and showed him a lot of love and attention during the time he lived with us.

With her graduate program in archival preservation and research completed, it came time for Connie to find a job in the field. Unfortunately, the chance to work with the Menninger archives was blocked. For some reason, my brother Roy and my cousin Robert vetoed that opportunity. I'm not sure what they were afraid of. I had recently been named chief of staff of the Menninger Foundation, but I didn't feel I was in a position to fight too fiercely for my wife to be given the position. Connie had to look for a job elsewhere.

The railroad industry had been highly influential in the history of our hometown of Topeka. Of course, the history of railroads was deeply intertwined with the history of the Midwest in general. Connie had done quite a bit of work on records of railroads, and she saw great potential in this field of study. She had been working on the records of the Atchison, Topeka & Santa Fe Railway (ATSF) as part of her responsibilities at KSHS. With the encouragement of her friends there, she decided to submit a proposal for a grant from the Santa Fe Southern Pacific Foundation. To the joy of KSHS and our family, Connie received approval for a five year, $238,000 grant for her organizing and computer processing of the foundation's records, to begin on January 1, 1986.

Joseph Snell, KSHS Executive Director, observed that the archives were significant to the state of Kansas as well as to the Santa Fe Southern Pacific Foundation specifically. He said: "An original purpose of the historical society's founding fathers was 'to rescue from oblivion the memory of its early pioneers.' As the state and the railroad have grown and flourished from the same roots, we have undertaken a major program of preserving both the history of the state and the history of the railroad."

We were somewhat disappointed, of course, that Connie was not allowed to jump right into work on the Menninger archives. But she was genuinely excited by the prospect of working with the railroad records. She dove into her work as Project Archivist, a full-time staff position at the KSHS.

Connie inherited mountains of uncatalogued documents, photos, and artifacts. It would have been daunting to even the most veteran of archivists. But Connie was determined, and she was thorough and well-organized.

While it was a lot of work, the job was also a lot of fun. Connie and I took an Amtrak train to Arizona to ride the restored section between Williams, Arizona and the South Rim of the Grand Canyon, spending a night at the unique El Tovar Hotel at the canyon. We also took a car trip west paralleling the Santa Fe railway route from Raton Pass in New Mexico through Tehachapi Pass in California. We served as excursion train car hosts at the annual Topeka Railroad Days.

In addition to her work on the ATSF project, Connie became involved in several peripheral activities. She organized a program for the long-term protection of photo and video material for archivists. She also chaired an advisory board of the Kansas University Museum of Anthropology.

In 1986, Connie was appointed to the brand-new advisory board of the Hall Center for the Humanities at Kansas University. When the center was struggling, Connie boldly challenged the board members to pledge to donate $1,000 apiece annually. "I am challenging this board...here is my check," she said, plopping the check down on the table in front of the director. The board chairman loved telling that story.

In 1987, Connie joined the Historic Topeka Board of Directors, and in 1988 she served as president of the Shawnee County Historical Society. She was also appointed to the board of directors of the Brown Foundation for Educational Equity, Excellence and Research—the same Brown of the famous *Brown v. Board of Education* decision that had its genesis in Topeka.

Connie loved her work with the ATSF archives at the KSHS. It was with a great deal of sadness that she left after the five-year grant ran out at the end of 1991. Even after she moved on from the position, Connie remained somewhat of an expert on railroad history. She did some work with the archives of the Gulf, Colorado & Santa Fe Railway, a subsidiary of the ATSF. In 1997, she was interviewed by the History Channel for a series on early railroads. She was a mainstay in the Railroad Days of Topeka celebration, as well as on the restoration committee of the Great Overland Station, a historically significant railway station in Topeka. That building held personal significance to Connie as well. The first time she visited Topeka, she and I rode the train from Stanford to visit my family for Christmas of 1951. She noted upon arriving in Topeka that the train station reminded her of the one in Pittsburg, Texas, where she spent part of her childhood. That sense of familiarity had helped her warm quickly to my hometown. She was therefore enthusiastic about the efforts to preserve the historic depot.

Connie began 1992 ready for a new challenge. The concerns that previously prevented her from engaging the Menninger Archives no longer existed. As consultant archivist, she was finally permitted the opportunity to make the improvements the collection so desperately needed. She prompted the creation of a 12-member Menninger Museum and Archives Advisory Council to redefine the scope of the collection and consider automation of the collection. They formulated a collection policy for the institution's archives and exhibits.

Alice Brand Bartlett, a member of the council, was quoted in an article at the time, saying: "We are fortunate to have Connie Menninger as our consultant. Her nine years of experience in museum and archives administration plus a master's degree from the University of Kansas Historical Administration and Museum Studies program will provide us with much needed expertise and good connections with Kansas museums and archives."

Connie brought professional organization to the Menninger collection. She enhanced the exhibits in the Menninger Tower building lobby. She helped gather artifacts and photos for the Topeka Institute for Psychoanalysis' 50th Anniversary. And she arranged for the transfer of artifacts inappropriately housed at Menninger to other museums, particularly Native American artifacts, which she had delivered to the Kansas University Museum of Anthropology.

In addition to better organizing the existing archives, Connie undertook collection of records and papers from various Menninger staff and important players in the early history of mental health, analysis, and psychotherapy, including oral history recordings. Through this effort in particular, Connie made a great contribution to the historical record of developments in mental health.

In 1996, she became the official Menninger archivist on staff. She held that position until 2002, when she retired at the age of 71.

In addition to working with the Menninger archives, Connie continued to volunteer at KSHS for the next decade, averaging more than 800 hours of service to the museum each year. She became the de facto mother of the group of fledgling archivists at the KSHS, throwing staff parties, and offering cooking and sewing lessons and parenting advice.

Connie was passionate about education and learning, and about providing opportunities for everyone. This passion made her a longtime advocate for the public library in Topeka.

The Topeka & Shawnee County Public Library (TSCPL) was an award-winning library in the 1980s. But by the 1990s, improvements were needed. In 1996, a bond issue was passed to enhance the library's facilities. Connie and I participated in efforts to raise money for the remodeling and expansion. But as was her wont, Connie quickly gained a leadership role in the project.

She learned the Denver Central Library was designed by the architect selected to design the TSCPL renovation, so on a trip to Colorado we paid the Denver building a visit. After touring the facility, Connie came away a convert to this architect's design. She reached out to the architect—Michael Graves—and we subsequently visited him at his home in Princeton, New Jersey. Connie communicated with him during the development of plans for the Topeka building. We wound up making a substantial donation to the project.

Many of Connie's interests came into play in one particular endeavor related to the library.

We learned that a set of stained-glass windows in the original Topeka public library building on the Statehouse grounds had contained the words "History," "Science," and "Art," while three others conveyed a quote by Sir Francis Bacon: "Reading maketh a full man; conference a ready man; and writing an exact man." When the former library building was demolished in 1961, the six stained glass windows were auctioned independently. My uncle Karl had purchased the one displaying the word "History."

In the 1990s, Connie discovered in the Menninger Archives the window Karl had purchased and was intrigued by the long since divided set. She had a vision for incorporation of the windows in the new construction, which she communicated to the architect. Using her research skills, she started trying to locate the other five windows.

Four of the windows had been purchased by a member of the Stauffer media corporation who, naturally, liked the phrase, "writing an exact man." She struggled to locate the final piece of the puzzle, but by the time of the renovation, she had secured five of the six. The final piece, she finally learned, was in the possession of a person in another state who was unwilling to part with it. But the family agreed that, upon the owner's death, they would sell it. We purchased it for the library after his passing.

James McHenry, Director of Development TSCPL, said: "Connie was always the sleuth and bloodhound—out there with her eyes one-hundred yards over the rim and ahead of the wagon train. Hers was an attitude of discovery and a 'this-is-interesting' spirit. Repeatedly, her 'what-if's pried for future options… Connie was a frontier woman with a can-do energy… When she walked into a room, the voltage would ramp up. When she took charge, I could expect dynamite."

In recognition of our donation to the renovation, TSCPL includes a Menninger Conference Room. People probably assume it is named for the Menninger institution, but it is actually in recognition of Connie and me. We were designated as "pacesetters" for our role in the TSCPL Great Expectations Campaign. In January of 2002, we were honored at a Library Gala Night, an event attended by then First Lady Laura Bush.

Life was exciting for us in the 1990s. We were approaching 70 at the start of the new millennium. I was CEO of Menninger. Connie was happy laboring over the archives of the organization. We knew we couldn't work for many more years, but we were relishing this period of our lives.

More important than our work, however, was the joy we took from family and friends. Our children were all grown and pursuing their own endeavors. And Connie and I were blessed by our friends in Topeka and across the nation.

40

Family

N o man succeeds without a good woman behind him. Wife or mother, if it is both, he is twice blessed indeed."

The quote by the British actor and writer Godfrey Winn couldn't be any more true about my life. In addition to having the love of my wife, Connie, for more than 70 years, I was twice blessed because I also had the nurturing and encouragement of my mother, Catharine "Cay" Wright Menninger.

I have talked at great length about my father. I've discussed his many contributions to the world, and how I set out to follow in his professional footsteps. But it was my mother who deserves the lion's share of the credit for my upbringing. While Dad was perpetually on the move, Mom was there for us. Every time we were sick, sad, stressed, or uncertain, Mom was our rock. Even as we became adults, Mom remained a wise and calming influence, never more so than when our daughter Claire died unexpectedly in the mid-1960s. We were fortunate that, because we were living in Topeka at the time, my mother was there to take care of details and assuage Connie's grief.

Being married to a prominent man, Mom was consistently loyal. She was totally committed to protecting Dad from the world and fostering a home environment in which he could succeed. She was an unsung hero throughout his entire career. When he arrived home from work each day, she would greet him warmly and allow him time to relax. She then ensured that our home was a welcoming place for him to host guests, or a place to address his remaining tasks in a peaceful atmosphere.

My mother was more than just a great housewife. She was an active volunteer in organizations like the League of Women Voters, the American Women's Voluntary Services during World War II, and the local Red Cross. Her talents were on full display when she was picked by the Red Cross to direct all volunteer activities in the Topeka area in response to a major flood of northeast Kansas in 1951. A book which printed a letter from my mother about the flood said, "Mrs. Menninger kept quite busy during the flood, working eighteen to twenty-hour days…during the height of the emergency." In the letter, my mother wrote that "order reigned" during the crisis, but there was still much "heartbreaking work yet to do."

As her three sons became young adults, she took on more and more of a role as Dad's assistant with work. Mom became his fundraising partner, helping him with his organization, scheduling, and correspondence with donors. (Dad kept three secretaries busy at the office too!) She accompanied him on many of his fundraising trips. They frequently traveled by train and worked in the overnight compartments, as well as in hotel rooms on multinight visits to New York, Los Angeles, Chicago, or wherever else they could meet with potential donors. Somehow, they sent out thousands of Christmas cards each year without the help of computers and copiers!

To the surprise of none of her sons, my mother blossomed after Dad passed away. She had been entirely dedicated to the success of her husband and her sons. But after Dad was gone, it was her time to shine. She had always enjoyed traveling, either on vacations or in support of my father. So, it was only natural that she became involved in an organization that took her around the globe.

Her passion for helping others and her interest in the world led her in the late 1960s to become involved with the organization People to People, started by Kansas' own President Dwight Eisenhower in 1956 "to enhance international understanding and friendship through educational, cultural and humanitarian activities involving the exchange of ideas and experiences directly among peoples of different countries and diverse cultures." In People to People, my mother found a place to really invest herself. She was appointed to the board of People to People, and soon she was traveling all over the world on its behalf. She visited more than a dozen countries as an ambassador of the organization.

People to People was headquartered in Kansas City. When the CEO of the organization suffered a heart attack, Mom stepped in to temporarily fill his position. She received all kinds of recognition for that.

After nearly 40 years, my mother finally moved out of the big house on Collins Avenue. Removing all the accumulated possessions from the house was such a monumental chore, I didn't really have time to get too sentimental about it. Mom moved into an independent living community connected to an assisted living facility. With nothing to tie her down, she remained constantly on the move. When she wasn't working for People to People, she visited her grandchildren or took vacations. Her mind remained sharp enough that, in 1988, when Connie served as president of the Shawnee County Historical Society, my mother assisted her with projects there.

Finally, in the early 1990s, my mother's health began to seriously deteriorate. At around 90 years of age, she began suffering brain damage due to hypertension, which impaired her mobility and ability to communicate. This was tough on her because she so relished her independence. After falling and breaking her hip, Mom moved into the medical unit of her living facility.

My mother passed away on September 6, 1994, just short of her 92nd birthday, and—more significantly—on the same day as my father's passing, 28 years later. While she had blossomed in her nearly three decades as an independent, self-sufficient widow, it still seemed fitting that she pass away on the anniversary of her husband's death.

I said at her memorial: "She was both traditional and forward-looking. She was unaffected and deeply committed to service. She was generous, caring, sensitive, loving. She raised us with that model and quietly encouraged us to be likewise. Notes we have received since her death attest to the fact that many others were similarly touched by her at some point in their life, and that she has made a difference in this world, leaving it a much better place as a result."

The next year, with my brothers Roy and Phil and I in attendance, the Catharine Wright Menninger Childcare Center for Menninger employees' children was dedicated to honor my mother, who 60 years earlier had helped start the first nursery school in Topeka.

As I mentioned previously, Connie's widowed father lived with us for a few years until he passed away in 1984. So, my mother was the last of our living parents. I'm thankful that my children had many years to know their remarkable grandmother.

———————

For obvious reasons, my brother Roy is featured prominently in my story. I am happy that, despite the stress of our careers, our personal relationship remained strong. My oldest brother and I were generally of the same mind in our profession, and we got along well outside of work. He has his own story to tell, so I won't delve into his personal life.

Much less prominent in my memoir is my middle brother, Phil. While growing up, I was actually much closer to my middle brother than I was to Roy because there was less of an age gap between us. While Roy and I are physically similar to my father—tall and lean—Phil had the physique of our mother's father—short and stocky.

As I mentioned earlier, all three of us had an ocular defect. Phil's was dyslexia. This presented a tremendous challenge to him in school. Because of this, my parents presented different options for him, trying to foster his other abilities.

Phil's attendance at Washburn University was interrupted by the Korean War. While Roy and I had commissions, Phil enlisted in the Army as a non-commissioned soldier. He was honorably discharged with a rank of Master Sergeant. He then entered the Army Reserve, from which he ultimately retired with a rank of Captain. After his discharge from active duty, he graduated from Washburn University with a bachelor's degree of Business Administration.

Phil worked at Menninger for more than 40 years in the fundraising office. Though he was limited by his ability to read, he had good business sense and he related well with people. He married and had two children.

Phil's greatest joys were in community service and bicycling. He served as president for both the Downtown Topeka Lions Club, and Boys and Girls Club of Topeka. He became very adept at personal computing when that was still a new thing. He created newsletters and publication materials for organizations in Topeka. He was perhaps best known in town as a founder of the Kaw Valley Bicycle Touring Club.

My brother Phil passed away in 2016 at age 87.

———————————•———————————

As I've mentioned, Connie told me on one of our first dates that she wanted to have six children. I was fine with that proposition. Aside from the loss of our infant daughter Claire, we were blessed with six healthy, talented, and immensely enjoyable children. We started with Fritz, who was born while I was finishing up medical school in New York. Next came John and Eliza while I was in my psychiatric residency in Topeka. Marian was born in Oklahoma while I served a stint with the Public Health Service. Will and David came after we returned to Topeka in the latter half of the 1960s.

I am proud and delighted by the accomplishments of each of my children. But I want to avoid delving too much into their accolades and achievements. To do so would risk emphasizing that what they do is more important than who they are. Most important is that they are kind, respectful, and conscientious people. They each made Connie and me proud in their own unique way. But for this memoir, I won't discuss their private lives, and will only briefly mention their endeavors.

If and when they decide to write their own memoirs, they can brag on themselves.

Fritz was a rambunctious, active boy with a perfectionist streak. Even as a young boy he demonstrated unusual kindness and concern for others. He realized as a young adult that he liked working with his hands and was particularly adept at endurance competitions. He experienced success as a bicycle racer, but he actually found his greatest passion was "orienteering," a sport of navigation using tools such as a map and compass. Fritz also discovered a passion for coaching young children in various sports. A community center in the Topeka area once named him "After School Hero" for his contributions to their programs.

Each of my children is special and dear to my heart. But the experience of having the first child move away from home is particularly difficult. I wrote an "In-Sights" column in the mid-1970s sharing with readers the experience of Fritz's move to MIT in Boston entitled, "When the Fledgling Leaves the Nest":

> I'm aware that the bald eagle keeps its fledgling in the nest for one year and then boots it out and forces it to leave the home territory. But they don't have the feelings we have.
>
> Sure, we enjoy the normal parental satisfaction that our child has come this far and has accomplished this much. We also recognize that we can't really expect to keep a child forever, no matter how much we might want

to.

But now, somehow all that fades and the feelings take over.

Mother can choke up and express distress. But Dad's not supposed to show feelings. Phooey! It hurts, and I'm not going to pretend it doesn't depress me.

...this insistent parental urge persists: "Dad, your job is incomplete. There are so many things you haven't told him. So many things you haven't shown him."

My concerns for the first fledgling were unnecessary. Fritz would eventually be the one fledgling who returned to the nest. Fritz was trained in childcare and nursing. His skills were immensely useful—and appreciated—when Connie's health took a downturn in the early 2000s. Fritz moved in with us and cared for his mother with remarkable love and tenderness. He has been a tremendous help to me in my "old age" as well. A father has a special connection to his firstborn son, and I greatly appreciate that I have had Fritz close by in my later years.

We would experience five more times a fledgling leaving the nest. It certainly gets easier. But the love Connie and I felt for each of our children was demonstrated in our emotion over the first leaving home.

Fritz learned early on that he was not interested in studying psychiatry. But our second child, John, decided to enter the family tradition. He was a sensitive, diligent, artistic, and expressive child. He continued in my footsteps by attending Stanford for undergraduate school and Cornell for med school. What a pleasure to visit John at those schools about three decades after I had attended them. In 1985, John became the first fourth-generation "Dr. Menninger." John embarked upon psychiatric residency at the University of Colorado. I greatly enjoyed attending conferences with John, sharing with him the professional bond that I'd had with my father.

While music was Fritz's strong suit, John found art more to his liking. His talent for models and building things manifested itself in a skill for woodworking as an adult.

Our first daughter, Eliza (often called Liza or Lize), was born in 1960. Having a daughter delighted Connie.

Eliza loved animals as a child and bonded with her grandmother on a trip to Kenya for a wildlife safari. Not surprisingly, she initially set out to become a veterinarian. She worked for a local veterinarian while in high school, then interned with both large- and small-animal vets at Middlebury College in Vermont. Because she anticipated attending the Kansas State University College of Veterinary Medicine, she thought it would be wise to spend one undergraduate year at Kansas State.

While Eliza was home over the holiday break of her sophomore year at Middlebury, those plans changed. She accompanied me while I did rounds at the Topeka State Hospital. We had a memorable time talking to staff and residents. I'm not sure if that one event made a big impact on my daughter. But a few days later, she informed us that she had decided to switch her major to pre-medicine.

Due to the change of plans, there was now no need for Eliza to spend an undergraduate year at Kansas State. Eliza stuck with the plan to leave Middlebury for a year, however, deciding to return to Topeka for a year at Washburn University. This allowed her to experience a different college and to spend time with her family. Connie relished that year with her adult daughter back in our home. They really bonded during that experience.

After a year, Eliza returned to Middlebury without missing a beat. She earned valedictorian honors. The university chose to present me an honorary degree at that same graduation, leading to a heartwarming moment for a proud father. I was seated on the stage for the ceremony. As the valedictorian, Eliza was the first to be presented her diploma. The university president told me, "You can hug your daughter when she comes up."

Subsequently, Eliza attended Harvard Medical School and did her psychiatric residency at McLean Hospital in Boston. Eliza continued to work in the Boston area, which made Connie quite happy to make frequent visits. Eliza became medical director of the partial hospital services at McLean. She also served as an assistant professor of psychiatry and on the admissions committee at Harvard Medical School.

Our fourth child, Marian, was born during my two-year stint as Chief Medical Officer and Psychiatrist at the Federal Reformatory, El Reno in Oklahoma. Marian was a vigorous and tenacious child, and one with a consuming passion: Marian was a voracious reader. Her talents with language made her a natural fit for spelling bees in elementary school, and for debate competitions in high school.

Marian wasn't just bookish, however. She was musically inclined, athletic, and competitive. Probably partly due to Connie's influence, Marian loved horses. Despite getting kicked in the chin by a horse as a child, she was not afraid of them. In fact, she competed on the polo team at Stanford.

Marian also found time to perform in the famous—or should I say "infamous"—Stanford marching band. Known officially as the Leland Stanford Junior University Marching Band, the group had metamorphosed since Connie and I left the university in the early 1950s. Gone were the straight lines and traditional marches. Playing the mellophone, our petite but fiery Marian enjoyed being a part of the creative, irreverent bunch of musicians. By joining the group in the spring of 1983, she just missed being a part of history. She was not amongst the Stanford band members who prematurely assembled on the football field while the final play of the famed 1982 Stanford-Cal game was still going. Otherwise, she might have been one of the musicians bowled over in the end zone on "The Play."

Marian's older sister Eliza had surprised us by changing her course from veterinary studies to medicine. Marian, initially interested in psychiatry, changed her interest to pediatrics. From my standpoint, this was not a matter of chance. Marian was almost three years old when her baby sister Claire died unexpectedly. I believe she was influenced by this early life experience and wanted to ensure the same fate didn't befall other infants. Marian became a neonatal medicine specialist.

After the passing of three-month-old Claire in 1964, we added a third son to the family in 1966. This quiet, serious boy was the third generation of Menningers to take the name William. After having four children enter the medical field, the odds were against that streak continuing. Will was infatuated with numbers from the start. He hit middle school about the time personal computers made their appearance. At his behest, we purchased a computer around 1980 and he amazed us with his intuitive sense of what could be done with it even in those early days. He became so knowledgeable that he was invited to make a presentation on "applications of the mini-computer in education" to a Kansas School Board Association convention while just 13 years old.

Gifted in math and technology, Will eschewed medicine, opting to study electrical engineering at Stanford. He worked summers doing computer programming for the Menninger Foundation. He went to MIT for a doctorate, then moved back to California to work for a company that specialized in microwave tubes that are used in satellite communications. Born in the early days of the space race and a child when the U.S. sent rockets to the moon, Will contributed technology to a moon-mapping spacecraft in 2009.

Last but not least, our son David was born in 1968. Compared to his siblings, David was laid back and sociable. Similar to his older brother John, David enjoyed putting together models. He also had a talent for photography. So, like Will, David studied something besides medicine while at Stanford. He received awards for his photography and graphic design abilities.

David's artistic abilities opened doors in animation and design in California. This led him to work for the internet company America Online, implementing its My Calendar feature. Since then, he has worked in computer user-interface design, development of personal digital photography software, and on web design for well-known genealogical websites.

I could go on about the special qualities of each of my six children. But instead, I will simply say that I am thankful that we have remained a close-knit unit. Other than the typical childhood grievances and annoyances, my children have cared for and supported each other. Our regularly scheduled reunions in Park City, Utah, have helped the Menninger clan stay united despite its growth. My six children produced eight grandchildren, and now some great-grandchildren. I cherish every opportunity to sit with those grandchildren and great-grandchildren, to learn about them, and to try to share a morsel of love, wisdom, and encouragement.

The popular philosopher Og Mandino said, "The greatest legacy we can leave our children are happy memories." For the Menninger family, many of those great, happy memories were made traveling. That was certainly true for Roy, Phil, and me. The most precious times for us, therefore, were when Dad would pack up our car and we would break away from home for a family adventure on the road.

Recalling all those happy memories with my parents and my brothers,

I was determined to have similar adventures with my own family. While our numbers were growing in the 1960s, we didn't do a lot of traveling as an entire family. But in 1969 we made a purchase that brought equal amounts of joy, excitement, and frustration. We bought a Winnebago motor home, a 24-foot-long recreational vehicle popular at the time. We put over 6,500 miles on it that first summer, rambling through the Southwest and up the West Coast.

Nearly every year for a decade or so, we loaded the vehicle with our kids and multiple dogs and headed out in search of adventure. Many of our trips were to visit friends we'd made along the years.

In 1941, when I was nine years old, my parents took me and my brothers on a car trip to all the great natural wonders of the west: Yellowstone, the Great Salt Lake, Bryce and Zion National Parks, the Grand Canyon. The experience was one of the best of my childhood. Perhaps it became more meaningful once the war started and my father spent so much time away from us after that. For whatever reason, that family vacation meant a great deal to me, and I wanted to repeat it with my own family. We did, 30 years later, in 1971. We drove our "land yacht" more than 4,000 miles through Colorado, Utah, Arizona, and New Mexico, visiting many of the sites my parents showed us when I was ten. Our version of the trek was "highlighted" by a harrowing drive in southeastern Utah. Little did I know that I would be inching our behemoth down the cliff on a narrow, one-way dirt road.

Over the years, we made road trips throughout the Southwest, up to the Badlands of South Dakota, through the Ozarks, up to New England, and out to the Pacific Northwest.

One incident that left an indelible impression on our family was a broken drive shaft while driving in Colorado in 1975. The plight of the drive shaft, and the intervention of several guardian angels, prompted me to such introspection that I wrote an "In-Sights" column about the ordeal. Following are some excerpts from that column:

> While sitting and waiting for the tow truck, a lot of thoughts crossed my mind.
>
> First were the recriminations: "You—fool, why did you do that?!" My family didn't have to say it. I said it to myself with emphasis. Then I repeatedly reviewed how it

happened. It is a pain to be in a situation where you can't solve the problem yourself.

When the tow truck finally arrives, it's most reassuring. The driver acts with confidence and assurance. He makes me feel better when he tells me he's been here before. I'm not the first fool to make such a stupid mistake and get stranded. Others have gone through it, and they've survived.

We ride down the mountain road in the cab of the truck, except for the kids who are enjoying a glorious view of the mountain scenery from the back and delighting with the blare of the horn as we round each tight curve. However, at the service station, the next stage of concern sets in.

The service manager tells me that it will take a week to get a new part—Aaahg! However, it might be possible to take a partially-damaged drive shaft forty miles down the road to the nearest dealer and get a used shaft which has the part I need; then I could see if the good sections could be welded together at a machine shop.

I borrow a car, take a couple of kids, and I'm off. Lo and behold, the dealer has a suitable used shaft and the machine shop can do the job. We're saved from a week's stranding.

I'm not sure if any of our Good Samaritans ever read the column, but needless to say the experience increased my faith in humanity, and probably diminished my faith in my own good judgement.

I won't bore you with more stories from our family vacations. But I can summarize the trips by saying that travel accomplishes many things besides recreation. It was wonderful bonding for us to pile into the car—or later the Winnebago when we outgrew our station wagon—and go careening off on an adventure. You're together 24/7, but in an ever-changing environment. You have to learn to get along, to entertain each other, and to appreciate your differences.

It's interesting how the unplanned detours, the unforeseen incidents, are what families remember most from such trips. It's not the view of the

Grand Canyon from some perfect spot that kids remember most. It's the bologna sandwich on the side of the road while the parents try to decipher a map or await a tow truck. Things rarely go exactly as planned on a trip. You have to learn to manage changes to your expectations. We had too many car problems, drives through treacherous weather, and other white-knuckle moments to list. Pretty much every vacation has its own hiccup. The amazing thing we experienced was that no matter what the issue or inconvenience, we got through. We survived. Often it was due to the benevolence of some stranger we encountered along the way.

41

Friends

While my wife and my children have been the joy of my life, friends have been the spice. I've been blessed to know people from every stratum of the social ladder and from every walk of life. I made friends who were completely unlike me in every way while serving in the Peace Corps. Some friends were nearly exactly like me and shared similar passions and interests, while others challenged me, caused me to view the world differently, and opened my world to things I would never have otherwise experienced.

I concluded the previous chapter describing some of the trips on which our family embarked over the years. Part of what we endeavored to do on our trips was maintain close connections with lifelong friends. We would return to Stanford regularly to connect with old classmates and teachers. To a degree we did the same with friends from Cornell, and from our other stops along the way. We would also make a point to visit the friends who had passed through Topeka and gone on to other places. Keeping up those relationships was important to us, so we invested in them.

Connie's hospitality to the choir of Topeka's First Presbyterian Church produced a lot of close friendships. For years she hosted a meal for members of the group prior to Thursday night rehearsals. The meals were particularly popular with choir members who either were single or who traveled to Topeka for the rehearsals.

One friend we endeavored to follow throughout his career was vocalist David Holloway. David was a paid soloist at the church during his time as a student at the University of Kansas. He and his first wife, Doris, were frequent guests during the late 1960s. They babysat our kids once when Connie and I went on a trip.

After their graduations from KU, we followed David and Doris' careers. In 1970, they were in the Kansas City Lyric Opera, with David as the lead in *Of Mice and Men*. David made his way up through the ranks as a vocal performer, working in Denver, Chicago, San Francisco, San Diego, and New York. We saw him perform twice at the Kennedy Center in Washington, D.C. He performed lead roles at the Metropolitan Opera and the New York City Opera. Sadly, we were not able to catch any of his performances as lead baritone in an opera in Düsseldorf, Germany. But we maintained close ties with David and his second wife, Deborah, over the years. He concluded his career by overseeing the apprenticeship program at the Santa Fe (New Mexico) Opera for over a decade. It was our pleasure to be able to see David perform on several occasions throughout his long and successful career.

Music was an important part of our lives. We tried to expose our children to a variety of musical styles and to allow them to learn diverse instruments and to meet talented musicians. I personally wouldn't have known much about opera had it not been for David. Following his career was a blessing.

Art was equally important in our family. We sought to help our children appreciate art while developing their own creative talents. A man who had an influence on our family was sculptor John Whitfield. Connie met the artist at a Washburn University Art Fair in 1964, and they struck up a fast friendship. One of the things that drew them to each other was their mutual love of sailing. From her childhood in New England, Connie had a lifelong passion for sailing, and John filled this void in her life by treating her to occasional excursions on the lakes of Kansas.

John's art adorned our home, and he became a mentor to our children. Our second child, John, was particularly influenced by John Whitfield. While in high school, our son took a course in metal working from Whitfield at Washburn, and he apprenticed under the artist one summer. Thanks in large part to the encouragement and instruction he received from Whitfield, our son John became quite an accomplished artist himself. Though he eventually pursued a career in psychiatry, our son's training in art led to a lifelong hobby.

When the idea arose in the early 1980s to honor my uncle Karl on his 90th birthday with a piece of art on the Menninger campus, it was only natural that we looked to John Whitfield. John proposed a beautiful sculpture titled "The Vital Balance," which took its name and inspiration from a 1963 book by my uncle. John's proposal was selected by the Menninger Foundation and was unveiled at a birthday celebration for Karl in 1983. Our last child, David, was as passionate about art as his brother John, and he also apprenticed under Whitfield. David assisted in the creation of "The Vital Balance," an interesting connection between great-uncle and great-nephew. Over the years, the sculpture was a reminder of the concepts and ideals of my grandfather, my father, and my uncle. Future CEO of the organization, Ian Aitken, told the *Topeka Capital-Journal* of the sculpture:

> The Vital Balance sculpture is important to the Menninger staff and our community-at-large because it represents our founders and our charge to carry out their legacy of patient-focused treatment. It's a daily and visible reminder…that everything we do is centered around our patients and helping them regain their balance.

Indeed, the sculpture is viewed daily by current Menninger staff and patients in its place of honor on the Menninger Clinic campus in Houston.

You never know what will result from a chance meeting and an act of hospitality.

When our family was growing in the late 1960s, we found ourselves in need of some support around the house. Connie's involvements in the community were expanding and I was traveling a lot for work. The idea of hiring someone to help with the care of our children was inspired in part by the tornado that struck Topeka in 1966. The destruction wrought by the storm produced a shortage of housing options for Washburn University students. We thought we might offer our guest room to a student willing to help us keep up with our five children that ranged in age from infant (Will) to nine years (Fritz).

Connie inquired of a friend who happened to be the head of the Washburn women's physical education department. That friend recommended a young female student named Lin who had just transferred into the program. We offered Lin a live-in position helping Connie with our kids.

Lin had transferred to Topeka from a college in Iowa because she was dating another transfer student to Washburn, a young man named Davey Lopes. Davey was an athlete who was mentored at his previous college—Iowa Wesleyan University—by the school's athletic director, Michael Sarkesian. When Sarkesian was hired as athletic director at Washburn in 1966, he brought Davey with him.

Lin moved in with us and was a huge help around the house. We got to know Davey immediately. Davey was an instant standout on the Washburn basketball team, and he played baseball as well. He occasionally joined us for meals at our house. The only problem was that Connie didn't anticipate the appetite of a two-sport athlete. We attended a handful of Davey's games. Our kids adored him. So, when Lin and Davey told us they planned to get married and wondered if Davey could move in with us, we happily accepted.

Davey was working toward a degree in elementary education and practiced teaching sixth grade while in Topeka. He came to Washburn primarily as a basketball player. But things took a bit of an unexpected turn in his one season on the baseball team in the spring of 1967. He earned All-American honors for a tremendous season and was drafted by the San Francisco Giants. Davey decided to forego that opportunity to stay at Washburn. He played basketball the next season and won All-American in that sport as well. But at just 5-foot-9, it was going to be tough for Davey to make a living playing basketball. Despite his love of basketball, baseball became his best hope for a professional career. He was drafted by the Los Angeles Dodgers that offseason and left Washburn—and our home and his new bride—to go to the Dodgers' winter league program. Lin stayed with us to finish the school year.

Our sixth and last child was born in January of 1968. Due to our friendships with musician David Holloway and athlete Davey Lopes, we decided to name this son David.

We gleefully followed Davey's matriculation through the Dodgers' minor league system. He was not a young player—he was 23 years old when he entered the organization at one of the lowest levels. It took five years, but he finally was promoted to the Dodgers' big-league team in 1972. Once there, he made up for lost time, quickly developing into a star second baseman who excelled at stealing bases. They eventually settled in Los Angeles, but Davey and Lin visited us occasionally over the next several years.

All of our children loved Davey, but the one who most passionately followed his career was Will. The statistical and strategic elements of baseball piqued the interests of our analytical, mathematically gifted son. When he wasn't out playing baseball himself, Will would clip from newspapers the box scores of the Dodgers games and pore over the stats. We made a trek to St. Louis to see the Dodgers play the Cardinals in the summer of 1973.

In October of 1977, I took Will and his childhood friend Daniels Benfer to Los Angeles for the World Series, which pitted the Dodgers against the New York Yankees. Forget that the Yankees were my favorite team growing up, our allegiances were fully with Davey and the Dodgers.

Davey had had a marvelous season, but he was mired in a slump when we arrived in Los Angeles. We went to the game that Friday afternoon, then went to Davey's home after the game. We'd just witnessed a game pitched marvelously by Yankee Mike Torrez, coincidentally from Topeka. After three games, Davey had no hits in 13 at bats and had struck out three times. He agonized over his poor showing.

I recounted our conversation and what ensued in our Christmas letter that December:

> Scene I. The time: late Friday evening, October 14, after the third game of the 1977 baseball World Series. The place: the kitchen of Los Angeles Dodgers' second baseman, Davey Lopes, who had gone hitless in the series to that point. A young admirer asks Davey, "Why don't you hit a home run tomorrow?" Davey almost guffaws; he's a base stealer, not a home run hitter; he'd just like to get any kind of hit.
>
> Scene II. The next day, in Dodger stadium, the fourth game of the series. With that young fan (our Will) looking on, Davey, in his second at-bat, strokes his first series hit—a screaming line drive home run over the deep center field fence!
>
> That's how it really happened when Will, his dad and his close friend Daniels Benfer traveled to Los Angeles for the middle three games of the series. Though Will and Daniels anguished over the games (and series) the

Dodgers lost, it was a marvelous experience. The boys came home with glorious memories—including a clubhouse visit for autographs—and wonderful souvenirs.

The boys had actually been invited to visit the Dodgers' clubhouse following Game Four, but the Dodgers lost despite Davey's home run. Facing elimination, Los Angeles manager Tommy Lasorda restricted any visitors from the clubhouse. Fortunately, the curse seemed to be lifted off Davey. He hit a triple and a single the next day. The Dodgers won Game Five and Will and Daniels made it into the clubhouse after all. Will got his glove autographed and they had all the excitement a youngster could want.

The Dodgers eventually lost the 1977 World Series, but we remained friends with Davey, following him throughout his career and catching games in various cities when possible.

———————•———————

Not all of our friends were famous, but they were all equally important to us. As much as we hoped to encourage and influence others, we received more in return. Friends from church, civic organizations, and our various jobs helped us become more well-rounded and considerate of different perspectives.

In the end, family and friends are life's greatest treasures. I was blessed by relationships with many more than I can list—from childhood friends like Fritz Fenster and college mates like John Menaglia to professional colleagues like Joe English, they have made my journey a joy. In my later years, my life has been enriched by friendships with people like Topeka mayor Michelle de la Isla and First Presbyterian Church pastors Sandra Stogsdill Nichols and Pat Yancey.

Above accomplishments, accolades, and wealth, friends and family would give meaning to my life and sustain me through the next phase. In the 2000s I would be in for professional and personal challenges like I'd never faced.

42

Nothing Gold Can Stay

Nature's first green is gold,
Her hardest hue to hold.
Her early leaf's a flower;
But only so an hour.
Then leaf subsides to leaf.
So Eden sank to grief,
So dawn goes down to day.
Nothing gold can stay.

–Robert Frost

In our 60s, Connie and I felt as though our relationship had entered a golden phase. We were delighted with the "empty nest," traveling to visit our children, who now had careers and families of their own. We were blessed with wonderful friends and co-workers at jobs we both enjoyed.

The Menninger Foundation confronted the same challenges facing all mental healthcare providers: seeing more patients for shorter periods of time while receiving less compensation for those services. But we retained a spirit of optimism and control over the situation. The Menninger trustees endorsed a plan developed by management to reconfigure our operations and reduce overhead expenses. We planned to continue specialized treatment programs for professionals in crisis and difficult treatment problems on the Topeka campus. We continued our efforts to expand our partnerships with other hospitals while remaining committed to excellence in education and research. I turned 68 years old in 1999 and was as energized as ever to ensure the future success of the Menninger organization my grandfather, father, uncle, and brother had worked so hard to build.

Connie continued her work with the Menninger Archives and relished her many volunteer commitments. In 1999, we fulfilled one of her longstanding ambitions by taking a ten-day tour of the country of Panama and its famous canal. We also traveled for work and to visit our children and longtime friends. Our bodies were healthy, and our children were happy. I wrote in our family Christmas card at the close of the millennium: "This year has had its share of crises and concerns, but for us the glass has still been much more full than empty."

But as Robert Frost so insightfully wrote, "nothing gold can stay."

The Menninger Clinic turned 75 in 2000. With the new millennium came strong indications that the Menninger Foundation could no longer retain its current course. By the mid-1990s, what had been termed "behavioral health's golden age" had come to a close. Changes in the rules of reimbursement for psychiatric and other mental health care required Menninger patients to assume more and more of their total bill for treatment. Admissions rapidly declined.

Income, therefore, didn't keep pace with expenses. In 1999, Menninger operated with an annual budget of $74 million, with 1,250 full-time employees. Staff costs, maintenance of the campus (90 acres and 30 buildings), declining admissions and shortened hospitalization, and an oppressive debt load were all weighing us down. We relied upon an endowment of more than $120 million committed to education and research. Losses far exceeded new contributions, seriously depleting the endowment. Estimates forecast that, without a major change, the endowment would be tapped out within about three years.

Menninger was hardly alone in this crisis. In fact, by comparison, we were better off than most. At least we were surviving. A number of similar private psychiatric hospitals—prominent names in the industry like Timberlawn, Chestnut Lodge, Institute of the Pennsylvania Hospital, Institute of Living—had gone out of business or had sought some affiliation in order to survive.

As CEO, I worked to balance my responsibilities of administration, trustee relations, fund raising, clinical consultation, teaching, and clinical research as changes in health care rapidly advanced. Times were tough, but I was blessed with a dedicated group of trustees from all over the country and extraordinary support from philanthropic resources.

The strength of our reputation and the size of our endowment ensured that Menninger had some time to chart a new course. But what should that new course be? In that time of crisis, we sought to stay true to the vision of our founders. Our heart was always in inpatient services. We understood that people didn't get well in just a few days or a week. Our treatment programs required longer stays. But the new rules made longer stays cost prohibitive.

The other problem was the cost of research and education. I wanted us to be able to explore neuroscience and breakthroughs in brain imaging techniques, but we couldn't put together the financing. Despite our history of dedication to research and incorporation of new techniques, Menninger just couldn't afford to keep up with the rapid advances in technology.

It was also evident that we could no longer fund education the way that we wanted to. The entity that drove the growth of Menninger in the 1940s—the Menninger School of Psychiatry—could no longer be maintained in its current form. This was particularly sad. The MSP had trained more than 3,200 practitioners in its formal training programs, while also providing training and continuing education for mental health professionals across the country. The benevolent nature of my grandfather had been carried on throughout the decades. The Menninger Foundation was not bent on hoarding knowledge for its own benefit. What was learned by Menninger staff was always shared with the mental health community at large.

For the sake of cost savings, we changed our practices in every way we could that would not affect our treatment model. We were seeing more patients than in the past but for shorter lengths of stay. Our "patient days" were cut by more than half from our peak year of 1986.

The changes we made kept up our hope and enthusiasm for the institution. But unfortunately, as I've mentioned before, the light at the end of tunnel is often the headlight of an oncoming train.

———————————

"In any moment of decision, the best thing you can do is the right thing, the next best thing is the wrong thing, and the worst thing you can do is nothing."

The words of President Theodore Roosevelt couldn't have been more true for the Menninger Foundation in 2000. We were in a "moment of decision." We longed to do the best thing—the right thing. We desperately wanted to avoid doing the wrong thing. But doing nothing was not an option.

With the help of a consultant team from Ernst & Young, the trustees of the foundation considered a number of options. We concluded that, in order to sustain our commitment to the full Menninger mission, the future viability of the institution necessitated an affiliation with a medical school and medical center. We started exploring all our options for affiliations. But one oppressive reality hung over the deliberations: An affiliation would likely require the relocation of Menninger.

Anyone in leadership long enough is eventually forced to make some hard decisions that will impact the lives of the people under them. I knew how hard it would be on our staff and their families if they were asked to relocate. I understood how challenging it would be to terminate staff who were not needed at a new location. And, as essentially a lifelong resident of Topeka, I knew just how impactful a move of the organization would be on the community.

I anguished over the reality. Connie felt the burden as well, and it affected her health. She began to struggle with depression and anxiety as the process moved forward. For the most part, we tried to keep the deliberations under wraps, but word gets around. As we sent out feelers to medical schools around the country to gauge their interest and evaluate their suitability, the staff and community inevitably heard the rumors that Menninger might have to move.

The trustees were encouraged by the response to our inquiries. More than 60 medical schools expressed interest in an affiliation with Menninger. A chance meeting with one school stood out in particular. During that period of investigation, Menninger Hospital Director Glen Gabbard attended a meeting in New York and happened to have a conversation with the chair of the Department of Psychiatry at Baylor College of Medicine (BCM) in Houston. He expressed to Gabbard his immediate enthusiasm for a potential partnership.

With the help of the consultants, the trustees narrowed the list of options to three. One of the finalists, BCM, in partnership with Methodist Hospital of Houston, was persistent in its overtures. They promised to match whatever other offer we received. After looking at all the factors, it was clear that the Houston partners represented Menninger's best option.

BCM was at that time (and still is) one of the top-ranked medical schools in the country. Methodist Hospital was a highly respected non-profit, comprehensive medical services and health care organization. These Houston partners offered a state-of-the-art medical complex, an internationally recognized teaching hospital, a top-ranked research medical school, an underserved patient market, and strong community financial support.

At our annual meeting in September of 2000, we made the incredibly hard but unanimous decision to relocate all Menninger services to the Texas Medical Center in Houston in order to partner with BCM and Methodist Hospital. A letter of intent with the Houston partners was agreed upon shortly after the board meeting. Involved in the transfer were residential programs for children and adolescents, professionals in crisis, complicated persistent treatment problems, and special psychiatric disorders such as eating and obsessive-compulsive disorders. The education and research programs would join the BCM Department of Psychiatry, which would be renamed the Menninger Department of Psychiatry and Behavioral Sciences at Baylor College of Medicine.

As the year 2000 came to a close, many details remained to be determined. But with the agreement made in principle, we had to make the decision public. The news was of international consequence. The Associated Press reported on the decision on December 5, 2000, in a fashion that wasn't very complimentary of Topeka.

Following are excerpts from the AP news article:

> Other parts of Kansas have long seen Topeka as culturally backward, nicknaming it "Slow-peka" and "Topuka." But in the Menninger Clinic, at least, Topeka had a source of intellectual pride.
>
> For generations, the psychiatric clinic has been a world-class center of new ideas and talent in the Midwest, established far from what were, at the time, the twin capitals of psychiatry, New York and Vienna.
>
> But now, after 75 years, the Menninger Clinic is leaving town for Houston.
>
> Topeka is mourning the loss of a major institution, hundreds of good-paying jobs, a rich pool of teaching

talent and a group of arts patrons. Many Topekans also ponder what the loss will mean to the city's reputation.

… The decision to move was a response to financial problems that have reduced Menninger's endowment from $129.2 million in 1998 to $104 million.

Dr. Walter Menninger, president and chief executive, said those problems are largely due to insurance companies' increasingly restrictive reimbursement practices regarding mental health treatment. He said the clinic would be out of business within six to eight years if it did not move.

As part of the deal, the three institutions have pledged to raise at least $200 million in endowment money, twice the size of a rejected package proposed by Gov. Bill Graves to keep the clinic in Kansas.

"It's a loss to Kansas because it's really kind of a Kansas icon," said Tom Bartlett, a psychologist at a Topeka mental health center. "It's sort of like saying they just pulled all the sunflowers out of Kansas."

Merle Blair, president and chief executive of the Greater Topeka Chamber of Commerce, said the loss of Menninger's annual payroll of $56 million surely will have an economic impact. But Blair also noted that Topeka, population 123,000, has low unemployment and said that Menninger staffers who choose to stay in town should have little problem finding work at hospitals.

But the city will lose more than just jobs. Menninger gave a certain cosmopolitan quality to a town where the restaurants still insist on serving practically everything with cream sauce.

"The Menninger staff brought a tremendous vitality to the community," recalled psychologist Harriet Lerner, who joined the staff in 1974. She called the clinic's departure "a tremendous drain of creativity and imagination."

The decision was met by some understandable skepticism. Many questioned whether Menninger could provide the same quality of care in this new setting. Would the leadership of BCM and Methodist Hospital grasp the concepts and practices we had employed for more than 75 years? Would our current staff be allowed to care for patients in the same way it did in Topeka? Would the enormous city and big medical school engulf us? Would urgency to make a profit override our dedication to quality?

Believe me, I understood the skepticism. I harbored these concerns myself. But I knew that doing nothing was not an option. My main concern was that our tradition of care for patients be continued. I was reassured through our extensive negotiations that Baylor Med and Methodist Hospital represented the best opportunity for that to happen. I was convinced we had found a partner who possessed a complementary view of our perspective. I believed our tradition of careful and thorough examinations would now be augmented by new knowledge and new techniques developed by the medical school. I felt particularly reassured when about a third of our staff in Topeka stated they planned to relocate to Houston when the clinic moved.

What it came right down to for me personally was the need to ensure that what my grandfather, father, uncle, and brother had dedicated their careers to would live on. My ultimate concern was that what they created would not end on my watch.

Connie and I had been through crises before. Job changes and moves of our family. The loss of an infant daughter. The passing of my father and the resulting turmoil at Menninger. Being pushed out of the organization to the state hospital. The substantial financial loss we incurred with the bankruptcy of a Burger King franchise.

None of those occurrences, however, was quite like the announcement of the move of Menninger. An entire community was affected.

While the details of the move to Houston were still being hammered out in late 2000 and early 2001, some of the necessary steps were already being taken. We began reducing the size of our staff in Topeka to prepare for the transition. Activities in Kansas City, both in hospitals and outpatient services, were terminated at the end of 2000. Acute psychiatric services in Topeka were transferred to a separate facility operated by Stormont Vail Health in February 2001. Partial hospital services were closed at the same time, and outpatient services for local and regional patients closed shortly thereafter. A Community Residence Program for patients who were severely and persistently mentally ill was transferred to the local community health center in Topeka, Valeo Behavioral Health. The Karl Menninger School of Psychiatry was to be transferred to BCM in July of 2001.

Also closing its doors was the Topeka Institute of Psychoanalysis (TIP). This was no small part of the story that was unfolding. TIP had been one of the most productive psychoanalytic institutes in the country. Its faculty had made large contributions to the theory and practice of psychoanalysis.

In the summer of 2001, in conjunction with the formal ceremony for the final class of graduates from the MSP, we held a week-long celebration of the school and of TIP.

Testimonials poured in of the impact of Menninger's years in Topeka. In one which we shared at the ceremony, a former patient wrote:

> Following my admission to Menninger, I spent a total of ten weeks hospitalized as an inpatient. Thanks to the superior staff of professionals, my life was spared... I have been free of symptoms of depression since the end of 1999... Additionally, I have been given the tools necessary to maintain my sobriety. In short, I've been granted a second chance at living a productive and healthy life. Everything I see and do – watch a sunset, talk with my parents, visit a friend, play with my dog, or say a prayer – I remember that my life is possible because of the Menninger Clinic.

Overseeing the changes taking place in 2001 was difficult for me personally. I tried to approach each step with pragmatism, but it was impossible not to be emotionally affected. I had to pep talk myself during that period: *Life is not always fair. And no one is without pain. Bad things do happen to good people without necessarily being the fault of some evil person or force.*

At the celebration of MSP and TIP that summer, I spoke frankly about the inevitability of sadness and disappointment. I told those gathered that we may lament change, but we must accept the new realities, adapt, and move on. I shared four points:

1. We should respect our past and our heritage, but we must live in the future.
2. We must respect change as ubiquitous, inevitable, and discontinuous.
3. We must continue to learn and enhance our coping skills.
4. We must view what is happening to us in a healthy perspective.

While we celebrated the past, I shared a quote by Kierkegaard that seemed fitting: "Life can only be understood backwards, but it must be lived forward."

43

Houston, We Have a Problem

O ne of my favorite bromides is particularly fitting looking back on the year 2001: "If everything seems to be going well, you have obviously overlooked something."

The close of the previous year had seen the announcement of the move of the Menninger Clinic and Hospital to Houston. We entered the new year bearing the emotional weight of moving the programs from Topeka—their home for more than 75 years. But we also felt excited to have a plan in place that we believed would ease the organization's financial burdens for the foreseeable future. The emotion I felt most was relief, knowing that the programs developed by my grandfather, uncle, father, and brother would endure.

The search for an affiliate partner was done, but much work lay ahead. To prepare to move the Menninger programs to Texas, many transitional steps were taken. One of the big ones was to locate a site in Houston that could temporarily house the programs in the time between the move out of our Topeka facilities and the construction of a new, permanent home near the Texas Medical Center.

In the spring of 2001, we identified a former psychiatric hospital facility suitable for temporarily housing our operations in Houston. With trustee approval, but prior to the finalization for the agreement with BCM, we signed a ten-year lease for the Houston facility.

If I were given to superstition, a summer storm which ensued might have been interpreted as a bad omen.

After the lease was signed on the Houston facility, Tropical Storm Allison produced major flooding that caused significant damage to the buildings in June of 2001. This was another costly headache that took a toll on the morale of the Menninger staff at the time the negotiations were taxing us all.

I could not help but recall the famous words of James Lovell, mission commander of the Apollo 13 rocket, on April 13, 1970: "Houston, we have a problem."

———————————•———————————

Despite the sadness produced by the imminent move (and the damage to the Houston facility notwithstanding), we felt good about the arrangement with our partners in Texas. But when final details were being hammered out, the negotiations hit a snag.

Our partners from BCM and Methodist Hospital arrived with final paperwork that stated that they would have sole control over the selection of the primary administrator of the hospital. There was apparently doubt in the minds of some of our counterparts at BCM and Methodist Hospital regarding the capacity of the Menninger management team to manage the operation. We, on the other hand, felt strongly that the head of the hospital needed to be someone from the Menninger ethos, who would be loyal to our history and would ensure that our concepts were maintained. I had been planning to relocate temporarily to Houston to serve as CEO throughout the transition period, which I anticipated taking a year or two.

This one sticking point scotched the deal. We planned to sign the final paperwork at a meeting in Topeka in late summer of 2001. But feeling blindsided by this new proviso, representatives of Menninger decided to terminate the negotiations.

No word but "devastated" seems to fit how we felt following that meeting.

We were frustrated that a suitable solution hadn't been reached. We were sorry that we had to tell our employees and the Topeka community that this painful process would be prolonged. We were fearful that our best option for relocation had been lost.

The financial crisis facing the Menninger Foundation went to another level at that point. We were sitting on a ten-year lease on buildings in Houston. We were already in the middle of several processes to move from our Topeka facilities. And now we no longer had a dance partner.

Connie and I had been through the wringer by this point. We read the headlines and heard the talk all over town of the impact the move to Texas would have on Topeka. We were confronted with skepticism that the Menninger programs would be diminished in the partnership. In addition to the financial pressures and the burden of the impact the move would have on our hometown, Connie was saddened that her work with the

Menninger archives would soon be ended. We decided as a couple that regardless of where Menninger eventually relocated, we would remain in Topeka. I had planned to remain CEO through the transition period, to eventually be replaced. Perhaps another role within the organization would be suitable for me at that time. I couldn't worry about that, however. I was completely focused on negotiating the move.

When the move to Houston was aborted in 2001, my role as CEO needed to be reevaluated. The breakdown of negotiations with our Houston partners caused us to look at the situation differently.

After discussion with key trustees, it made sense for a change of leadership to happen immediately. John McKelvey, the Chairman of the Menninger Board of Trustees, stepped in as acting CEO on a transitional basis. He was winding up his career with Midwest Research Institute in Kansas City and had a strong background in business management.

My resignation and McKelvey's appointment as CEO were formalized at the board's annual meeting on November 1, just a few days after my 70th birthday. I became Chairman of the Board of Trustees. In that role, I continued to provide clinical and administrative consultation, to assist with fundraising, and to advise McKelvey as he took over the search for a suitable affiliate partner.

We summarized this new development in our annual Christmas card at the end of 2001:

> When he succeeded his brother Roy as president and CEO in 1993, Walt expected to carry the responsibility for 6 to 10 years; as it turned out, it was 8 1/3 years. During this period, the economics of healthcare have profoundly compromised the traditional role of the private psychiatric hospital. Nonetheless, Menninger was able to sustain its national and international reputation, evidenced in a consistently high ranking in the annual *U.S. News & World Report* surveys (cited as #3 this past year, ranked #1 in 1995). Similarly, our philanthropic support has continued to be extraordinary, with more than $71 million raised in this period, over $30 million of that in the past three years.

Stepping out while the move was still up in the air was the hardest part of my resignation. Moving an organization is one of the hardest things a CEO can do. I knew the impact it would have on Topeka. I knew the impact it would have on the staff and their families. But I felt honored to be the Menninger who led the decision to move, because it was the right thing for the organization.

Under McKelvey's leadership, the board of trustees renewed the search for an affiliate. We hired Bear Stearns to restart the process. We made solicitations to more than 60 medical schools in the renewed search.

One would think that the Menninger staff would have been beaten down by the prolonged search for a partner. Surprisingly, the interest shown by a new round of potential affiliates energized the board and the staff alike. It reminded everyone that we had a product others wanted. Thirteen serious offers were considered.

One of those 13 was, surprisingly, the same Houston partners with whom we'd just severed negotiations. One might assume that the Houston well would have been poisoned by that point. But BCM and Methodist Hospital resubmitted their proposal.

In an interesting twist, both BCM and Methodist Hospital had undergone changes in leadership during the months after our partnership dissolved. When talks were renewed, the poison pill of the choice of hospital administrator had been removed. The Houston partners demonstrated the same enthusiasm we had seen from them in the first round. And this time, we knew much more about each other and what was needed to make the alliance work. After several months of deliberations, it was decided that Houston remained the best option for Menninger. A new agreement with BCM and Methodist Hospital was formally signed by the Menninger directors and trustees on December 4, 2002. The new transition plan was for Menninger to move to Houston in the summer of 2003.

On December 5, 2002, Menninger released the following statement:

The Menninger Clinic announced today that its boards of directors and trustees unanimously approved a partnership with Baylor College of Medicine and The Methodist Hospital to create a comprehensive, world-class center for psychiatric care, research, and education.

This partnership will enhance Menninger's capabilities as a center of excellence in psychiatry and the behavioral sciences by combining Menninger's clinical program with Baylor's College of Medicine and The Methodist Hospital's educational and research environment. Menninger will move its Topeka, Kansas-based clinic to 2801 N. Gessner Road, Houston, during the spring and be fully operational in its new location by early June 2003.

"Baylor College of Medicine and The Methodist Hospital were selected because their proposal best reflected a true partnership among equals and enabled Menninger to preserve its treatment approach," said John McKelvey, Menninger Foundation president and chief executive officer. "They fulfilled the required criteria, which included an internationally recognized medical center; compatibilities in cultures, treatment, and education concepts; and a strong research center with a top-ranked medical school. All of these lead to the ability to recruit world-class clinicians and researchers, and fulfill our mission that was set by Drs. C.F., Will and Karl, and continued forth by Drs. Roy and Walt Menninger."

"As chairman of Baylor's Department of Psychiatry and Behavioral Sciences, I and our faculty are delighted and enthusiastic that Menninger will be joining us in Houston to advance psychiatric treatment locally, nationally, and internationally," said Stuart Yudofsky, M.D., Baylor College of Medicine Department of Psychiatry chairman and chief of psychiatry service at The Methodist Hospital.

"We respect the accomplishments of the Menninger team, and we feel honored and look forward to continuing to build on the richly deserved Menninger reputation and heritage," said Yudofsky. "This historic partnership among Menninger, Baylor College of Medicine, and The Methodist Hospital brings together the most highly qualified healthcare professionals to care for those among us who suffer from psychiatric illnesses. We intend to provide the most effective, patient-centered psychiatric care available anywhere—care informed and enriched by breakthrough research from our science laboratories."

The fateful day arrived on May 30, 2003. Ten semi-trucks loaded with furniture and supplies were en route to Houston when carloads of staff and 29 patients drove out of the Menninger campus, headed for the airport. A chartered plane delivered the staff, patients, and a load of records and prescriptions to the hospital campus in Houston leased two years earlier.

With that, more than 75 years of history in Topeka came to a close. Quotes in *The New York Times* contrasted my brother Roy's disappointment with my pragmatism:

> "I can't stand here without many more feelings than I can accommodate, much less explain," Roy said.
> "I'm nostalgic, but I also recognize you can't live in the past," I said.

Our emotions aside, neither Roy nor I were involved in the details of the move. With McKelvey's work negotiating the partnership completed, Menninger named a new president and CEO, Ian Aitken, who would guide the transition. Aitken became the first non-physician to hold the role of CEO (McKelvey's short term in the role notwithstanding).

Aitken had come to Menninger as an administrator helping with outreach efforts. He had previously been the administrator of a hospital in Chicago. He had only been at Menninger for a few years, but he exhibited the type of common sense, humility, and people skills that were required to make the partnership with BCM and Methodist Hospital work. Though he was a non-physician, the Menninger Board of Directors saw that Aitken embodied the values of caring intrinsic to the organization.

Making the move to Houston with Aitken were 83 employees—about a third of the Topeka staff—including all the key administrative and clinical leaders. That fact assured me that the Menninger tradition would remain strong through the transition.

The city of Houston heralded the arrival of Menninger. The following are excerpts from the May 31, 2003, *Houston Chronicle*:

> The famed Menninger Clinic officially arrives in Houston today, filling the city's longtime gap in the elite treatment of severe addiction and other serious mental illnesses.
>
> Operations will be transferred from Kansas to 2801 Gessner when 29 patients arrive this afternoon by chartered jet. The clinic, considered the nation's foremost psychiatric-care facility for much of the 20th century, will begin accepting new patients Tuesday.
>
> "After working on this partnership for three years, I'm overjoyed it's finally happening," said Dr. Stuart Yudofsky, chairman of the psychiatry department at Baylor College of Medicine and chief of psychiatry at The Methodist Hospital, Menninger's two new partners. "There has been a hole in the heart of the Texas Medical Center, a gaping hole. We are going to sew that hole closed."
>
> Yudofsky said Houston psychiatrists have long had to refer such patients out of state, to Menninger and other clinics.
>
> Menninger arrives in the midst of a crisis in mental health care in Houston and the state. Fifty percent of psychiatric inpatient beds in the greater Houston area have closed since 1996 and the state's Mental Health and Mental Retardation agencies have begun rationing care to the indigent because of budget cuts and cost increases.

In that summer, the departure of Menninger from Topeka was complete. At the end of the process, the affiliation and move had taken three and a half years and cost over $10 million.

Skeptics of the move anticipated that the three partners in the new venture would have trouble co-existing. Those fears were not unfounded. The most common cause of the failure of organizational mergers is cultural incompatibilities.

In the case of transplanting the Menninger programs and people, there certainly was a culture shift. The change was much greater than mere location, but the geographical settings couldn't have been more different. For the past few decades, Menninger was situated on rolling hills overlooking Topeka, with the gentle Kansas River as its backdrop. Inner-city Houston couldn't have been a bigger contrast. Though a campus on several acres was anticipated, you couldn't escape the fact that the new location would be within a bustling metroplex.

Additionally, Menninger had always been a stand-alone entity with complete autonomy. Now it would be part of a consortium collaborating with BCM and Methodist Hospital.

A new clinic board, with six representatives of Menninger Kansas, three of BCM, and three of Methodist Hospital, could have easily turned into an ugly turf battle. But as the transition played out, the group admirably set aside differences for the purpose of making a new Menninger leadership team.

Almost as soon as the 83 staff and 29 patients settled into temporary facilities in Houston, Menninger started admitting new patients. Everyone was a bit shocked when demand was instantly much higher than they anticipated. The Menninger Clinic broke even in its third year in Houston. A 50-acre parcel of land just a short drive from the Texas Medical Center was located for a new facility, and in 2011 Menninger broke ground on a 120-bed, $65 million facility.

The happy ending of the story is that Houston became home to a world-class psychiatric hospital.

Unfortunately, the other side of the coin is less pleasant. The move left a big hole in Topeka. The departure of Menninger from Topeka had a significant impact on both the general and the professional community.

The most immediate loss, obviously, was an industry that had recently employed over 1,000 people. Many of those staff were highly educated, well-paid professionals with families. These families were particularly prominent in Topeka's educational and artistic circles.

Regrettably, it became more difficult for Topeka to recruit mental health practitioners. Many who were employed in the community had initially come to Topeka as students in the Menninger School of Psychiatry. With the departure of Menninger, Topeka's access to that talent pool was lost.

Sadly, for some Topekans, the long-standing pride in the national and international reputation of Menninger shifted to feelings of anger and bitterness. Not only had the city lost a landmark, it had lost a substantial employer and an institution that brought significant revenue and talent into the community. Some perceived Menninger's affiliation with Baylor Med as a rejection of Topeka and the state of Kansas. Some resented that we hadn't managed to affiliate with University of Kansas Medical Center in Kansas City.

I was more or less unaffected by the community reaction. I was focused on what I believed to be best for the institution. My sole desire was to ensure that Menninger not meet its end while on my watch.

———————————

As I mentioned above, Menninger executed its move to Houston in the summer of 2003. Until all the facilities could be prepared, clinical services would continue at the Topeka campus. So, the wind-down of all operations in Kansas took some time. A new Menninger-Baylor-Methodist Foundation was created to provide oversight for the operations in Houston. The Menninger Kansas Foundation, on which I served, oversaw maintenance, development, and sale of property and other matters, and continues even to the present to handle matters within the state pertaining to the organization.

I also provided consultation to the Houston foundation. In 2003, I was elected chairman of the newly-formed Board of Visitors for Menninger in Houston, which was created to solicit interest and philanthropic support for the Houston-based programs. I was pleased to serve in these capacities because it allowed me to observe the transition and to develop relationships with the new leadership in Houston. I can happily say that my fears of what would happen to the Menninger ethos were gradually assuaged. The new leadership was respectful of Menninger traditions and solicitous of former directors, including Roy and myself. We always felt welcomed and appreciated when we visited the new location.

My involvement became important a few years after the move when a crisis of leadership befell the clinic. As the head of the Menninger Kansas Board, I was kept abreast of the problems and had some insight that the board in Texas didn't have. I was appointed to the Menninger Texas board of directors at that time to assist in resolving the matter.

I would continue in another role which I had assumed in 2001, that of editor of the *Bulletin of the Menninger Clinic*. I had been one of the publication's primary contributors since I became Menninger's Director of Education in the mid-1980s. I had overseen the content of one of the quarterly editions of the bulletin, drawing material from presentations at the Park City winter psychiatry conferences. Even after the move of Menninger to Houston, I continued in the role of editor of the bulletin for more than a decade.

There are not many "institutionally sponsored" journals that have stood the test of time and remained of quality and reference. The *American Journal of Psychiatry* by the American Psychiatric Association is their organizational journal. But I don't know of a comparable "institutional journal." I think it reflects on the commitment of the organization not just to practice, but to expand the knowledge of the psychiatric community. It's a reflection of organizational values. It has maintained a commitment to education in the profession.

It was also a way for us communicate the big events of the institution, to tell the story and retain the values of Menninger. It serves as a valuable archive of the history of the institution. And the papers were always of high quality on important topics. For these reasons, I was honored to serve as editor. The work appealed to my journalistic interests. It kept me connected to the Menninger programs in Houston. And it allowed me to occasionally remind readers of the institution's rich history.

Another piece of the Menninger world evolved following the move. The Topeka Institute for Psychoanalysis, closed in the summer of 2001, took on a new life. A number of faculty and students of the institute joined forces with colleagues from the Kansas City Psychoanalytic Society and

Institute to establish the Greater Kansas City and Topeka Psychoanalytic Center.

I had come to another transition point in my life.

My career had unfolded in roughly ten-year increments. After a little more than a decade of training in college, medical school, and residency, I spent nearly a decade transitioning through roles with the U.S. Public Health Service and as a young doctor at Menninger.

Then came the decade of the 1970s at the Topeka State Hospital. Next, I spent the 1980s in various directorial positions at Menninger. And finally, I spent just short of a decade as CEO of the organization.

Thus, I had dedicated approximately half a century to the mental health of my fellow man. During that final phase of my career, I encapsulated much of what I had learned in two speeches describing the lofty goal I pursued throughout my career: to heal broken people in a broken world.

44

Healing Broken People

After years of study and observation, I learned one thing: The world is full of hurting people.

Another thing I learned: Hurt people hurt people.

As a psychiatrist, I learned a great deal about the types of wounds and injuries people carry around inside. These wounds are different than a broken leg or a broken arm, obviously. These unseen injuries manifest themselves in the thoughts, feelings, and behaviors of the wounded person. In nearly every case, it's easier to diagnose and treat a physical wound than a psychological one.

I was asked on occasion to talk about healing people and healing the world. These are, obviously, two very different topics. But when you think about it, it is wounded people who cause most of the problems in the world, directly or indirectly.

The following are thoughts on the subject of healing the person, taken from talks I gave in the latter years of my career.

> In the course of becoming a physician, one learns that, try as one might, you cannot save everyone. Pain is ubiquitous and loss is inevitable in life. People do suffer and die, despite heroic efforts of healers.
>
> But life also teaches us that the capacity of individuals to deal with life's adversities is not the same for all people, nor is it the same for any one of us at different times. We all have our limits, and they can be surpassed by a fulminating infection or a powerful explosion.
>
> Life is full of adversity and experiences that wound us. Several years ago, I came across a cartoon portraying a newborn nursery with cribs and infants. Prominently displayed on the wall was a sign saying: "Caution: Living

may be hazardous to your health."

And it most certainly is! There are hazards all around us that we must inevitably negotiate if we are to live a normal life.

Life thus becomes a series of trade-offs, of calculated risks and probabilities. When a painful event does occur—and one will, sooner or later—you react with hurt and resentment and bitterness. It shouldn't have happened. It's unfair, unjust!

We search for someone to blame, and all too often in today's world, someone to sue! But adversity and pain are not always someone else's fault; and in any case, we are faced with the challenge of adapting to our life's encounters.

A major adaptational challenge in life is to maintain a sense of control and mastery over one's self, particularly in relation to the external world. Each individual is challenged to balance inner strivings, inner restraints, and the demands and rewards of the external world.

Effective coping or adaptation in life is a function of our capacity to master these demands.

The "loss of control" over one's life can be profoundly unsettling, as seen in persons who have experienced overwhelming trauma and suffer from a post-traumatic stress disorder. When one is confronted with a situation that significantly impairs the ability to sustain a sense of autonomy, adequacy, and effective control over one's destiny, one's overall survival can be threatened.

In response to most of life's insults, whether it is a cold virus, or a cut finger, or a personal rebuff, we rely on our internal healing processes. But we will all, at one time or another, have some kind of injury which requires the assistance of some external agent to facilitate or enhance the healing process.

The primary healing process occurs within the wounded individual. The presumptive or designated "healer," physician, or other supportive person, plays a role of facilitator.

How is this accomplished? What is it that the "healer" does? Certainly, he empowers the wounded person to cope more effectively with the injury or illness, by providing caring, education, insight, support, and other appropriate and necessary interventions such as medicine and or surgical attention.

Caring is an important part of this process… We are keenly aware of physicians who are absolutely superb technicians, but who approach patients in such a cold manner as to prompt doubt and distress in the patient.

Caring has long been identified as an important part of health care quality. Dr. Francis Peabody said it eloquently (in his 1927 paper "The Care of the Patient" published in the *Journal of the American Medical Association*):

> The good physician knows his patients through and through, and his knowledge is bought dearly. Time, sympathy, and understanding must be lavishly dispensed, but the reward is to be found in the personal bond which forms the greatest satisfaction of the practice of medicine. One of the essential qualities of the clinician is interest in humanity, for the secret of the care of the patient is in caring for the patient.

As we discuss caring, we should consider the elements of healing: Love, Faith, Hope, Humor and Relationships.

Love:

Caring may be identified as one aspect of the "intangible": love. Love is a most powerful force, countering alienation, loneliness, low self-esteem, and self-doubt. Love is an affirming experience that reinforces life.

Consider the unexpected outcome in a laboratory research study of the cholesterol deposits in rabbits. In a routine study, it was discovered that some of the rabbits had remarkably reduced cholesterol deposits when compared to other rabbits in the study.

Initially, the researchers had no explanation for this phenomenon, for they had tried to carefully control all the factors and make sure all the rabbits in the study were treated comparably.

Then they discovered that a night worker in the laboratory had been playing with some of the rabbits. Lo and behold, the rabbits he gave special attention and affection to as he cleaned the lab were the ones with fewer cholesterol deposits.

After the researchers discovered this, they repeated the experiment, deliberately building into the experimental protocol the fact that some rabbits got more attention, fondling, and affection. Again, the rabbits that received the tender, loving care had fewer cholesterol deposits; and the researchers published their findings in *Science* in 1980.

My uncle, Dr. Karl Menninger, noted in *The Vital Balance* in 1963 that "the interference with the giving and receiving of love disrupts and demoralizes the integrative patterns of life and makes us feel ill and act in opposition to our desires." Likewise, a loving environment can have a significant therapeutic impact.

Faith:

Faith is likewise a powerful influence on the course of healing, although in the secular world, many practitioners may pay it little heed.

When one is damaged and distressed, faith can play an important role in helping place the adversity in a broader context. Further, religious faith can play a role in healing that secular efforts cannot.

This is especially the case for an emotionally troubled person to achieve a sense of forgiveness, particularly in the case of a sense of guilt for some presumed or real transgression/"sin." Often it is much easier to forgive others than to forgive oneself, or to truly believe in the forgiveness of sins.

In relation to faith, one can consider the healing power of prayer. A systematic review of the available data on the efficacy of any form of distant healing including prayer was reported in the *Annals of Internal Medicine* by J.A. Astin, E. Harkness, and E. Ernst in 2000: Of five studies that examined prayer as a distant healing intervention, two trials showed a significant treatment effect on at least one outcome in patients being prayed for.

One of those was a study of 990 patients suffering from life-threatening cardiac conditions at Kansas City's St. Luke's Hospital. Of that group, 466 were randomly assigned to be prayed for daily by five separate individuals from a pool of 75 volunteers who knew nothing about the objects of their prayer except for their first names and that they were ill. Overall, those who were prayed for did 11 percent better than the control group.

In a Catholic congregation in my home community, parishioners suffering from stress or illness are given pager instruments that have a vibration mechanism activated by a phone call that other members of the parish make as they offer a prayer on behalf of the hurting person.

While it has not been subject to scientific study, a patient with whom I worked felt a great benefit and reassurance as she felt the vibrations associated with the prayers on her behalf.

Power of expectations represents another facet of faith—the degree to which our faith and expectations prompt certain behaviors and responses.

Hope:

The formal dictionary definition of "hope" speaks of desire with expectation of obtaining what is desired, or belief that is it obtainable. Synonyms are trust and reliance. But that definition does not really capture the psychological power and meaning of hope.

In *The Vital Balance*, my uncle ascribed hope to "the mysterious workings of the repetition compulsion, the very essence of which is a kind of relentless and indefatigable pursuit of resolution and freedom. I would see in hope another aspect of the life instinct, the creative drive which wards against dissolution and destructiveness."

In "A Life Setting Conducive to Illness, the Giving-Up–Given-Up Complex," published in the *Annals of Internal Medicine* in 1968, George Engel reviewed 100 reports of sudden death under some unusual circumstances, such as receiving news of the death of a loved one; death during situations of danger like a riot, storm, earthquake or personal assault; death after being accused of a serious offense; or death during what should have been an occasion for joy like a reunion after a long separation.

Engel compared these phenomena to circumstances under which patients become ill, and he found one particular psychological pattern especially associated with disease onset, a pattern he labeled "The Giving-Up–Given-Up Complex." He wrote:

> What are its essential elements? …a sense of psychological impotence, a feeling that for briefer or longer periods of time, one is unable to cope with changes in the environment… In place of the smooth, almost effortless integration of behavior and the sense of confidence and mastery of the environment that mark effective

functioning, there is a disruption, a pause, an interruption, while the mind seems to search in vain for a solution.

Characteristics of the "Giving-up – Given-up complex" according to Engle are:

(1) affects of helplessness and hopelessness—feelings of being at the end of his rope, at a loss, bewildered, uncertain, at an impasse. When hopeless, he holds himself to account for his failure or inability to cope, and he has no expectations that any change in the environment is possible or will help; help, even if offered, will be of no avail;

(2) a depreciated image of oneself—one who is no longer competent, in control, or capable of functioning in his accustomed manner;

(3) a loss of gratification from relationships or roles in life;

(4) a disruption of the sense of continuity between past, present and future; and

(5) a reactivation of memories of earlier periods of giving up.

While hopelessness can lead to disease, hope can make you well—reflected by the anecdotal experiences with hopeless cases cited by Bernie Siegel in his 1986 *Love, Medicine and Miracles*. Siegel observed that "Exceptional Cancer Patients" have an attitude that doesn't dispute the diagnosis, but does defy the prognosis.

Norman Cousins wrote in *Head First: The Biology of Hope* in 1989:

Intense determination and hope...can have a physiological effect. Positive feelings...actually can stimulate the spleen, producing an increase in red blood cells and a corresponding

increase in the number of cancer fighting cells....
All the positive forces—love, hope, faith, will to
live, determination, purpose, festivity,
laughter—are powerful antagonists of depression and help to create an environment that makes
medical care more effective.

Suzanne Kobasa studied groups of middle and
upper-level executives to determine differences between
those who experienced high levels of stress without
becoming ill and those who did become ill. In "Stressful
Life Events, Personality, and Health: An Inquiry Into
Hardiness" published in the *Journal of Personality and
Social Psychology* in 1979, she identified the difference
as a function of "hardiness," and she characterized hardy
persons as having three general characteristics:

(1)   they believe that they can control or
influence the events of their experience;
(2)   they feel deeply involved in or
committed to the activities of their lives; and
(3)   they anticipate change as an exciting
challenge to further development.

Humor:

After his follow-up study of Harvard students who
participated in a study funded by the William T. Grant
Foundation, George Vaillant concluded that humor is one
of the truly elegant defenses in the human repertoire. He
wrote in his 1977 book *Adaption to Life*, "Few would
deny that the capacity for humor, like hope, is one of
mankind's most potent antidotes for the woes of Pandora's
box."

Vaillant identified humor as one of those ego
mechanisms associated with successful, healthy
adaptation in the 94 individuals whom he followed up 30
years after they were originally studied as healthy

Harvard undergraduates.

Psychoanalyst Martin Grotjahn observed in his 1957 book *Beyond Laughter*:

> The humorist...behaves as if he knows the misery of this world but resolutely proceeds to disregard it. He remains aware of the valley of tears but behaves as if it is still the Garden of Eden. He proceeds not by denying the existence of misery but by pretending to be victorious over it. He illustrates for us the hope for the victory of infantile narcissism over all experience.

A vigorous proponent of the positive effects was William F. Fry, who found both the arousal and cathartic effects of humor in psychological terms are paralleled in physiological processes. He noted that laughter increases breathing activity and oxygen exchange, increases muscular activity and heart rate, and stimulates the cardiovascular system, the sympathetic nervous system, and the production of catecholamines like epinephrine— all of which in turn stimulate the production in the brain of endorphins, the body's natural pain-reducing enzymes. (Taken from Bernard Saper's "Humor in Psychiatric Healing," published in *Psychiatric Quarterly*.)

Relationships:

> Healing has, as its centerpiece, relationship. Relationships provide the invaluable role of support, and support is repeatedly noted as a factor in enhancing recovery or response from stress... Support systems provide love, faith, hope, and ideally, humor.

William Tarnwater wrote in "The Experience of Seeking and Receiving Help," published in the *Bulletin of the Menninger Clinic* in 1969:

The relationship of the healer to the individual in search of healing is enhanced by the healer's appreciation of the ambivalent feelings of individuals who need help. That is, the person in need of help may experience inevitably some anxiety, sometimes a sense of shame, inadequacy, failure, humiliation, resentment, feelings of worthlessness and being "not okay."

It's important to note that healing is not a "zero sum" process. In the act of healing, the healer also benefits.

45

Healing a Broken World

A psychiatrist devotes himself to helping individuals sort out their personal lives, to help them recognize the ways they distort reality, and to cope with the challenges they face. This is their attempt to change the world on the micro level, one life at a time. In the previous chapter I shared excerpts from talks on the subject of healing the individual.

I was occasionally asked, however, to look at mental health on a macro level, to try to assess why the world is the way it is. Why does so much hate exist? Why do people cause so much destruction? Why does the world seem broken?

There is no way to definitively answer these questions. But I tried on various occasions to shed some light on the universal problems of hate, violence, and destruction. The following are comments from one of those occasions, the Pastoral Institute Seminar in Columbus, Georgia, on April 21, 1995, at which I delivered the speech "Healing a Broken World."

Let me begin with words from my late uncle's book *Man Against Himself*:

One would expect that in the face of...overwhelming blows at the hands of Fate or Nature, man would oppose himself steadfastly to death and destruction in a universal brotherhood of beleaguered humanity. But this is not the case. Whoever studies the human behavior of human beings cannot escape the conclusion that we must reckon with an enemy within the lines. It becomes increasingly evident that some of the destruction which curses the earth is self-destruction; the extraordinary propensity of the human being to join hands with external forces in an attack upon his own existence is one of the most remarkable of biological phenomena.

In the context of that book, Dr. Karl Menninger was thinking about literal self-destruction, suicide. But the fact is, the greatest destruction that curses the earth is the violence human beings wreak on each other. Indeed, homo sapiens is one of the only two species that kill its own indiscriminately. The other: the rat!

The Power of Emotions:

The French philosopher René Descartes, conjuring the essence of being, concluded after much deep thought, "I think, therefore I am." He opined that the only proof he could make for really existing was the fact that he was able to think. Our intellect is one reason our species— homo sapiens, "wise man"—has been able to so completely and effectively master our planet. Certainly, our extraordinary forebrain, an incredible computer with 10 to the 13th power connections, has allowed us to take our experience and organize it in symbols which we call language, which can be communicated across time and space.

If we were totally intellectual beings, without emotions, we would presumably function reasonably and without conflict—much like robots. Were we to bump into each other, we might be programmed simply to say, "I'm sorry," and to proceed without further incident. But we are not robots. We are more than just intellectual. We are also emotional beings. Indeed, I am as impressed with "feeling" being the proof that we do indeed exist, as Descartes was with thinking.

How often have you heard the idea that if you think you may be dreaming, you should pinch yourself. Why? Because it is in the process of feeling that pinch, that pain, that you are assured you do indeed exist. Which is to say, "I feel, therefore I am."

Emotions—a reflection of our state of feeling—are a powerful part of our lives. Our emotions represent the "spice" in our life, the highs and the lows, the excitement and thrills and pain and anguish. From our earliest infancy throughout life, we strive to achieve pleasure and to avoid pain. Although often frustrated in our quest, this striving is prompted by powerful emotional forces within us—forces evident in young children well before they have a capacity to intellectually understand what is happening. Further, a pattern is set whereby feelings may overwhelm our intellectual understanding and thus direct our behavior.

Sigmund Freud expressed it this way in "The Disillusionment of the War," 1915:

> Students of human nature and philosophers have long taught us that we are mistaken in regarding our intelligence as an independent force and in overlooking its dependence on emotional life. Our intellect, they teach us, can function reliably only when it is removed from the influences of strong emotional impulses; otherwise, it behaves merely as an instrument of the (emotional) will and delivers the inference which the (emotional) will requires.

The emotions which have been identified as the driving forces in human behavior are love and hate. Of these, the force of love is associated with positive and constructive activity, and the force of hate with negative and destructive activity. Both emotional forces are relevant in the context of healing.

Origins of Hate:

From whence cometh hate? I would cite three

402

sources. First, its roots appear to be in the nature of our being. Second, its expression evolves as part of the normal development from infancy through childhood into adulthood. Finally, it is reinforced and intensified in individuals who are exposed to parental violence and childhood abuse and neglect.

With respect to the first source, from our birth, we have an innate striving which is self-centered, in search of pleasure, with aggressive activity and with rage when we are frustrated or hurt. Students of the development of aggression in young children have noted a striking upsurge in a child's aggressive drive at about nine months of age that may account for the development of obstinacy and willfulness. Anna Freud and Dorothy Burlingham observed in their "Hamstead Nurseries in London" as cited by Karl Menninger in his 1942 book *Love Against Hate*:

> Children between the ages of one and two, when put together in a play pen, will bite each other, pull each other's hair and rob each other's toys, without regard for the other child's unhappiness... (Y)oung children at play...will destroy their toys, pull off the arms and legs of their dolls or soldiers, puncture their balls, smash whatever is breakable, and will only mind the result because complete destruction of the toy blocks further play... We often say, half-jokingly, that there is a continual war raging in a nursery. We mean by that, that at this time of life, destructive and aggressive impulses are still at work in children in a manner in which they only occur in grown-up life when they are let loose for the purpose of war.

The second origin develops from capacity of the helpless, dependent young child to deal with conflicting feelings which he/she experiences. These include the good, pleasurable feelings when he is cared for and nurtured by mother; and the distressing, uncomfortable feelings when his needs are not responded to by that same mother. Indeed, when frustrated or hurt, he can do little but verbally protest, since he is a Lilliputian in the land of powerful, giant, grown-up adults.

The young child, who doesn't have the capacity to understand how someone can be both good and bad, solves the dilemma by mechanisms of splitting, externalization, and projection. The infant splits off good feelings and bad feelings and attributes them to separate entities. By externalization, the child gets rid of unpleasant self-images and their accompanying feeling states, attributing them to a handy target. Thus, a child who falls and hurts himself may avoid chagrin and self-blame by saying the doll was responsible. Projection is a defense mechanism which occurs at a later stage of development, and attributes unacceptable thoughts or impulses to some other person in an effort to be rid of them.

As the child matures, he incorporates images and concepts associated with good feelings which enhance a sense of identity and self-esteem. Simultaneously, there is an externalization of images and concepts associated with bad or undesirable attributes onto persons or groups of persons who are suitable targets and who are generally different in ethnicity or nationality. Psychoanalyst Vamik Volkan wrote in his 1988 book *The Need to Have Enemies & Allies* that "the mind of the developing child starts creating the concept of 'enemy' and this concept goes far and above the animal phenomenon of fear of danger." Volkan experienced this personally, being raised a Turk on the island of Cyprus, where Greeks and Turks have always been mutual antagonists even though they lived side by side for centuries until 1974, when the island was divided.

Finally, some of the anger and hate in children is the

result of their experience at the hands of significant adults in their life. As Karl Menninger noted in *Love Against Hate,* "Parents often treat their child as they themselves were treated by their own parents, many years previously, thus achieving a long-deferred and displaced revenge for the indignities and suffering they endured." Further, research has increasingly demonstrated that children who have been the victim of extraordinary violence and abuse grow up to pass it on.

Hate Begets Hate:

Of one thing you can be certain, anger begets anger and hate begets hate. I came to appreciate this truism many years ago in those moments of tension in my marriage when a disagreement escalated to an angry outburst. It became obvious that shouting back in a louder voice never helped. It only increased the intensity of the dispute. Similarly, when the exasperating behavior of an offspring moved me to lose my cool, the anger would escalate. Certainly, parental control must be established over a child who is out of control, but if that control is administered in anger or rage, the emotions will just fester in the child.

An Exemplary Solution—The Lawrence Experience:

In 1970, the community of Lawrence, Kansas was in great distress and crisis. Lawrence, at that time, was a community with a population of approximately 40,000 persons, plus an additional 25,000 University of Kansas students, located some 40 miles west of Kansas City. It was also known among the "hip" populations as "River City," where one could find "clean" drugs. The city had experienced incidents of civil unrest, firebombings, student riots, a young Black man killed by police gunfire, a curfew, and vigilantes patrolling the streets. The community was split, with much enmity between groups. The police were caught in the middle, under attack from every group in the community as being either too soft or too hard.

The city manager and the police chief called on the Menninger institution for help with a program to help improve police-community relations. It became clear that the community needed more than some public relations activity; it needed to find a way to bring the community together to address the problems.

While the larger community was at the edge of an abyss, the initial challenge was to identify the leaders of the various communities that made up the larger community. These groupings included the city government, the merchant group, the "vigilantes," the Native Americans, African Americans, "street" people, University of Kansas students and administration, and the police. Our staff started by canvassing various stated leaders in the community about who they believed influenced decisions in the community, and a "power structure" of some 30 persons was identified. These 30 persons were brought together to review and support the proposal for what needed to be done.

That leadership group helped identify the significant communities within Lawrence who felt aggrieved and organized those subgroups to designate a representative to be a part of a steering committee or "board of directors" for the ongoing project. Once created, it met weekly to formulate and implement a series of all-day workshops involving participants from the different communities. Meeting on neutral turf, each workshop would start by defining the problems of Lawrence and end by recommending solutions. Between these two tasks was unstructured chaos, with each representative outlining his or her complaints about Lawrence's problems: intolerance; prejudice; insufficient employment opportunities; insufficient vocational training; inadequate public transportation; inadequate housing; inadequate compensation for police, firemen and other public employees; and difficulties in the school district. The issues most frequently cited were black/white, town/gown, street/straight, and rich/poor.

In the process of meeting together, individuals were confronted with the myths perpetuated about each other. Everyone agreed that the police had an impossible job, and the police officers ended up smelling like roses. The participants came to assume that people had reasonable motives for what they did, and misunderstandings were exposed in the process of formulating recommendations for the larger community. Overall, the ten retreats resulted in some 80 recommendations, published in the local newspaper and presented to the City Council, regarding housing, public policy, police actions, etc. Virtually all were adopted in one form or another. Physical confrontations were markedly reduced. And neighborhood groups which originated at that time continued to function for a number of years thereafter.

Healthy Communities:

In May 1970, Lawrence was not a healthy community. What is a healthy community? It is a community with a vision which reflects concern for the common good, for something higher than individual needs. It is a community which promotes health by being a nurturing place to live. It is a community committed to a clean, safe physical environment; a stable ecosystem; a diverse, vital and innovative economy; a high degree of participation and control by the public; and which is mutually supportive and non-exploitave. It is a community which encompasses three fundamental principles:

(1)   The recognition that health and well-

being are interconnected with social, cultural, physical, economic and other factors,

    (2)   With community-wide participation and collaboration in defining and meeting needs to improve health and the quality of life, and

    (3)   Intersectional responsibility for developing locally relevant solutions.

A New Paradigm for Healing:

According to the 1981 *New Webster's Dictionary of the English Language,* to "heal," as a transitive verb, means "to make hale, sound, or well; to cure of a disease or wound and restore health; to reconcile, as a breach or difference; to purify or cleanse." As an intransitive verb: "to grow sound; to return to sound state." How do we apply this concept of healing to the larger world?

In their 1991 article "Healing and Empowering Through Community Narrative," Julian Rappaport and Ronald Simkins proposed that the term "healing" should not be limited to repair of past hurts. "Healing is something everyone needs. ...healing is a process that is proactive as well as reactive. Everyone who experiences healing is better equipped to enter into new life challenges. Thus, healing, prevention and empowerment are interwoven products of community beliefs, attitudes and behaviors that apply to the entire community." Utilizing a narrative of a religious community, they cite the value of individuals to become healers and the power of the people in a community to care for one another.

How do we go about healing? Rappaport and Simkins suggested that we must make "efforts to change existing social institutions and to create new settings that operate by different 'rules of the game.'" They also suggested developing "settings, either within traditional social institutions or as alternatives to them, designed to facilitate the empowerment of people by means of citizen participation in the decisions and activities that affect their lives."

An additional perspective regarding healing in the context of the larger society was offered by Richard Katz in his 1984 article "Empowering and Synergy: Expanding the Community's Healing Resources." He noted that a "scarcity paradigm dominates Western thinking about the existence and distribution of a wide variety of resources." But from his study of community healing systems, he posited that "resources created by human activities and intentions, such as helping and healing, are intrinsically expanding and renewable, and need not be assumed under a scarcity paradigm."

To establish this environment in Western industrialized society, Katz believed there must be a radical paradigm shift. It depends upon a belief that self and community can work toward a common good while seeking to fulfill their own perceived needs.

How Can We Do This?

Communities are made up of individuals, and the healing of a community must be paralleled by the healing of individuals who can create a new context for "enemies and allies." The old focus on differences and scapegoating of others as being "not one of us" must be overcome. We must deal with hate without responding in kind.

One thing is clear—when you experience or are confronted with such intense emotion, rational intellectual discussion is not possible. Sometimes, the only suitable response is to just listen, allow the angry person some distance and give him/her time to cool down. Insofar as possible, avoid a confrontation that puts the other person down or in a position of losing face or self-esteem. Recognize that hate is often a projection of some underlying unhappiness with oneself. Ideally, you should search for ways to help that person actually enhance his/her self-esteem.

Yet, as I speak of hate in others, I realize that I fall into the common trap. That is, the implication is that hatred and bigotry are "out there" somewhere. We must remember the wisdom of Walt Kelly's Pogo who observed: "We have met the enemy and they is us!" All of us tend to externalize or project unacceptable parts of ourselves on others and make them the "enemy." It is much easier to focus on others as the cause for our difficulty than to come to grips with our own inner "enemy."

In reality, there may be little we can do about changing most of those "others." We must begin with ourselves, and how we deal with our own bigotry—which is there—and our rage; how we respond when we are hurt and feel wronged. The natural impulse is to strike out, hit back, demand our pound of flesh, without acknowledging that our anger begets more anger and our hate begets more hate. It is all too easy to claim an eye for an eye and not recognize how that retaliation perpetuates the hate.

Nonetheless, again and again, both here and abroad, the solution to individual or group hatred is an effort to eliminate and destroy the hated "enemy." It is as if we are safe only if we achieve some kind of external "cleansing"—individual or ethnic. But killing or reviling others does not truly solve the problem of hate, either in others or in oneself.

So what can we do? We must address the problem of hate from two perspectives: within and without. First, we must start by looking within ourselves, at our own insecurities and our own love for ourselves. Do we truly love ourselves, or are we so angry and so questioning of our own self-esteem and worth, that we can do naught but pass that anger on? Look for ways to become a better person, to take part in activities or work that makes the world a better place without having to put others down. Accentuate the positive in oneself and in the world.

Secondly, we must find some way to acknowledge our commonality with those with whom we may disagree. Let me again quote my uncle, Dr. Karl Menninger (from *Love Against Hate*):

> The world is made up of people, but the people of the world forget this. ...It is hard to believe that there are not some supermen and some archfiends who manipulate the rest of us and guide our destinies.

We do need to be cleansed of our own rage, and to help others be cleansed, but not by "ethnic" cleansing. Rather we must search out constructive opportunities to help others, to "clean" by enhancing the lives of others, not destroying them. In so doing, we will find ourselves cleansed, emotionally, spiritually, in every way. We will then experience the wisdom articulated by a marvelous Nigerian proverb which I learned from Peace Corps volunteers: "When the right hand washes the left hand, the right hand becomes clean also."

46

Transitions and Love Lost

I spent the majority of my life either preparing to work at the Menninger Clinic, or, finally, in positions of directorship within the organization.

After all those years of striving, it was suddenly gone. In 2003, the clinic relocated to Houston.

You might suspect that was a tremendous loss to me personally and to my family. But the truth is, I didn't experience it as such. Certainly, there was a huge shift in how I spent my time and how much direct influence I had on the organization. But challenges and opportunities continued to present themselves daily, keeping me busy. I was hardly at a loss for things to do.

That's not to say there weren't a lot of emotions connected to the events of the preceding couple of years. I was saddened that Topeka had lost a landmark institution, not to mention jobs for hundreds of the city's citizens. Of course, I couldn't help but feel disappointment that we weren't able to find a way for the organization to continue on its same course. I felt the weight of the work and sacrifice put forth by my grandfather, father, uncle, brother, and so many others to build the institution. I took solace in knowing that I had helped to ensure its continuance under unfavorable conditions. It wouldn't end on my watch, and for that I was thankful.

The truth is, I didn't experience the move of Menninger as a loss because I remained involved with the Menninger Clinic in its new location. I made regular trips to Houston during the first few years to assist in the transition, provide clinical and forensic consultation, and ensure that the spirit of the Menninger Clinic carried on. It was a pleasure to be so warmly welcomed on my visits to the Houston campus. I was elected chairman of the newly-formed Board of Visitors for Menninger in Houston, which solicited interest and philanthropic support for the organization. This tapped my fundraising experience and perpetuated many of the relationships Menninger had forged with donors over the years.

I also continued to serve as editor of the *Bulletin of the Menninger Clinic*, which allowed me to help the organization retain its history and perpetuate its long-held values. That seemed of particular importance in light of the move and influence of new leadership.

Through these areas of engagement, I didn't disconnect from Menninger in 2003, but rather continued involvement in the organization in a variety of ways.

———————————

While I did remain connected to Menninger Texas, I nonetheless had more free time to invest in outside interests than I'd had in years. Upon the closure of the Menninger Campus in Topeka, I set up an office on Topeka's Wanamaker Drive, where I saw a handful of patients as a private psychiatrist. After years of administrative duties—focusing on staff, facilities, and finances all day long—it was refreshing and rewarding to reengage in therapy with a few patients, learning about their lives and helping them.

Mary Donohue was instrumental in the successful move of my base of operations. I kept a busy schedule of speaking and serving as a consultant to a host of organizations while Mary ran the office, organized my files, and managed my schedule. For nearly four decades, Mary's assistance was crucial to my success.

There's no question that in any kind of administrative role, the help of an executive assistant is essential. I observed that my father sometimes needed as many as three secretaries to keep track of all he did. But I'm not sure they were all that capable. I swore that if I were ever in that position, I would make sure to have a competent secretary.

Through my career that spanned the Topeka State Hospital, Menninger, and private practice, Mary adapted masterfully, keeping me organized and informed. She was adept at shorthand, so I could dictate reports and letters which she handled efficiently. She made sure all the administrative tasks were done. All my records and reports and correspondence and bills, she took care of. There were a lot of things for which I was theoretically responsible in the running of our office, but which she handled for me.

I think most people will agree, if you want to get something accomplished with a CEO or head of an organization, you really don't need to deal with that leader, you deal with his or her secretary or executive assistant. Those are the people who know everything. They can refer you to where to go or what to do to navigate the system. Mary taught me that. She was excellent at dealing with people. But if you disrespected or slighted her, you had much more difficulty getting access to me.

During the tenuous phase in which we sought a new home for the Menninger Clinic, I received a couple of awards that lifted my spirit: I was awarded the Silver Buffalo Award, the highest volunteer recognition of the Boy Scouts of America. After decades of involvement with the organization on the national level, I engaged with the Boy Scouts on the local level, a very rewarding new endeavor.

I was also honored to receive the John P. McGovern Compleat Physician Award, presented by the Houston Academy of Medicine and Harris County (Texas) Medical Society.

Connie and I celebrated 50 years of marriage in 2003. She was still just as beautiful, sweet, and kind as the day I married her. But sadly, things were not the same.

The move of the Menninger Clinic to Houston was hard for Connie. She lost her work with the Menninger archives. Her position was abolished in the fall of 2002. In her four years of work with the archives, she had gotten them all into proper storage in acid-free boxes, efficiently categorized. It was our understanding that the archives would all be moved to Houston. But my cousin Rosemary—Karl's daughter—didn't want her father's papers to be moved away from Topeka. She filed suit to prevent that from happening. Eventually the lawsuit was settled to keep all our papers at the Kansas State Archives. All my papers will go there when I have no more need for them.

Without her job at Menninger, Connie fell into what seemed like depression. She struggled to continue in the activities that brought her pleasure.

She remained on the board of the Hall Center for the Humanities at Kansas University, and she shifted some of her attention to the Topeka &

Shawnee County Public Library. It was in 2002 that she was awarded the Community Resource Council's 2002 Ramona Hood Award for her years of volunteerism in the community. That recognition and her outlets of volunteerism helped relieve her mind and give her a sense of purpose.

But still her condition worsened. It became evident by summer of 2004 that what she suffered from was not merely depression.

I wrote in that year's Christmas card:

> Connie's depression has evolved into an Alzheimer's-like-situation with compromised mental and motor function. Although the etiology is unclear, a late summer CT brain scan shows she has advanced atrophy (loss of substance) of the frontal lobes, which severely compromises her executive decision-making capacity and affects her recent memory. She also has limits in her motor abilities, as well as her attention span and patience.
>
> It is difficult to accept a gradual process occurring in a long-standing partner, one who has been so integral to making life meaningful. As we face the fact we will not be here forever, we are challenged to revisit what life is all about. We think about what will remain when we pass on—the works in which we have been engaged and the progeny who will survive us.

The impact of this development on me was both emotional and practical. I was distraught watching my beloved Connie become less and less herself. Our playful, affectionate interaction faded as she grew less able to communicate and respond. She became easily confused and fearful. Whenever I was not with her, even for just a few minutes, she would ask, "Where's Walt?"

My focus shifted from outside activity to caring for Connie. I gave up most of my engagements in order to be with her. Soon Connie required round-the-clock care. Our son Fritz, with his training in nursing, was invaluable. He moved back into our home and attended to Connie with both skill and affection. He shared with me the responsibilities of household management, meal preparation, and her personal care. As her condition deteriorated, we received invaluable help from friends from church. Eventually we engaged hospice to assist with her care.

Connie developed muscular weakness on the left side of her body and her stamina was sapped. She had considerable trouble walking and could no longer negotiate stairs. She spent most of each day sitting in a recliner or lying on our bed, dozing, watching television, or listening as I read aloud to her. Thankfully, she retained the ability to recognize family and friends, flashing her heartwarming smile, and willingly giving hugs to visitors. She remained gracious and affectionate, without anger or resentment.

I found I was able to be grateful for our blessings and not dwell on what was lost. I found joy in caring for my affectionate companion who was the source of so many rewarding moments in my life, repaying Connie for all she had done for me and our children. She had more than earned it.

I reflected on the developments in the 2007 Christmas card:

> We imagined that retirement would allow us more time together doing more traveling, visiting friends and enjoying our progeny. Connie's condition certainly modified that plan, but we have indeed spent more time together, albeit under different circumstances. We still enjoy deeply satisfying moments together, and neither of us is yet fully prepared for the relationship to come to an end. Obviously at some point it will, and reality suggests that will occur sooner rather than later. Such is life. In the meantime, we are both deeply grateful for the precious moments we continue to enjoy.

In late March of 2008, Connie manifested the final signs of dementia's downhill course—the loss of the ability to smile and to hold her head up. Until then, she was able to respond to my affectionate overtures. Her appetite diminished, and over her last seven to ten days, she stopped eating and drinking. We shared our bed until she left, in peace, on Sunday morning, April 13, just a couple of months short of our 55th wedding anniversary.

In June, the family gathered to inter her ashes and celebrate her life with a memorial service I described at the time as "soaring."

The First Presbyterian Church choir performed a stirring rendition of "When I Survey the Wondrous Cross." Musicians including David Holloway, 40 years earlier our choir baritone soloist, and Bob Jacoby, formerly Connie's boss at the private medical clinic, blessed us with poignant selections. Sensitive memories were presented by daughter Eliza. Fritz offered an allegory comparing Connie to Dorothy in the *Wizard of Oz*. The homily by Neil Weatherhogg, First Presbyterian pastor at the time, focused on hope.

The following is the benediction response from the memorial service:

Go now in peace, Never be afraid.
God will go with you each hour of every day.

Go now in faith, steadfast, strong and true.
Know He will guide you in all you do.

Go now in love, and show you believe.
Reach out to others so all the world can see.

God will be there watching from above.
Go now in peace, in faith, and in love.

By Don Besig and Nancy Price

Kind words from Connie's friends and associates, creatively edited by Faith Adams, were integrated and illustrated by son David in an extraordinary memorial booklet about his mother entitled "Perspectives of a Vibrant Life." Some especially touching adjectives shared to describe Connie included: open, caring, passionate, determined, fiery, sharp, generous, nurturing, and advocating for others.

"She lived in such a way that when she died, we all knew her love would survive and continue to grow," wrote Susan Garlinghouse, Connie's close friend and partner in many community projects.

The dedication for the booklet was provided by son David's wife, Monica Eppinger, who had been close to Connie since her teen years. An excerpt from the dedication read:

Connie was sunshine and thunder. She could radiate delight—in giving a good ribbing, getting a good pun, booming a Bach organ toccata, taking on a good fight—more actively than practically anyone I know. She could positively beam approval, victory, joy. Connie could also thunder. Woe unto the son, daughter, or hapless USD 501 administrator who aroused Connie to anger. She could hurl thunderbolts with a look, ignite phone lines to scorching with a well-placed call. What most struck me as a kid was her ability to be in those moments without filtering. I wouldn't call it "expressing her feelings" even; to shine or to thunder manifest her very self.

Though she was gone, Connie remained ever present to me as a companion in spirit. Our home, with all her creative expressions, kept her spirit fresh and alive.

A couple of years after Connie passed away, our neighborhood association posthumously recognized her with a plaque on the College Hill Wall of Fame. (We moved into the College Hill neighborhood when we returned to Topeka more than a half century ago.) The citation read:

Constance Libbey Menninger (1931-2008)
Lived at 1505 Plass Avenue.
Archivist, Santa Fe Railway Records.
Served on State and Nat'l Boards.
Exhibited Megalopsukhia. "Greatness of Soul"

-47-

Retirement and Reflection

Widowed at 76, I realized more than ever how profoundly blessed I am by the love, compatibility, and accomplishments of my six children and their spouses and offspring. Because Connie didn't like for me to be away from her side as her condition deteriorated, I limited my travel during her final years. Once she passed away, I made trips to visit each of my children—flung from Massachusetts to California—in their homes. I attended every grandchild's recital, performance, ball game, and graduation I could.

Free to roam, I also visited friends and classmates from across the country. I traversed portions of the Minnesota and Dakota Northern railways, attended Shakespeare Festivals in Oregon with the Stanford Travel Study program, and attended college and medical school reunions.

When I turned 80 in 2011, I noted in my annual Christmas card:

> So the years do pass, although you never feel as "old" in your own mind as your chronological years attest. There is something, however, about a milestone year that challenges that feeling, especially #80! As I reached that date this October, I had to acknowledge, "Now, I am an old man!" Some days that is more heartfelt than others. But I have been extraordinarily healthy and have yet to be compromised by any significant physical or mental limitations.

Not ready to become an old man just yet, I resumed some of the involvement in the community I had discontinued during Connie's convalescence.

Prompted by the end of a ten-year office lease, I closed my clinical practice in 2013. The process of closing the office occupied the better part of five months, clearing out old files, shifting some to archives, discarding many, moving some home, and disposing of my professional library. Instrumental throughout the process of closing the office, Mary Donohue retired that year, ending 43 years of work as my personal assistant.

I no longer needed an office, but I wasn't done working. It marked a bit of a milepost in my career as I focused on the activities and organizations that seemed most worthy of my time and attention.

I took the role of board chairman of the Tower Mental Health Foundation, an entity originally funded by the Menninger Foundation and overseen by the Kansas Attorney General to make grants in support of mental health activities across the state. I also began making numerous visits to the Larned State Hospital at the invitation of my friend Bill Rein, providing consultation to the administration and training for the staff. They asked me to meet with a few "problem patients" while on my regular visits.

Meanwhile, my involvement with the Boy Scouts of America endured. Having served on the National Health and Safety Committee since 1970, I added a role on the national Youth Protection Committee. In 2011, prompted by my work as chair of the local Boy Scouts capital campaign, the Association of Fundraising Professionals Topeka Chapter on Philanthropy honored me as the year's Outstanding Volunteer Fundraiser (Individual).

I am a longtime member of the Kansas Historical Society. Over the years, I was involved in fundraising and supported the organization. In November of 2020, when an officer of the board passed away unexpectedly, I was nominated to fill his seat as president-elect and became president the next year. This endeavor quickly turned into much more than I anticipated. I've been more active than presidents usually are. A major renovation, the COVID pandemic, the unanticipated retirement of the executive director of the Historical Society Foundation, and the untimely death of the executive director of the Historical Society, made my years on the board much more challenging than I expected them to be.

I connected with the memory of my beloved wife by serving on the Friends Council for the Hall Center for the Humanities at University of Kansas. Connie served on the Hall Center's Board of Directors from its inception in 1986 and was named their first board member emerita when she could no longer actively participate. In 2014, I was added to the Hall Center's Board of Directors.

After Connie's passing, I resumed singing in the First Presbyterian

Church chancel choir, an activity we so relished. The church had been such a source of support throughout Connie's decline, and after her passing I found new opportunities to serve at church. I was invited to assist the church's Stephen Ministry, a program of Christian caring for members of the congregation enduring life's challenges such as death of a spouse, divorce, job loss, illness, or relocation. This ministry has provided me an ongoing opportunity to help others in their time of need as the church helped me in mine.

I am always particularly pleased to serve at church, but that willingness recently pushed me out of my comfort zone to a degree. One afternoon, First Presbyterian pastor Sandra Nichols happened to notice me conversing with some teenagers. She approached me soon after to ask if I would be willing to serve as a liaison to the youth program. She apparently saw something in the interaction that she thought was meaningful. The role has set up some quite interesting conversations between this "nonagenarian" and a group of "Gen-Zs."

I've always believed that, in order to remain young in heart and mind, one needs to stay curious and entertain new ideas. But I've recently been drawn into new realms that are a stretch even for me. A young Topekan I chanced to meet has now enlightened me to rap and hip-hop music. SJ Hazim, a local musician and entrepreneur, educated me on the specifics of these genres of music, going so far as to invite me to some of his performances and engagements in the community as he endeavors to be a positive influence on Topeka's youth.

Having quickly developed a friendship, SJ used a photo of the two of us on the cover of a book that accompanies his recent musical compilation. For the book, I wrote the following introduction:

> All my life, I have loved music. Especially choral music. For over a half-century, I have sung in my church choir, and resonated with the powerful emotion that is expressed in a magnificent composition. No less enjoyable are musical productions, which translate a full range of human experience and emotion through this medium we call music.
>
> But I must acknowledge, I haven't appreciated all forms of musical expression. That was the case for me

with Hip Hop. I could appreciate opera in a foreign language because I could resonate with the musical tones, although it is more meaningful if I get the translation. But I could not find a translator for Hip Hop.

Then an associate invited me to attend a program, which SJ Hazim was presenting for high school students... While I was unable to fully appreciate the Hip Hop articulation of SJ's message, I was fascinated with the alacrity with which the youngsters picked it up. And I loved their quickly joining in with SJ on each refrain. It was a remarkable experience.

I guess an old dog can learn some new tricks even in his nineties.

———————•———————

As time marches on for me personally, so it also has for the Menninger Clinic, which now occupies several buildings on 50 acres anchored by a 120-bed hospital in Houston. Although it is no longer located in Topeka, my involvement with the organization provided me some special moments in recent years.

In 2012, all six of my children joined me in Houston for the dedication of the new, state-of-the-art hospital located in southwest Houston, just minutes away from the Texas Medical Center. The occasion was special not only because it prompted the six children to come together for 36 hours, during which we shared thoughts, feelings, experiences, and love. It also presented them an opportunity, as adults, to appreciate what their great-grandfather, great-uncle, grandfather, uncle, and father had devoted their lives to. The new hospital represented an important milestone in the evolution of Menninger. The occasion evoked memories, nostalgia, camaraderie, and pride among us.

It's hard to imagine anything could top that special occasion, but what occurred the next year certainly comes close. On March 7, 2013, the Houston Menninger Hospital celebrated "Dr. Walt Menninger Day at the Menninger Clinic." This event followed the transfer of patients and staff to Houston nearly ten years to the day.

CEO Ian Aitkin, who served on the Menninger staff during my tenure as CEO in Topeka, stated, "This special day allows us to duly express our appreciation for all that you do to support us and the Menninger Clinic's mission."

My opportunities to contribute continued. I was drawn into some extensive consultation when conflicts arose with the leadership of Menninger after Aitken retired. Although I could hardly be considered an "outsider" at Menninger, I was able to provide a perspective that was unique in working through some of those challenges.

Menninger continues to have family involved. My son John, a psychiatrist in Colorado, was elected to the Menninger Clinic Foundation board in Houston in 2016. His great-grandfather and all the Doctors Menninger who have followed would be—and are—proud.

Meanwhile an interesting saga played out on the property in Topeka that was the former home of the Menninger Clinic.

With the Menninger Clinic and all its programs relocated to Houston, what was to become of the expansive campus and all its buildings on the west edge of Topeka? The Menninger Kansas Foundation went to work to find a new life for the property.

In 2007, the property was purchased by the Sisters of Charity of Leavenworth Health System, Inc. (SCL Health). Over the years, a number of buildings were torn down. A chapel on the property, funded in 1996 by a benefactor named Irene Nunemaker, was relocated to Washburn University when the programs moved to Houston in 2003, where it is utilized for programs, concerts, and weddings.

Of the more than two dozen structures that once occupied the land, three buildings remained standing on the property in the late 2010s. Unoccupied for several years, these buildings were in decline. Demolition appeared inevitable. But many in the community viewed the buildings as both historically and aesthetically valuable. Many conversations were held as to alternatives to the wrecking ball.

The CEO of the local non-profit Sunflower Foundation, Billie Hall, saw potential for two of the buildings, which formerly housed a power facility and nurses' dormitory at the bottom of the hill. That organization purchased the buildings from SCL in 2015 and began an ambitious renewal of the property, aided by industrial bonds issued by the City of Topeka. The Sunflower Foundation, which focuses on meeting the health needs of Kansans, including serving the poor, uninsured and underinsured, and supporting healthy lifestyles, moved its offices into one of the buildings. They endeavored to fill the facilities with tenants dedicated to health care, hoping to create a "culture of collaboration." They planned for a space to document the history of Menninger and the Knights and Ladies Benefit Society—now Security Benefit—which occupied the land before Menninger.

The most recognizable of the buildings—which became known as the Menninger Clock Tower—has stood high on a hill overlooking the city since 1924. Purchased by SCL Health in 2007 from the Menninger Foundation, the beautiful building modeled after Independence Hall in Philadelphia had earned distinction on the Register of Historic Kansas Places and the National Register of Historic Places but was in need of costly repairs. Unable to finance the repairs themselves, SCL Health sought a permit to raze the tower in 2020, claiming they had already invested half a million dollars in the building and could not afford more renovations. In January of 2021, the Topeka Landmarks Commission rejected the request, desiring to find an alternative to destroying the building. Since then, investments from the city and the state have been made to entice investors who could breathe new life into the elegant structure.

I appreciate the efforts made to preserve these beautiful and historic buildings. It's nice to know that people recognize the significance of not just the groundbreaking clinical work that took place there, but even more importantly, the thousands of lives that were changed for the better on that campus.

———————————————

While the buildings of the Menninger Hospital have attracted much attention in Topeka, the work done, and friendships forged within them have not been forgotten.

In 2015, what was first planned as an informal get-together of a few former co-workers turned into about 200 former Menninger employees gathering to reconnect. What was obviously needed was an actual reunion.

We went to work planning such an event, and in October of 2016, more than 300 former Menninger staff came together from across the nation and beyond.

The *Topeka Capital-Journal* described the event and how it came about:

> Alison Beebe, a registered nurse, worked for Menninger for 20 years and was on the committee that put together the reunion. She described what happened on Menninger's Topeka campus as "magical," an almost indescribable feeling of collaboration. It was that magic, she said, that made an informal reunion in 2015, published through social media and expected to draw 20 or 25 people to Topeka's Celtic Fox, bring in more than 200.
>
> For the official reunion in 2016, there was an exhibition at the Kansas Center for Historical Research of materials from the Menninger archives, a reception at the Washburn University Library with a display of Menninger related documents, and a banquet at Topeka's Capital Plaza Hotel.
>
> Speaking at the banquet, I said, "As we gather to reminisce this evening, our memories are of a special institution, with some extraordinary qualities that touched us all. I sometimes think of it as the Menninger virus, which we tried to do our best to transfer and infuse (in the ongoing institution in Houston)."

I read from a letter I received from a former patient many years ago:

> I've never been in any environment before, and never will be again, where I think everyone loves me specially for no reason at all except they love everything, so that includes me too… People who love just one person, or people close to them, are a dime a dozen, but this place is loaded with these rare creatures… It's a relief and joy to be part of something like that, because instead of love being a burden or responsibility making me an

uncomfortable jester in a spotlight, I can just luxuriate in it… It has the somewhat tremulous excitement of a brand-new happy experience, complete freedom from any strain or weight… It's as if the hospital has surrounding me a series of countless little doorways to love.

I concluded my address by saying, "Over the years, that love made a difference in the lives of our patients, and no less in our own. The lives also of our colleagues, our coworkers and the community. That love brings us all back together this weekend. Thank you for it. And God bless you."

There were several other noteworthy speakers at the reunion of Menninger employees in 2016. But one comment that stood out was made by Larry Wolgast, former Vice President of Development for Menninger who was serving as mayor of Topeka at the time. Mayor Wolgast had worked tirelessly to improve downtown Topeka, and he was instrumental in the development of numerous "pocket parks" commemorating famous and influential Topekans on the city's most historic commercial street, Kansas Avenue. A question posed to the crowd gathered at the reunion was recorded by the *Topeka Capital-Journal*:

> "Who is missing? No. 5 on the poll of Topekans to be recognized was Dr. Karl Menninger, further down was Dr. C.F. and Dr. Will," he said. "If the votes for all three of those were to be added together, they would be No. 1. I strongly support efforts to place statues of these three leaders on Kansas Avenue."

The idea of a pocket park honoring the Menninger family gained momentum and finally became a reality in 2023. It features a statue of my grandfather striding along Topeka's Kansas Avenue on his way to the location of his first office at 727 South Kansas. Complete with a tablet of Menninger history and busts of C.F., Karl, Will, Roy, and me by nationally-recognized sculptor Joe Skeeba, the pocket park was dedicated on May 9, 2023, in time for the 100th anniversary of the Menninger Clinic, which will occur in 2025.

Armando Colombo, the current CEO of the Menninger Clinic, attended the dedication and talked about the important role Topeka played in the growth of the clinic. Roy and I both made remarks to the gathering. I was sure to credit Wolgast for making his vision for the pocket park become a reality. Topeka's mayor from 2013 to 2018, he spearheaded the steering committee through challenging deliberations, solicited funds from a wide range of donors, and negotiated a thicket of roadblocks to see it through years after his tenure as mayor was completed.

I have said many times that I deemed my greatest responsibility was to ensure that Menninger not die on my watch. While it was none of my doing, I am pleased that the pocket park ensures the memory of the Menningers will live on in Topeka as well.

———————•———————

After Connie passed away in 2008, I embarked on a period of travel and activity, refreshed and energized after a couple of years spent primarily caring for her. But it wasn't without acknowledging my own ongoing challenges of aging over the next several years. First, I admitted my need of hearing aids. Then a couple of falls produced a need for physical training to improve my balance, posture, strength, and stamina. In my early 80s, I began a regimen of regular physical training with Nan Gatewood, a personal trainer in Topeka. This has been one of the important stabilizing relationships over the past decade. Nan has been a valuable monitor of my health and helped me to stay active in my later years.

In addition to the glorious Menninger reunion of 2016, a sad reunion was held that same year. My brother Phil passed away at 87. His memorial service brought back to Topeka all the grandchildren of Will and Cay Menninger.

While the death of my sibling helped to cement the knowledge of my advancing age, nothing hammered the fact home quite like the birth, in 2018, of my first great-grandchild.

I turned 90 in 2021. A few years prior, I experienced some word-finding difficulty and submitted to multiple examinations, imaging, consultations, and observations. What they identified was a "lacunar infarct in the left cerebellum." In just six hours, the symptoms were gone.

Doctors prescribed a blood thinner to prevent a recurrence.

The experience of losing some short-term memory and haziness about other recollections served as a motivator to put down on paper some "Lessons I Have Learned."

I recognized that much can be learned about oneself through the process of writing. I also believed that I had a few thoughts on life which I didn't want to take with me to the grave. My years of study of psychiatry and human nature, my observances of political and world events, and my experiences as a husband, parent, community volunteer and head of a major organization gave me a few thoughts I wanted to share.

The question, as you will read in the final chapter of this memoir, is just how reliable are my memories? I am quite aware of the tendency to remember things not as they were, but rather how we wanted them to be. It's in our nature to rewrite history. More of my thoughts on that phenomena are the subject of my final chapter.

-48-

Memories

R emembrance of things past is not necessarily the remembrance of things as they were."

Those words by French novelist Marcel Proust have always struck me as profound, and they become increasingly weighty as I age. This thought was at the forefront of my mind as I endeavored to record the story of my life and career in this book.

Were the contents of this book tainted by wishful thinking? Was it written like Dorothy would have recorded her memories of Oz—a hazy interpretation of what might have been merely a dream?

I think not. When I couldn't recall something clearly, I opted to leave it out of the book. I did not want to muddy the historical record, and I certainly didn't want to portray anything or anyone in a false light.

I tried to corroborate my memories with historical documents. Throughout my career, I devoted great effort to retaining records of the past. With the heroic assistance of my secretary Mary Donohue, I kept both paper and electronic files of nearly every speech I delivered and every paper or article I wrote, as well as notes and artifacts from meetings, conferences, and commissions.

The history of the Menninger Foundation is painstakingly preserved at the Kansas State Historical Society, an organization which I have served in various official capacities out of a recognition of the importance of the preservation of all history. Additionally, the *Bulletin of the Menninger Clinic* published a record of the organization's history for anyone to read throughout the years. That source, and countless other public resources, were utilized to ensure the accuracy of this book. An invaluable record of my personal life was the annual Christmas letter Connie and I began sending to friends in the late 1950s. The mailing list grew from a few dozen friends and family in our early years to over a thousand. When my memory was fuzzy, I was able to look back at more than 60 years of yearly highlights.

For those reasons, I had a reliable set of resources for this book. That being said, the fallibility of memory has long been of significance to me. This is more than just an extracurricular interest. It is a crucial concept in helping psychiatric patients sort out their experiences and organize their lives. Getting a proper read on our life history is important to our mental health.

One of the more unique and enjoyable talks I gave was a presentation about memory at a joint meeting of the Midwest Archives Conference and the Society of Rocky Mountain Archivists held in Topeka in October 1995. The talk was printed in a professional journal published by the Midwest Archives Conference called *Archival Issues* in 1996. The preface to the article described my concern with the problem of memory:

> Dr. Menninger…has a long-standing interest in the problems of history, especially in relationship between human memory and historical reality. His psychiatric practice and his professional research have afforded him ample opportunities to consider the complexities of human memory and its relationship to historical documentation.
>
> His plenary remarks…center on the idea that memory can rarely be depended upon to faithfully recall past events, especially those in which the subject directly participated. For various reasons—including self-protective mechanisms in the mind and the disaggregated fashion in which the mind stores memory fragments—we tend to remember past events unreliably and our recollection changes over the course of our lives. As Dr. Menninger points out, this calls into question historical documentation that is predominantly based on people's recollections of past events.

I concluded my talk to the group of archivists and historians gathered at the meeting with a warning specific to their profession:

> Clearly, the historian seeks to be objective in the assessment of historical materials and to draw appropriate

inferences from those materials. Nevertheless, we all need to keep in mind the limitations of data based on human memory and reminiscence. In terms of your work, you must recognize the limitations of oral history and reports of past events based just on later memory. Autobiographers should check memories against other verifying information with regard to one or another historical event. We must acknowledge the human propensity to replace reality with wishful thinking, toward the end of an enhanced self-esteem, and an affirmation of worth and meaning for one's lifetime.

This was a fun topic for me to study and speak on. But it is humbling to think about how your own recollections can be distorted. As I grow older and time puts distance between me and the significant events of my life, I recognize that my memory is fallible.

The following is the updated version of my talk, a William Allen White lecture in Emporia, delivered in 2009, entitled "Memory and History: What Can You Believe?"

Over 20 years ago, it was my privilege to keynote the annual meeting of the American Association of State and Local History when it met in Topeka, where I was asked to share some thoughts on the relationship of the human mind and history. At the time, I had been intrigued with the vicissitudes of human memory. All too often, I came across instances of individuals recalling history as it wasn't. In a period when modern technology has enhanced the recording—tape and video—of oral history, I thought it advisable to explore the validity and reliability of memories.

In the 1990s, the subject of memory was explored in patients with posttraumatic stress disorder with a new twist. A number of individuals reported "recovered" memories of early childhood abuse and made allegations toward parents or care takers resulting in litigation. Such allegations had some devastating consequences for the persons involved, both accusers and accused. In response, the False Memory

Syndrome Foundation was organized to support accused parents. Yet, as my psychologist colleague Jon Allen observed, "As apt as the term 'false memory' may be for legal purposes, it starts scientific and clinical discussion off on the wrong foot."

As a psychiatrist and psychoanalyst, I am keenly aware of the importance of the past as prologue. As part of a clinical evaluation, it is essential to take a careful history. Knowledge of an individual's past experiences and behavior is vital to understanding his or her present difficulties. Yet, as a result of any number of processes, an individual's perceptions and memories can be distorted. Usually, the distortion is a function of an emotional need to preserve one's self-esteem or protect the individual from the emotional consequences of what actually happened. For whatever reason, historical reality is modified.

In 1985, psychologist Daniel Goleman authored a book about this phenomenon entitled: *Vital Lies, Simple Truths: The Psychology of Self-Deception*. He included an extraordinary example of this process—John Dean's memory. You may recall that John Dean was the legal counsel for President Nixon at the time of the Watergate cover-up. When he came forth to testify at the Senate investigatory hearings in June of 1973, Dean submitted a 245-page statement recounting, in specific detail, events and conversations over the many months he was involved in the Watergate affair. When queried about his facility for recalling details of conversations which took place many months before, Dean responded: "My mind is not a tape recorder, but it certainly receives the message that is being given."

Little did he apparently realize how his remarks might be checked. For when the tapes of Nixon's conversations of his staff were ultimately revealed, it was possible to check the accuracy of Dean's detailed recollections. (This comparison was actually done by Ulric Neisser.) On the day of the grand jury indictment of the five Watergate burglars,

Dean met in the Oval Office with Nixon and (his chief of staff, Bob) Haldeman. Dean reported the meeting as follows:

> The President asked me to sit down. Both men appeared to be in very good spirits and my reception was very warm and cordial. The President then told me that Bob (Haldeman) had kept him posted on my handling of the Watergate case. The president told me I had done a good job and he appreciated how difficult a task it had been and the President was pleased that the case had stopped with Liddy. I responded that I could not take credit because others had done much more difficult things than I had done... I told him that all I had been able to do was to contain the case and assist in keeping it out of the White House. I also told him there was a long way to go before this matter would end and that I certainly could make no assurances that the day would not come when this matter would start to unravel.

When this statement is compared to the taped session:

> Comparison...shows that hardly a word of Dean's account is true. Nixon did not say any of the things attributed to him here: he didn't ask Dean to sit down, he didn't say Haldeman had kept him posted, he didn't say Dean had done a good job (at least not in that part of the conversation), he didn't say anything about Liddy or the indictments. Nor had Dean himself said the things he later describes himself as saying: that he couldn't take credit, that the matter might unravel some day, etc. (Indeed, he said just the opposite later on: "Nothing is going to come crashing down.") His account is plausible, but entirely incorrect.

To understand these distortions, one must conclude that Dean's testimony described not the meeting itself but his fantasy of the meeting as it should have been. In Dean's mind, Nixon *should* have been glad that the indictments stopped with the five burglars, Haldeman *should* have told Nixon what a great job Dean was doing, and Dean *should* have told Nixon that the cover-up might unravel instead of actually telling him it was a great success. The key to understanding this phenomenon is wishful thinking.

Autobiographical Memory:

Students of memory identify different kinds of memory. There is the short-term or "working" memory which occurs when you look up a telephone number and keep it in mind until you dial. There is long term memory of events in the distant past like your childhood home. There is "implicit" or "procedural" memory which refers to behavioral knowledge of an experience without conscious recall, such as a skill once learned like riding a bicycle or swimming, or an affective reaction in response to a stimulus without understanding the basis for that reaction. There is "explicit" or "declarative" memory which is the ability to consciously recall facts or events. There is "episodic" memory for specific events which have occurred in your life.

Autobiographical memory is largely episodic memory for both unique events occurring in one's life, like a graduation, and recurring events, like trips to grandmother's house. These memories typically include a great deal of visual imagery, but they are in no way like a video camera recording, because such events are not experienced objectively. Our perceptions are inevitably biased by a variety of factors: our age and capacity to understand what is happening, our expectations and knowledge at the time of the event, and the stress and bodily sensations experienced during the event. It is significant that no matter how accurately an event may be perceived and stored, when it is remembered, it is not simply replayed as on a videotape, it is reconstructed.

From a review of the literature, Jon Allen differentiates "conditioned-emotional" memory from "narrative-autobiographical" memory. Conditioned-emotional memory is present from birth, established in infancy, and operational throughout life. This memory is expressed through images, behaviors, and emotions. Narrative-autobiographical memory emerges during the preschool years and comprises personal memories for unique and generic events as well as autobiographical facts about oneself. While personal memories may include visual imagery, autobiographical facts are more verbal.

There is accumulating research on the accuracy of autobiographical memory. With regard to memory for life events, memory for recent events is more accurate than that for remote events. As time goes by, details get lost, though memories for unique events are likely to be more accurate than memories for recurrent events. With recurrent events, we may recall generally what happened and reconstruct details according to what is plausible. Or (as Allen said), "we may sharply remember a few details and then reconstruct the whole from them: 'Out of a few stored bone chips, we remember a dinosaur.' Alternatively, consider this library metaphor: 'memory is not so much like reading a book as it is like writing one from fragmentary notes.'"

Psychologist Elizabeth Loftus characterizes human memories as being stored in mental drawers in our brain, drawers which "are obviously extremely crowded and densely packed. They are also constantly being emptied out, scattered about, and then stuffed back into place... As new bits and pieces of information are added into long-term memory, the old memories are replaced, crumpled up, or shoved into corners. Little details are added, confusing or extraneous elements are deleted, and a coherent construction of the facts is gradually created that may bear little resemblance to the original event."

From her work with eyewitness testimony in legal cases, Loftus has found, "Memories don't just fade, as the old saying would have us believe, they also grow. What fades is the initial perception, the actual experience of the events. Every time we recall an event, we must reconstruct the memory, and with each recollection the memory may be changed—colored by succeeding events, other people's recollections and suggestions, increased understanding or a new context." Indeed, Loftus offers some striking examples of instances where eyewitnesses have clearly had their memories strongly influenced by the subtle suggestion of law enforcement officers.

Tell It Like It Is:

At times, we are challenged to "tell it like it is," or in the words of TV Dragnet's Detective Joe Friday: "Give me the facts, ma'am. Just the facts." Yet, if you look more carefully, you discover that people for one reason or another don't really want to hear it "like it is;" they want to hear it like they want it to be.

Historically there is a tradition of rejecting findings from knowledge or science when they challenge our sense of the world as it should be and wound our self-esteem. Recall the degree to which Copernicus was vilified because he had the gall to suggest the earth was not the center of the universe but instead revolved around the sun. And there is still much resistance to the concept of evolution as presented by Charles Darwin.

We are often as threatened by the truth about ourselves as by the truth about the world. Many of Sigmund Freud's ideas have been rejected because people are reluctant to accept the idea that there exist within our minds thoughts, feelings, memories, and past experiences which are not accessible to our conscious awareness, but which, nonetheless, influence our behavior and conscious thoughts.

Further, we are troubled that others might learn the "truth" about us. At one time or another, nearly all of my patients have reluctantly shared with me the fear that if I knew the awful truth about them, I would have nothing more to do with them. Yet all of us have crazy and unacceptable thoughts and feelings, which we share with no one, because if we did, we would be "exposed." No one is immune to these feelings, no matter what station in life. We pretend, and we hold forth pride. We deny our limitations. And we work hard to defend ourselves from seeing it "like it is" and facing up to any emotional and embarrassing consequences of that reality.

Rewriting History:

In George Orwell's *1984*, the central character, Winston Smith, worked in the Ministry of Truth where he rewrote newspaper articles in the archives each time there was a change in alliances. He would have to change the old enemy to a new ally and make it appear as if it had always been as it now was, and vice versa. We now know that what Orwell fantasized indeed occurred in recent history, with a rewriting of records behind the old Iron Curtain.

While that activity represents an obvious and overt threat to the search for accuracy in the past, there is another more subtle rewriting of history. This is the rewriting that occurs as people in their mature years reminisce and recall events of their earlier lives—but do so incorrectly. Some historians have recognized this propensity—at least Carl Van Doren did in his Pulitzer prize-winning biography, *Benjamin Franklin*. Early in the book, Van Doren observes:

> So far in this history, Franklin, speaking of himself in his own words, has almost always spoken in the words of the Autobiography which he wrote 45 years after the departure from Gravesend, when he was sage and famous and

writing for his son, the governor of New Jersey. Perhaps then he tempered the account of his youth, saw his course as straighter than it was, left out or had forgotten his ranker appetites, remembered too clearly the mind and will which had outlasted the lost years.

Similar findings were reported in the research of psychiatrist George Vaillant, who interviewed 30 years later 95 subjects of a study begun in the late 1930s and early 1940s at Harvard. The original study was funded by the W. T. Grant Foundation as a longitudinal study of young adults in good health. Vaillant notes that:

> Psychologically, the Grant Study subjects in adult life fared much better than the population as a whole, but it is hard to say how much better. Originally chosen for good health, there were none who experienced difficulties too severe to master, but there were also none who had survived the game of life without pain, effort, and anxiety.

As he organized his data from the follow-up interviews, Vaillant compared the data with questionnaire responses obtained at the beginning of the study. He writes:

> It is clear that the distortions produced by adaptive mechanisms may, over a period of years, become part of the individual's world view. Truth too awful to bear is unconsciously altered or postponed; the altered truth then becomes subjectively true. In other words, the men's adaptive styles affected their childhood environment as much as childhood affected choice of adaptation.

Observes Vaillant, "Repression is the prototype of all the adaptive mechanisms—if you cannot bear it, forget it."

Certainly, some individuals use this adaptive mechanism more than others. It is not surprising for persons to recall a past which is simply consistent with their present views. Indeed, some have observed that history is a record of present beliefs and wishes, not a replica of the past. Remembering is a reconstruction using bits of past experience to describe a present state.

In describing the childhood memories of Leonardo da Vinci, Freud wrote:

> [Childhood memories] are not fixed at the moment of being experienced and afterwards repeated, but are only elicited at a later age when childhood is already past; in the process, they are altered and falsified, and are put into the service of later trends.

Consider, in this context, the case of Robert Jordan, one of the composite Grant Study subjects interviewed by Vaillant. At age 19, Jordan was extremely conservative and attended Catholic mass four times a week. He also reported to the study psychiatrist a dream that he experienced perhaps 40 times. When Vaillant interviewed him 30 years later, Jordan maintained that as soon as he arrived in college, he had doubted the validity of religion and given up church altogether. He also said that he could only recall one recurrent childhood dream—which was not the same one reported during his college years. Concludes Vaillant:

> A dream repeated 40 times and church going repeated four times a week had been forgotten. How then may we obtain truth about the adult life cycle? Clearly it must be studied prospectively. It is all too common for caterpillars to become butterflies and then to maintain that in their youth they had been little butterflies. Maturation makes liars of us all.

Vaillant cites other instances of forgetting. One man

originally reported a class standing in military school of third out of 150. At the time he was 50 years old, he had become second out of 900. Another Grant Study subject did not approve of his adolescent children's use of marijuana. Yet in 1940, he had praised the pot-like effects of alcohol, when he wrote: "I get gentler, sweeter, less sarcastic, and enjoy dancing more. My mind is usually quite bright; I feel closer to music than ever, more open to people. Alcohol is always a pleasant experience." Vaillant notes that this man, in worrying over his adolescent children, had almost forgotten that in his own adolescence, he too had been a long-haired university dropout who wandered across Europe.

Memory as a Self-Portrait:

From all this, it seems apparent that what one recalls at any given moment is consistent with one's self-concept at the time. As articulated by my colleague, Jon Allen, the tendency is to reconstruct past events in a way that is consistent with your current self-image and the rest of your knowledge about yourself. What you remember is consistent with what should have happened in light of your current self-portrait. If you're feeling depressed, you'll remember your failure; if you're feeling confident, you'll remember your success. As your self-concept changes, you revise your autobiography. Further, nothing stays still in the brain. Every reconstruction is always a partially new construction. Especially as you recall an event many times, the connections become changed in the process. Under the guidance of your self-portrait, when you reconstruct, you may weave in fantasy and wishful thinking, reshaping your "memory" in your brain.

In his autobiography, *Dreams from My Father*, Barack Obama expresses reservations about his grandfather's memories of early racism experiences in Texas. He cites his grandfather's "tendency to rewrite his history to conform with the image he wished for himself." Obama goes on, "And yet I don't entirely dismiss Gramps's recollection of events as a convenient bit of puffery…, precisely because I know how strongly Gramps believed in his fictions, how badly he wanted them to be true, even if he didn't always know how to make them so."

As Elizabeth Loftus has put it, "Truth and reality, when seen through the filter of our memories, are not objective facts, but subjective, interpretative realities. We interpret the past, correcting ourselves, adding bits and pieces, deleting uncomplimentary or disturbing recollections, sweeping, dusting, tidying things up… We are innocent victims of our mind's manipulations." She notes Mark Twain's rumination on memory: "It isn't so astonishing, the number of things that I can remember, as the number of things I can remember that aren't so."

Recollections of Childhood Trauma – True or False?:

As noted earlier, in recent years there was increasing controversy about the recollection by some patients of childhood traumatic experiences, particularly incidents of sexual abuse. The uncertainty of how to interpret adult recollection of childhood memories was reflected in Freud's early work. As his patients recounted such experiences, he first assumed they were based in some factual past event. Then he came to the conclusion that some of such reports were more likely a reconstruction and not an actual experience. An increased awareness of the considerable extent of child abuse in recent years has prompted clinicians to reconsider that position.

We had an explosion of such recollections in clinical psychiatry as we gained more understanding of patients struggling with multiple personality disorder and other personality disturbances associated with early trauma. At the same time, the zeal of some therapists in search of presumed early childhood trauma led to the phenomenon of the so-called "false memory syndrome." It is quite clear that not all recovered memories in these patients accurately reflected past events. Indeed, the American Bar Association Journal featured an article on "Buried Memories, Shattered Lives" which cited legal cases where judges and juries were beginning to view with skepticism some sex abuse claims based on so-called recovered memories.

The American Psychiatric Association was prompted to formulate a statement addressing the issue of memories of sexual abuse. It acknowledged that some individuals who have experienced documented traumatic events may nevertheless include some false or inconsistent elements in their reports. Further, it noted that memories can be significantly influenced by questioning, especially in young children. Also, memories can be significantly influenced by a trusted person, such as a therapist, who suggests abuse as an explanation for symptoms or problems, despite initial lack of memory of such abuse; and repeated questioning may lead individuals to report "memories" of events that never occurred.

In his review of this phenomenon, Jon Allen cites a wide array of impinging factors which can cloud autobiographical memories: time; infantile and childhood amnesia; limbic system dysfunction; fantasy proneness; ego defense mechanisms of dissociation, repression, denial, projective identification, displacement, intellectualization, rationalization, suppression and splitting; and the social context. All of us must be disabused of illusions about memory as a video recorder with hypnosis as the route to the "play" button.

Memory in Old Age:

Numerous studies have found changes in memory associated with the aging process. Typically, with the loss of brain cells, there is impairment of short-term memory, the immediate recall of recently learned information. Long-term memory is less impaired, although such recollections may well be distorted.

Virginia Revere and Sheldon Tobin studied reminiscence data from two population groups, one middle-aged and the other older-aged. They hypothesized that the older group would relate to the past in a different way, suspecting the older person no longer has a need to see the past realistically. "Rather," they opined:

> ...the need is to see the past in such a way as to achieve some measure of immortality, to see oneself as a hero of a life worth remembering. Stated another way, to see oneself as a hero of a drama worth telling, a drama worth having lived for.

Revere and Tobin found that the intensity and involvement with the memories and the extent of dramatization were, as anticipated, much greater in the older group than in the middle age group. There was no significant difference between the two groups in the consistency of values and acceptance of life as it was. But in the older group, the researchers more often found a positive affirmation of life or a greater incidence of viewing significant figures positively.

The researchers conclude, "older persons were not only more involved with their pasts, but involved in the special way of mythicizing their recollections." This mythicizing of significant figures "can be interpreted as an adaptational response that is different from making sense of one's life... These aged persons have recast their memories to make the uniqueness of themselves vivid. In this sense, the past becomes more real and more poignant. The myth is the reality."

The Search for Truth:

In our exploration of memory and our pursuit of "the

truth," a theme persists: our memories may not be completely trustworthy, and our recollections may be more wishful thinking than true reality. Our memories re-create a past that justifies and sustains our self-esteem. Further, as psychologist William James observed, we have within us an indomitable desire to cast the world into a more rational shape in our minds than the shape into which it is thrown there by the crude order of experience.

These observations differ little from the observations of Freud and other students of human nature and the human mind. We seek to order our universe to make it reasonable and predictable and manageable. But we are human and subject to human frailties and limitations. We search for the truth, but only half-heartedly when we fear the truth may not be in our best interests. So, we are inconsistent and self-serving in our recollections, despite our best intentions to be otherwise. As often as not, we may not fully understand why we feel or act the way we do, and we struggle after the fact to come up with a rational explanation for our feelings and actions.

In my clinical practice, I try to take an objective position with regard to patients who come to me. I will confront my patients with any disparity between the truth as they perceive it and the truth and reality as I see it. Yet I know that reactions within me can bias my own perception if I am not careful. I have been most impressed with the unevenness of memory, and I acknowledge the human propensity to replace reality with wishful thinking, toward the end of an enhanced self-esteem, and an affirmation of worth and meaning for one's lifetime.

So how important is it to know the "truth?" An answer to this question, notes my colleague, Jon Allen, is offered by Lewis Thomas in his "Late Night Thoughts on Listening to Mahler's Ninth Symphony." Thomas proposes that "unconscious minds" must have evolved for a reason, and we should respect them. "Stock them up, put more things into them, and make use of them. Forget whatever you feel like forgetting." That would appear to be good advice for our overzealous colleagues and reassuring advice to many patients.

When I composed and delivered the preceding talk in the mid-1990s, I had no intentions of producing a memoir. But now here I am, in my 90s, sharing the story of my life. I believe I have accurately portrayed the events of my life and the history of the Menninger Clinic and Foundation, adhering to the facts as contained in reliable documents.

I didn't embark on this endeavor for self-aggrandizement or self-justification. I simply felt there were some things worth telling. I felt some of the lessons learned during my career were worthy of presenting anew in the present day. I believed some people deserved to be celebrated and events deserved to be remembered. And I thought the history of the Menninger Clinic in Topeka and its wonderful staff merited praise 20 years after its relocation to Houston.

When the Right Hand Washes the Left Hand

I found great joy and satisfaction in looking back on my life and compiling these memoirs. I had a lot of fun and met a lot of wonderful people.

But rather than some great narcissistic exercise, I hope that the purpose for writing my memoirs was what should have been the goal for my life: to leave the world a better place than I found it.

As I'm sure with every person, I have lived up to this goal at times, and at other times I've fallen far short. But I can talk a good game, and in 1986, I shared a message about loving, helping, and giving— a message I feel is relevant for all times, and particularly in this current age.

I was invited to deliver the commencement address at Ottawa University, a college about an hour from my hometown of Topeka. There is nothing like looking out at the fresh faces and hopeful eyes of a bunch of graduates to fill your heart with optimism. And in the case of these students, there was true cause for optimism. As part of their curriculum, they had gained extensive experience in the area of service. The university's Statement of Purpose is "to provide an education developing appropriate sensitivity to service to humankind and involvement in social concerns." It states that the university "seeks to prepare students for lives of service, and the servant ministry of Jesus Christ is upheld as the example most worthy of emulation."

This group of students was already dedicated to making the world a better place. So, I shared the following words (excerpted from a speech entitled "When the Right Hand Washes the Left Hand") to encourage them to that end.

Giving and Taking

Giving and taking are basic activities in which we engage throughout life. When we first enter this world, we do not have the capacity to give to others in any meaningful way.

Our earliest months are spent entirely in taking. Of course, in our infancy, we could not survive if someone did not look out for us and provide our basic needs for food, shelter, and love. The infant tends to take this for granted, expecting to be taken care of; thus, it is a rude awakening when we discover that others will not always automatically meet our needs.

As we become aware of that fact, we must find ways to get those things we need for survival. Most of us learn early in childhood that some way to get what we want is by what actor John Houseman calls the "old-fashioned way—by *earning* it!" We may earn it by good behavior or by giving something to others, especially our parents. We search for some balance between just taking what we want from others and behaving in a way to prompt others to reward us.

Initially, we may feel coerced into giving. The natural, self-centered impulse does not view giving as the way to receive. Rather, it may view giving simply as a means to reduce discomfort, to avoid a personal rebuke or criticism or punishment, as opposed to giving as a means to gain a smile or compliment or tangible reward. However, in the normal course of growth, there comes a recognition of pleasure to be derived from giving. Not only is there the satisfaction in the positive feedback from those on the receiving end, but ultimately there is an altruistic pleasure in making the world a better place because of your efforts.

Clearly not everyone learns the lesson to give in order to get. The reason why is not always clear, although it certainly has to do with one's early life experience and role models. For a person to be able to give of himself, he must have a secure sense of self and a sense of trust in others.

Altruism – An Adaptive Mechanism of Maturity

Between 1939 and 1942, some 268 Harvard undergraduates were recruited as participants in a longitudinal study of healthy and promising individuals.

These students underwent intensive medical and psychological study. At the time of the initial selection, all of the men in this study had achieved good academic standing. Most subsequently rose to the rank of officer and made distinguished records for themselves in the less academic atmosphere of World War II. Thirty-five years later, psychiatrist George E. Vaillant was able to follow up 95 men of the original 268 and assess their adaptation to life, chronicling his findings in a book with that same title: *Adaptation to Life* (Boston: Little Brown, 1977).

Vaillant notes that most of the original group were still alive after thirty years, without disabling illness, and over 90 percent had founded stable families. Virtually all achieved occupational distinction, but not one of those men had a completely pain-free life. Thus, Vaillant sought to identify the differences in approaches to adaptation to life. In the process, he looked at the mental health of these individuals and defined their adaptation in terms of various coping styles or mechanism. In his introduction, Vaillant writes:

> In writing of mechanism of adaptation, I am not writing about conscious avoidance of problems, or about willpower, nor do I mean perseverance or turning to others. These all serve as a means out of handling problems; rather I am discussing a far more subtle and almost entirely unconscious process.

In his survey of the mechanisms of adaptation, Vaillant identified five which he considered to be the most mature. He found these common among "healthy" persons from adolescence to old age; and he felt they integrate four sometimes conflicting aspects of human behavior—conscience, reality, interpersonal relations, and instincts. To the outside observer, however, these mature mechanisms appear to be "convenient virtues." What are these five? Humor, suppression, anticipation, sublimation, and altruism.

In the context of our gathering this afternoon, I would call particular attention to the last—altruism. *Webster's Third New International Dictionary* defines altruism as "uncalculated consideration of, regard for, or devotion to others' interests, sometimes in accordance with an ethical principle," in contrast to selfishness and egotism. Vaillant defines altruism as "getting pleasure from giving to others what you yourself would like to receive." The special psychological significance stems from the personal gain from being allied or identified with a cause or activity which is greater than oneself.

In the same way that George Vaillant considered altruism to be a mature adaptive mechanism, my father, Dr. Will Menninger considered the capacity to find more satisfaction in giving than receiving to be one of the criteria for emotional maturity.

Some Clinical Observations

In the course of my professional life, I have had the unusual opportunity to work both with people who have been primarily "takers"—criminal offenders sentenced to prison—and people who have dedicated themselves to giving to others—Peace Corps and VISTA volunteers.

In prison, one repeatedly encounters persons who are simply unable to trust anyone else or believe that anyone else would truly be concerned about them. It is as if they never have had a consistent experience with a caring person; in contrast, they have repeatedly experienced others as "using" or taking advantage of them. As a result, they conclude that the only one in life who is truly concerned about "number one" is "me;" and "if I am to survive, I just have to take from others before they take from me." Many of these persons feel they have been unfairly deprived in life and are therefore entitled to take what they want without giving anything in return. They often fail to appreciate how they turn that expectation into a self-fulfilling prophecy. By their attitude and behavior, they set up situations where they will inevitably be rejected and further deprived, such as being sent to prison.

In my work with psychiatric patients, I have likewise seen many people who were so restricted and self-limited that they could find no satisfaction in giving. Most remarkable is the transformation of these people as they begin to be able to give and to grow. It is exciting to observe a person who has never felt secure enough to invest outside himself begin to try it. As he does so, you can see him envision new horizons and find satisfactions never before appreciated.

At the opposite extreme from the selfish offender or the preoccupied and constricted emotionally ill patient is the person who reflects the security and contentment achieved by giving of himself or herself to others. Few experiences in my life have been as moving and impressive as meeting with a group of Peace Corps Volunteers overseas in a conference at the completion of their tour of duty, and hearing these persons share the new perspective of life which resulted from their service.

Which Are You?

A number of years ago, I came across a poem by Ella Wheeler Wilcox which contrasts the takers and givers of the world in an engaging way. Her poem is entitled, "Which Are You?"

> There are two kinds of people on earth today;
> Just two kinds of people, no more I say.
>
> Not the sinner and saint, for it's well understood
> The good are half-bad, and the bad are half-good.
>
> Not the rich and the poor, for to rate a man's wealth,
> You must first know the state of his conscience and health.
>
> Not the humble and proud, for in life's little span,
> Who puts on vain airs is not counted a man.

Not the happy and sad, for the swift flying years
Bring each man his laughter, and each man his tears.

No; the two kinds of people on earth I mean
Are the people who lift, and the people who lean.

Wherever you go, you will find the earth's masses
Are always divided in just these two classes.

And oddly enough, you will find too, I wean
There's only one lifter to twenty who lean.

In which class are you? Are you easing the load
Of overtaxed lifters, who toil down the road?

Or are you a leaner, who lets others share
Your portion of labor and worry and care?

It has always fascinated me how some people who have little are ready to give so much of themselves; and others who have much to give, give so little. And there are others who seem to give only when there is much recognition of the giving, in contrast to those who prefer to give of themselves anonymously.

'Tis Better to Give

In economics, it is generally understood that careful investment and reinvestment of capital is a key stimulus to the growth of an economy and at the same time, the best way to make money. This is in contrast to the stagnation which occurs when you just put your money in a sock. This principle of careful investment is no less true for one's emotional investment in life.

The Golden Rule says you should do unto others as you would have them do unto you. One may dwell on this rule as the "right" and "good" way to be, or as an obligation in life to be obeyed like other laws. However, when you "obey" that rule, you find that others are more likely to treat you in the same way. And you come to realize that behaving in that way is the most effective way to be assured that you will, in return, be treated comparably by others. Service to others is like making an investment. When it is done carefully, it does return dividends.

Altruism and service are indeed great and powerful forces, which I have seen played out in myriad ways… If you have that sensitivity and follow it through, you will inevitably serve yourself as you serve others. You will demonstrate a powerful truth, a truth which I learned at a completion of service conference of Peace Corps Volunteers in Nigeria, a truth conveyed in the simple yet eloquent Nigerian proverb: 'When the right hand washes the left hand, the right hand becomes clean also.'

I placed this message at the conclusion of my memoirs in hopes that you too would be motivated to leave the world a better place than you found it. Helpful in that mission are the following words of advice, given to me years ago:

"To whom much is given, much is required."

And "It's more important in life to like what you do than to do what you like."

50th Wedding Anniversary of CF & Flo Menninger with
extended family; Dr. Walt in striped shirt, circa 1935

Menninger family "stamping," 1938; Dr. Walt in another striped shirt

Walt, early 1940s

Dr. Will Menninger in uniform, 1944

Menninger family at 1724 Collins, circa 1948

Connie while at Stanford

Connie & Walt walking down
the aisle, Palo Alto, 6/15/53

Dr. Walt & Connie's family home in Topeka, 1964, prior to remodel

Will, Roy, Phil, & Walt: May 1956

Photo in front of the family home, Easter 1969

On left: Walt in Public Health Service uniform, El Reno, OK, 1963

On right: Joe English & Walt in their Peace Corps office,
Washington, DC, summer 1964

Dr. Walt & Fritz at Peace Corps booth, APA Meeting, Atlanta, 1964

Dr. Walt & Connie in New Mexico, 1963

Connie & Dr. Walt at Palisades Tahoe, 1967
(Known as Squaw Valley at the time of this picture)

Dr. Walt lecturing on the Morale Curve, May 1969

Dr. Walt with members of the Violence Commission,
including Dr. Milton Eisenhower (second from right), 1969

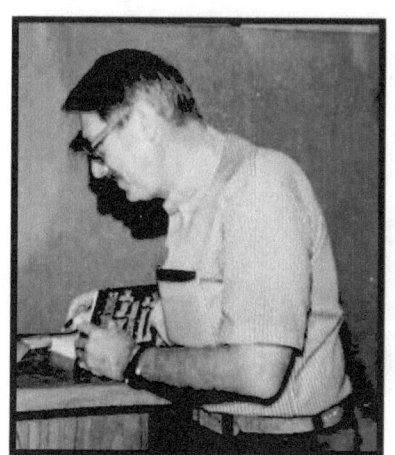

Dr. Walt signing copies of
Caution, 1978

Dr. Walt during his bearded
phase, circa 1981

Dr. Walt giving a speech at the National Press Club

Catharine Menninger celebrating her 80th birthday
with her three sons, 9/22/1982

Karl (seated), Roy, Walt, & John
Menninger posing for
US News & World Report
photo shoot, 1988

Mary Donohue in Dr. Walt's
office, May 1987

Dr. Roy and Dr. Walt in front of Tower Building,
Menninger grounds, Topeka, Kansas, 1980

Dr. Walt at his typewriter, working to make the
deadline for his "In-Sights" column

Walt, Phil, & Roy, September 1991

Dr. Walt with daughter Eliza and director Baz Luhrmann
at the premiere of *Gatsby*

Dr. Walt in his office, 2005

Dr. Walt with his six children on the occasion of his
90th birthday, 10/23/2021

Stay up to date with Dr. Walt:

www.waltmenninger.com

Scan this QR code with your mobile device

www.ingramcontent.com/pod-product-compliance
Lightning Source LLC
Chambersburg PA
CBHW021657120626
46545CB00004B/1279